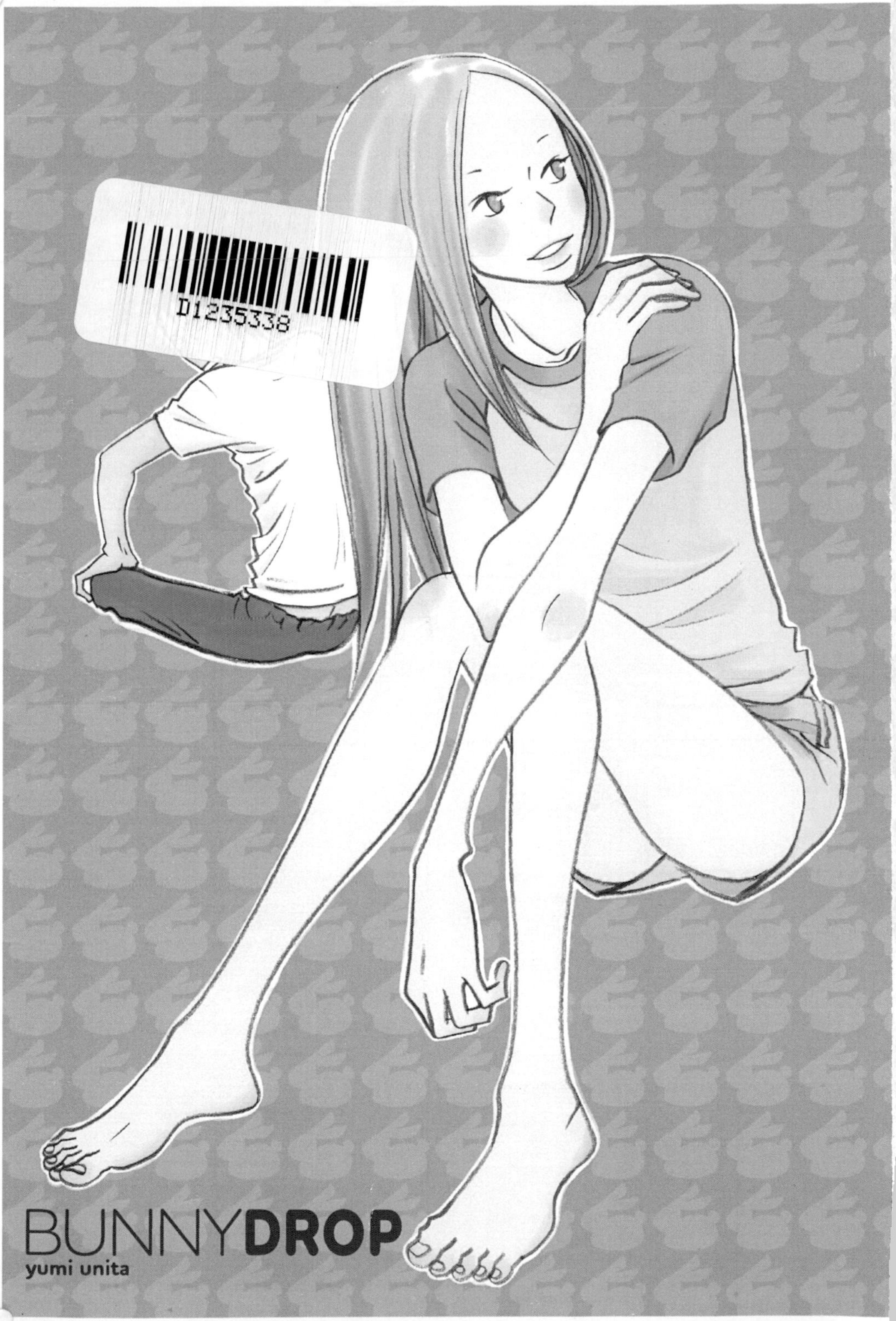

BUNNY**DROP**

yumi unita

BUNNY**DROP** 5

yumi unita

STORY

After taking in his late grandfather's love child Rin
out of necessity, Daikichi finds himself raising her.
When he finally meets Masako, Rin's biological (and
long-absent) mother, he resolves anew to raise
the little girl himself. And now, ten years later......

MAIN CHARACTERS

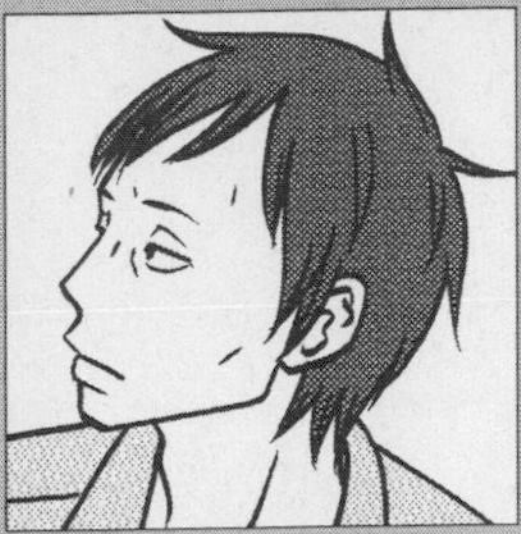

DAIKICHI KAWACHI
40 years old and single.
Used to be like a fish out of water around women and kids...

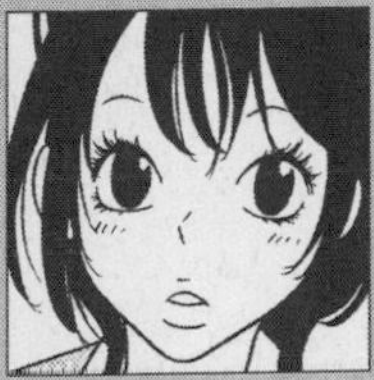

REINA
Daikichi's cousin's Haruko's daughter.
First-year in high school.

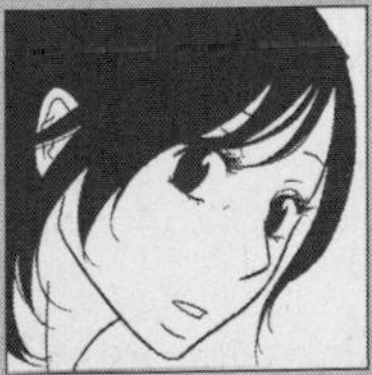

NITANI-SAN
Kouki's mother and a single mother.

RIN KAGA
A smart and responsible high school first-year.
Technically Daikichi's aunt.

KOUKI NITANI
Rin's childhood friend.
High school first-year.

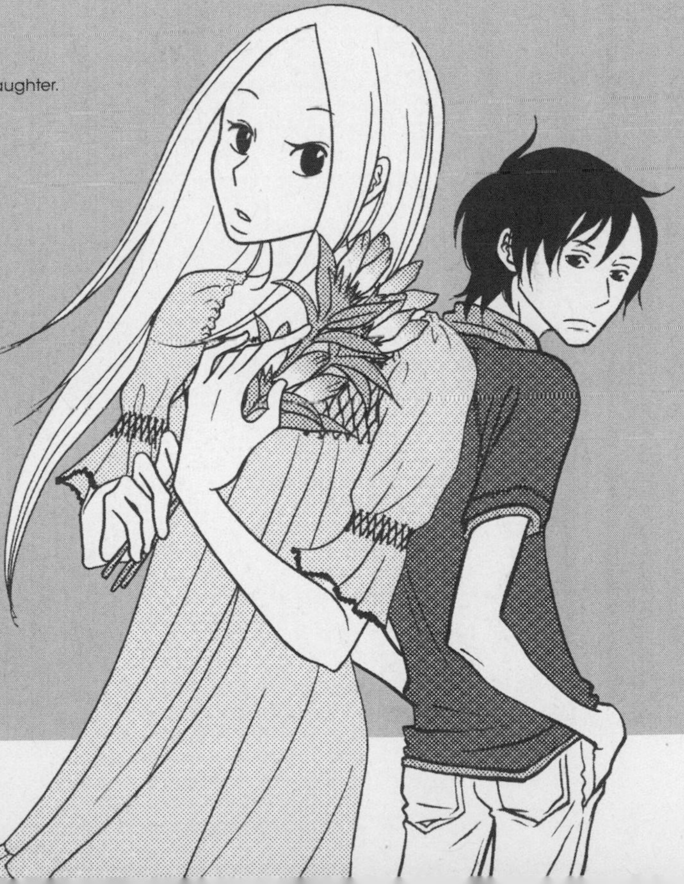

contents

BUNNY**DROP**

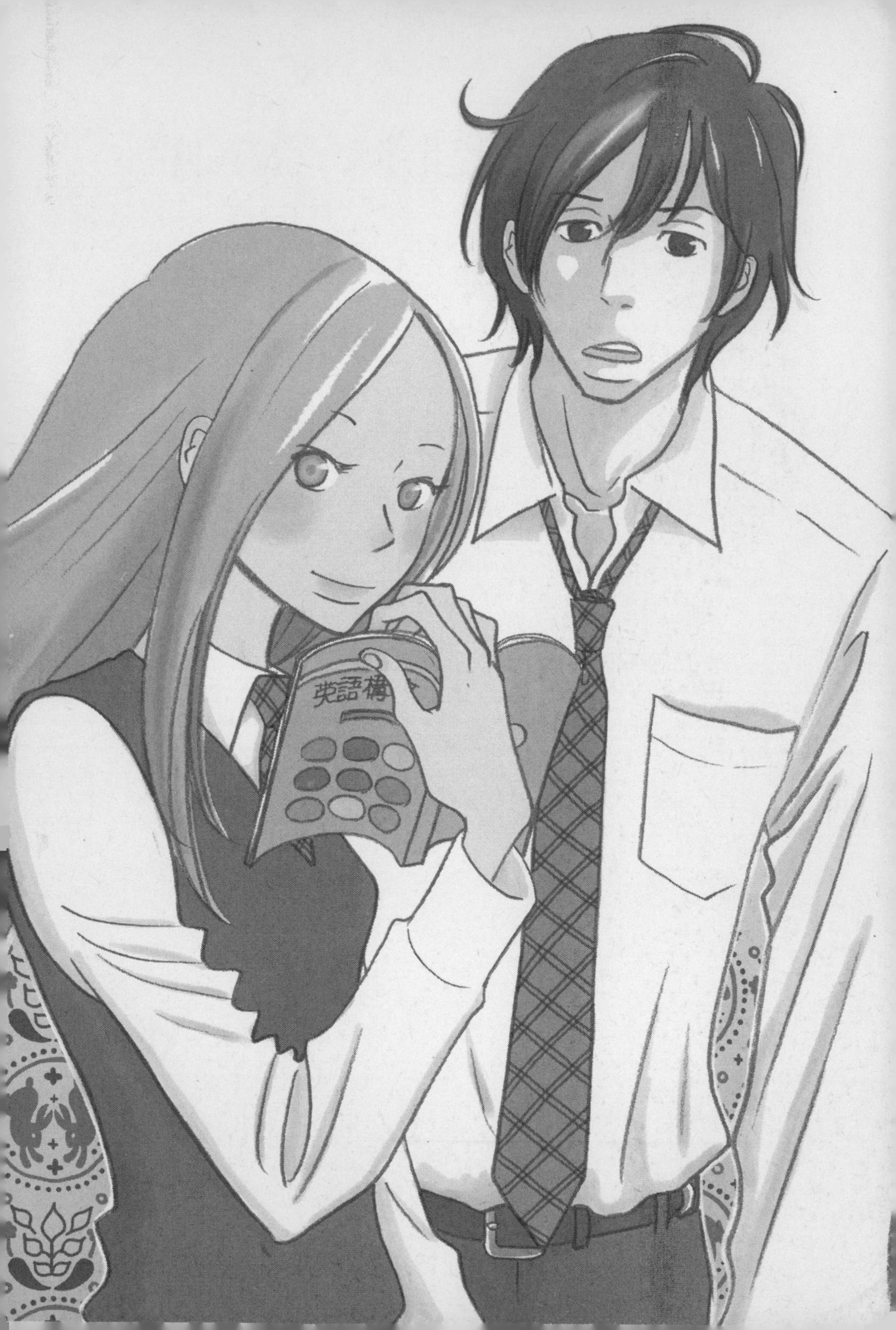
英語構

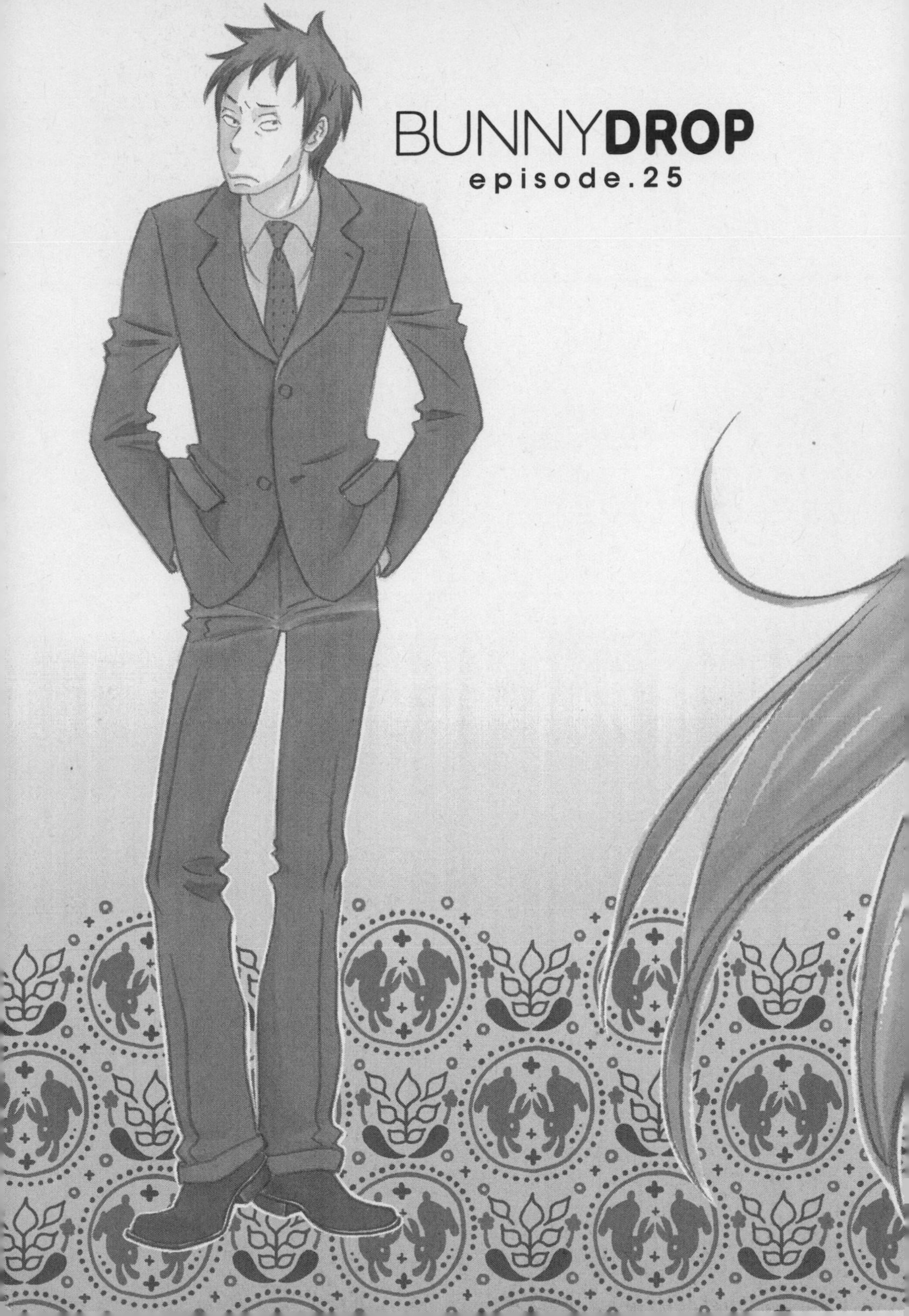
BUNNYDROP
episode.25

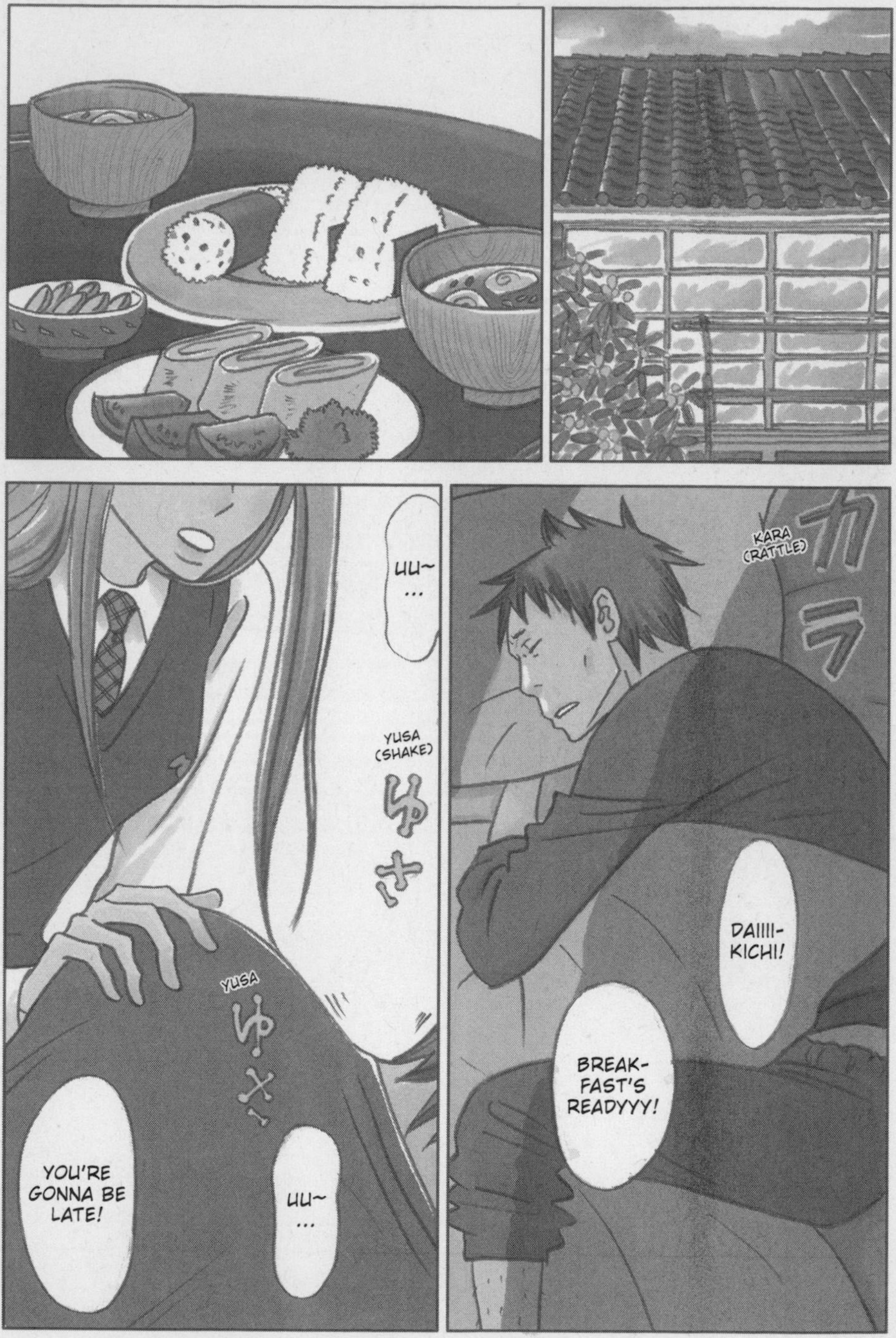
KARA (RATTLE)
カラ
DAIIII-KICHI!
BREAK-FAST'S READYYY!
UU~ ...
YUSA (SHAKE)
ゆさ
YUSA
ゆさ
UU~ ...
YOU'RE GONNA BE LATE!

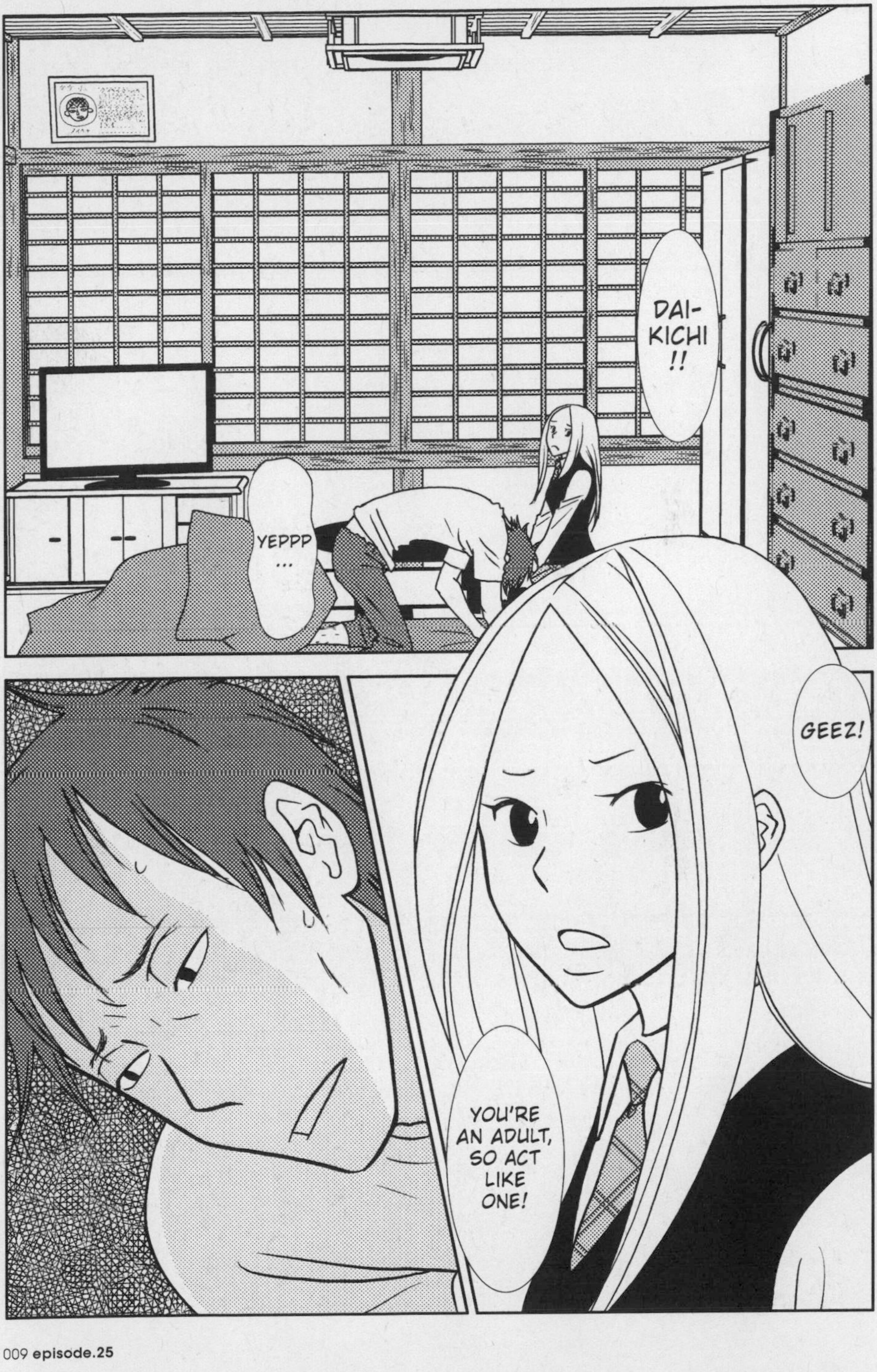
DAI-KICHI!!
YEPPP...
GEEZ!
YOU'RE AN ADULT, SO ACT LIKE ONE!

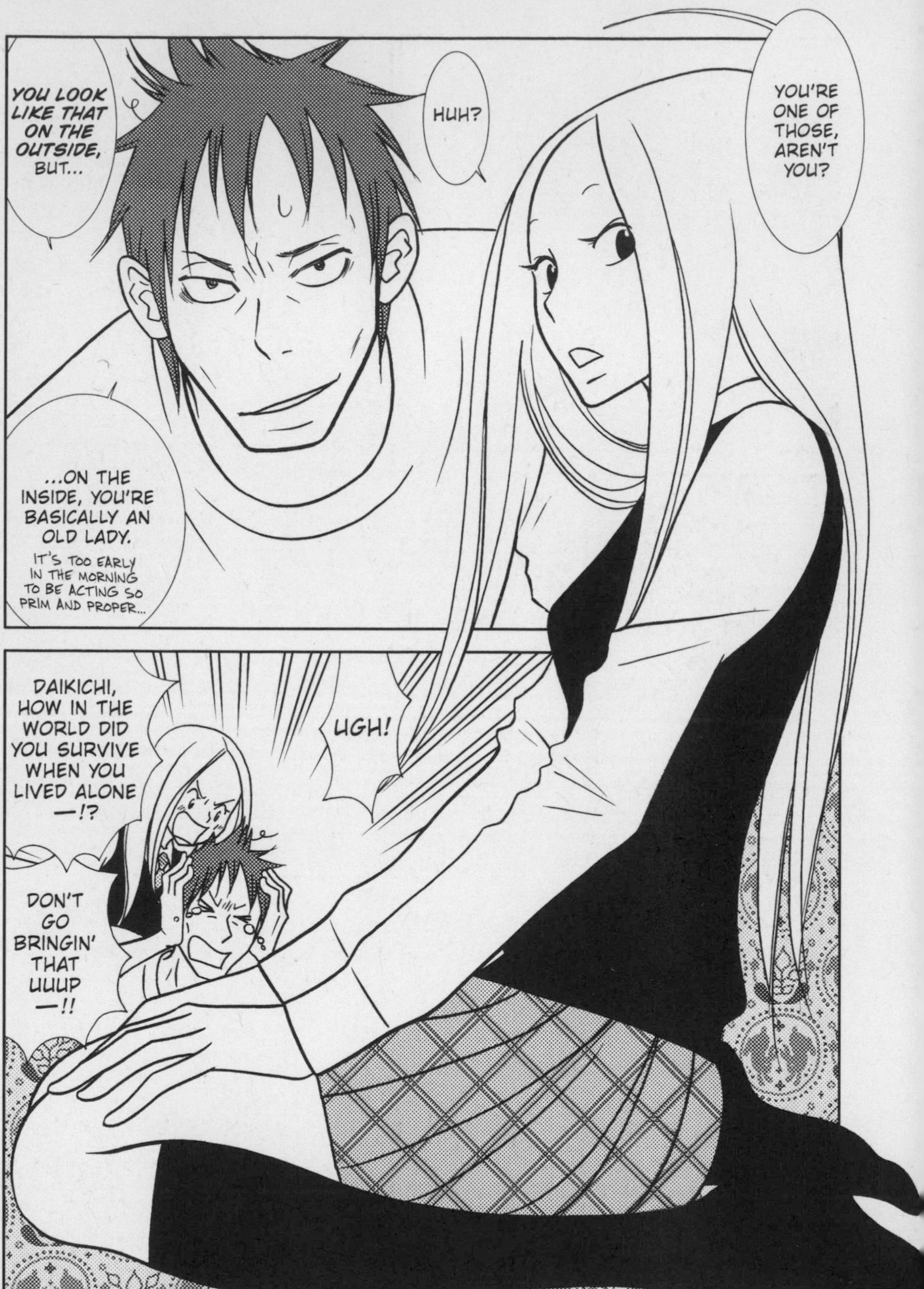
YOU'RE ONE OF THOSE, AREN'T YOU?
HUH?
YOU LOOK LIKE THAT ON THE OUTSIDE, BUT...
...ON THE INSIDE, YOU'RE BASICALLY AN OLD LADY.
IT'S TOO EARLY IN THE MORNING TO BE ACTING SO PRIM AND PROPER...
UGH!
DAIKICHI, HOW IN THE WORLD DID YOU SURVIVE WHEN YOU LIVED ALONE —!?
DON'T GO BRINGIN' THAT UUUP —!!

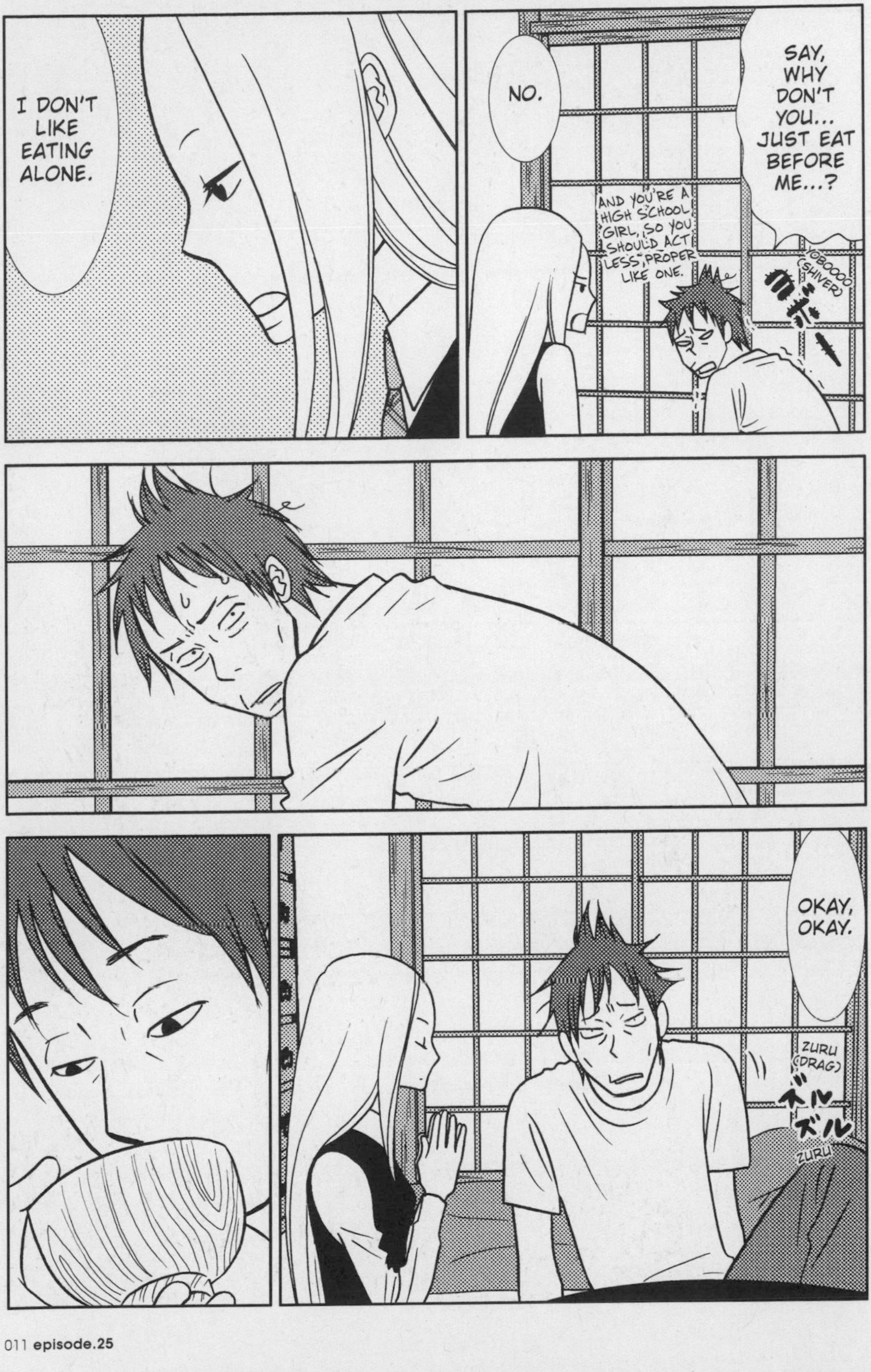

SAY, WHY DON'T YOU... JUST EAT BEFORE ME...?
NO.
AND YOU'RE A HIGH SCHOOL GIRL, SO YOU SHOULD ACT LESS PROPER LIKE ONE.
YOBOOOO (SHIVER)
I DON'T LIKE EATING ALONE.
OKAY, OKAY.
ZURU (DRAG)
ズル ズル
ZURU

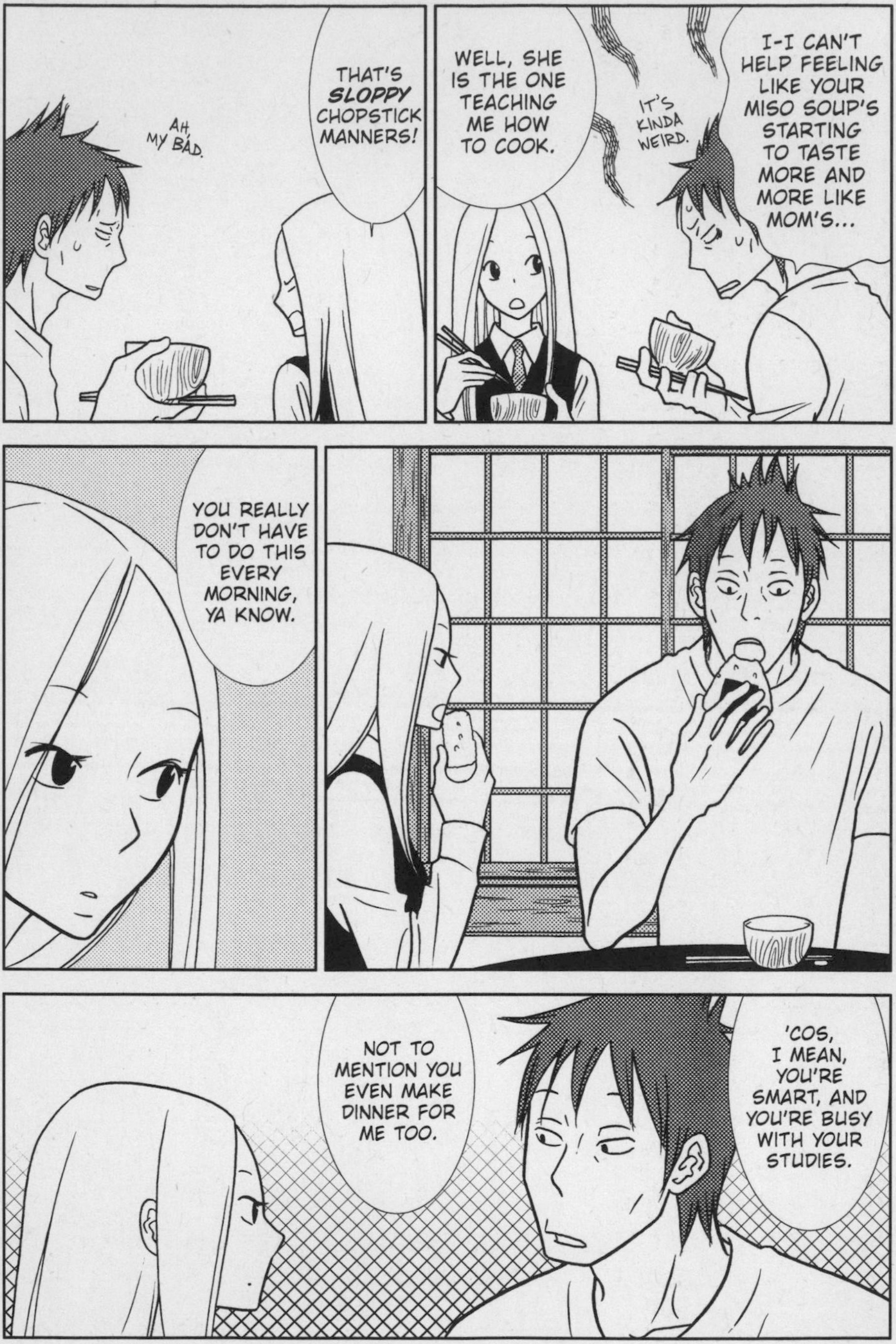
I-I CAN'T HELP FEELING LIKE YOUR MISO SOUP'S STARTING TO TASTE MORE AND MORE LIKE MOM'S...
IT'S KINDA WEIRD.
WELL, SHE IS THE ONE TEACHING ME HOW TO COOK.
THAT'S **SLOPPY** CHOPSTICK MANNERS!
AH, MY BAD.
YOU REALLY DON'T HAVE TO DO THIS EVERY MORNING, YA KNOW.
'COS, I MEAN, YOU'RE SMART, AND YOU'RE BUSY WITH YOUR STUDIES.
NOT TO MENTION YOU EVEN MAKE DINNER FOR ME TOO.

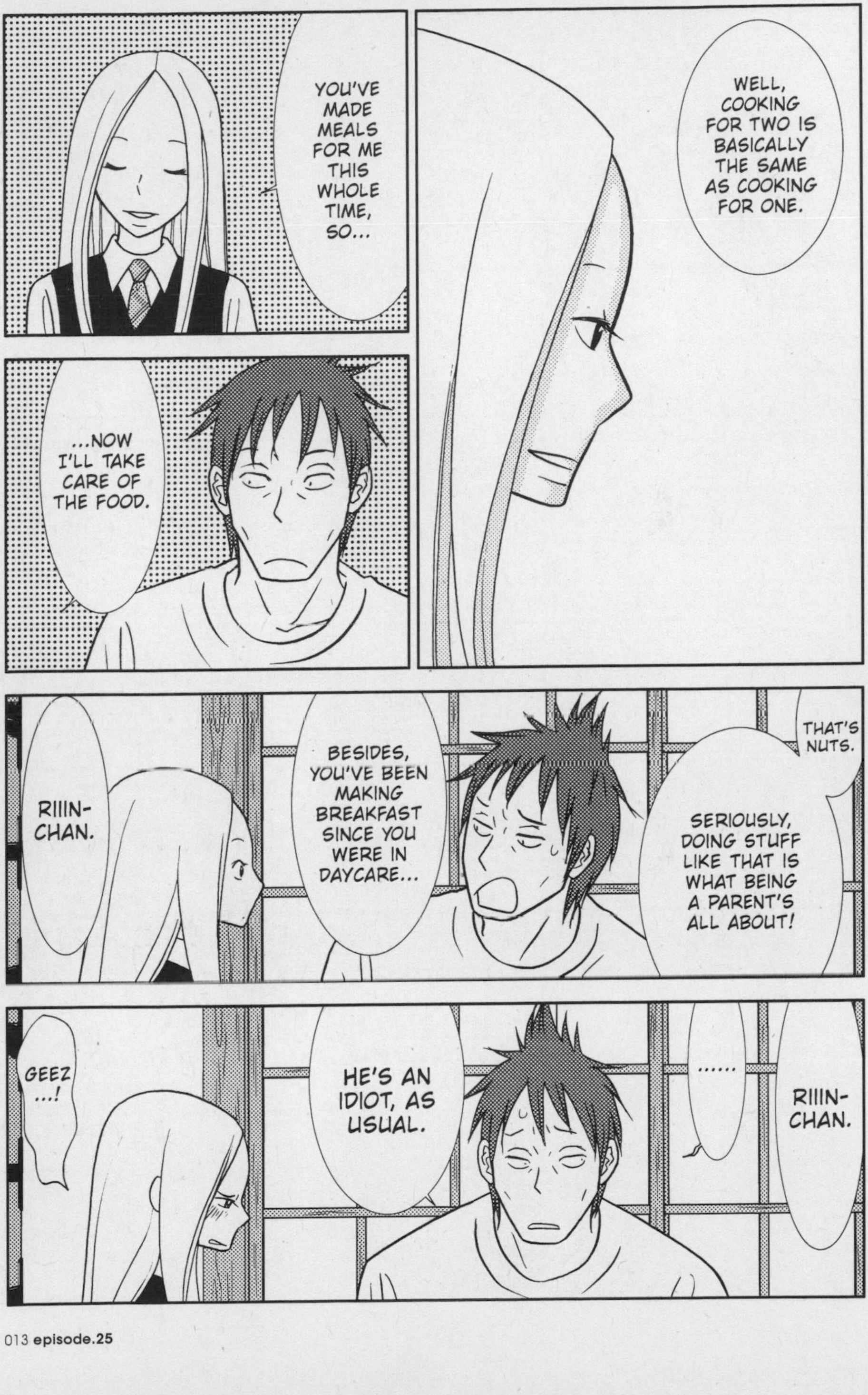
WELL, COOKING FOR TWO IS BASICALLY THE SAME AS COOKING FOR ONE.
YOU'VE MADE MEALS FOR ME THIS WHOLE TIME, SO...
...NOW I'LL TAKE CARE OF THE FOOD.
THAT'S NUTS.
SERIOUSLY, DOING STUFF LIKE THAT IS WHAT BEING A PARENT'S ALL ABOUT!
BESIDES, YOU'VE BEEN MAKING BREAKFAST SINCE YOU WERE IN DAYCARE...
RIIIN-CHAN.
RIIIN-CHAN.
......
HE'S AN IDIOT, AS USUAL.
GEEZ ...!

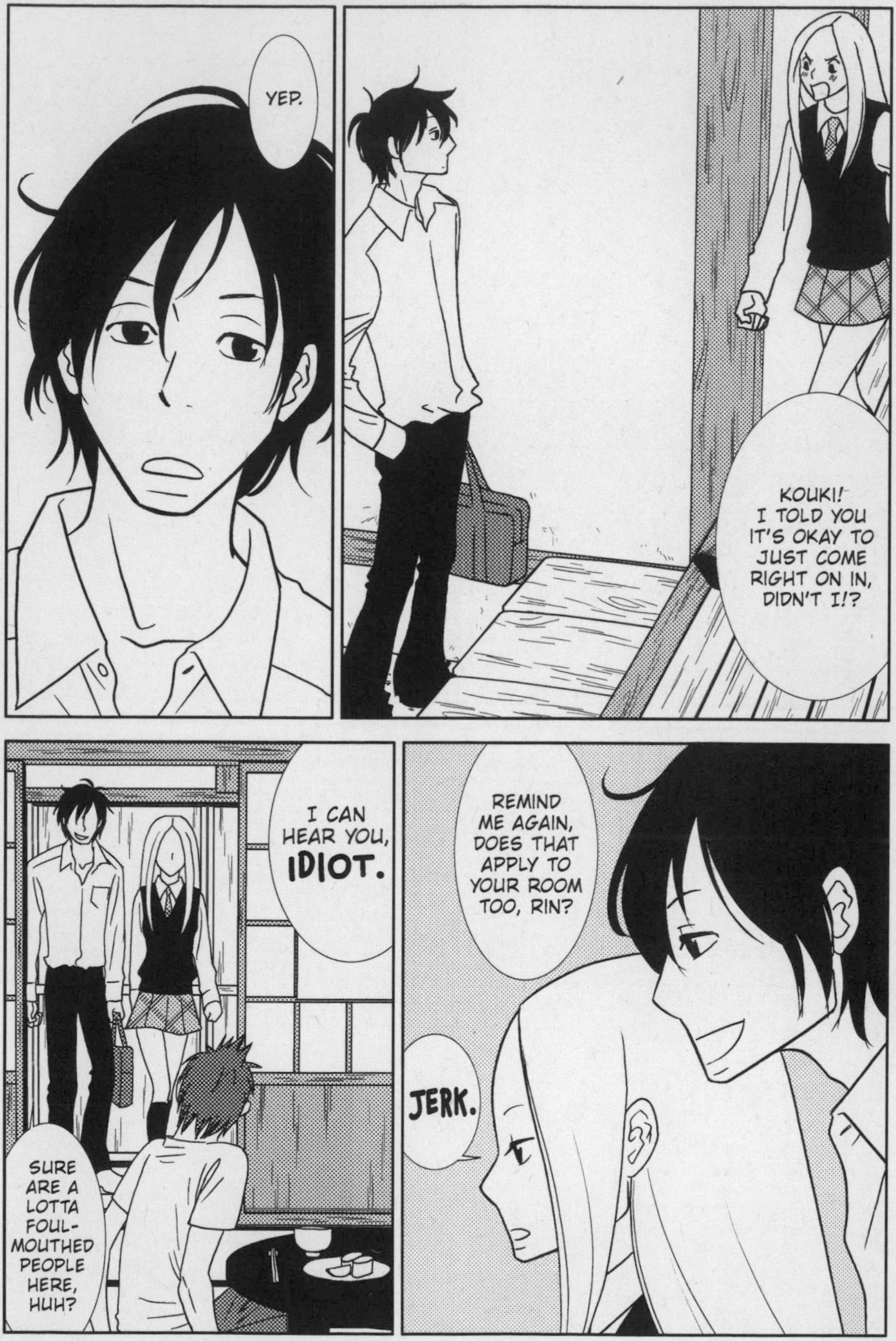
KOUKI! I TOLD YOU IT'S OKAY TO JUST COME RIGHT ON IN, DIDN'T I!?
YEP.
REMIND ME AGAIN, DOES THAT APPLY TO YOUR ROOM TOO, RIN?
JERK.
I CAN HEAR YOU, IDIOT.
SURE ARE A LOTTA FOUL-MOUTHED PEOPLE HERE, HUH?

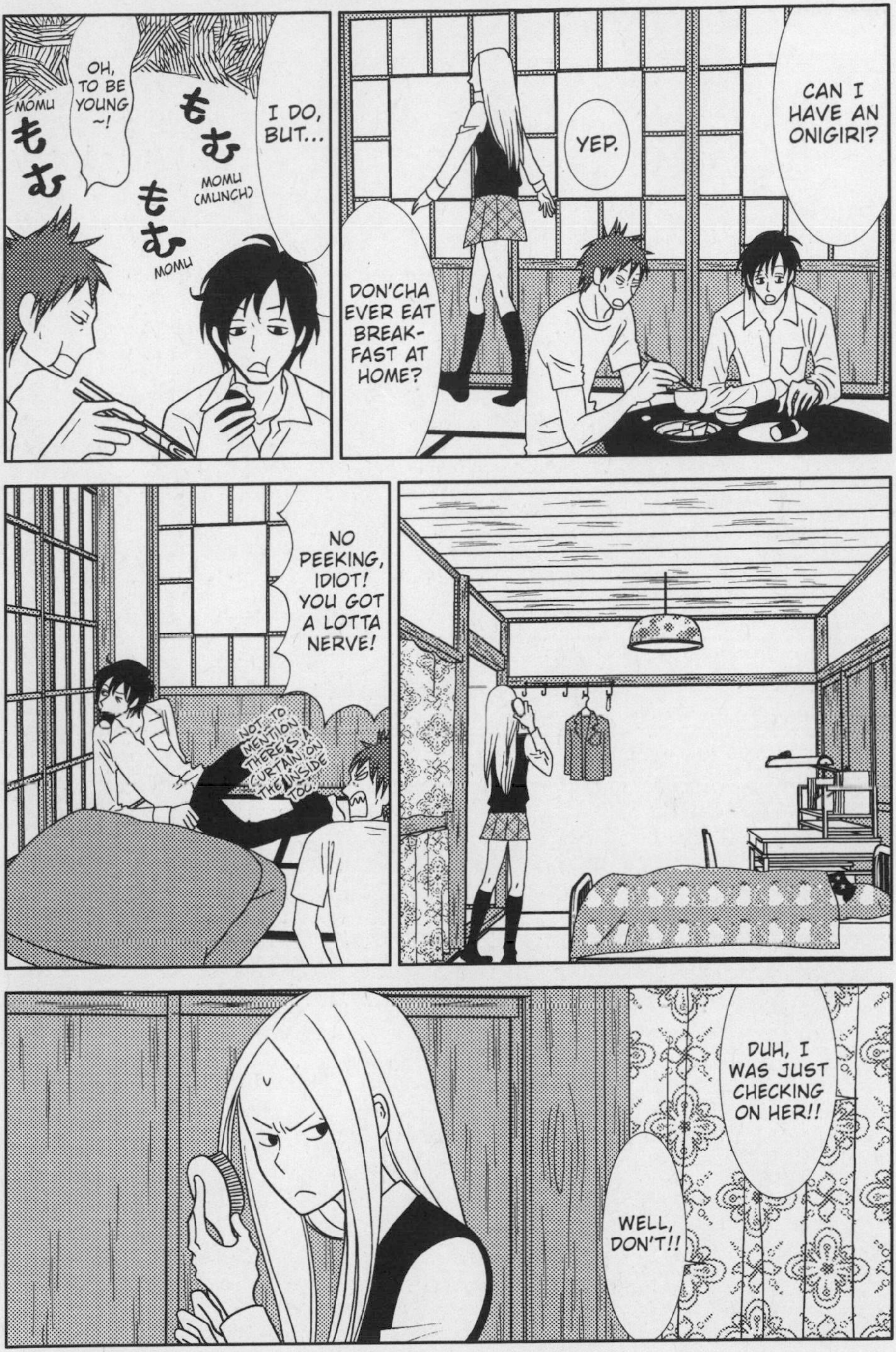
CAN I HAVE AN ONIGIRI?
YEP.
DON'CHA EVER EAT BREAK-FAST AT HOME?
I DO, BUT...
もむ
MOMU (MUNCH)
OH, TO BE YOUNG ~!
もむ
MOMU
もむ
MOMU
NO PEEKING, IDIOT! YOU GOT A LOTTA NERVE!
NOT TO MENTION THERE'S A CURTAIN ON THE INSIDE TOO.
DUH, I WAS JUST CHECKING ON HER!!
WELL, DON'T!!

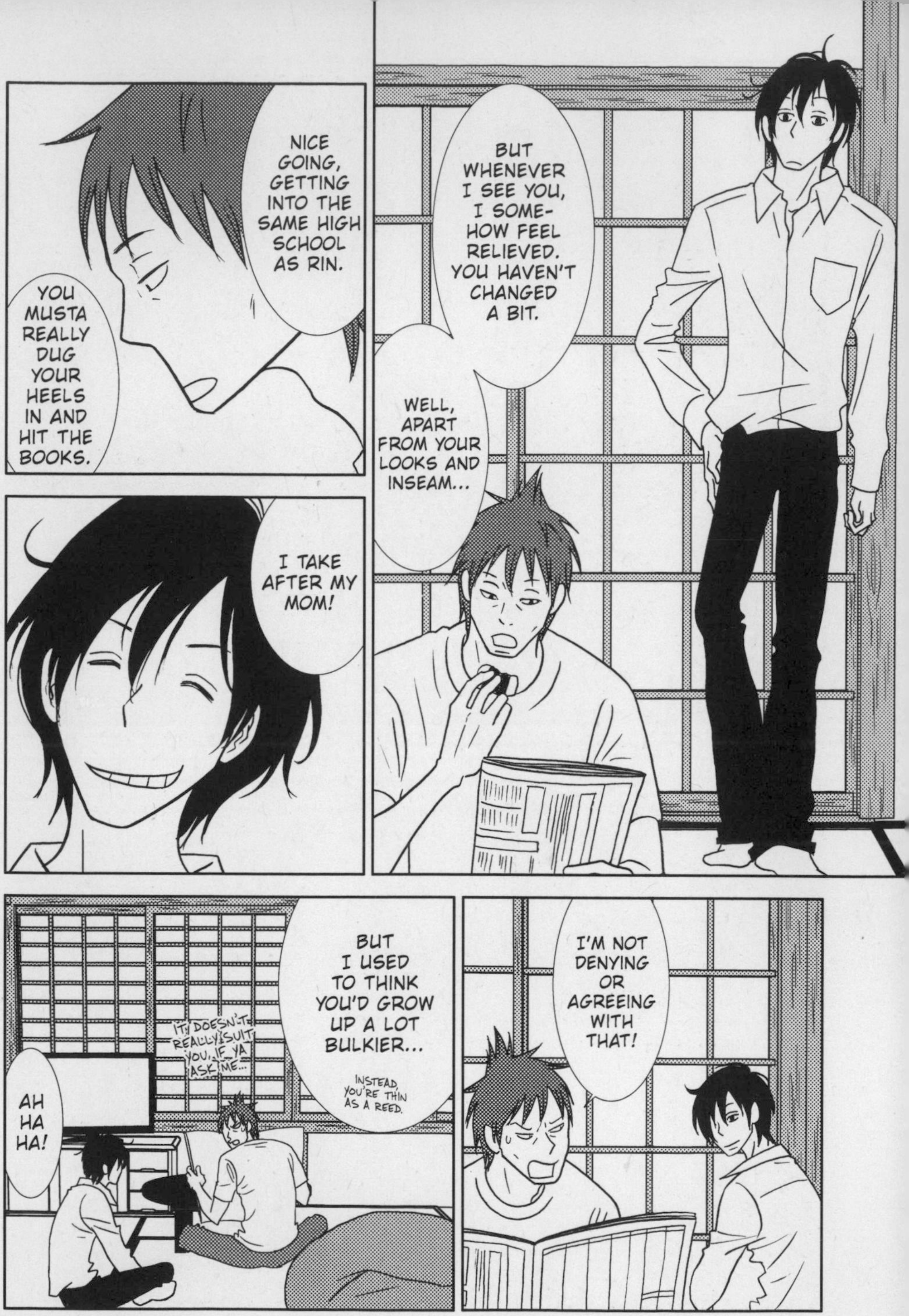
NICE GOING, GETTING INTO THE SAME HIGH SCHOOL AS RIN.
YOU MUSTA REALLY DUG YOUR HEELS IN AND HIT THE BOOKS.
BUT WHENEVER I SEE YOU, I SOME-HOW FEEL RELIEVED. YOU HAVEN'T CHANGED A BIT.
WELL, APART FROM YOUR LOOKS AND INSEAM...
I TAKE AFTER MY MOM!
BUT I USED TO THINK YOU'D GROW UP A LOT BULKIER...
INSTEAD, YOU'RE THIN AS A REED.
IT DOESN'T REALLY SUIT YOU, IF YA ASK ME...
AH HA HA!
I'M NOT DENYING OR AGREEING WITH THAT!

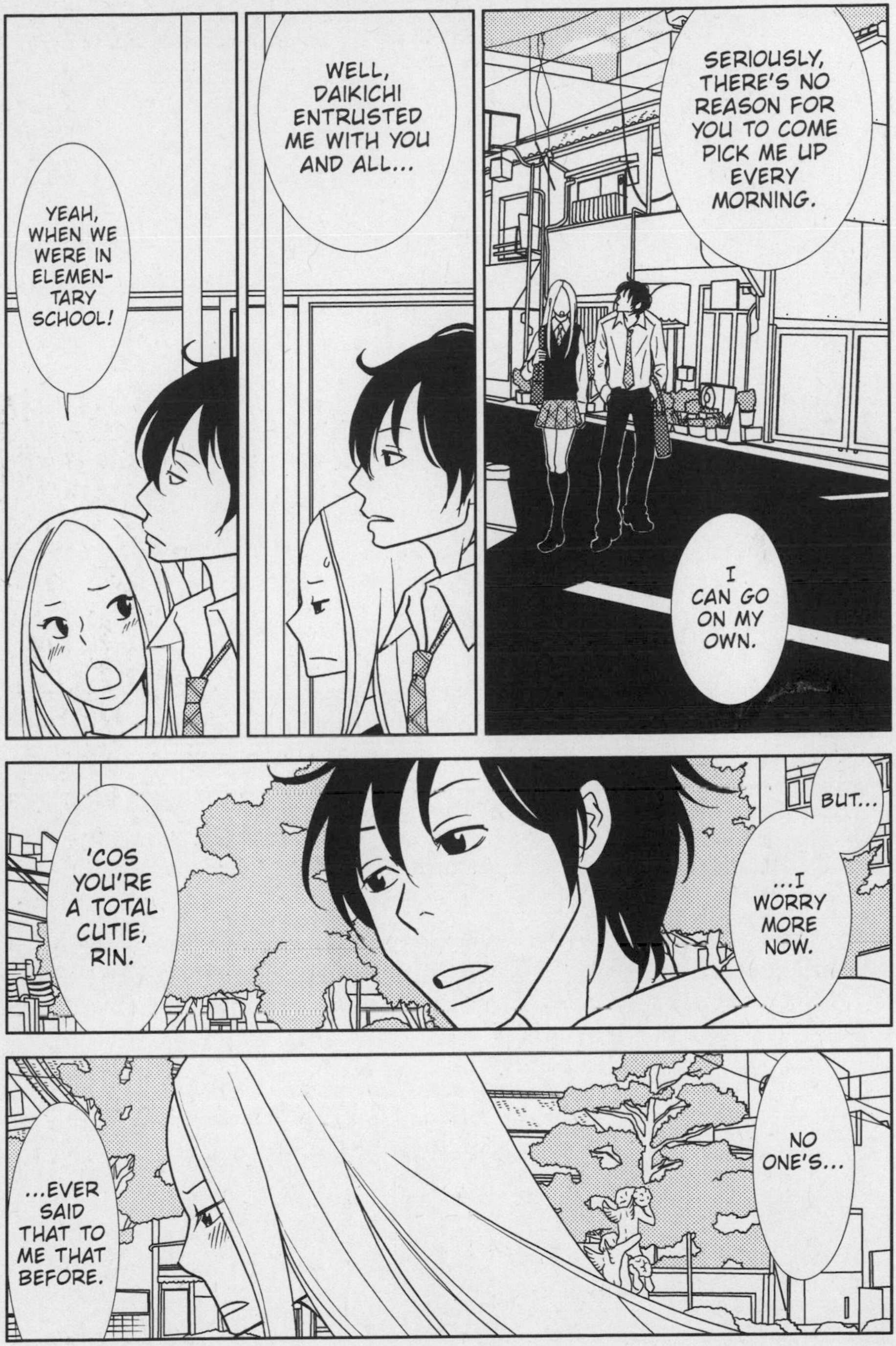
SERIOUSLY, THERE'S NO REASON FOR YOU TO COME PICK ME UP EVERY MORNING.
I CAN GO ON MY OWN.
WELL, DAIKICHI ENTRUSTED ME WITH YOU AND ALL...
YEAH, WHEN WE WERE IN ELEMENTARY SCHOOL!
BUT...
...I WORRY MORE NOW.
'COS YOU'RE A TOTAL CUTIE, RIN.
NO ONE'S...
...EVER SAID THAT TO ME THAT BEFORE.

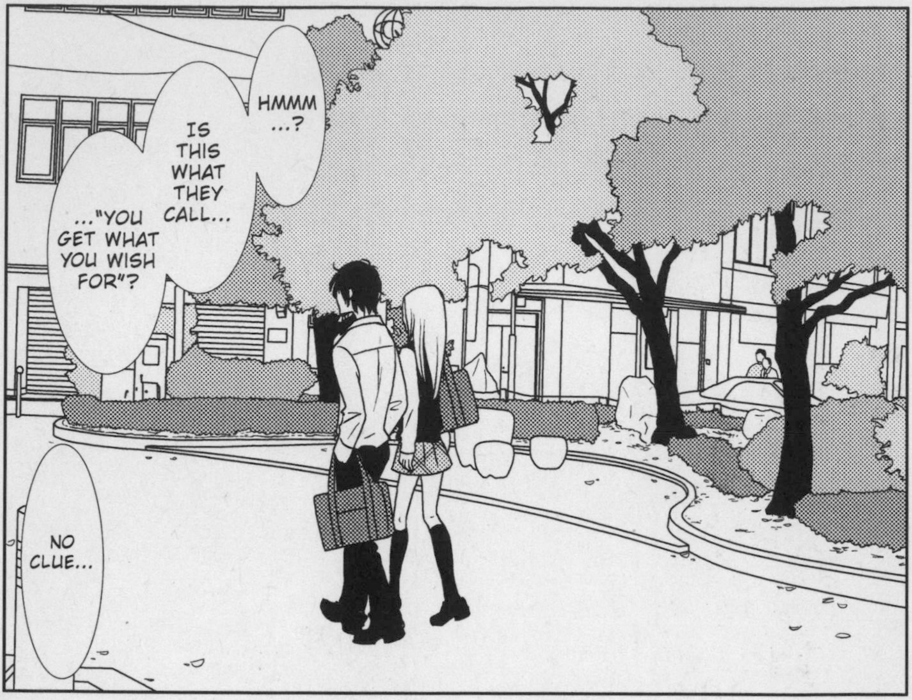
HMMM ...?
IS THIS WHAT THEY CALL...
..."YOU GET WHAT YOU WISH FOR"?
NO CLUE...

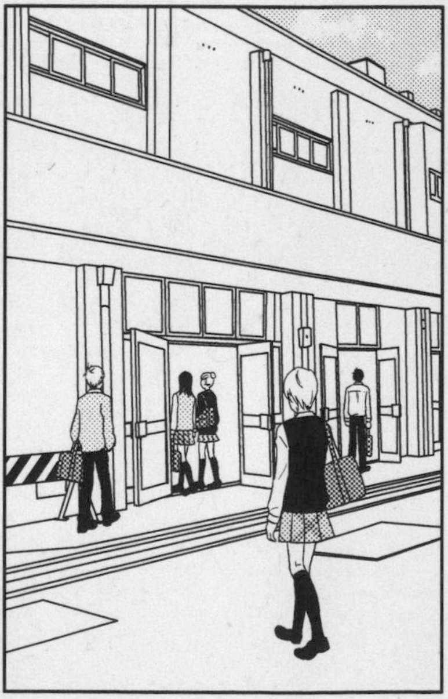

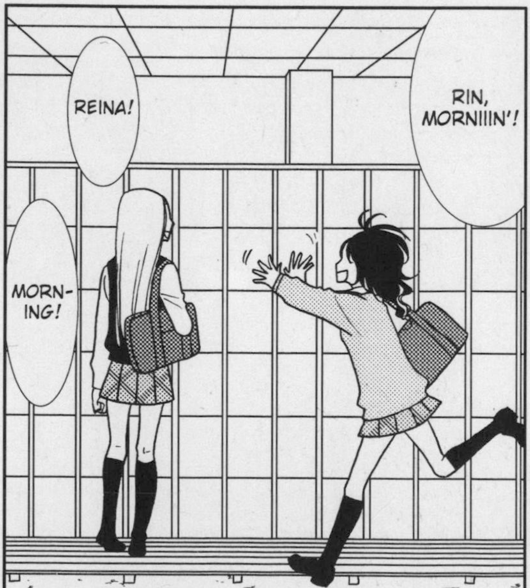
RIN, MORNIIIN'!
REINA!
MORN-ING!

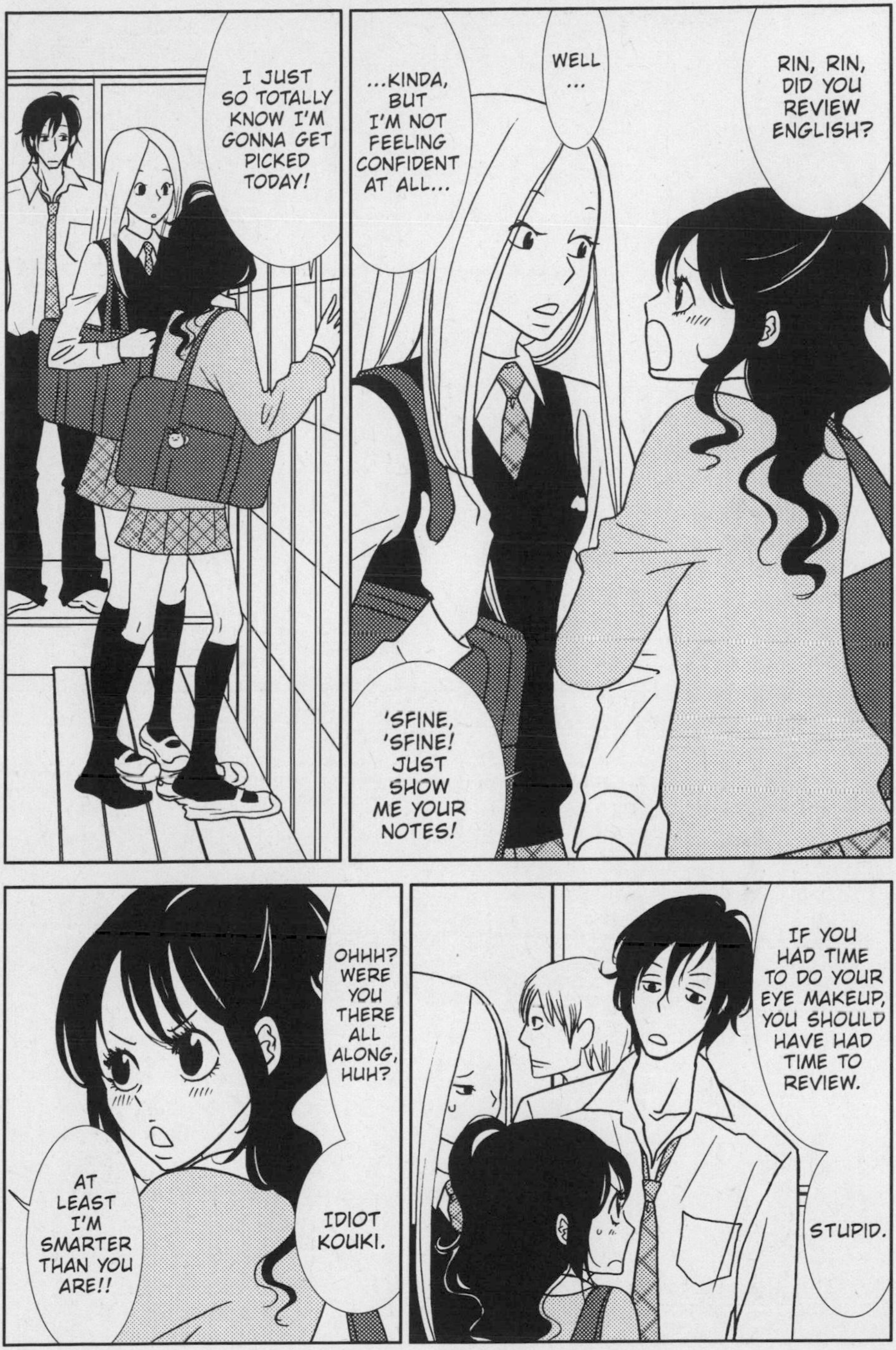
RIN, RIN, DID YOU REVIEW ENGLISH?
WELL ...
...KINDA, BUT I'M NOT FEELING CONFIDENT AT ALL...
'SFINE, 'SFINE! JUST SHOW ME YOUR NOTES!
I JUST SO TOTALLY KNOW I'M GONNA GET PICKED TODAY!
IF YOU HAD TIME TO DO YOUR EYE MAKEUP, YOU SHOULD HAVE HAD TIME TO REVIEW.
STUPID.
OHHH? WERE YOU THERE ALL ALONG, HUH?
IDIOT KOUKI.
AT LEAST I'M SMARTER THAN YOU ARE!!

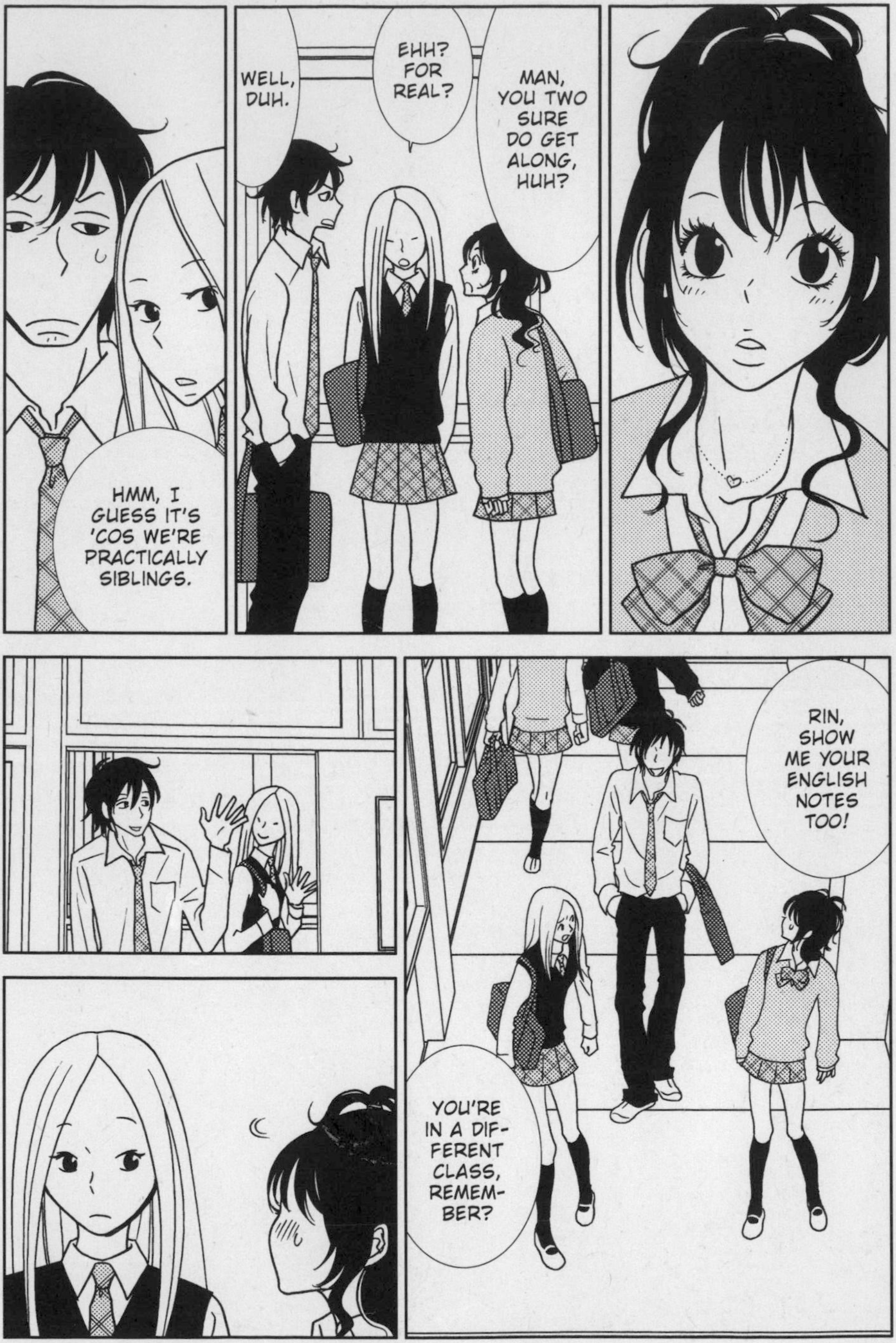
MAN, YOU TWO SURE DO GET ALONG, HUH?
EHH? FOR REAL?
WELL, DUH.
HMM, I GUESS IT'S 'COS WE'RE PRACTICALLY SIBLINGS.
RIN, SHOW ME YOUR ENGLISH NOTES TOO!
YOU'RE IN A DIF-FERENT CLASS, REMEM-BER?

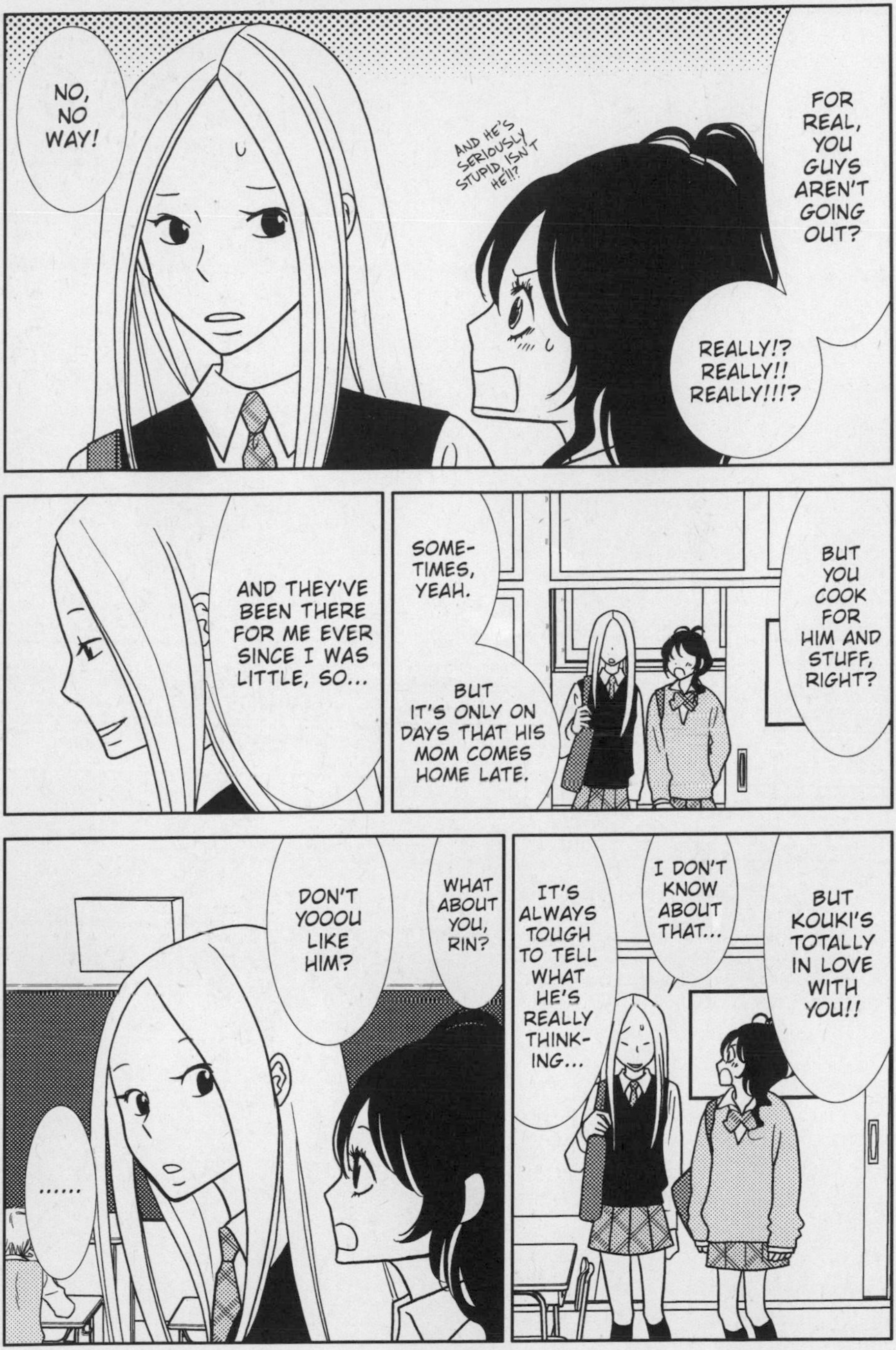
FOR REAL, YOU GUYS AREN'T GOING OUT?
AND HE'S SERIOUSLY STUPID, ISN'T HE!!?
REALLY!? REALLY!! REALLY!!!?
NO, NO WAY!
BUT YOU COOK FOR HIM AND STUFF, RIGHT?
SOME-TIMES, YEAH.
BUT IT'S ONLY ON DAYS THAT HIS MOM COMES HOME LATE.
AND THEY'VE BEEN THERE FOR ME EVER SINCE I WAS LITTLE, SO...
BUT KOUKI'S TOTALLY IN LOVE WITH YOU!!
I DON'T KNOW ABOUT THAT...
IT'S ALWAYS TOUGH TO TELL WHAT HE'S REALLY THINK-ING...
WHAT ABOUT YOU, RIN?
DON'T YOOOU LIKE HIM?
......

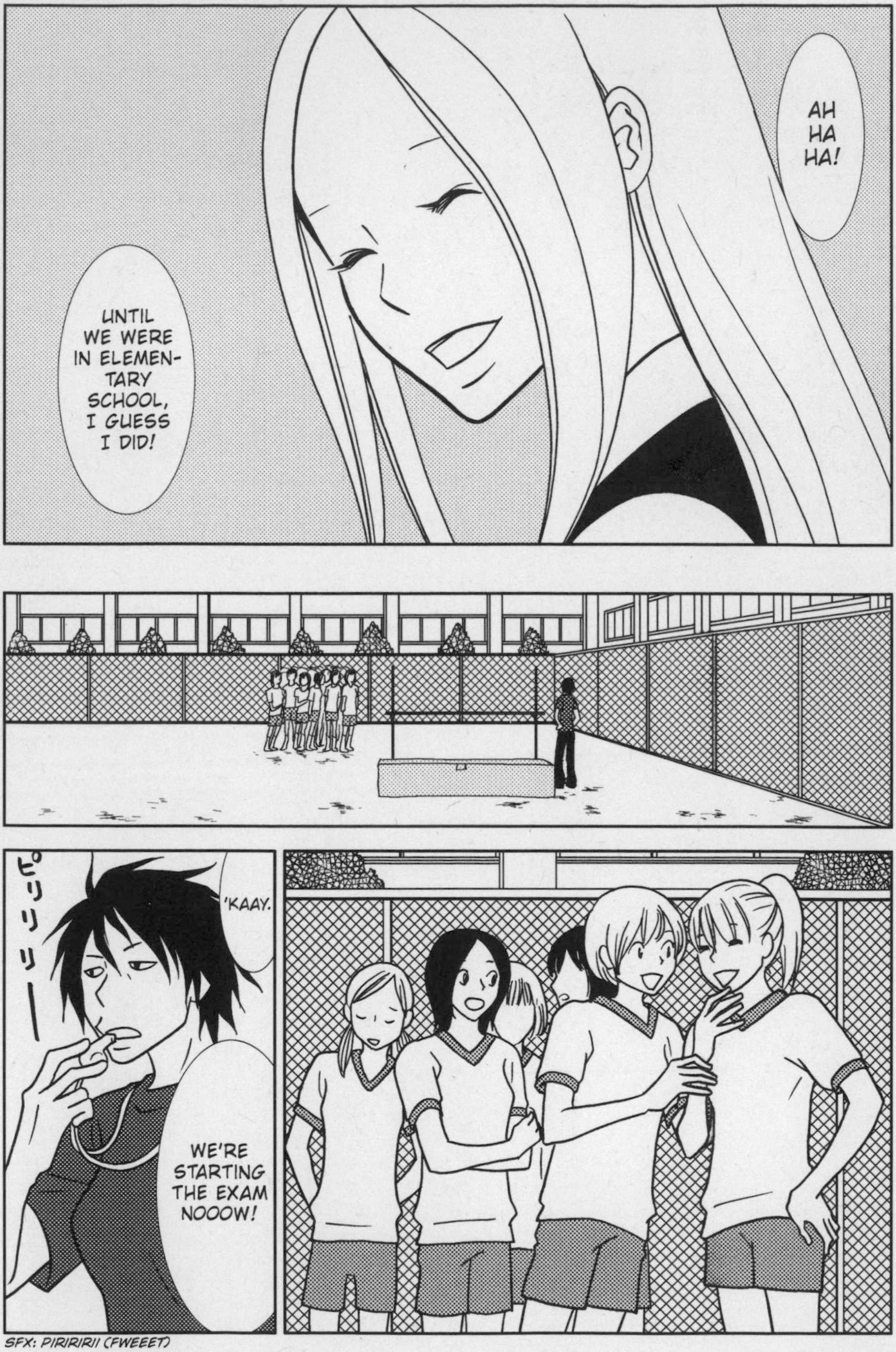
AH HA HA!
UNTIL WE WERE IN ELEMENTARY SCHOOL, I GUESS I DID!
'KAAY.
ピリリリー
WE'RE STARTING THE EXAM NOOOW!

SFX: PIRIRIRII (FWEEET)

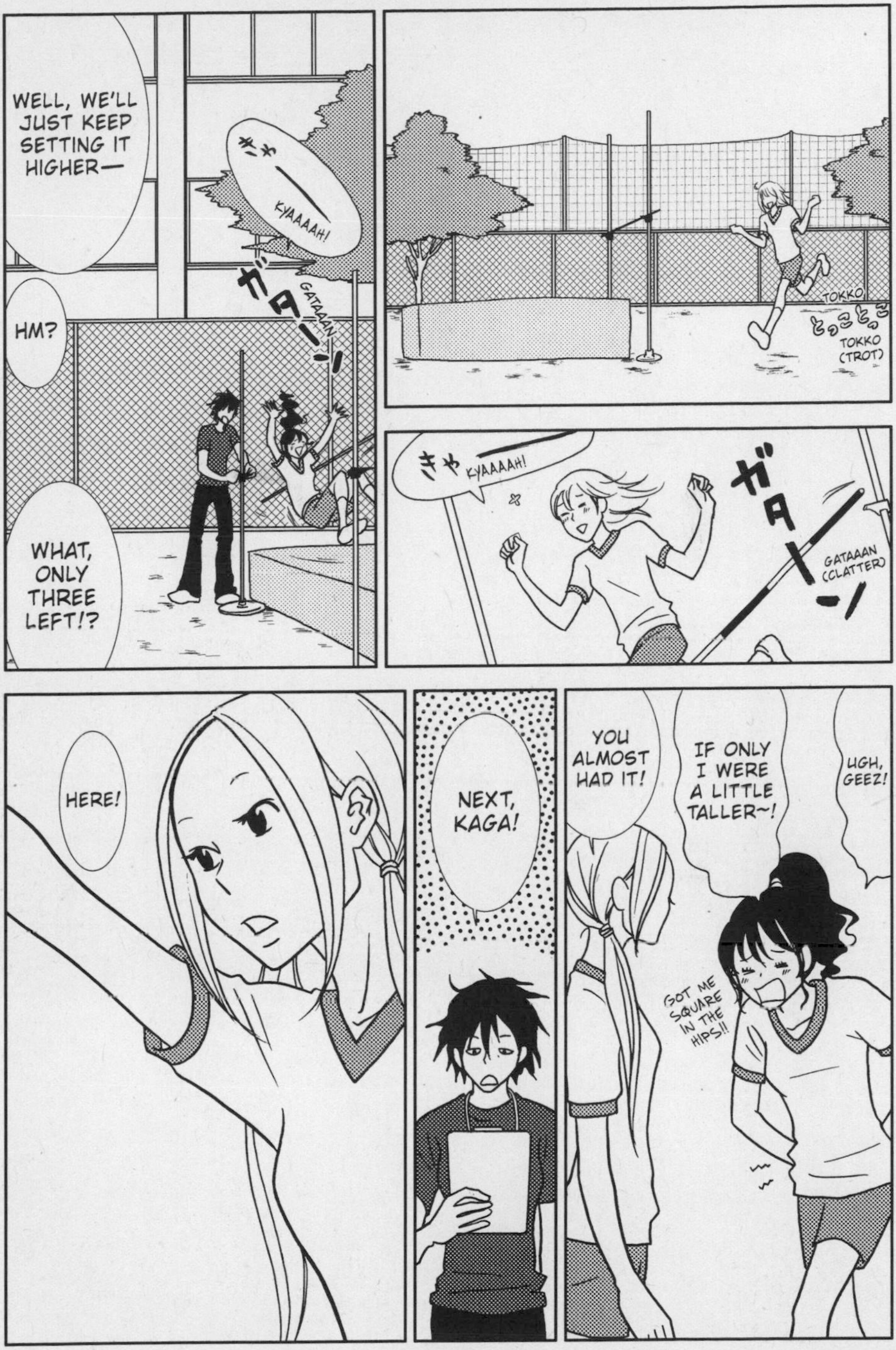
とっことっこ
TOKKO TOKKO (TROT)
きゃ KYAAAAH!
ガターン
GATAAAN (CLATTER)
WELL, WE'LL JUST KEEP SETTING IT HIGHER—
きゃ— KYAAAAH!
ガターン
GATAAAN
HM?
WHAT, ONLY THREE LEFT!?
UGH, GEEZ!
IF ONLY I WERE A LITTLE TALLER~!
YOU ALMOST HAD IT!
GOT ME SQUARE IN THE HIPS!!
NEXT, KAGA!
HERE!

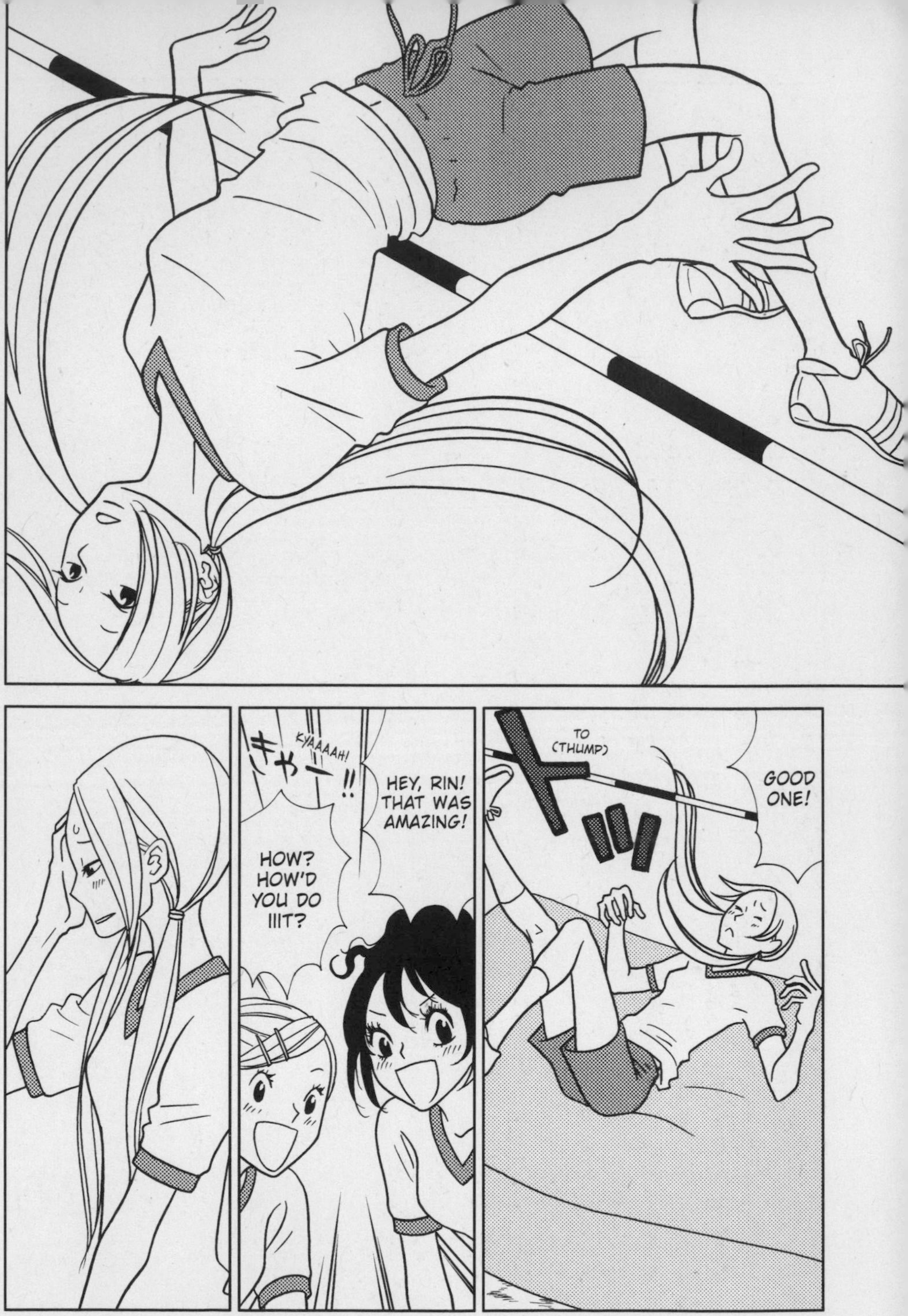
TO
(THUMP)
GOOD ONE!
KYAAAAH!
きゃー!!
HEY, RIN! THAT WAS AMAZING!
HOW? HOW'D YOU DO IIIT?

SFX: FURU (SHAKE) FURU

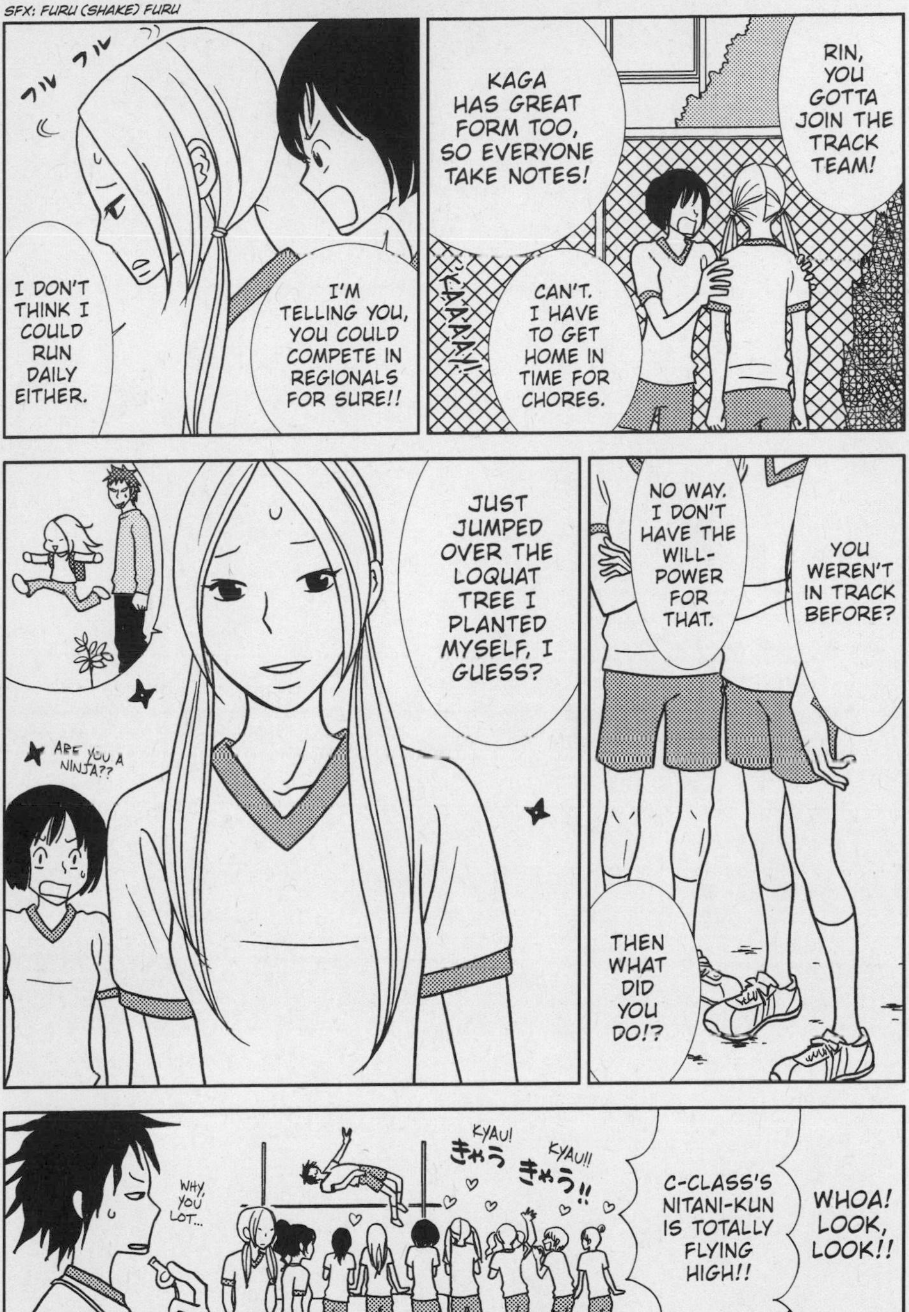

RIN, YOU GOTTA JOIN THE TRACK TEAM!
KAGA HAS GREAT FORM TOO, SO EVERYONE TAKE NOTES!
CAN'T. I HAVE TO GET HOME IN TIME FOR CHORES.
KYAAAA!!
I'M TELLING YOU, YOU COULD COMPETE IN REGIONALS FOR SURE!!
I DON'T THINK I COULD RUN DAILY EITHER.
YOU WEREN'T IN TRACK BEFORE?
NO WAY. I DON'T HAVE THE WILL-POWER FOR THAT.
THEN WHAT DID YOU DO!?
JUST JUMPED OVER THE LOQUAT TREE I PLANTED MYSELF, I GUESS?
ARE YOU A NINJA??
WHOA! LOOK, LOOK!!
C-CLASS'S NITANI-KUN IS TOTALLY FLYING HIGH!!
KYAU! きゃう
KYAU!! きゃう!!
WHY, YOU LOT...

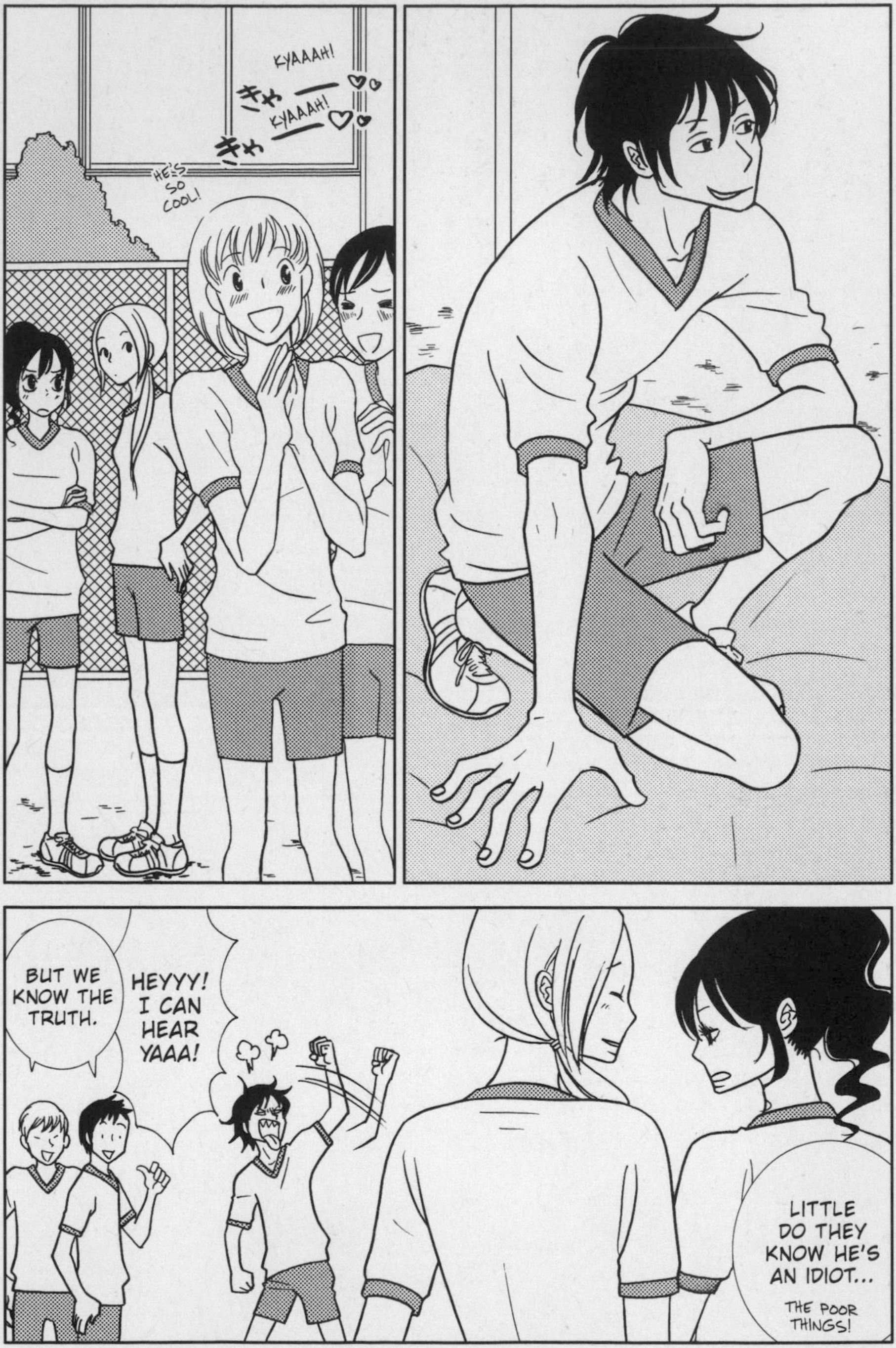
きゃー
KYAAAH!
きゃ
KYAAAH!
HE'S SO COOL!
LITTLE DO THEY KNOW HE'S AN IDIOT...
THE POOR THINGS!
HEYYY! I CAN HEAR YAAA!
BUT WE KNOW THE TRUTH.

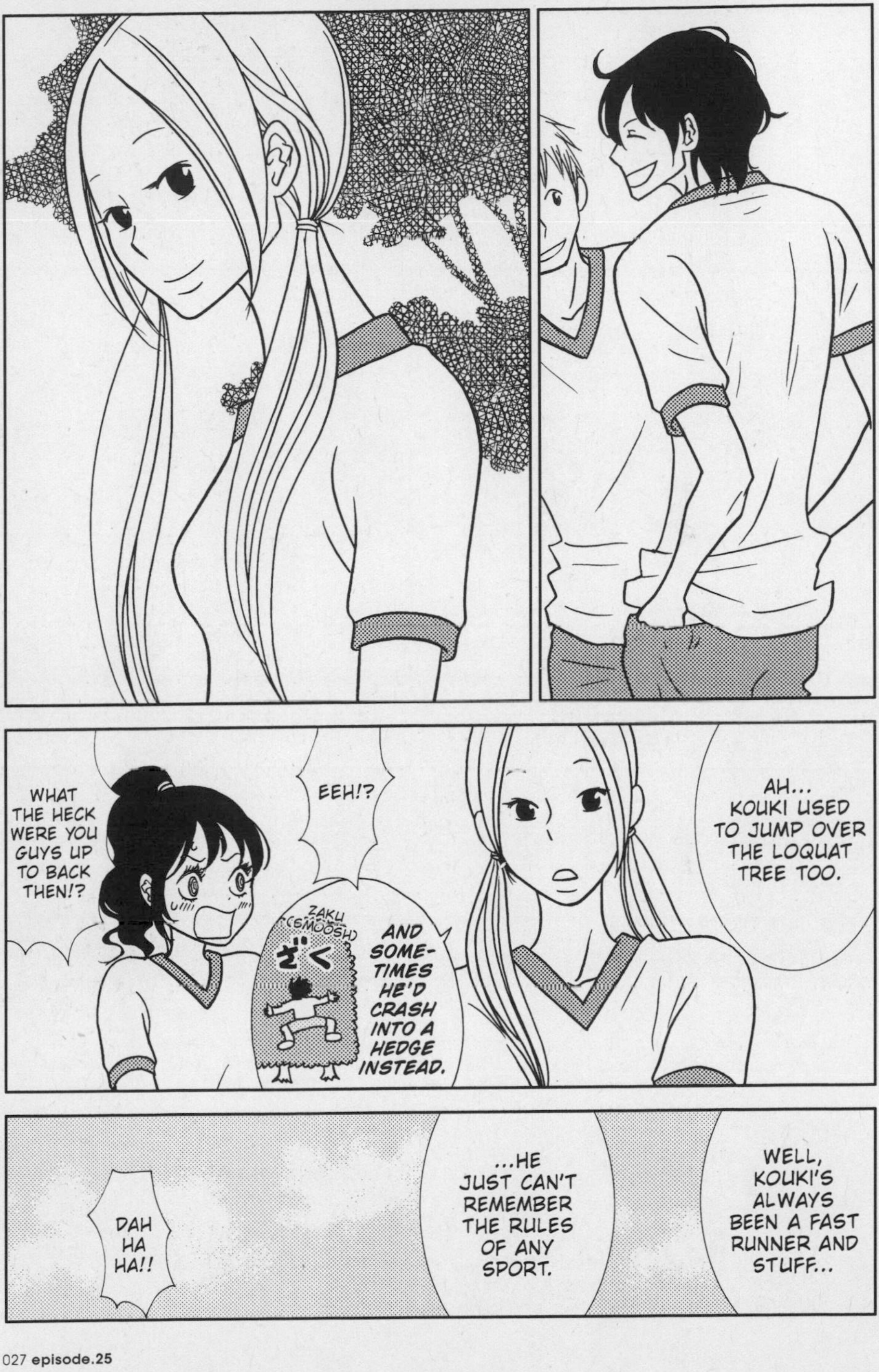
AH... KOUKI USED TO JUMP OVER THE LOQUAT TREE TOO.
AND SOMETIMES HE'D CRASH INTO A HEDGE INSTEAD.
ZAKU (SMOOSH)
ざく
EEH!?
WHAT THE HECK WERE YOU GUYS UP TO BACK THEN!?
WELL, KOUKI'S ALWAYS BEEN A FAST RUNNER AND STUFF...
...HE JUST CAN'T REMEMBER THE RULES OF ANY SPORT.
DAH HA HA!!

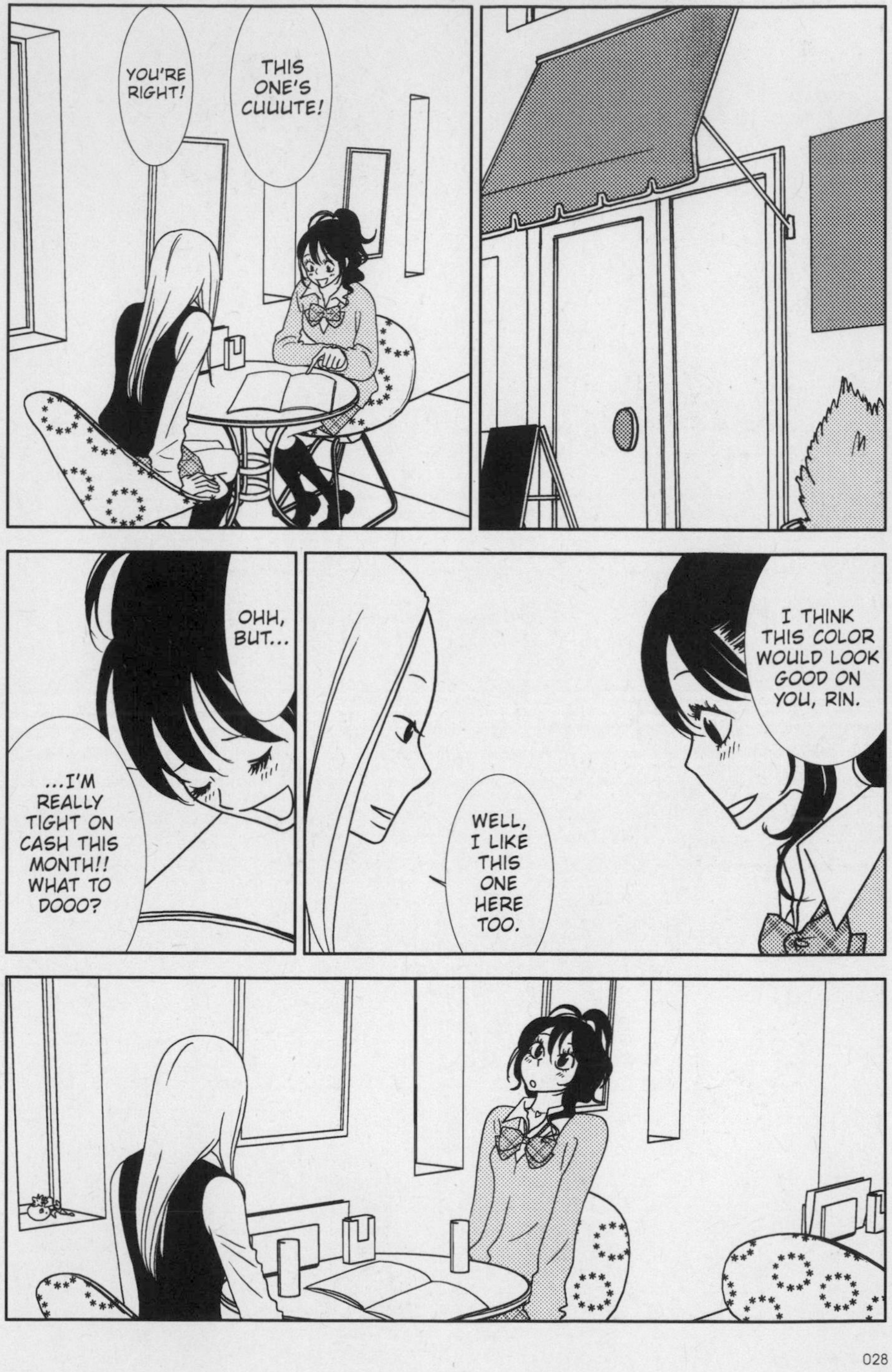
THIS ONE'S CUUUTE!
YOU'RE RIGHT!
I THINK THIS COLOR WOULD LOOK GOOD ON YOU, RIN.
WELL, I LIKE THIS ONE HERE TOO.
OHH, BUT...
...I'M REALLY TIGHT ON CASH THIS MONTH!! WHAT TO DOOO?

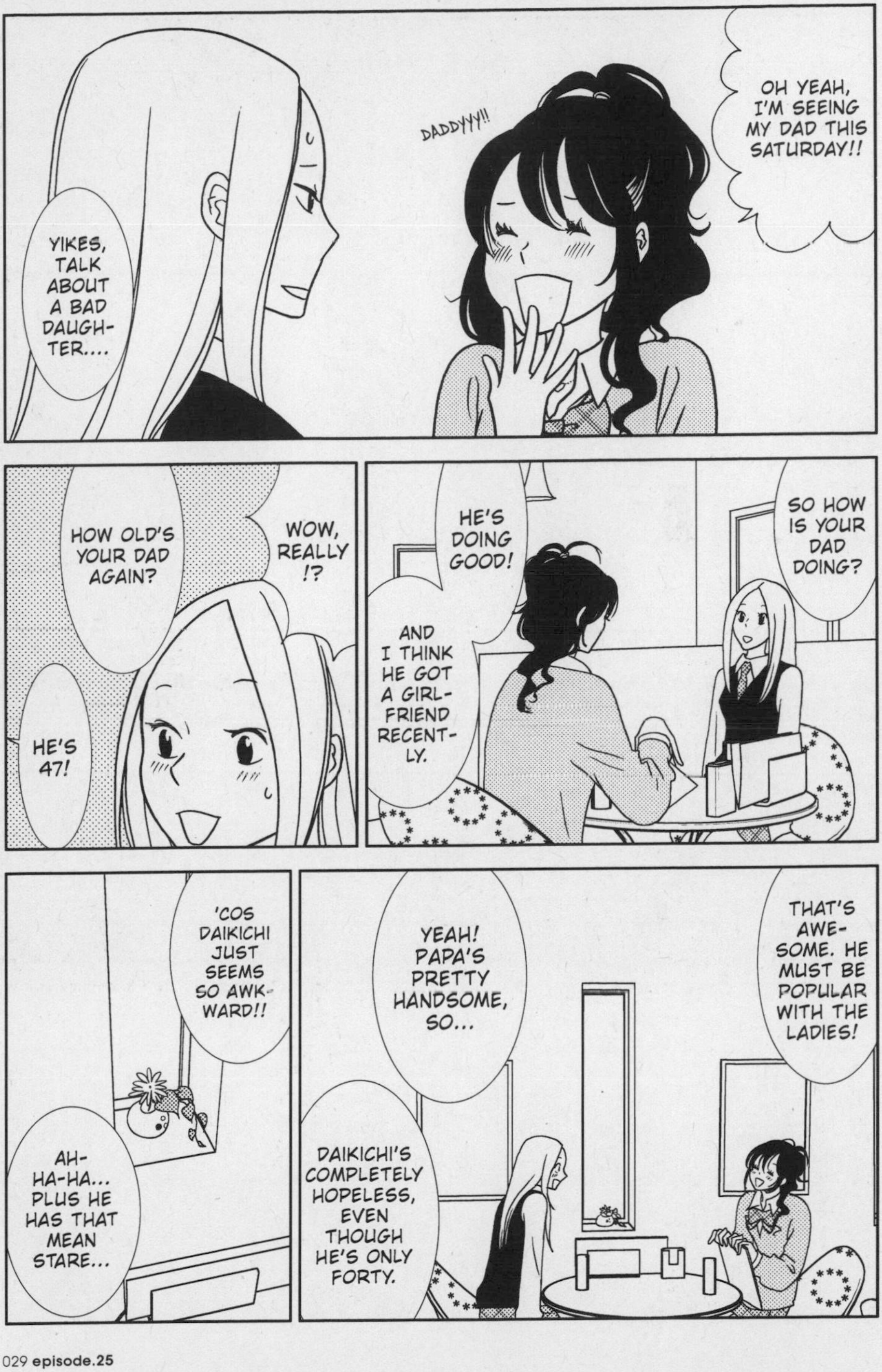
OH YEAH, I'M SEEING MY DAD THIS SATURDAY!!
DADDYYY!!
YIKES, TALK ABOUT A BAD DAUGHTER....
SO HOW IS YOUR DAD DOING?
HE'S DOING GOOD!
AND I THINK HE GOT A GIRLFRIEND RECENTLY.
WOW, REALLY!?
HOW OLD'S YOUR DAD AGAIN?
HE'S 47!
THAT'S AWESOME. HE MUST BE POPULAR WITH THE LADIES!
YEAH! PAPA'S PRETTY HANDSOME, SO...
DAIKICHI'S COMPLETELY HOPELESS, EVEN THOUGH HE'S ONLY FORTY.
'COS DAIKICHI JUST SEEMS SO AWKWARD!!
AH-HA-HA... PLUS HE HAS THAT MEAN STARE...

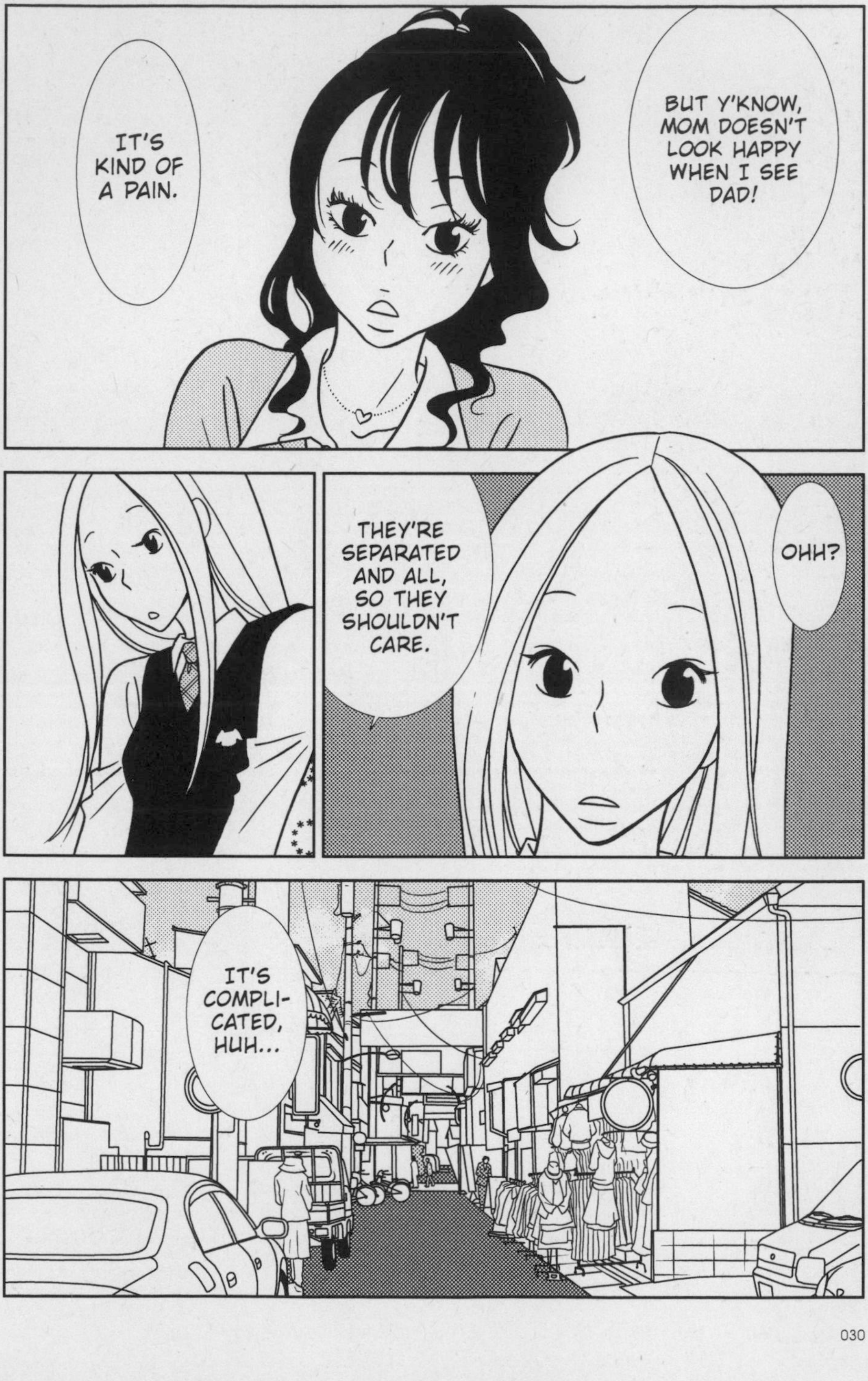
BUT Y'KNOW, MOM DOESN'T LOOK HAPPY WHEN I SEE DAD!
IT'S KIND OF A PAIN.
OHH?
THEY'RE SEPARATED AND ALL, SO THEY SHOULDN'T CARE.
IT'S COMPLI-CATED, HUH...

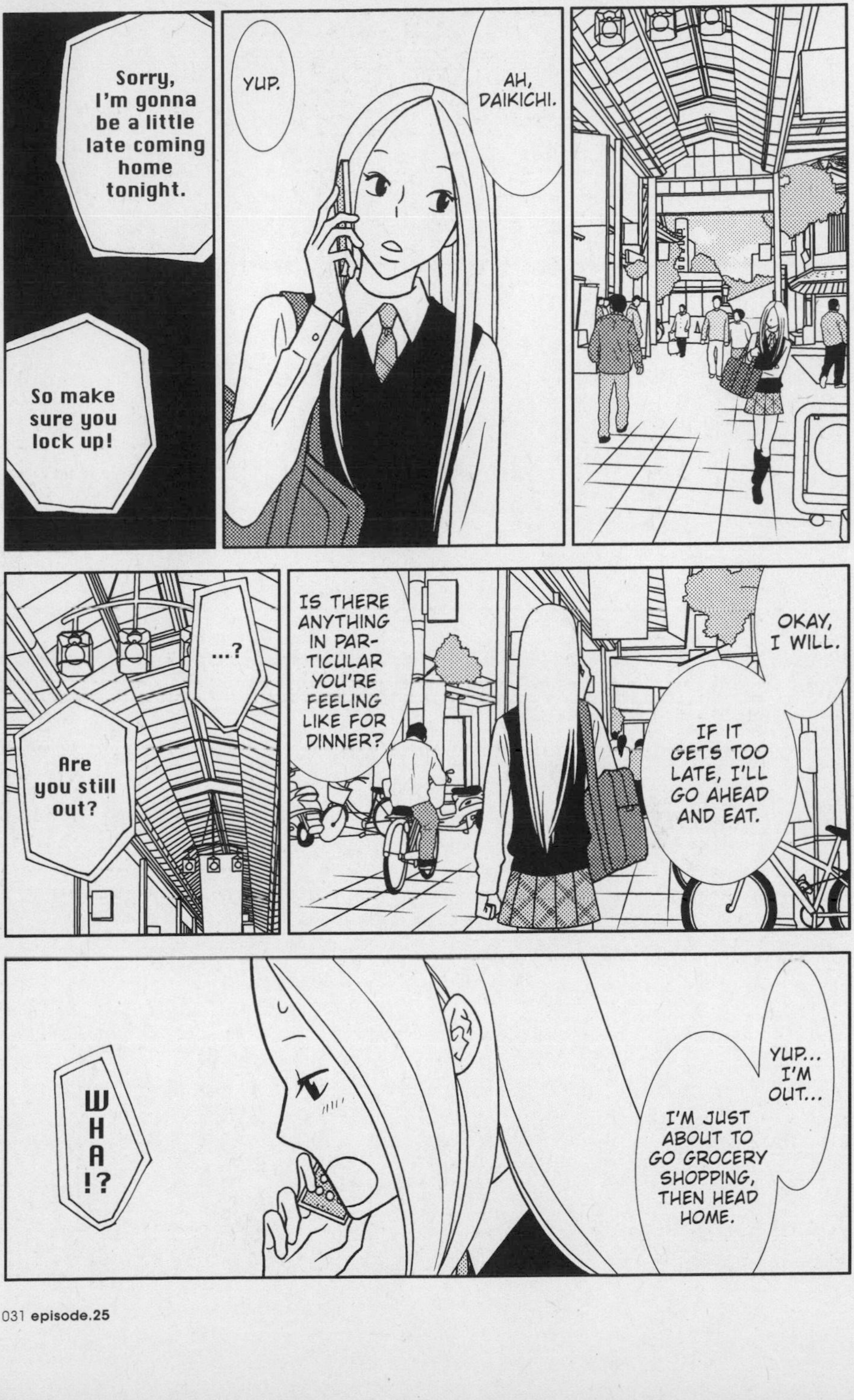
AH, DAIKICHI.
YUP.
Sorry, I'm gonna be a little late coming home tonight.
So make sure you lock up!
OKAY, I WILL.
IF IT GETS TOO LATE, I'LL GO AHEAD AND EAT.
IS THERE ANYTHING IN PAR-TICULAR YOU'RE FEELING LIKE FOR DINNER?
...?
Are you still out?
YUP... I'M OUT...
I'M JUST ABOUT TO GO GROCERY SHOPPING, THEN HEAD HOME.
WHA!?

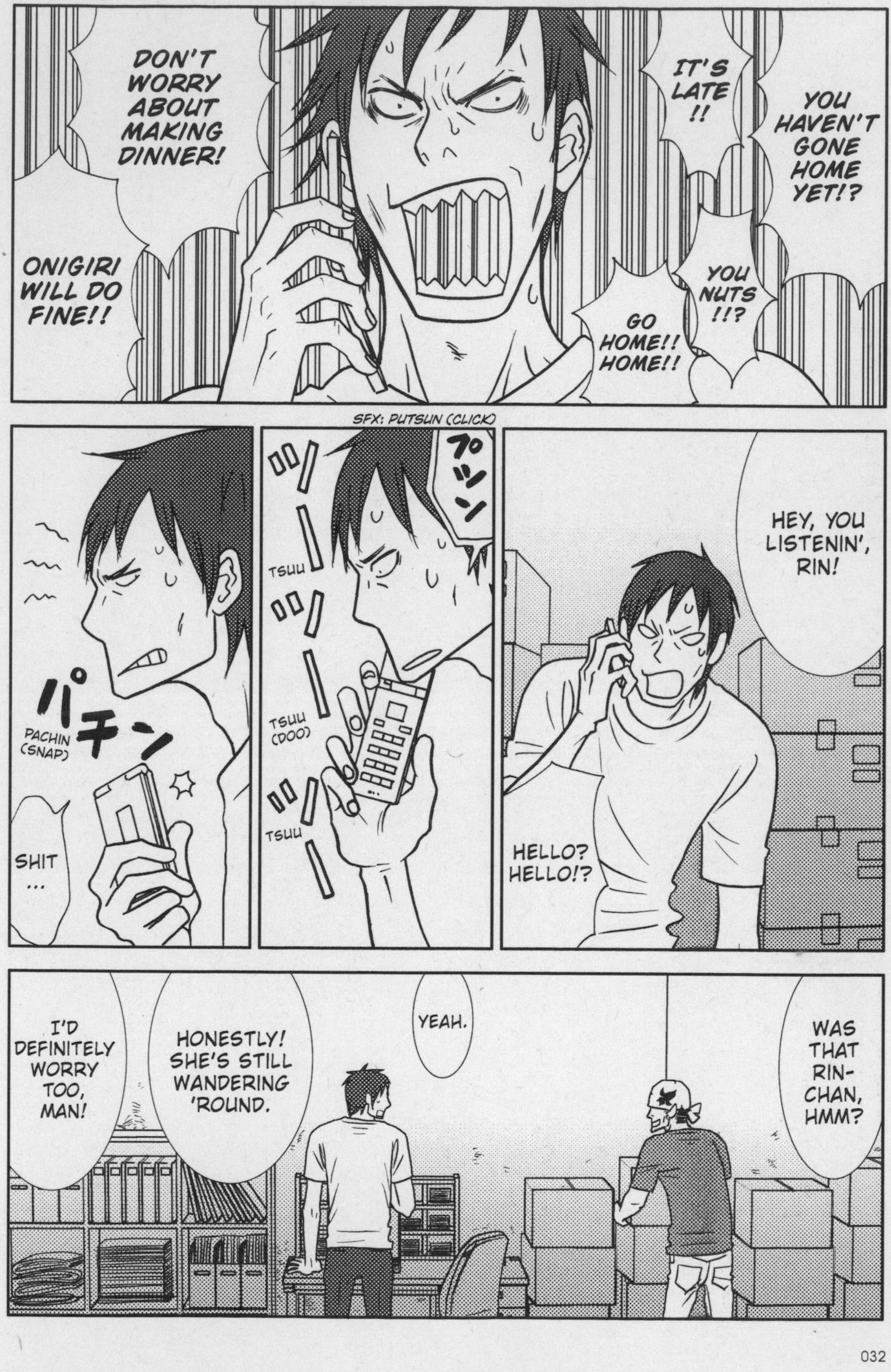
YOU HAVEN'T GONE HOME YET!?
IT'S LATE!!
DON'T WORRY ABOUT MAKING DINNER!
YOU NUTS!!?
GO HOME!! HOME!!
ONIGIRI WILL DO FINE!!
HEY, YOU LISTENIN', RIN!
HELLO? HELLO!?
SFX: PUTSUN (CLICK)
プツン
TSUU
TSUU (DOO)
TSUU
パチン
PACHIN (SNAP)
SHIT ...
WAS THAT RIN-CHAN, HMM?
YEAH.
HONESTLY! SHE'S STILL WANDERING 'ROUND.
I'D DEFINITELY WORRY TOO, MAN!

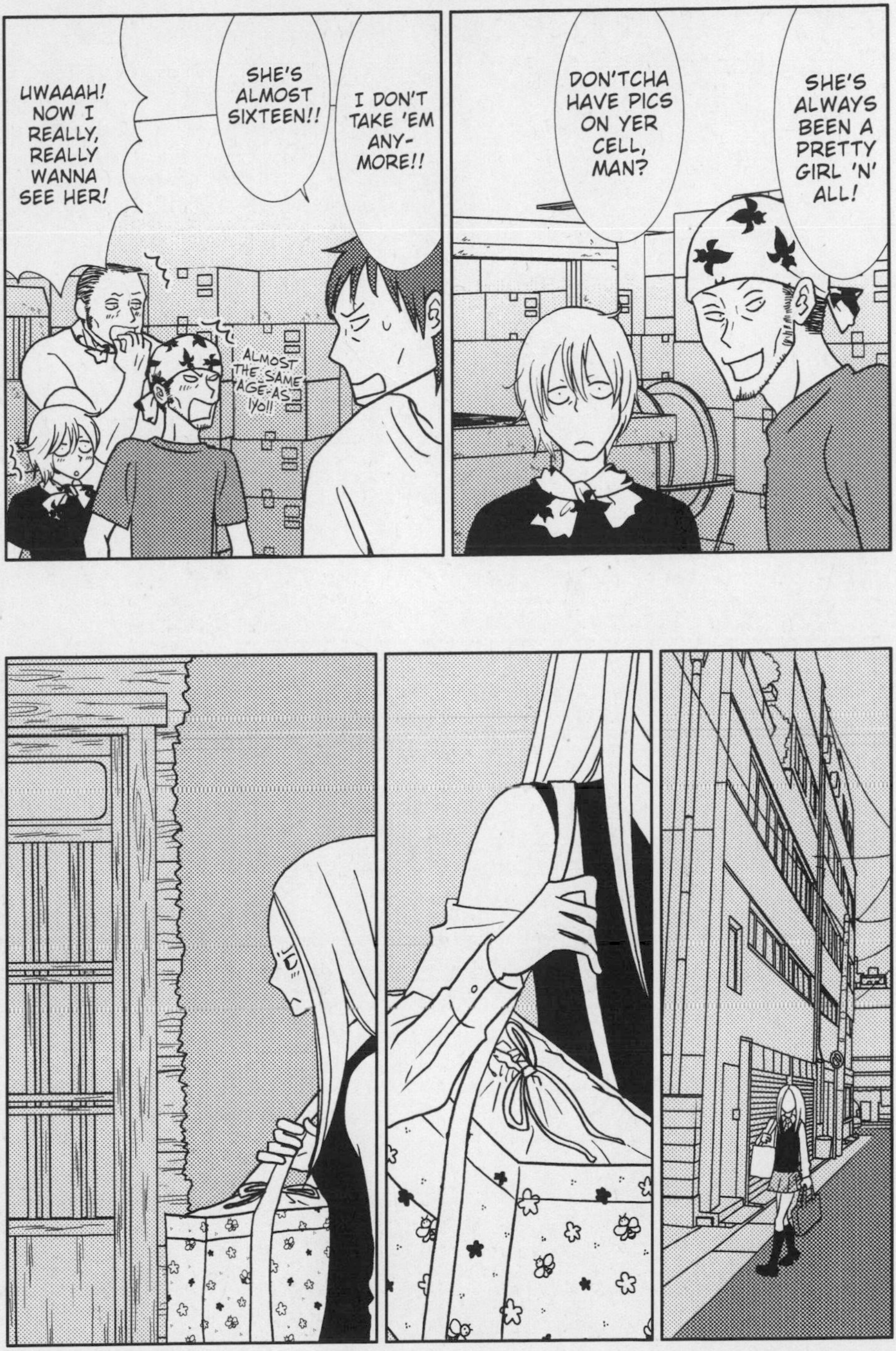
SHE'S ALWAYS BEEN A PRETTY GIRL 'N' ALL!
DON'TCHA HAVE PICS ON YER CELL, MAN?
I DON'T TAKE 'EM ANYMORE!!
SHE'S ALMOST SIXTEEN!!
UWAAAH! NOW I REALLY, REALLY WANNA SEE HER!
ALMOST THE SAME AGE AS IYO!!

BAG: RED BEAN BUN

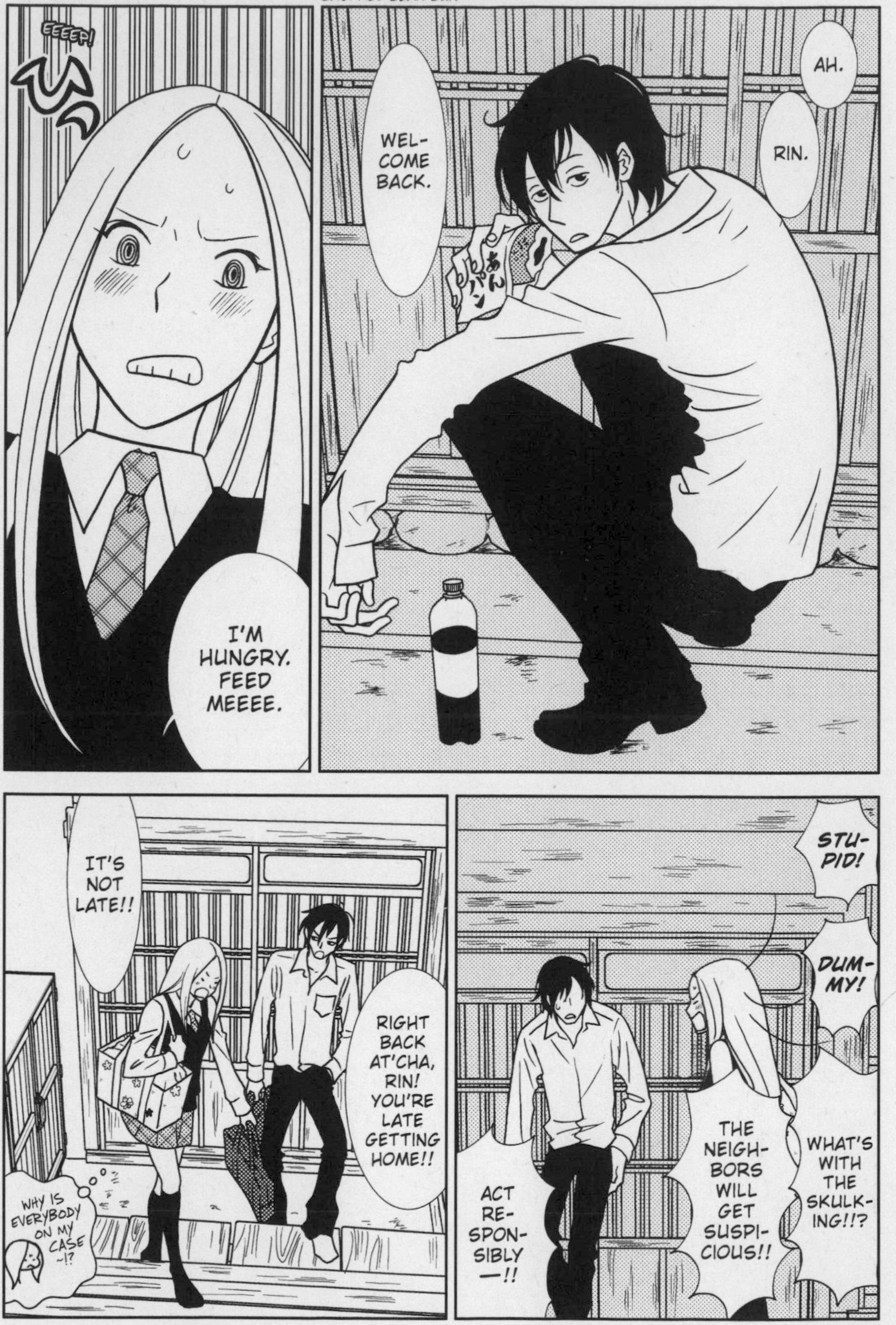
AH.
RIN.
WELCOME BACK.
あんパン
EEEEP!
ひっ
I'M HUNGRY. FEED MEEEE.
STUPID!
DUMMY!
WHAT'S WITH THE SKULKING!!?
THE NEIGHBORS WILL GET SUSPICIOUS!!
ACT RESPONSIBLY—!!
RIGHT BACK AT'CHA, RIN! YOU'RE LATE GETTING HOME!!
IT'S NOT LATE!!
WHY IS EVERYBODY ON MY CASE ~!?

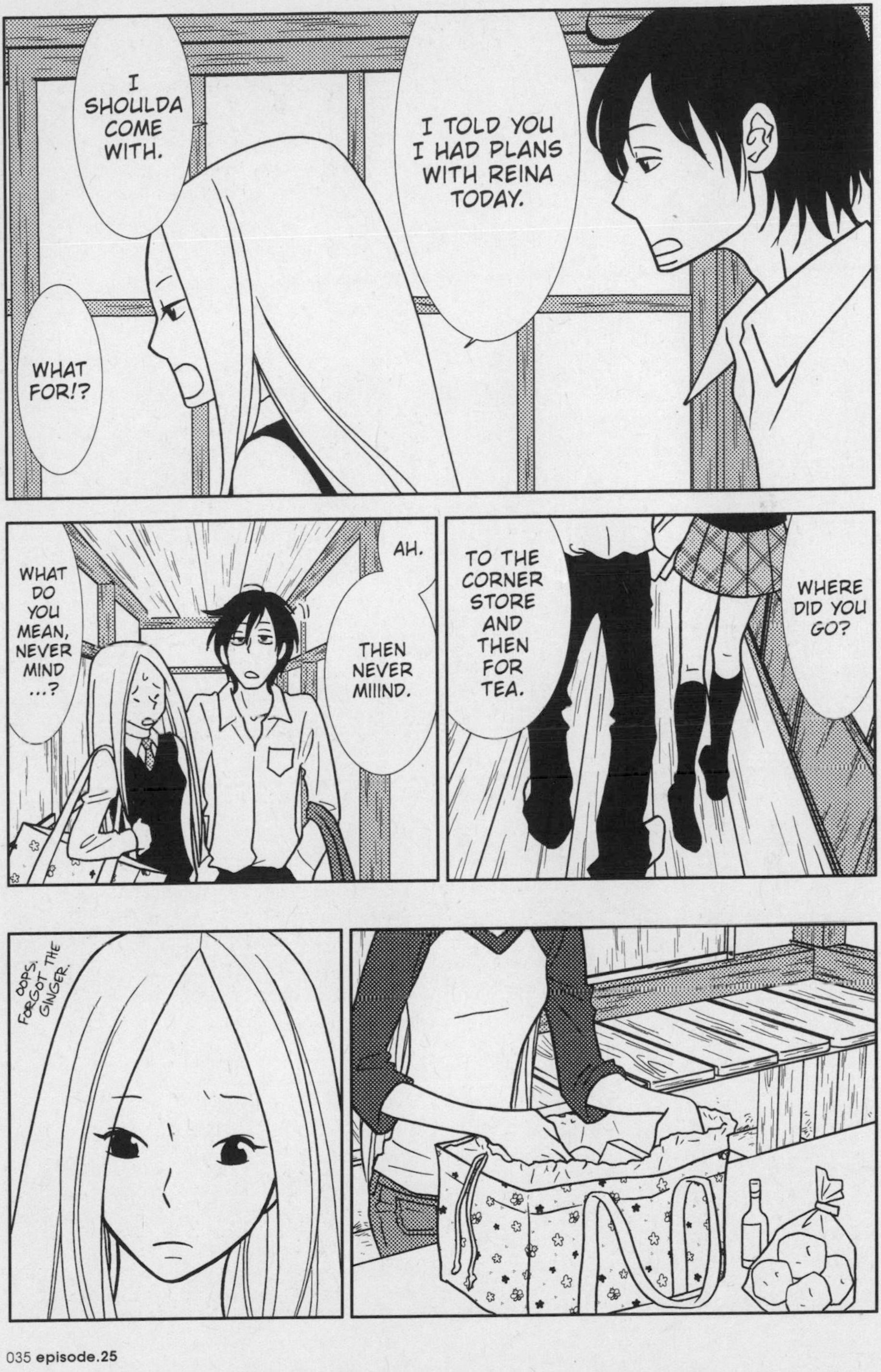
I TOLD YOU I HAD PLANS WITH REINA TODAY.
I SHOULDA COME WITH.
WHAT FOR!?
WHERE DID YOU GO?
TO THE CORNER STORE AND THEN FOR TEA.
AH.
THEN NEVER MIIIND.
WHAT DO YOU MEAN, NEVER MIND ...?
OOPS, FORGOT THE GINGER.

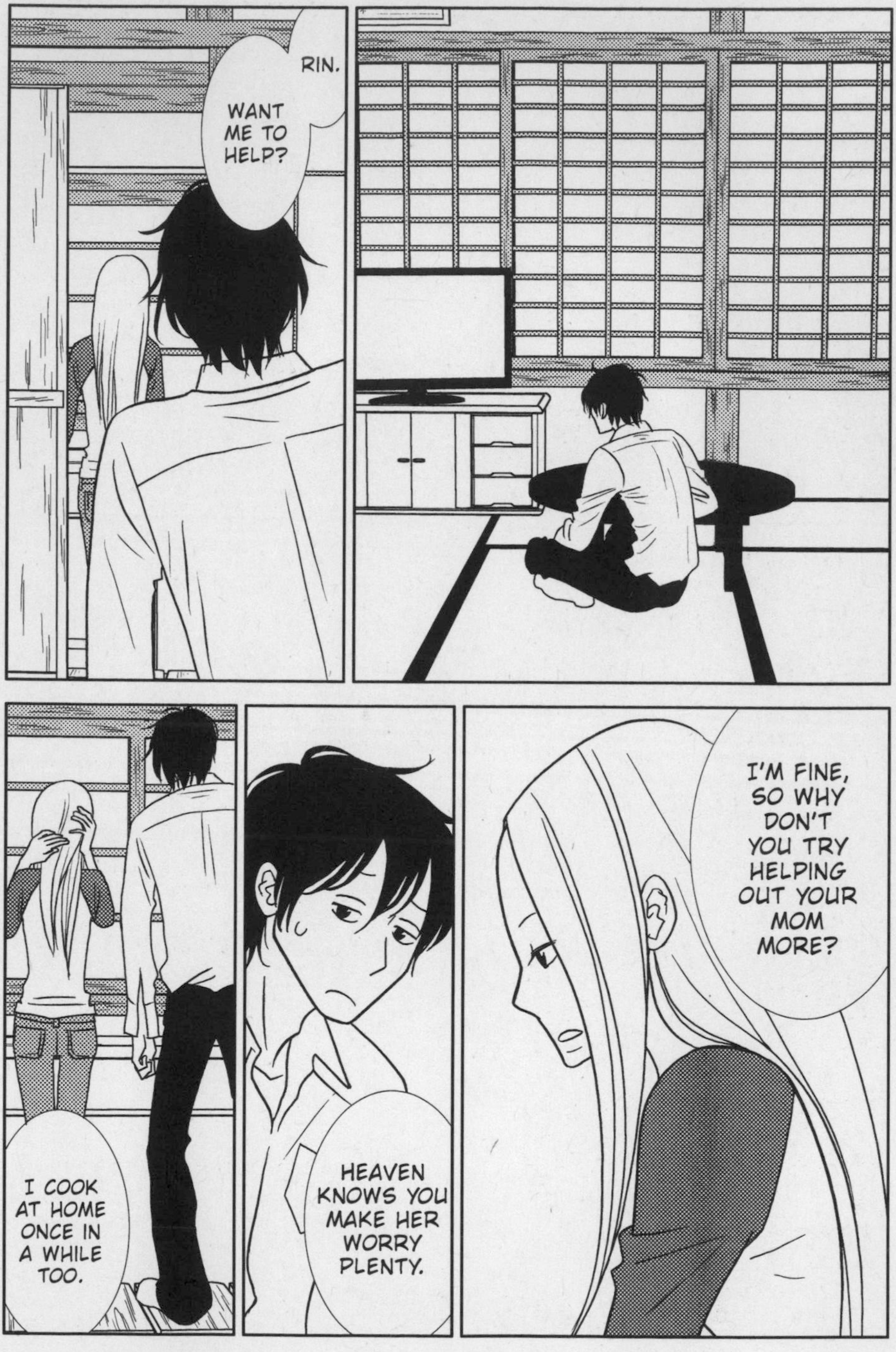
RIN.
WANT ME TO HELP?
I'M FINE, SO WHY DON'T YOU TRY HELPING OUT YOUR MOM MORE?
HEAVEN KNOWS YOU MAKE HER WORRY PLENTY.
I COOK AT HOME ONCE IN A WHILE TOO.

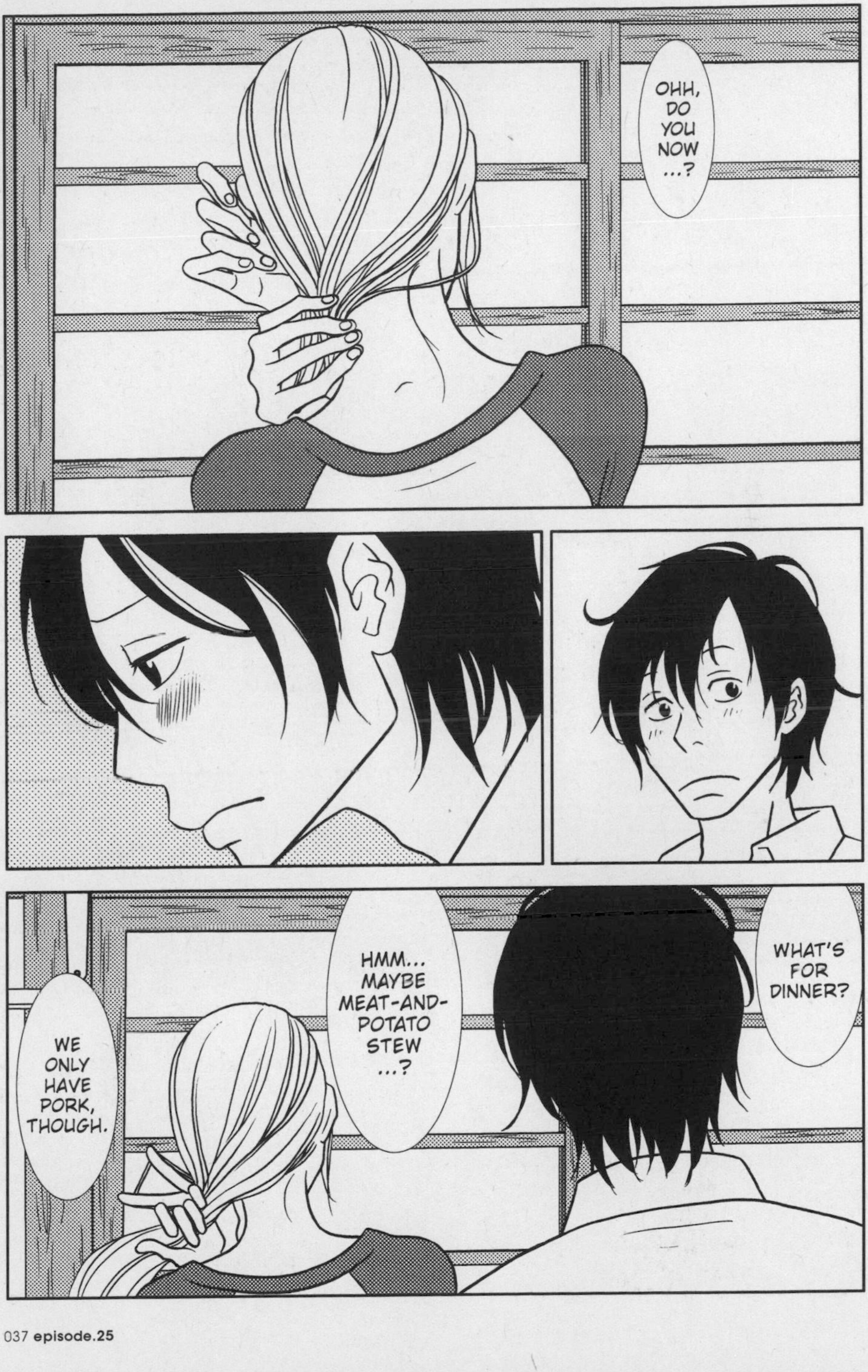
OHH, DO YOU NOW ...?
WHAT'S FOR DINNER?
HMM... MAYBE MEAT-AND-POTATO STEW ...?
WE ONLY HAVE PORK, THOUGH.

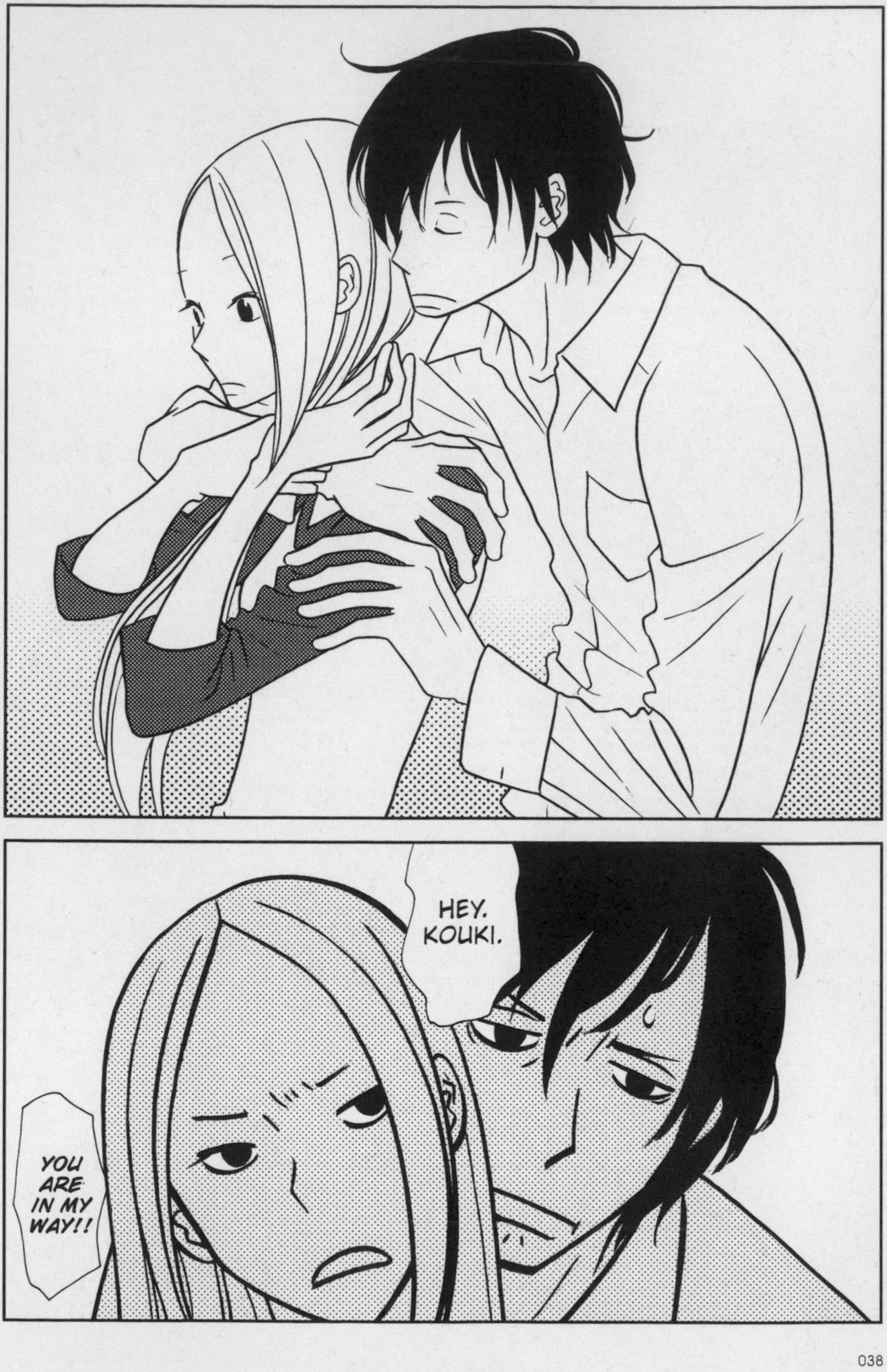
HEY. KOUKI.
YOU ARE IN MY WAY!!

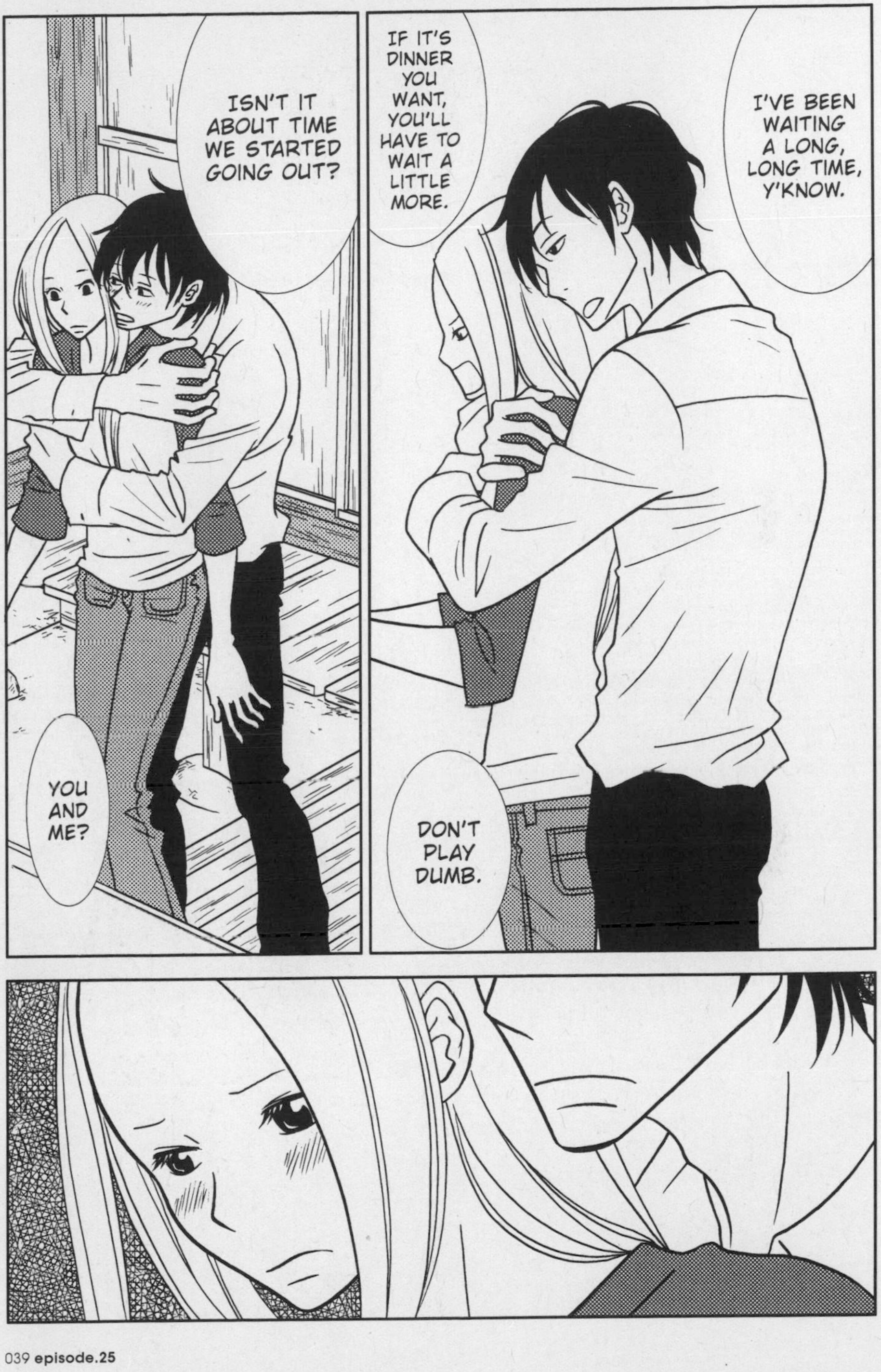
I'VE BEEN WAITING A LONG, LONG TIME, Y'KNOW.
IF IT'S DINNER YOU WANT, YOU'LL HAVE TO WAIT A LITTLE MORE.
DON'T PLAY DUMB.
ISN'T IT ABOUT TIME WE STARTED GOING OUT?
YOU AND ME?

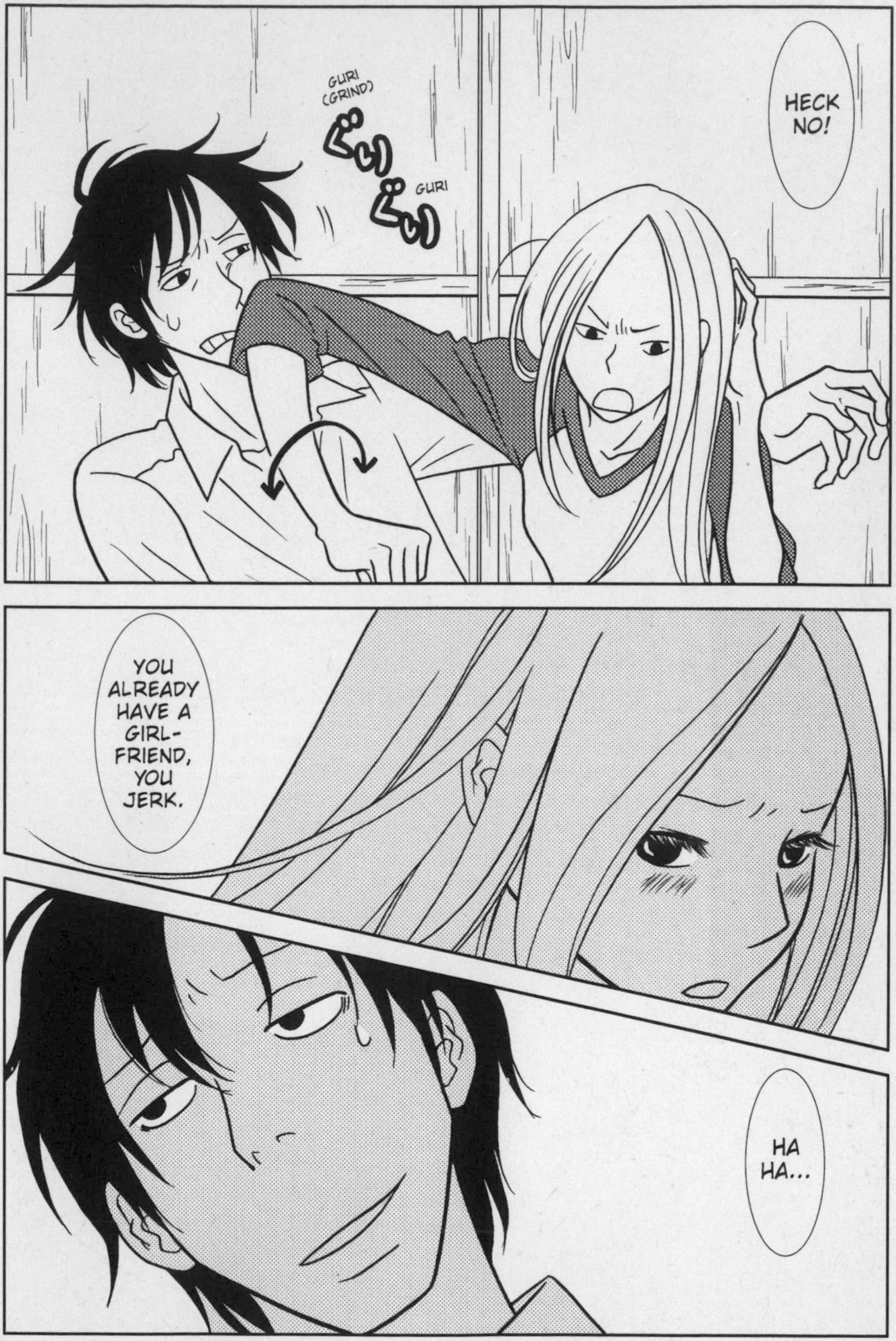
HECK NO!
GURI (GRIND)
ぐり
GURI
ぐり
YOU ALREADY HAVE A GIRL-FRIEND, YOU JERK.
HA HA...

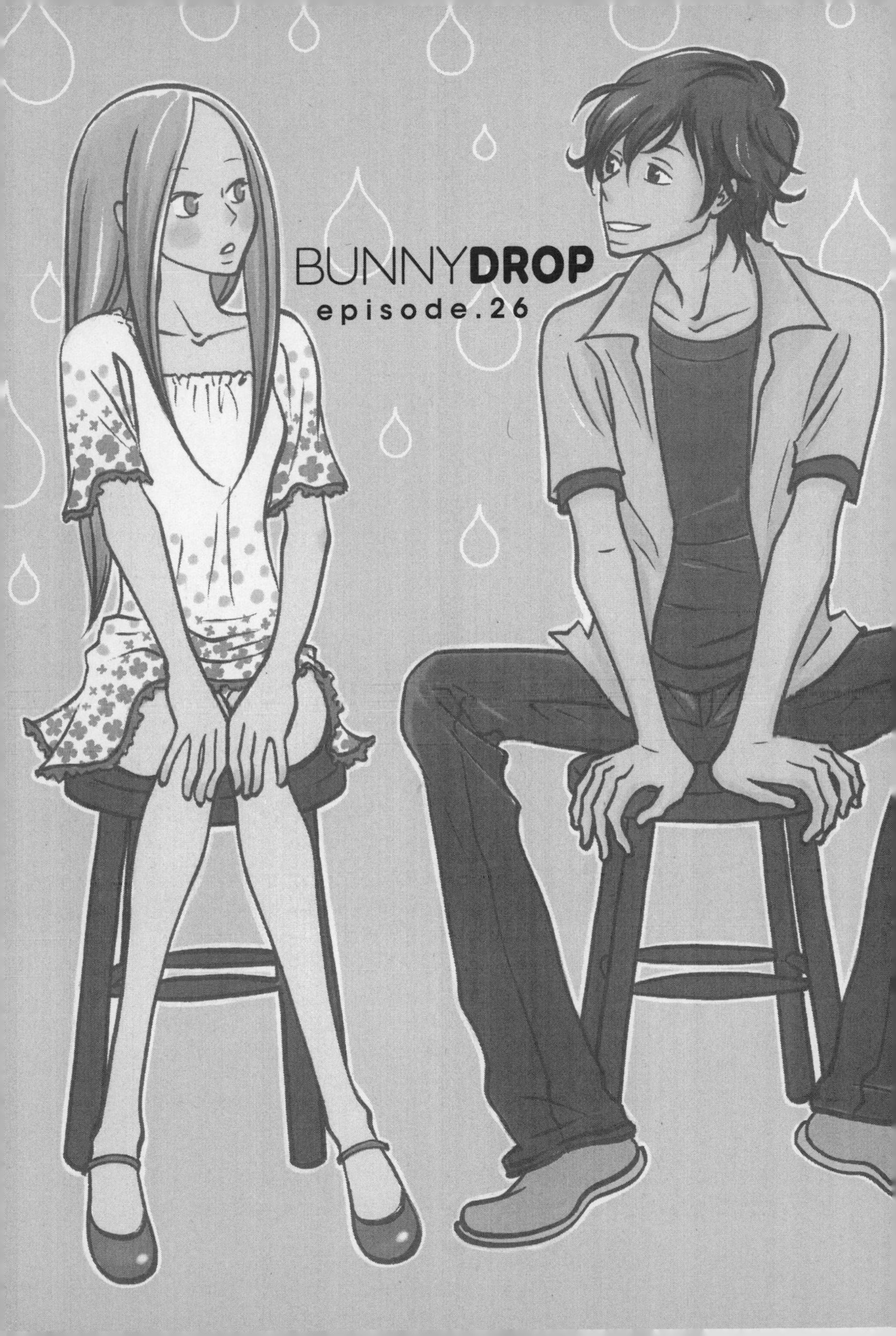
BUNNYDROP
episode.26

BUNNY**DROP**

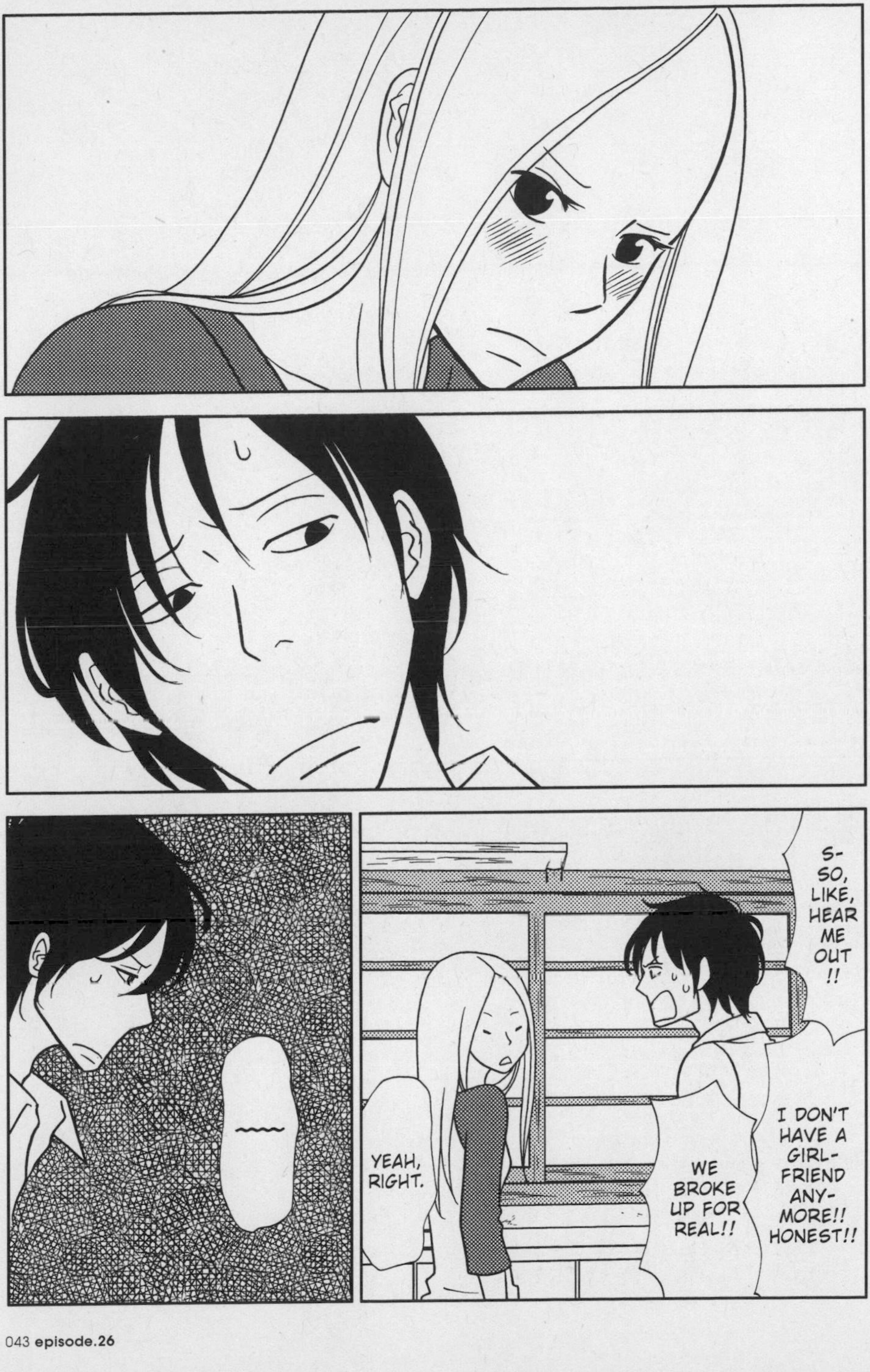
S-SO, LIKE, HEAR ME OUT!!
I DON'T HAVE A GIRL-FRIEND ANY-MORE!! HONEST!!
WE BROKE UP FOR REAL!!
YEAH, RIGHT.

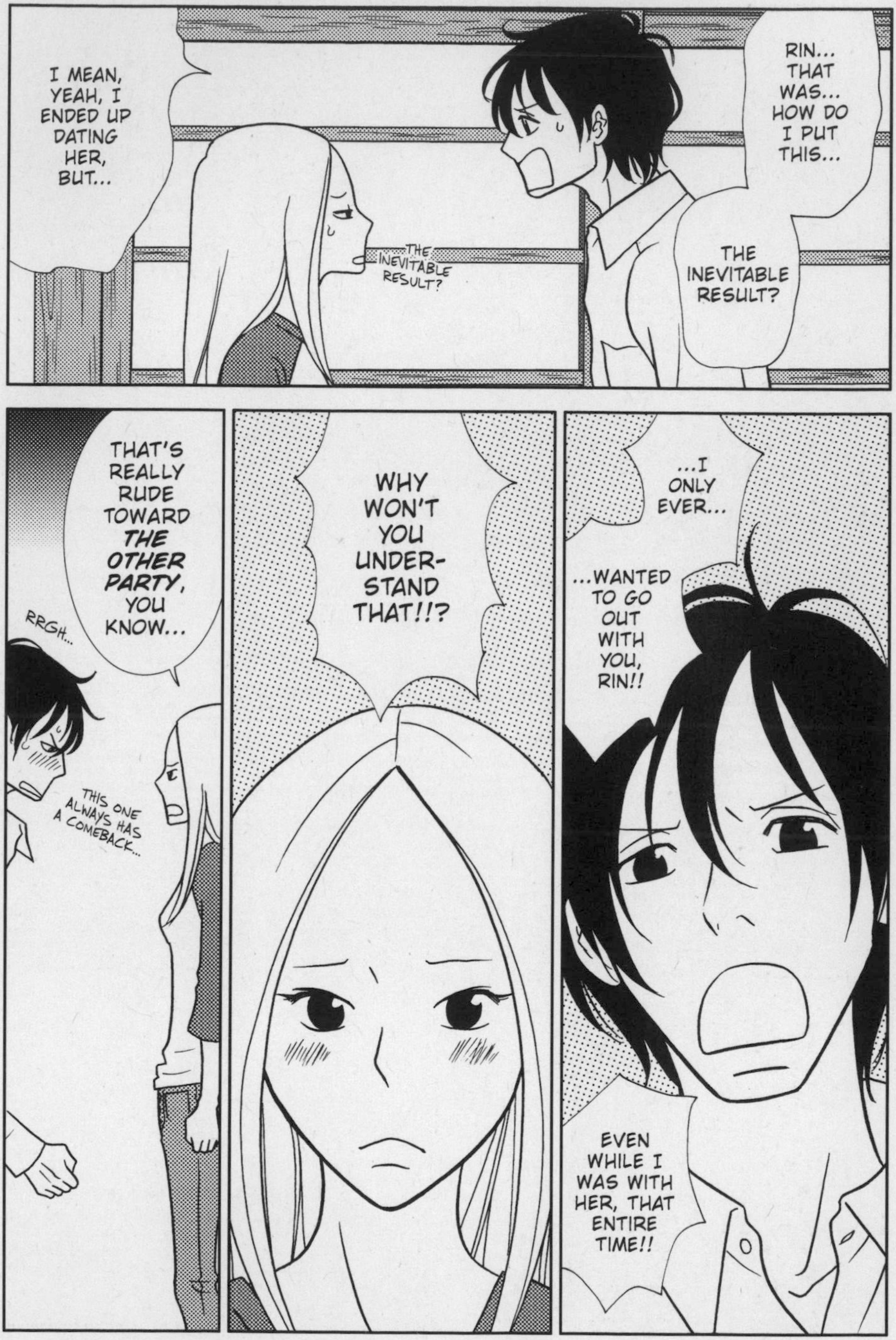
RIN... THAT WAS... HOW DO I PUT THIS...
THE INEVITABLE RESULT?
THE INEVITABLE RESULT?
I MEAN, YEAH, I ENDED UP DATING HER, BUT...
...I ONLY EVER...
...WANTED TO GO OUT WITH YOU, RIN!!
EVEN WHILE I WAS WITH HER, THAT ENTIRE TIME!!
WHY WON'T YOU UNDER-STAND THAT!!?
THAT'S REALLY RUDE TOWARD THE OTHER PARTY, YOU KNOW...
RRGH...
THIS ONE ALWAYS HAS A COMEBACK...

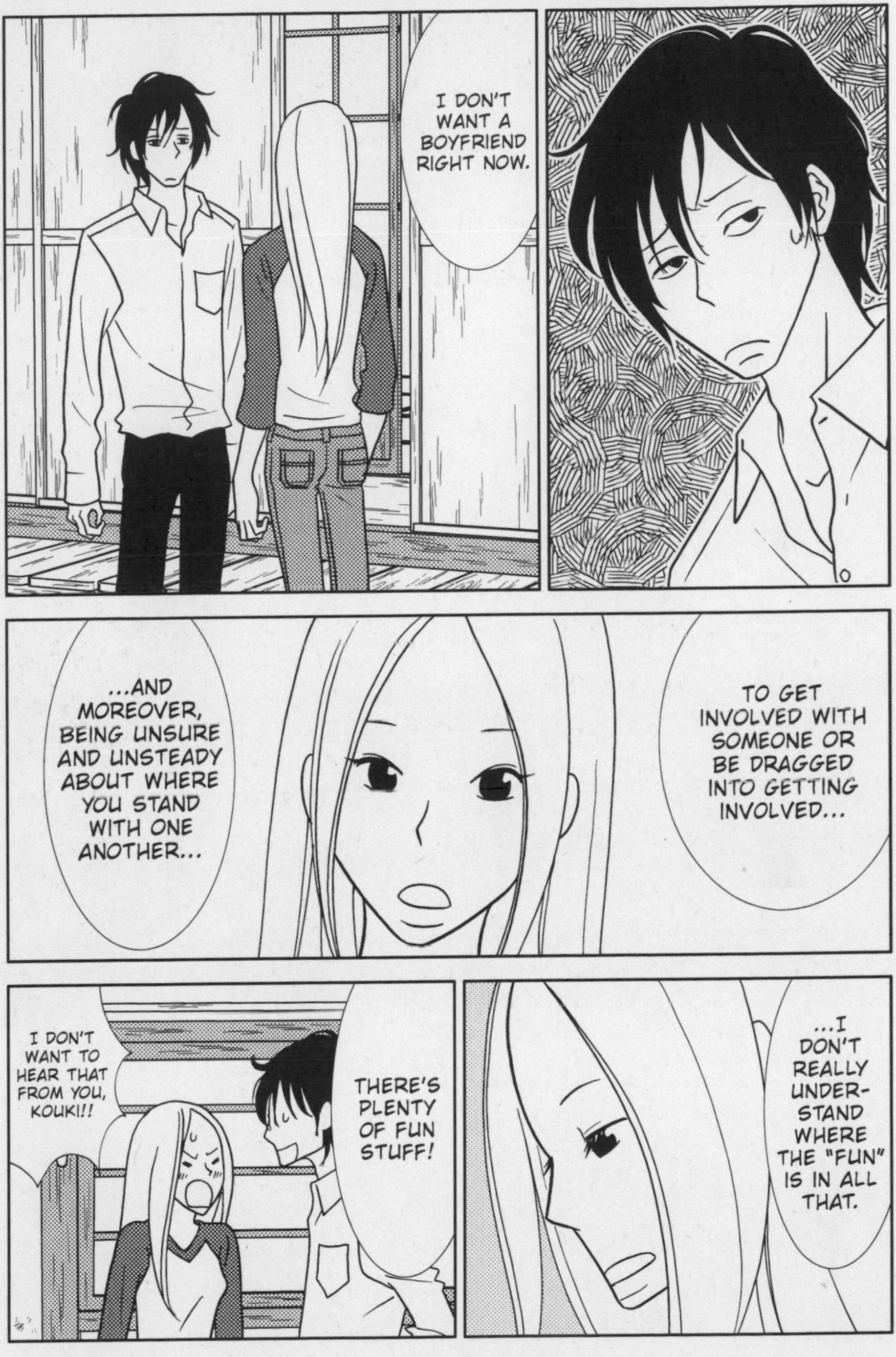
I DON'T WANT A BOYFRIEND RIGHT NOW.
TO GET INVOLVED WITH SOMEONE OR BE DRAGGED INTO GETTING INVOLVED...
...AND MOREOVER, BEING UNSURE AND UNSTEADY ABOUT WHERE YOU STAND WITH ONE ANOTHER...
...I DON'T REALLY UNDER-STAND WHERE THE "FUN" IS IN ALL THAT.
THERE'S PLENTY OF FUN STUFF!
I DON'T WANT TO HEAR THAT FROM YOU, KOUKI!!

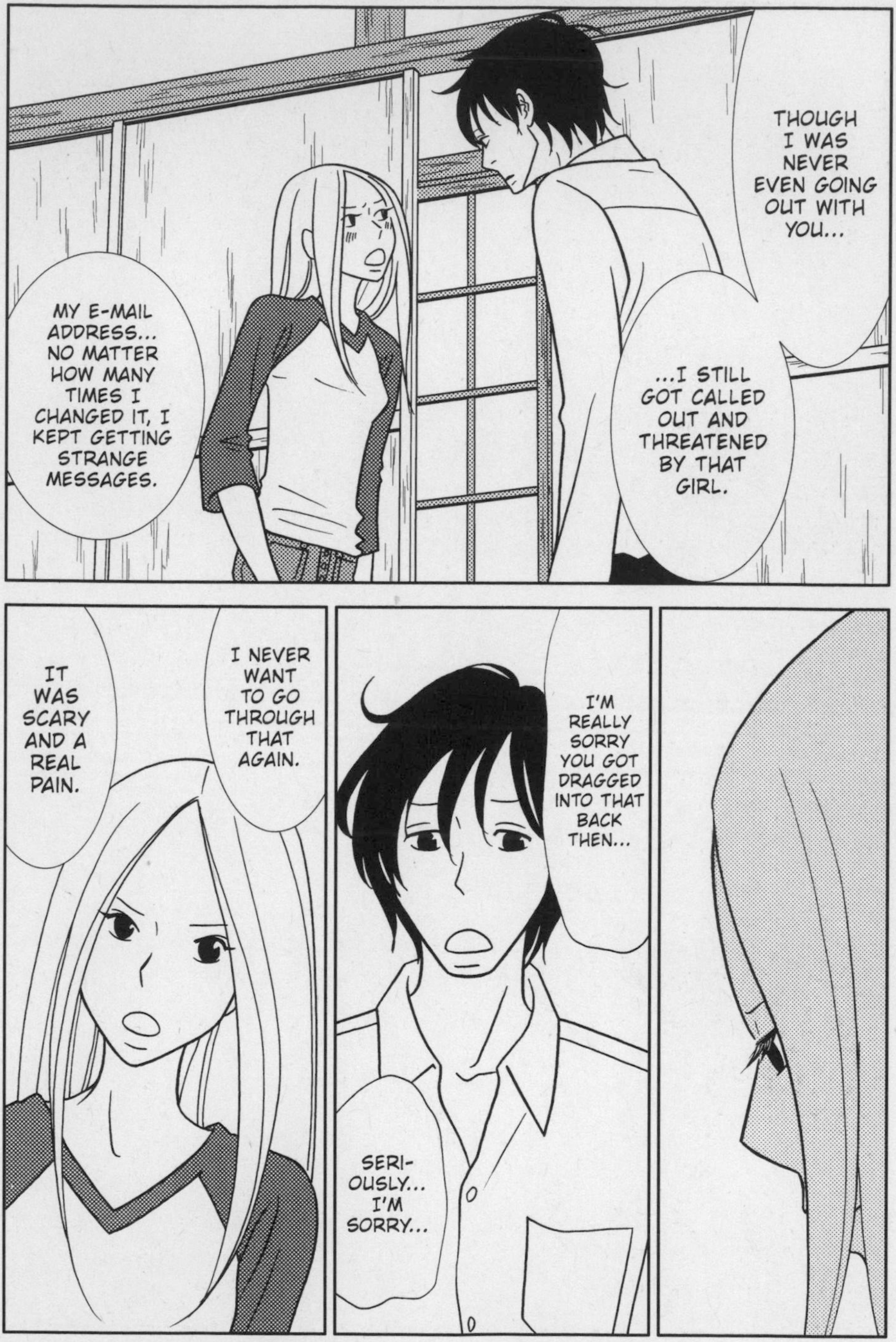
THOUGH I WAS NEVER EVEN GOING OUT WITH YOU...
...I STILL GOT CALLED OUT AND THREATENED BY THAT GIRL.
MY E-MAIL ADDRESS... NO MATTER HOW MANY TIMES I CHANGED IT, I KEPT GETTING STRANGE MESSAGES.
I'M REALLY SORRY YOU GOT DRAGGED INTO THAT BACK THEN...
SERI-OUSLY... I'M SORRY...
I NEVER WANT TO GO THROUGH THAT AGAIN.
IT WAS SCARY AND A REAL PAIN.

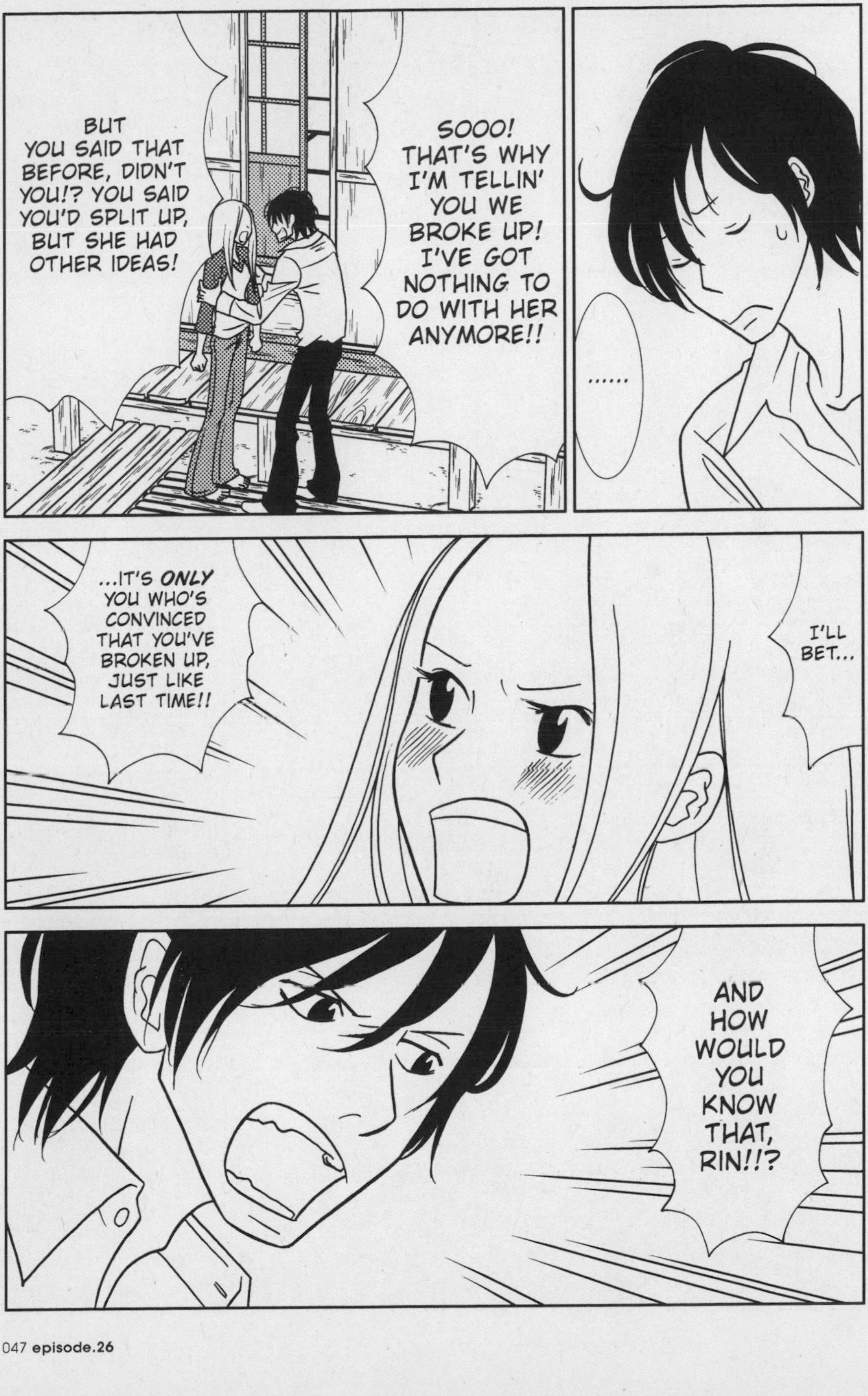
......
BUT YOU SAID THAT BEFORE, DIDN'T YOU!? YOU SAID YOU'D SPLIT UP, BUT SHE HAD OTHER IDEAS!
SOOO! THAT'S WHY I'M TELLIN' YOU WE BROKE UP! I'VE GOT NOTHING TO DO WITH HER ANYMORE!!
I'LL BET...
...IT'S *ONLY* YOU WHO'S CONVINCED THAT YOU'VE BROKEN UP, JUST LIKE LAST TIME!!
AND HOW WOULD YOU KNOW THAT, RIN!!?

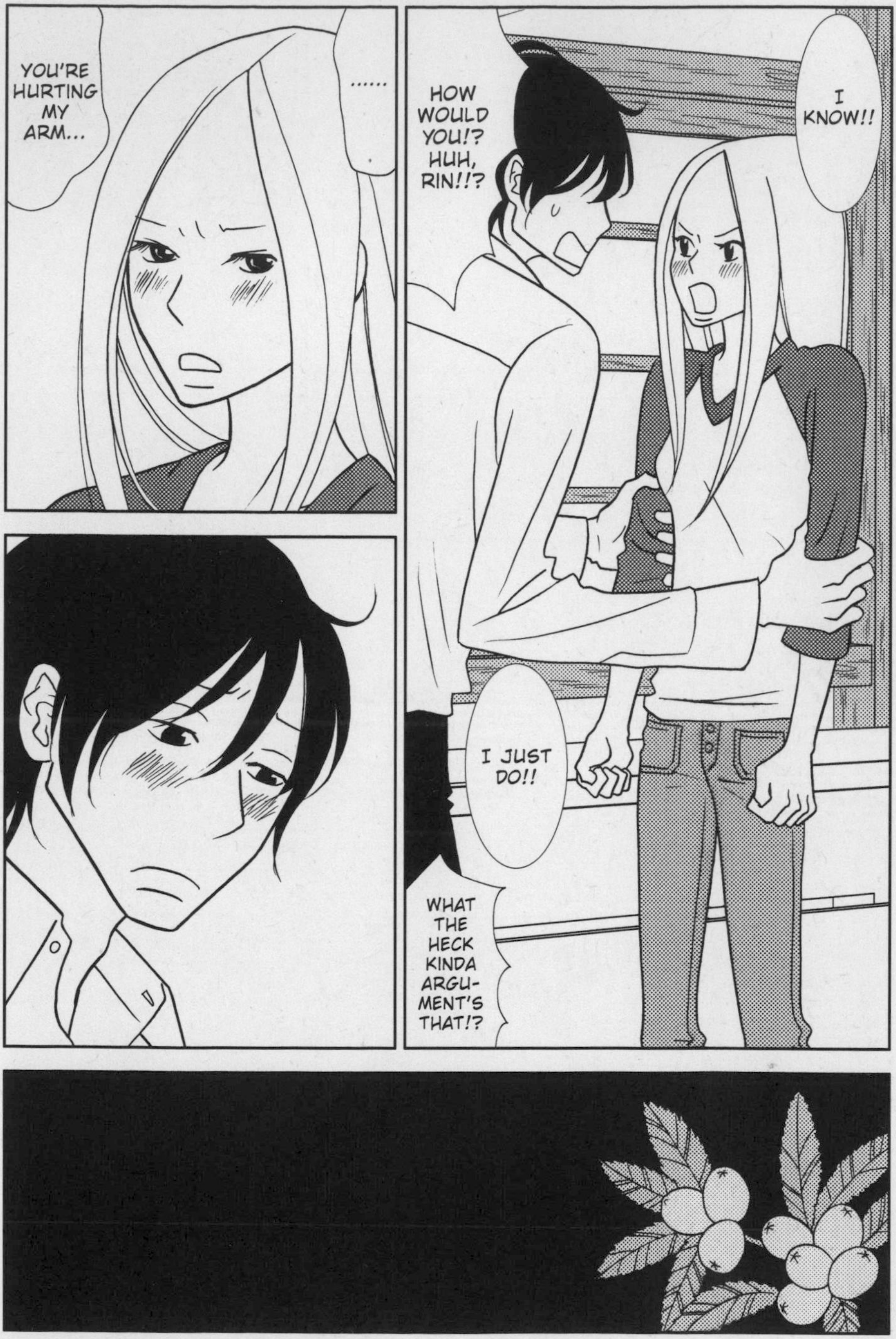
I KNOW!!
HOW WOULD YOU!? HUH, RIN!!?
I JUST DO!!
WHAT THE HECK KINDA ARGU-MENT'S THAT!?
......
YOU'RE HURTING MY ARM...

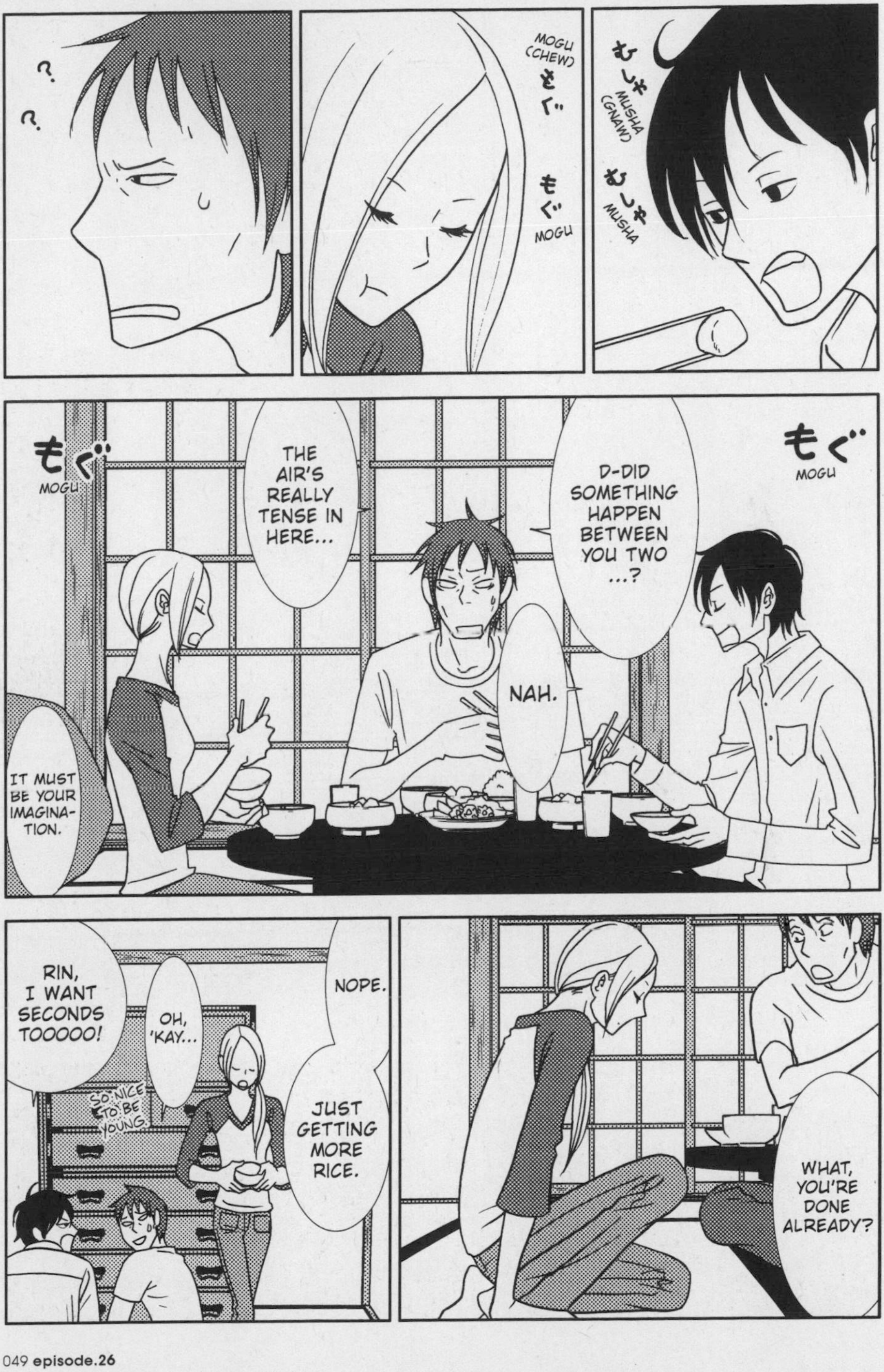
むしゃ
MUSHA (GNAW)
むしゃ
MUSHA
MOGU (CHEW)
もぐ
もぐ
MOGU
?
?
もぐ
MOGU
D-DID SOMETHING HAPPEN BETWEEN YOU TWO ...?
THE AIR'S REALLY TENSE IN HERE...
NAH.
もぐ
MOGU
IT MUST BE YOUR IMAGINATION.
WHAT, YOU'RE DONE ALREADY?
NOPE.
JUST GETTING MORE RICE.
RIN, I WANT SECONDS TOOOOO!
OH, 'KAY...
SO NICE TO BE YOUNG.

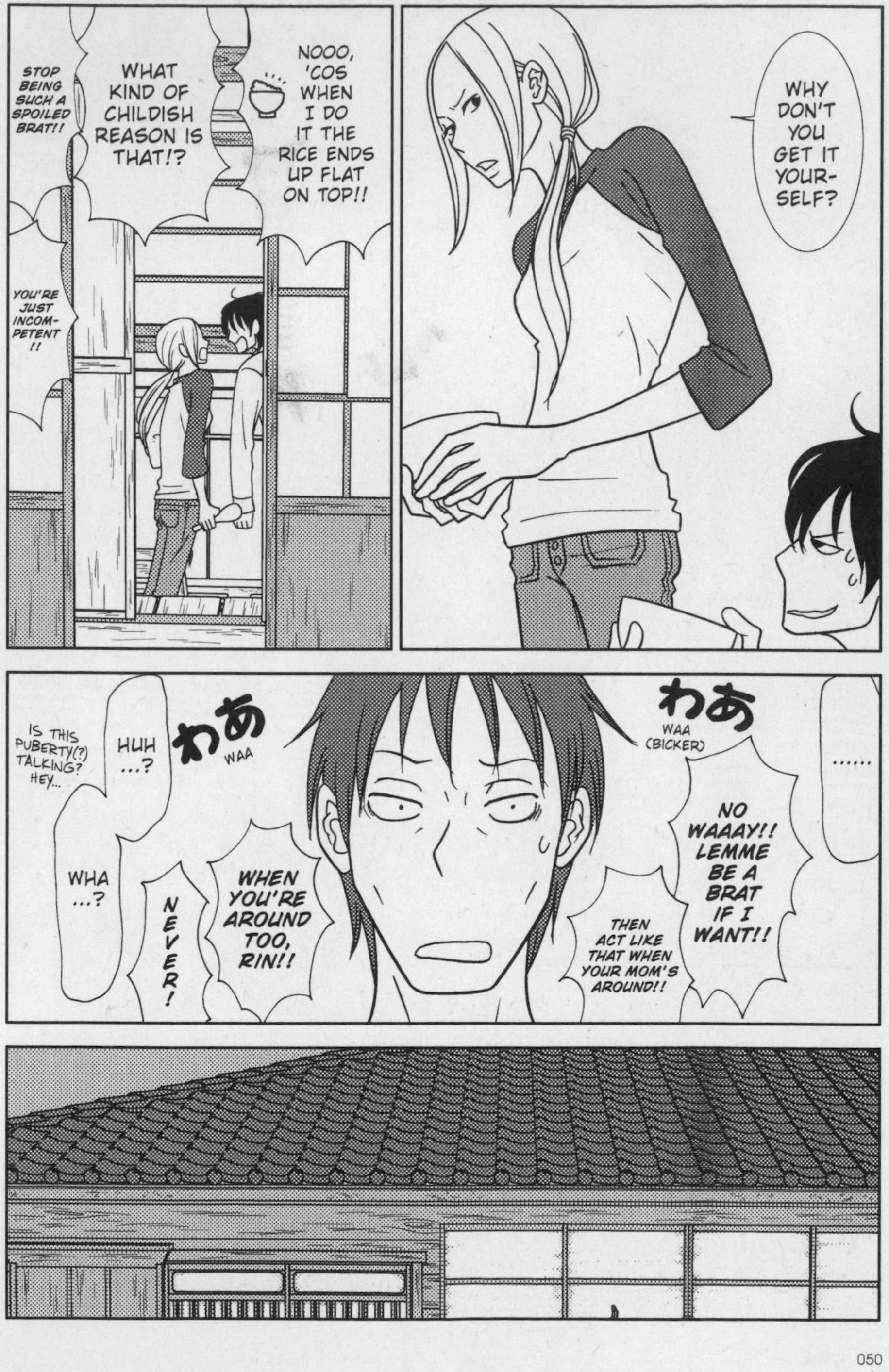
WHY DON'T YOU GET IT YOURSELF?
NOOO, 'COS WHEN I DO IT THE RICE ENDS UP FLAT ON TOP!!
WHAT KIND OF CHILDISH REASON IS THAT!?
STOP BEING SUCH A SPOILED BRAT!!
YOU'RE JUST INCOMPETENT!!
......
わあ
WAA (BICKER)
NO WAAAY!! LEMME BE A BRAT IF I WANT!!
THEN ACT LIKE THAT WHEN YOUR MOM'S AROUND!!
WHEN YOU'RE AROUND TOO, RIN!!
NEVER!
わあ
WAA
HUH ...?
WHA ...?
IS THIS PUBERTY(?) TALKING? HEY...

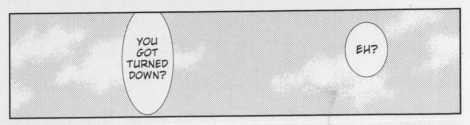

EH?
YOU GOT TURNED DOWN?
YEP...
NO WAY-YYY...!
I THOUGHT YOU TWO WERE GOING OUT...!!
NOT TRUE?
NOPE!
BUT YOU GUYS WALK TO SCHOOL ALL FRIENDLY EVERY DAY AND STUFF...
PRACTICALLY LIKE YOU TWO LIVE TOGETHER...
I'M SO JEALOUS...
YEAH, WE'RE CLOSE, BUT...
...UGH... THAT RIN KEEPS DREDGING UP THE PAST...
HUH? COME AGAIN?

SFX: BUTSU (MUTTER) BUTSU

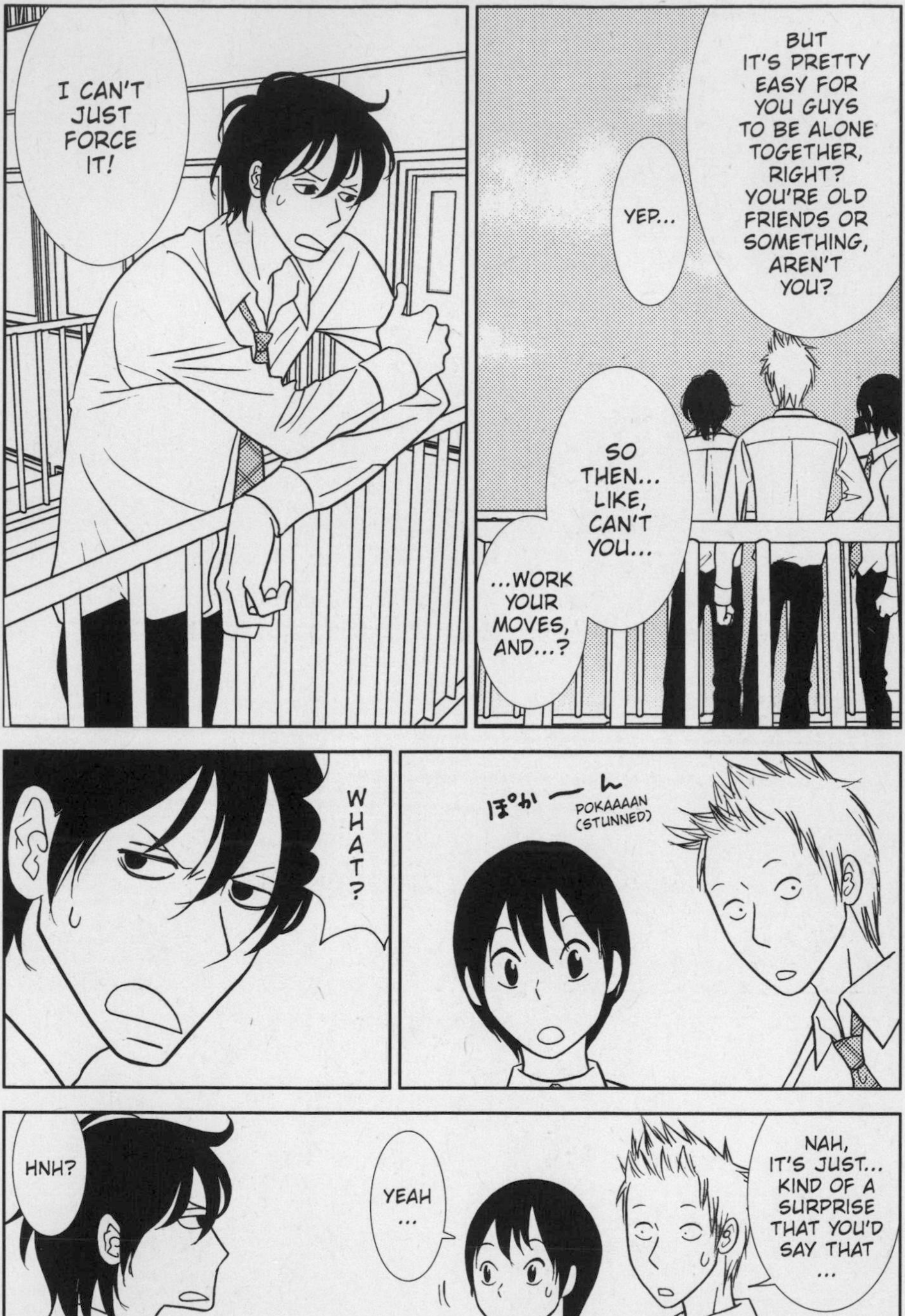
BUT IT'S PRETTY EASY FOR YOU GUYS TO BE ALONE TOGETHER, RIGHT? YOU'RE OLD FRIENDS OR SOMETHING, AREN'T YOU?
YEP...
SO THEN... LIKE, CAN'T YOU...
...WORK YOUR MOVES, AND...?
I CAN'T JUST FORCE IT!
ぽかーん
POKAAAAN (STUNNED)
WHAT?
NAH, IT'S JUST... KIND OF A SURPRISE THAT YOU'D SAY THAT ...
YEAH ...
HNH?

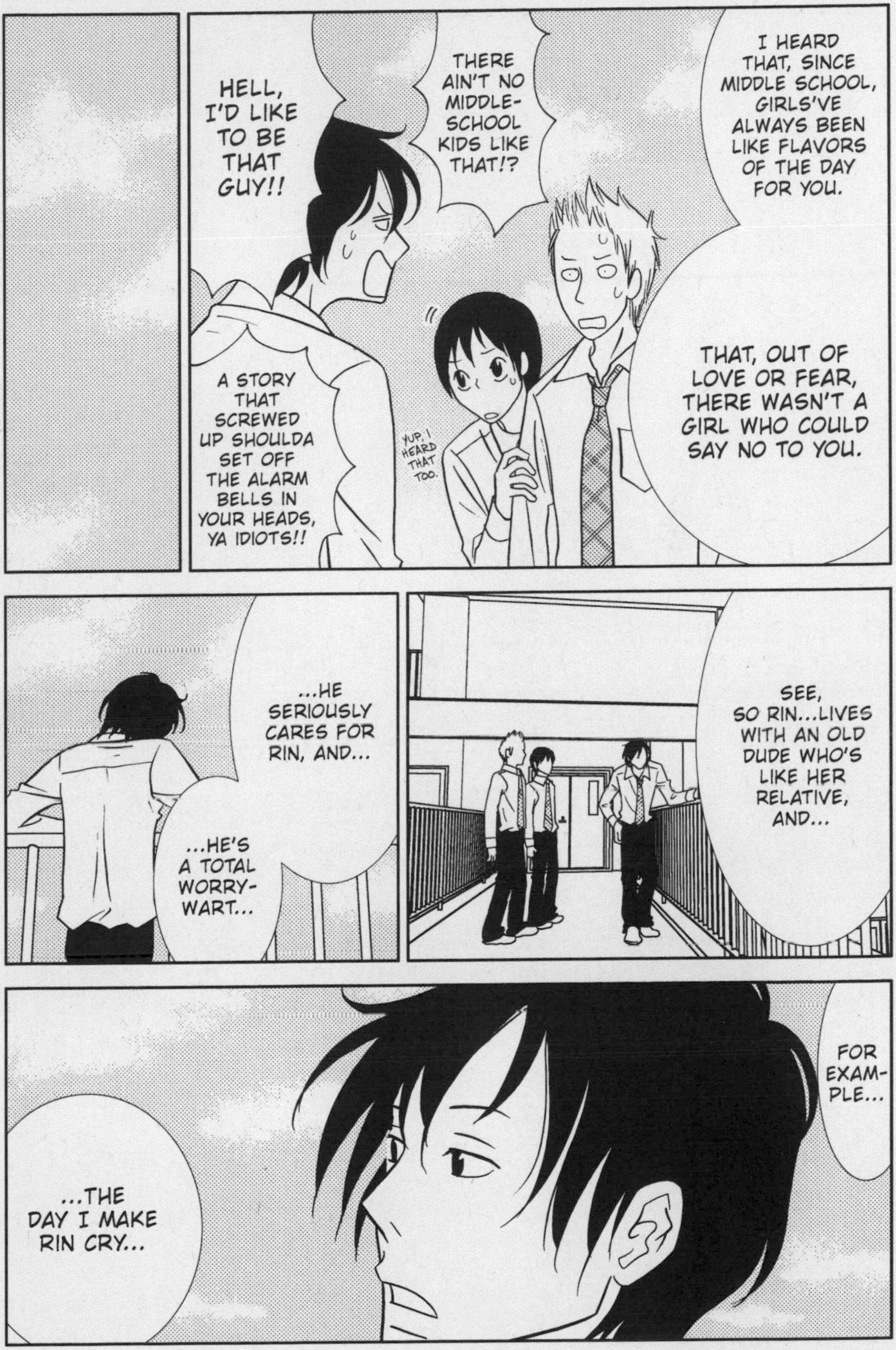
I HEARD THAT, SINCE MIDDLE SCHOOL, GIRLS'VE ALWAYS BEEN LIKE FLAVORS OF THE DAY FOR YOU.
THAT, OUT OF LOVE OR FEAR, THERE WASN'T A GIRL WHO COULD SAY NO TO YOU.
THERE AIN'T NO MIDDLE-SCHOOL KIDS LIKE THAT!?
HELL, I'D LIKE TO BE THAT GUY!!
YUP, I HEARD THAT TOO.
A STORY THAT SCREWED UP SHOULDA SET OFF THE ALARM BELLS IN YOUR HEADS, YA IDIOTS!!
SEE, SO RIN...LIVES WITH AN OLD DUDE WHO'S LIKE HER RELATIVE, AND...
...HE SERIOUSLY CARES FOR RIN, AND...
...HE'S A TOTAL WORRY-WART...
FOR EXAM-PLE...
...THE DAY I MAKE RIN CRY...

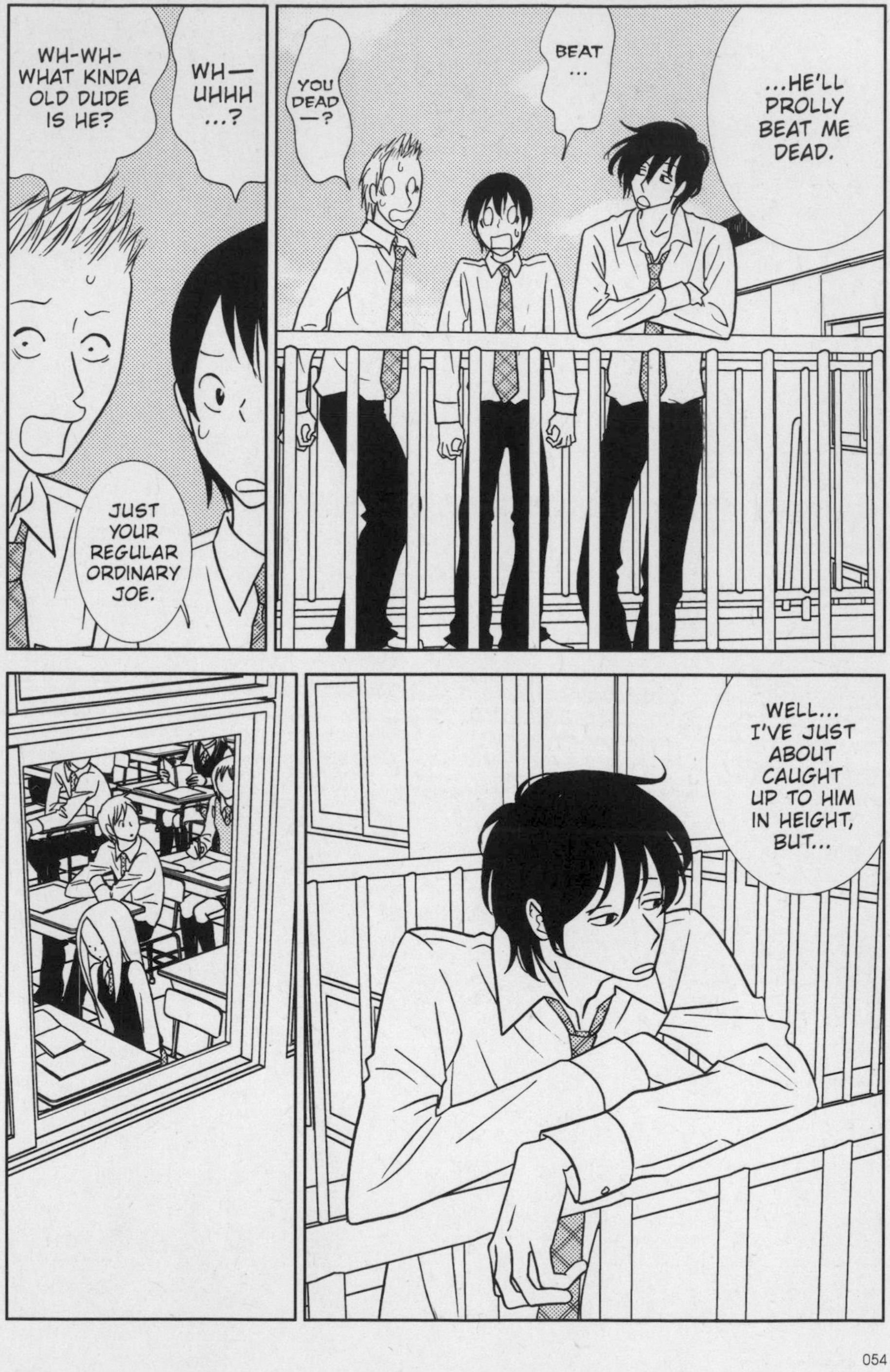
...HE'LL PROLLY BEAT ME DEAD.
BEAT ...
YOU DEAD —?
WH— UHHH ...?
WH-WH- WHAT KINDA OLD DUDE IS HE?
JUST YOUR REGULAR ORDINARY JOE.
WELL... I'VE JUST ABOUT CAUGHT UP TO HIM IN HEIGHT, BUT...

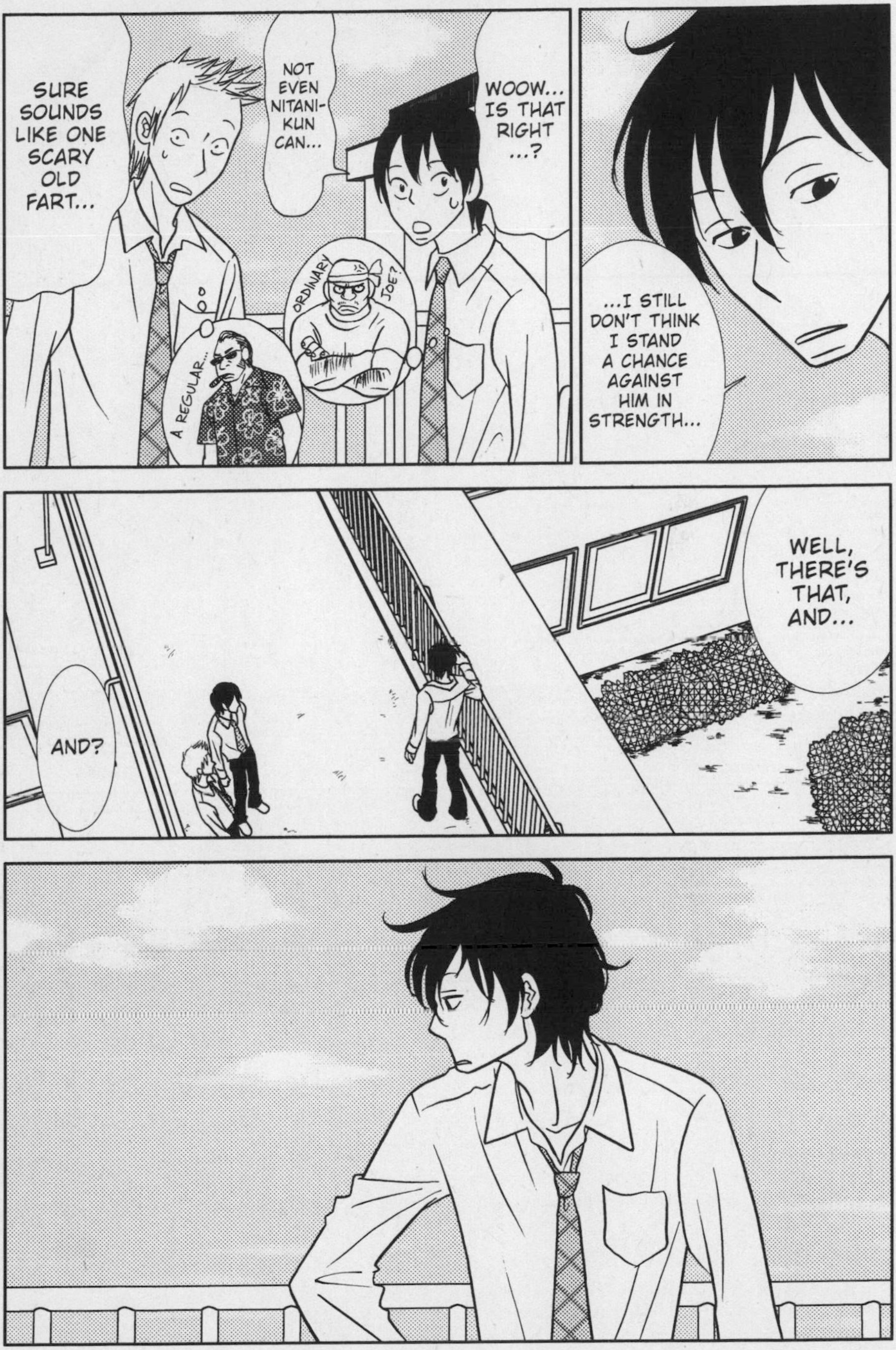

...I STILL DON'T THINK I STAND A CHANCE AGAINST HIM IN STRENGTH...
WOOW... IS THAT RIGHT ...?
NOT EVEN NITANI-KUN CAN...
SURE SOUNDS LIKE ONE SCARY OLD FART...
ORDINARY JOE?
A REGULAR...
WELL, THERE'S THAT, AND...
AND?

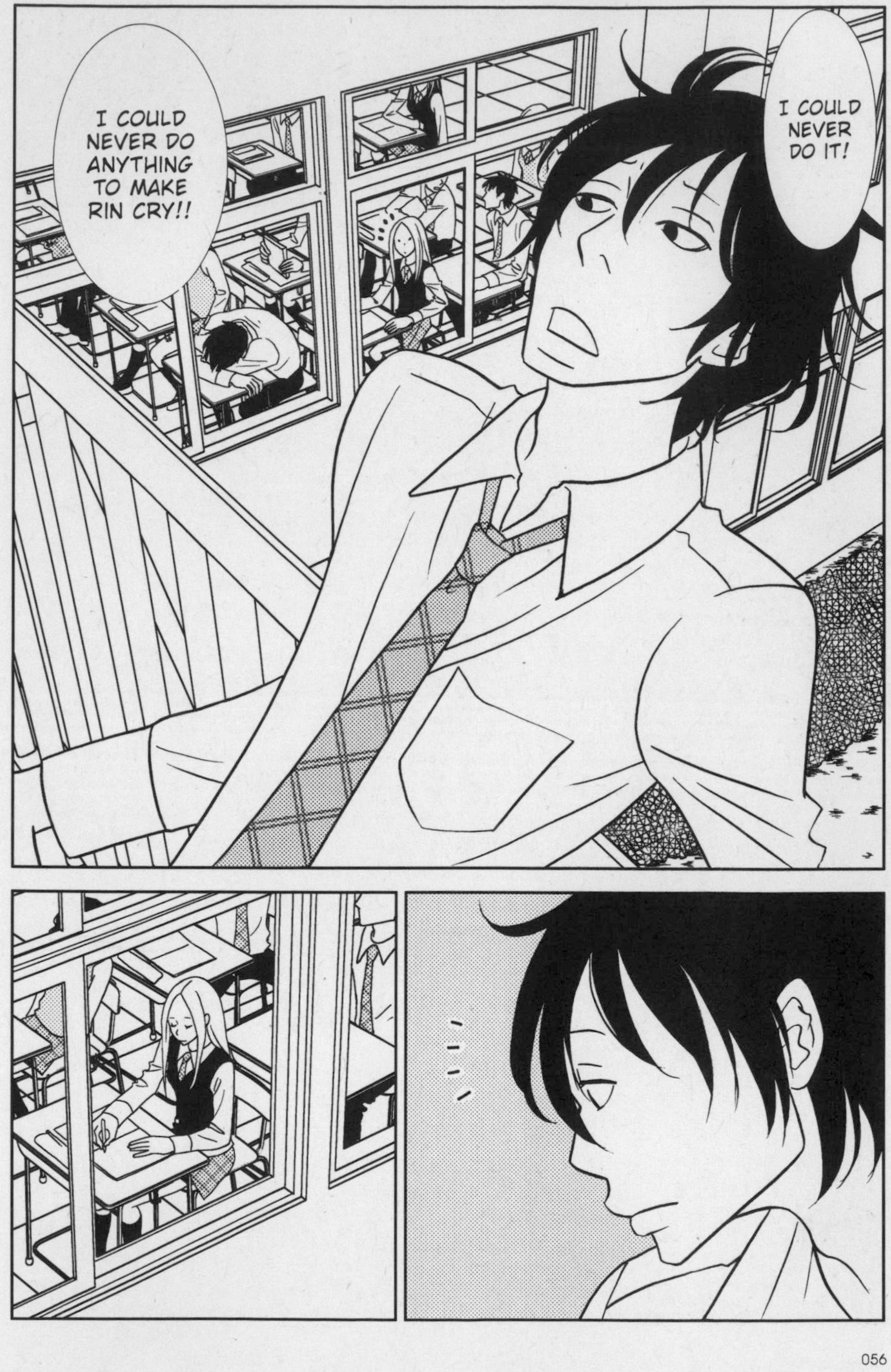
I COULD NEVER DO IT!
I COULD NEVER DO ANYTHING TO MAKE RIN CRY!!

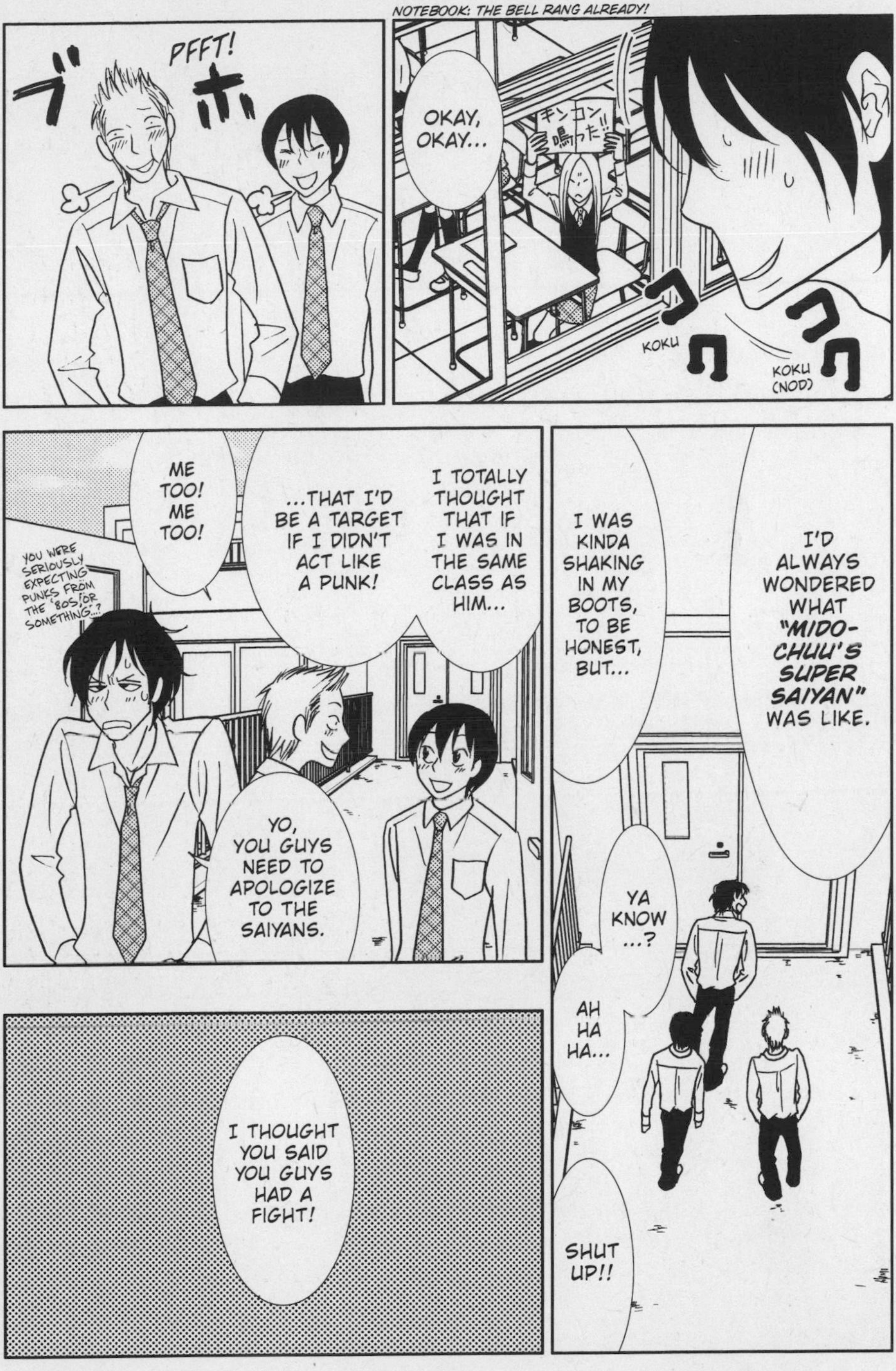
NOTEBOOK: THE BELL RANG ALREADY!
OKAY, OKAY...
キンコン 鳴った!!
KOKU
KOKU (NOD)
PFFT!
ブホ
I'D ALWAYS WONDERED WHAT "MIDO-CHUU'S SUPER SAIYAN" WAS LIKE.
I WAS KINDA SHAKING IN MY BOOTS, TO BE HONEST, BUT...
YA KNOW ...?
AH HA HA...
SHUT UP!!
I TOTALLY THOUGHT THAT IF I WAS IN THE SAME CLASS AS HIM...
...THAT I'D BE A TARGET IF I DIDN'T ACT LIKE A PUNK!
ME TOO! ME TOO!
YOU WERE SERIOUSLY EXPECTING PUNKS FROM THE '80S OR SOMETHING...?
YO, YOU GUYS NEED TO APOLOGIZE TO THE SAIYANS.
I THOUGHT YOU SAID YOU GUYS HAD A FIGHT!

NOTEBOOK: THE BELL RANG ALREADY!!

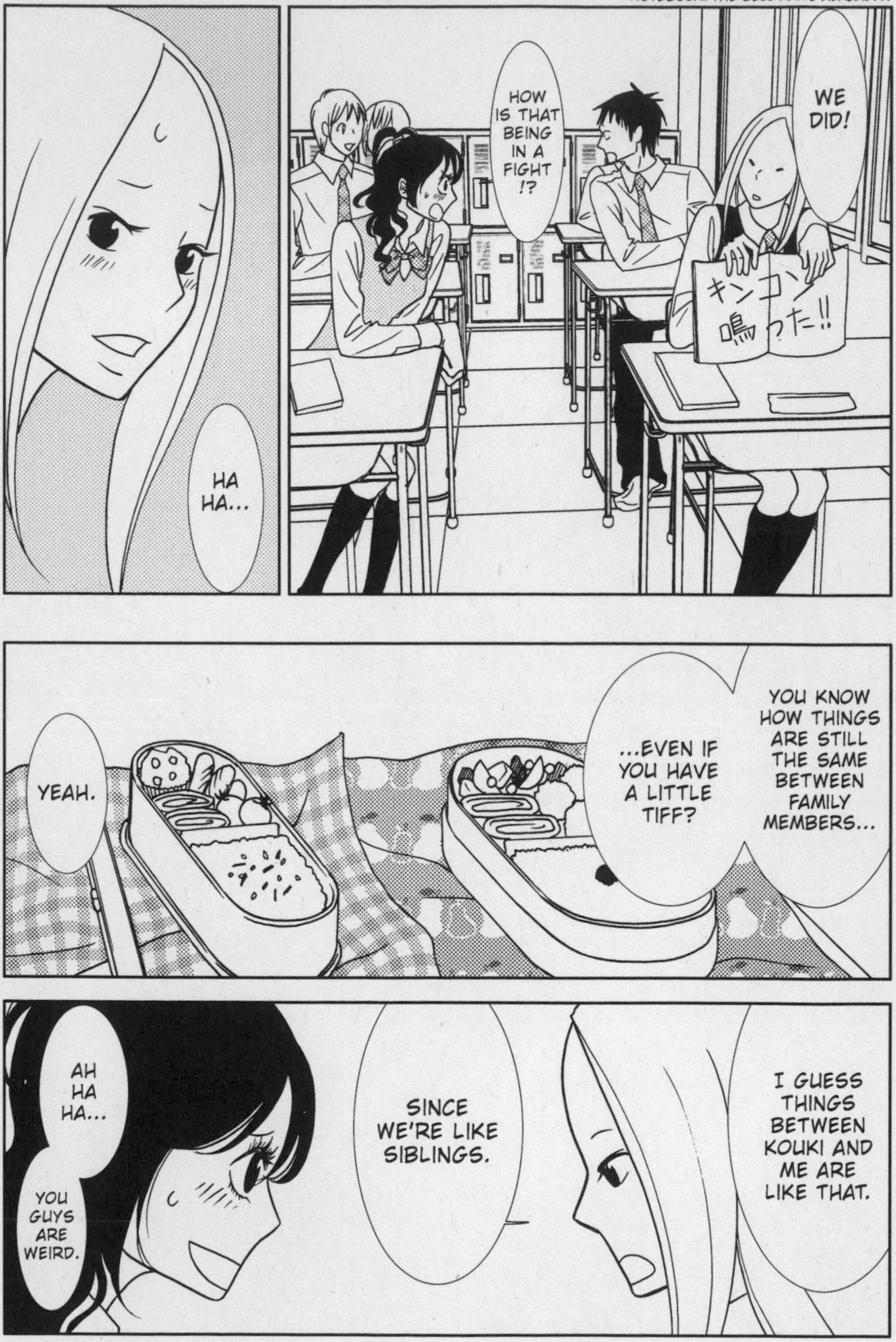

WE DID!
HOW IS THAT BEING IN A FIGHT!?
キンコン 鳴った!!
HA HA...
YOU KNOW HOW THINGS ARE STILL THE SAME BETWEEN FAMILY MEMBERS...
...EVEN IF YOU HAVE A LITTLE TIFF?
YEAH.
I GUESS THINGS BETWEEN KOUKI AND ME ARE LIKE THAT.
SINCE WE'RE LIKE SIBLINGS.
AH HA HA...
YOU GUYS ARE WEIRD.

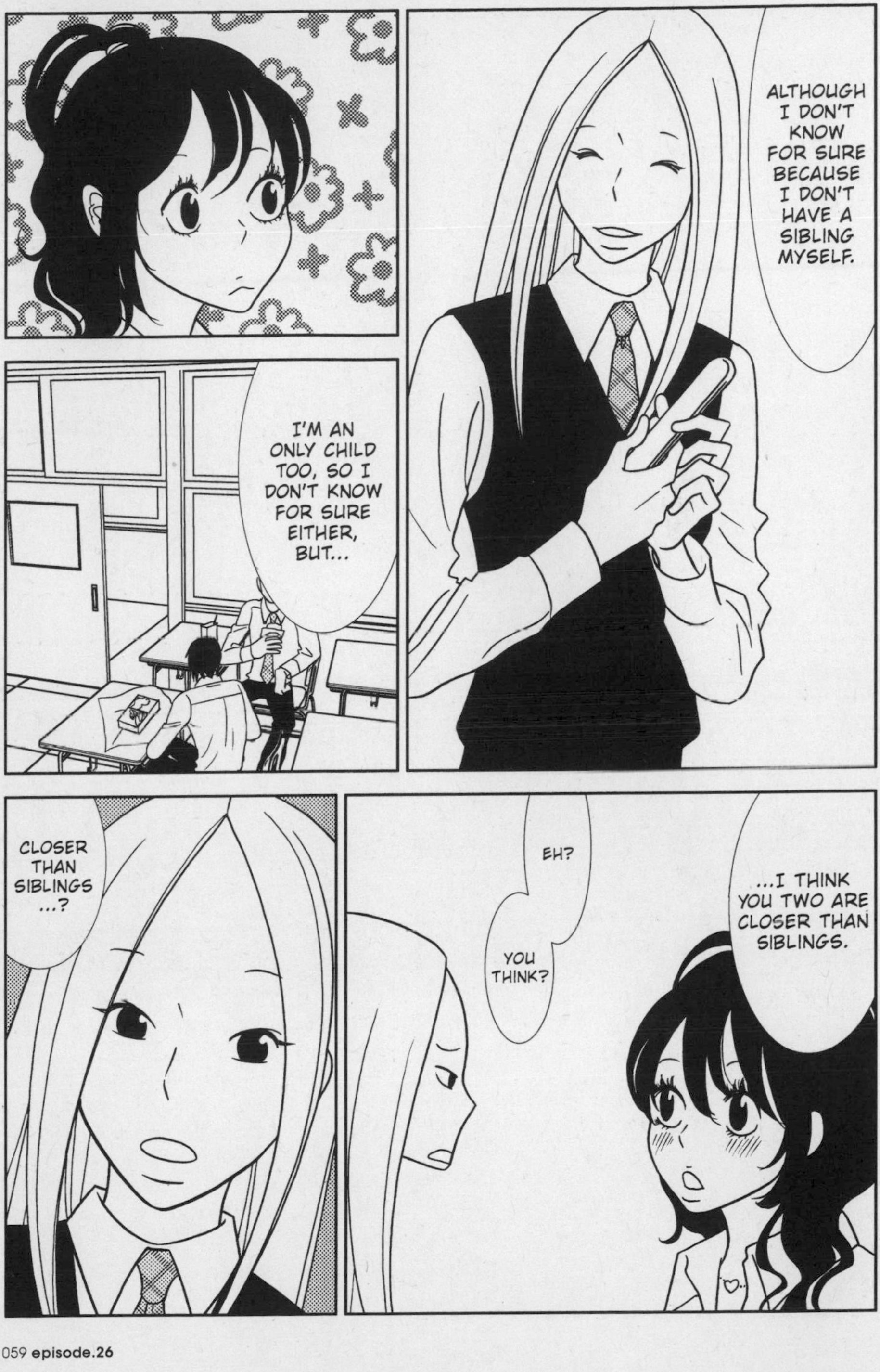
ALTHOUGH I DON'T KNOW FOR SURE BECAUSE I DON'T HAVE A SIBLING MYSELF.
I'M AN ONLY CHILD TOO, SO I DON'T KNOW FOR SURE EITHER, BUT...
...I THINK YOU TWO ARE CLOSER THAN SIBLINGS.
EH?
YOU THINK?
CLOSER THAN SIBLINGS ...?

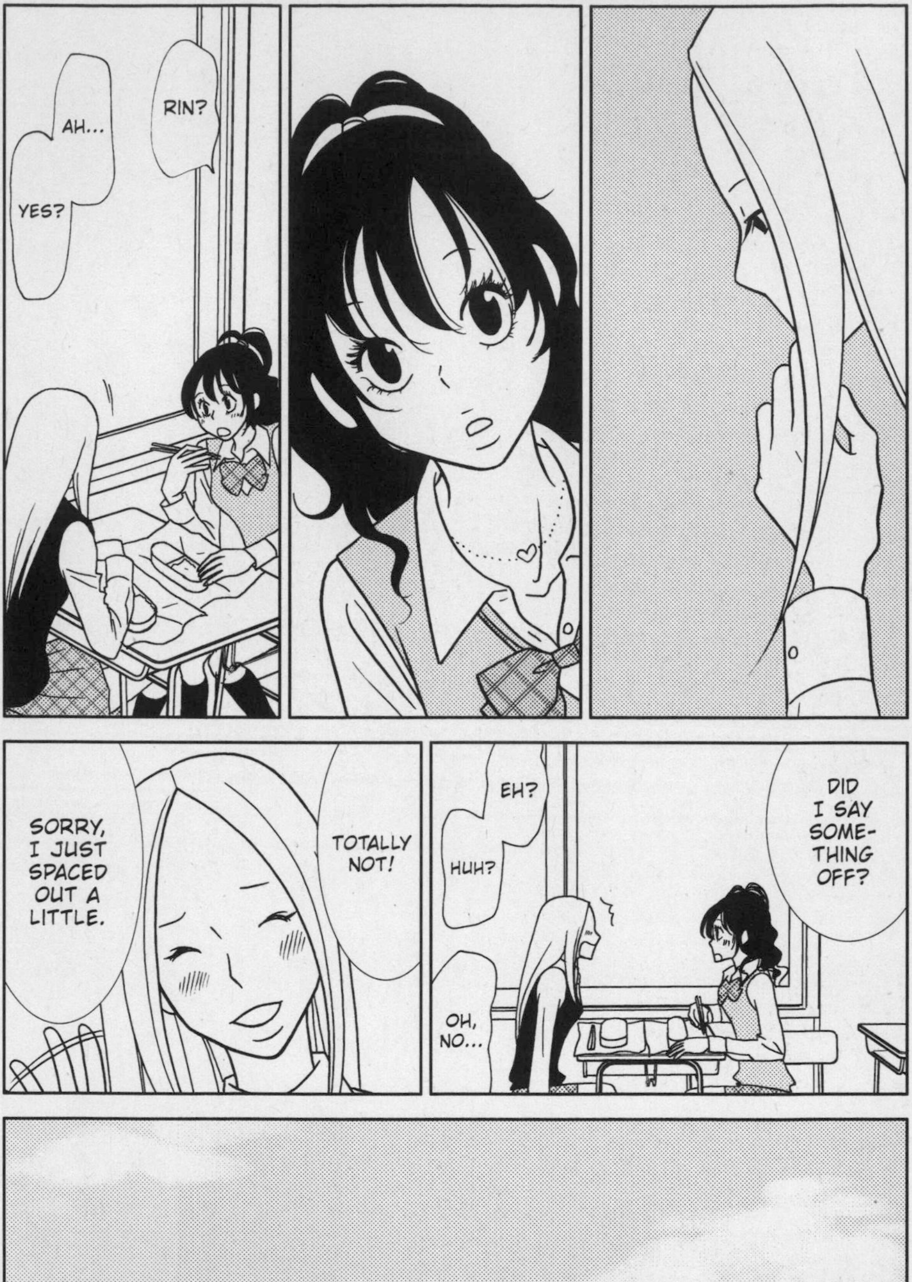
RIN?
AH...
YES?
DID I SAY SOME-THING OFF?
EH?
HUH?
OH, NO...
TOTALLY NOT!
SORRY, I JUST SPACED OUT A LITTLE.

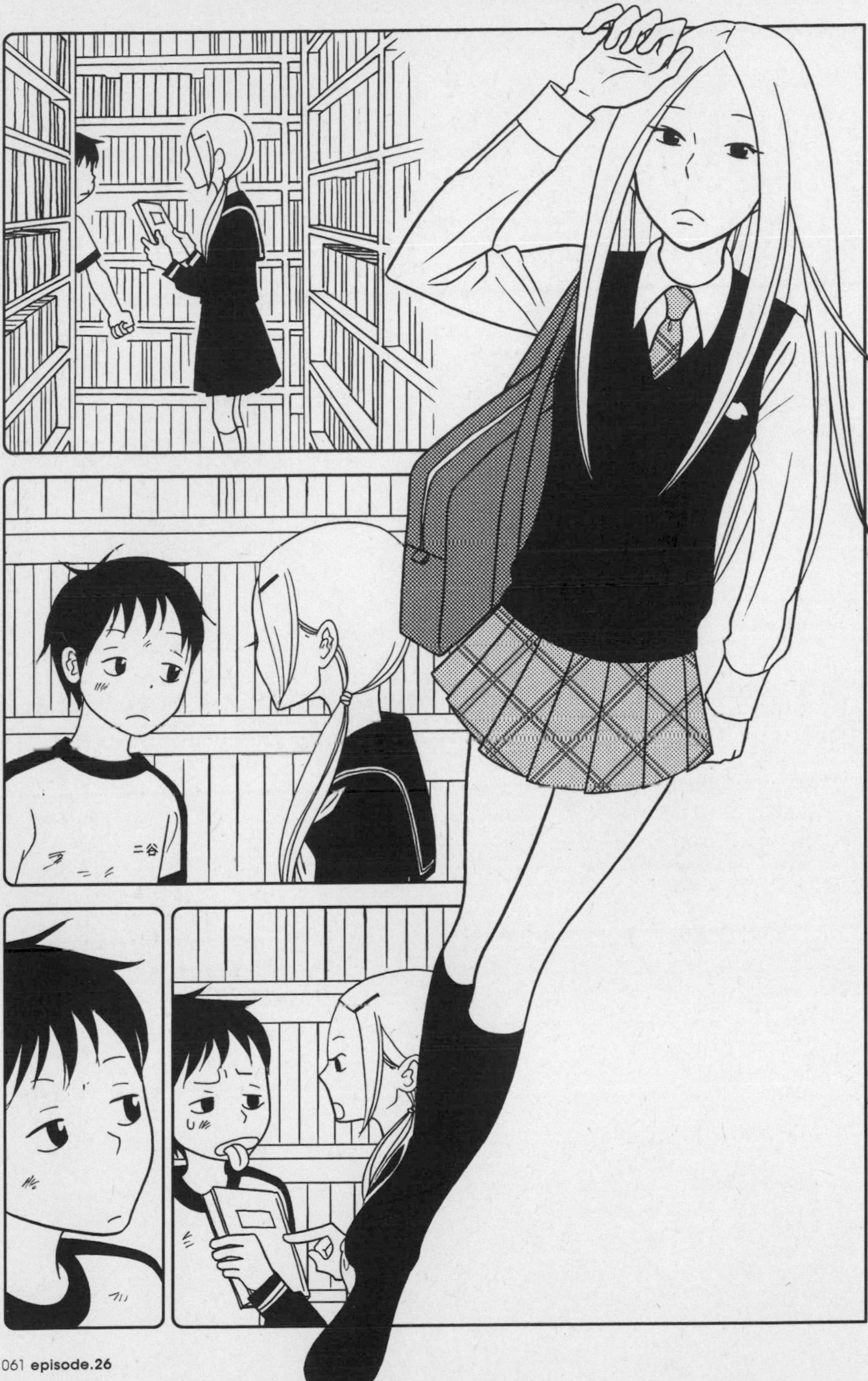
二谷

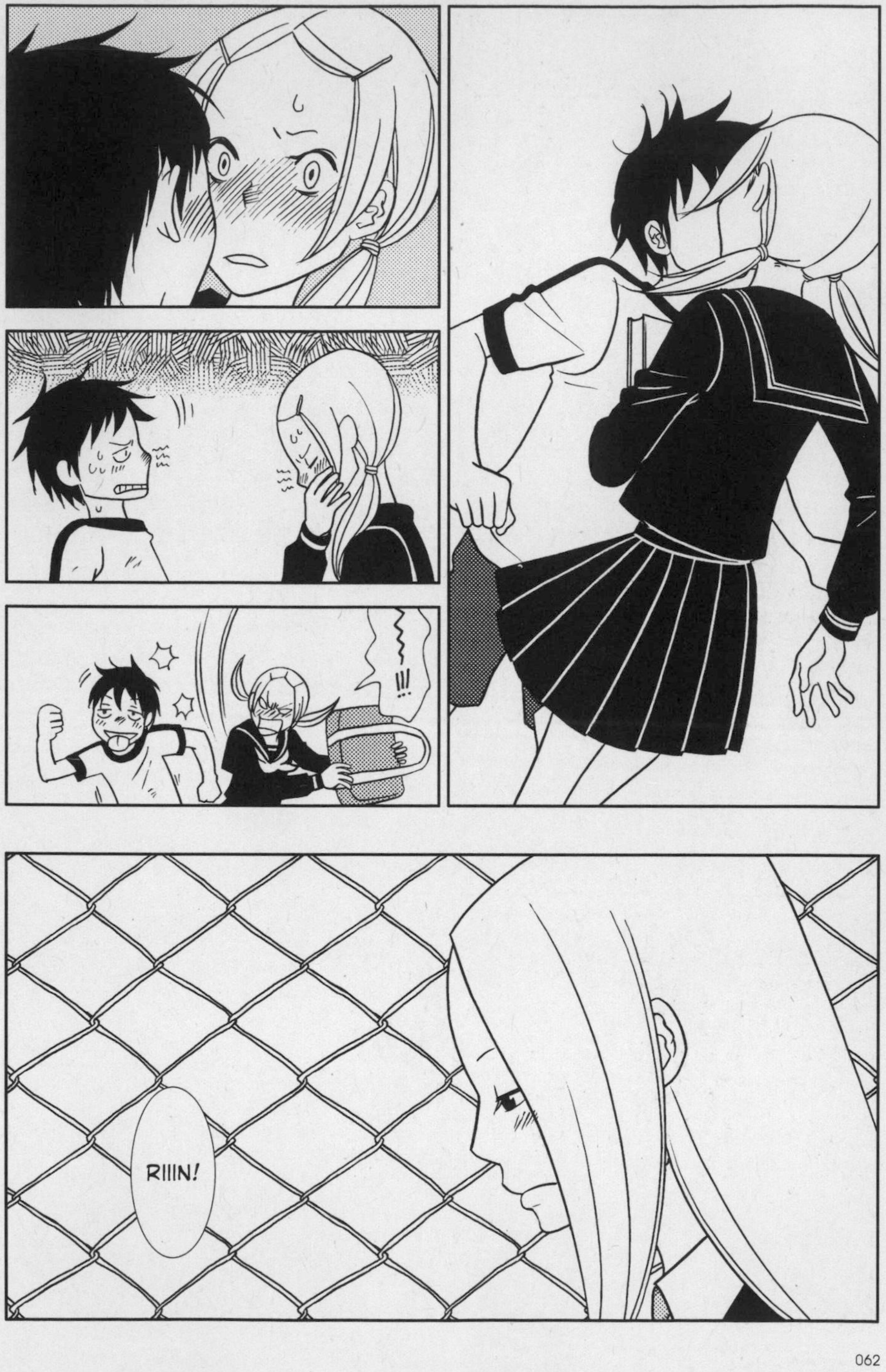
RIIIN!

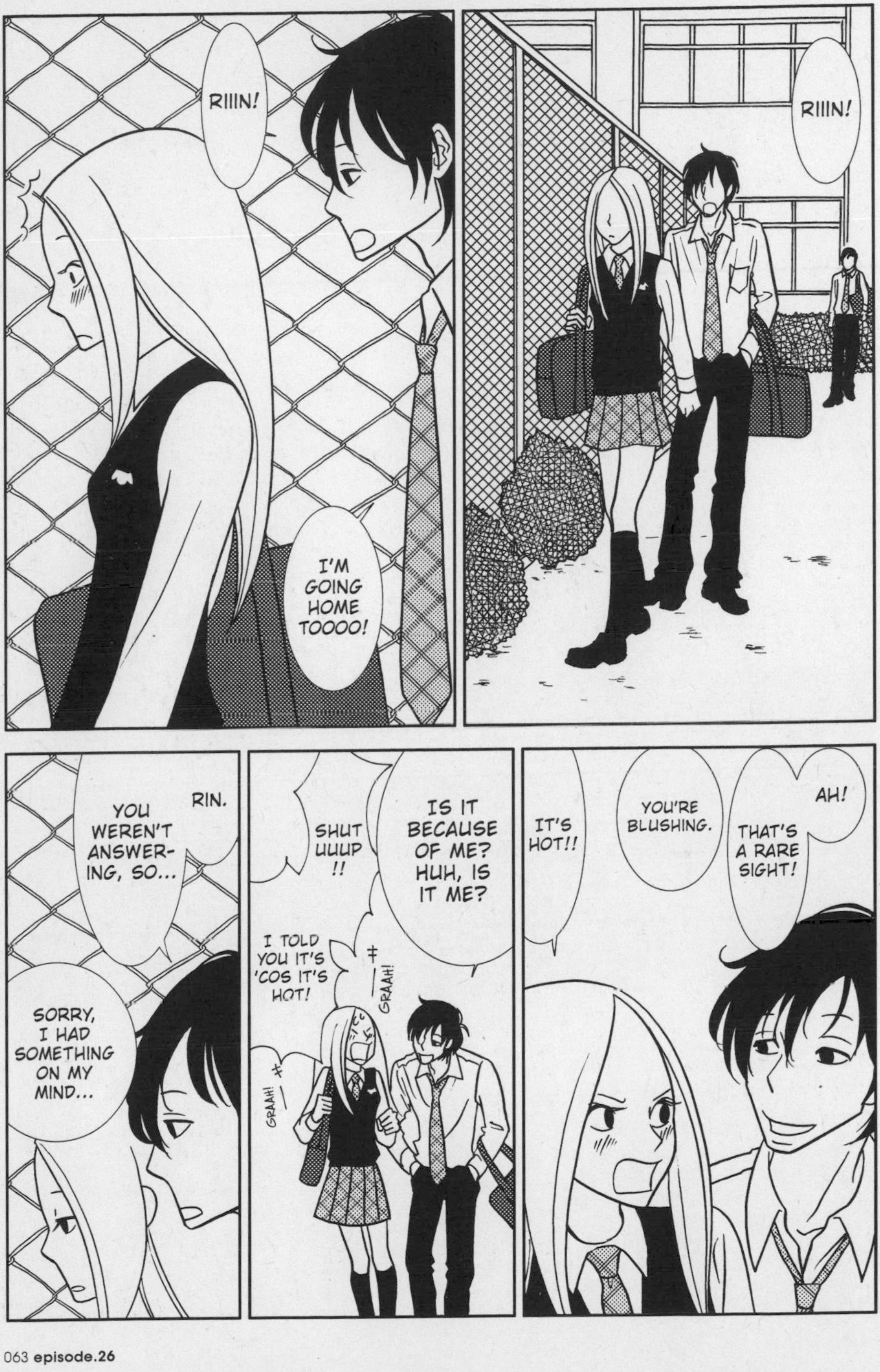
RIIIN!
RIIIN!
I'M GOING HOME TOOOO!
AH!
THAT'S A RARE SIGHT!
YOU'RE BLUSHING.
IT'S HOT!!
IS IT BECAUSE OF ME? HUH, IS IT ME?
SHUT UUUP !!
I TOLD YOU IT'S 'COS IT'S HOT!
GRAAH!
GRAAH!
RIN.
YOU WEREN'T ANSWER-ING, SO...
SORRY, I HAD SOMETHING ON MY MIND...

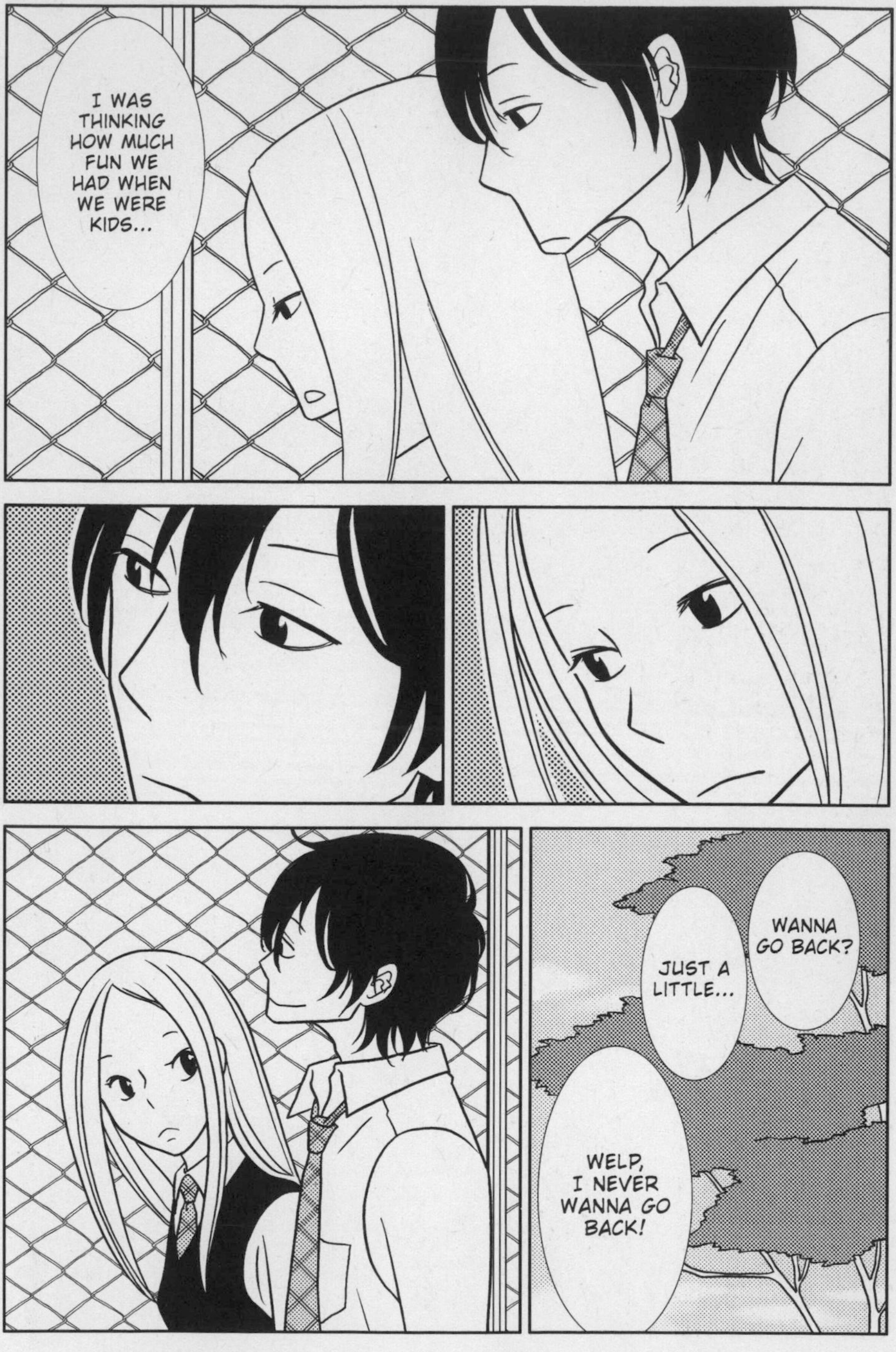
I WAS THINKING HOW MUCH FUN WE HAD WHEN WE WERE KIDS...
WANNA GO BACK?
JUST A LITTLE...
WELP, I NEVER WANNA GO BACK!

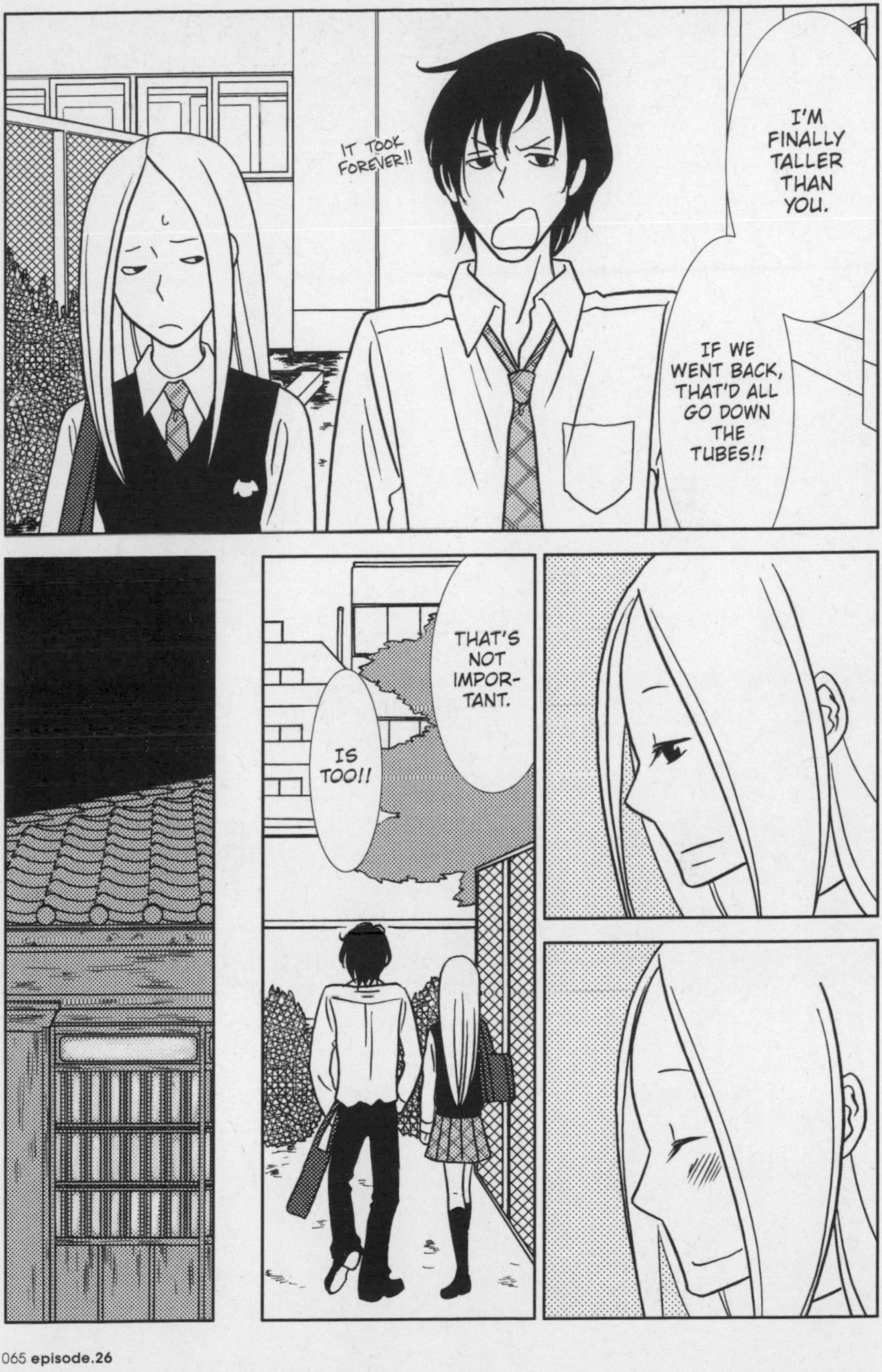
I'M FINALLY TALLER THAN YOU.
IF WE WENT BACK, THAT'D ALL GO DOWN THE TUBES!!
IT TOOK FOREVER!!
THAT'S NOT IMPORTANT.
IS TOO!!

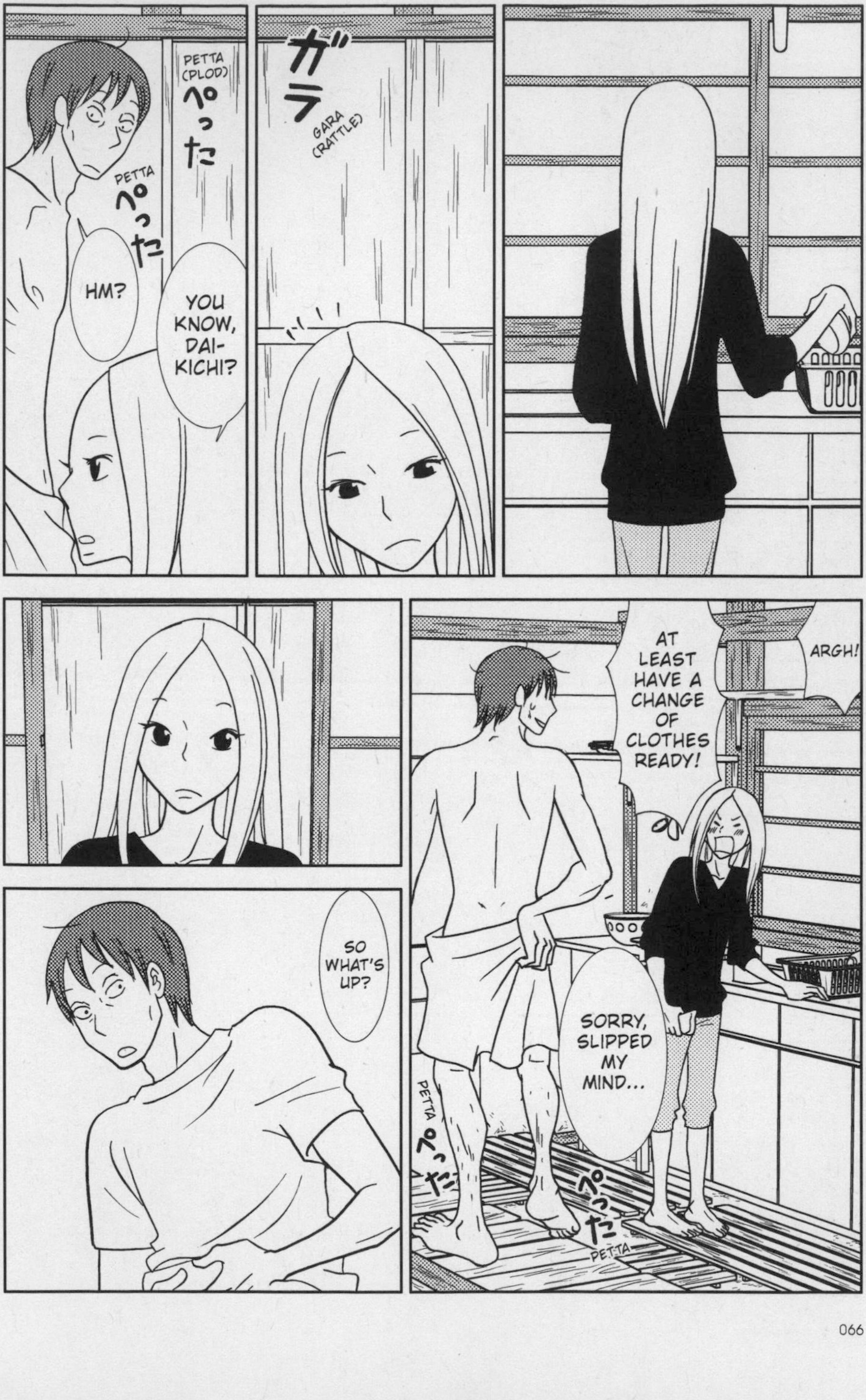
ガラ
GARA (RATTLE)
PETTA (PLOD)
ぺった
PETTA
ぺった
YOU KNOW, DAI-KICHI?
HM?
ARGH!
AT LEAST HAVE A CHANGE OF CLOTHES READY!
SORRY, SLIPPED MY MIND...
ぺった
PETTA
PETTA
ぺった
SO WHAT'S UP?

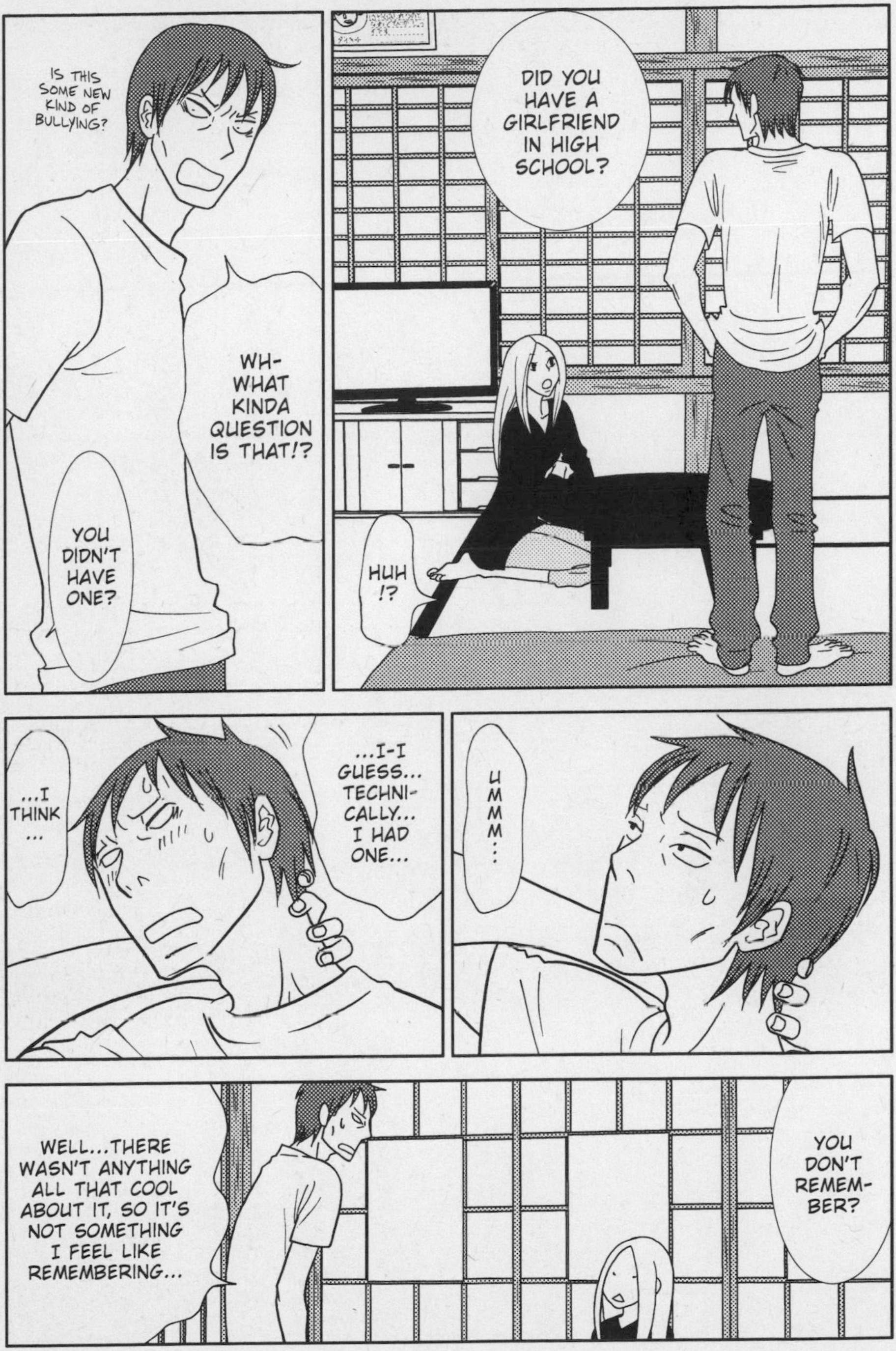
DID YOU HAVE A GIRLFRIEND IN HIGH SCHOOL?
HUH!?
WH-WHAT KINDA QUESTION IS THAT!?
IS THIS SOME NEW KIND OF BULLYING?
YOU DIDN'T HAVE ONE?
UMMM...
...I-I GUESS... TECHNICALLY... I HAD ONE...
...I THINK...
YOU DON'T REMEMBER?
WELL...THERE WASN'T ANYTHING ALL THAT COOL ABOUT IT, SO IT'S NOT SOMETHING I FEEL LIKE REMEMBERING...

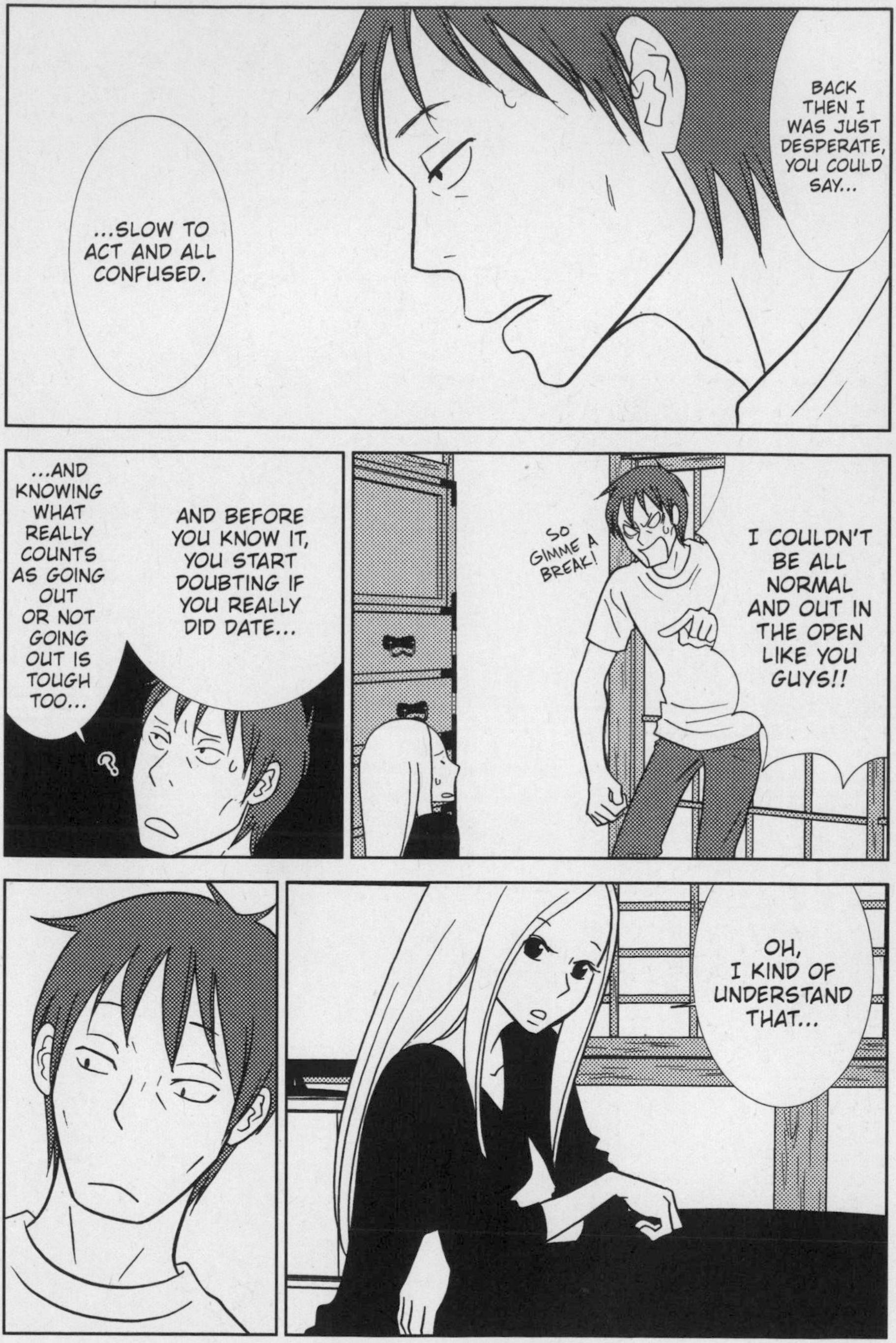
BACK THEN I WAS JUST DESPERATE, YOU COULD SAY...
...SLOW TO ACT AND ALL CONFUSED.
I COULDN'T BE ALL NORMAL AND OUT IN THE OPEN LIKE YOU GUYS!!
SO GIMME A BREAK!
AND BEFORE YOU KNOW IT, YOU START DOUBTING IF YOU REALLY DID DATE...
...AND KNOWING WHAT REALLY COUNTS AS GOING OUT OR NOT GOING OUT IS TOUGH TOO...
?
OH, I KIND OF UNDERSTAND THAT...

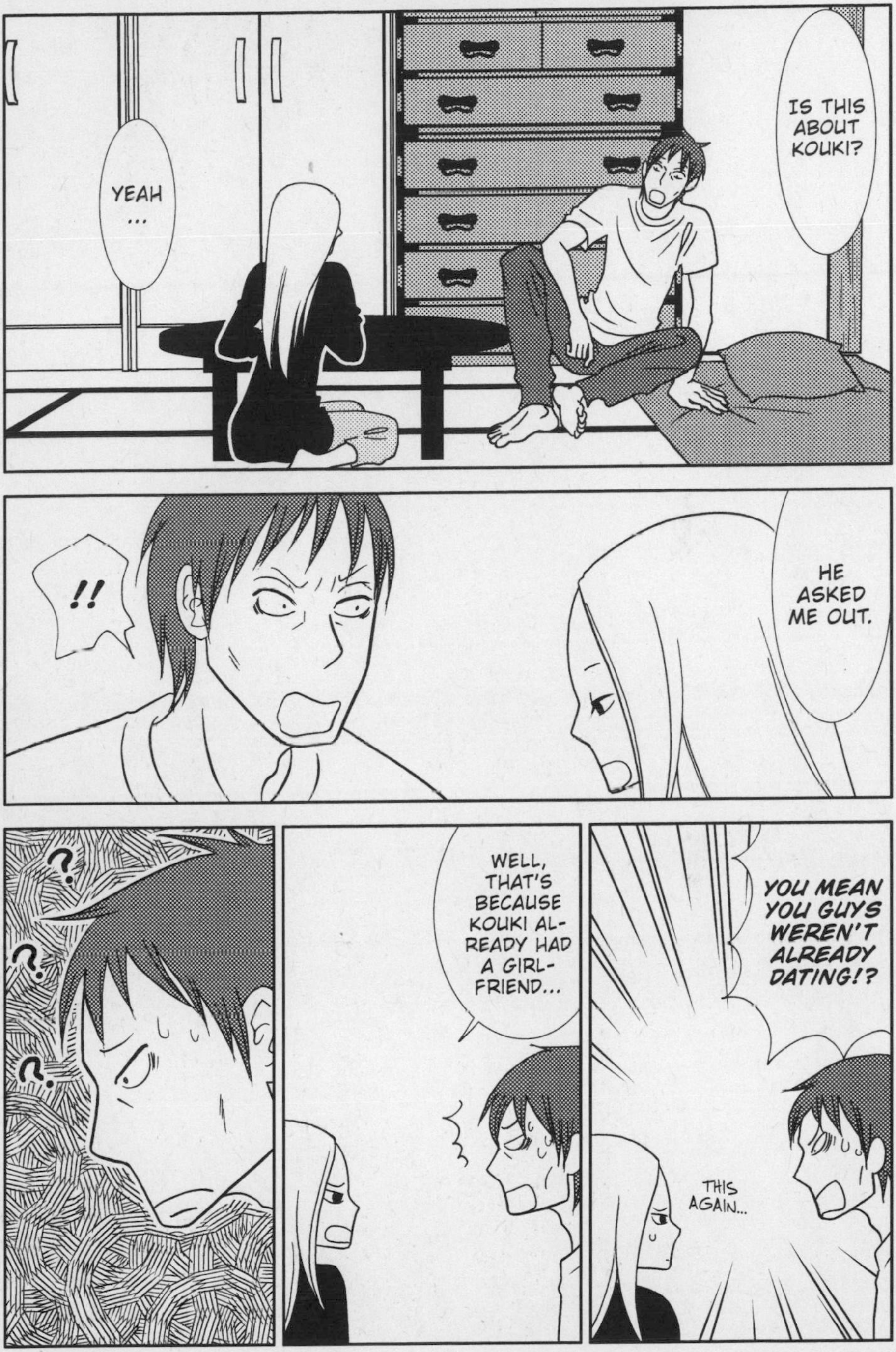
IS THIS ABOUT KOUKI?
YEAH ...
HE ASKED ME OUT.
!!
YOU MEAN YOU GUYS WEREN'T ALREADY DATING!?
THIS AGAIN...
WELL, THAT'S BECAUSE KOUKI AL-READY HAD A GIRL-FRIEND...
?
?
?

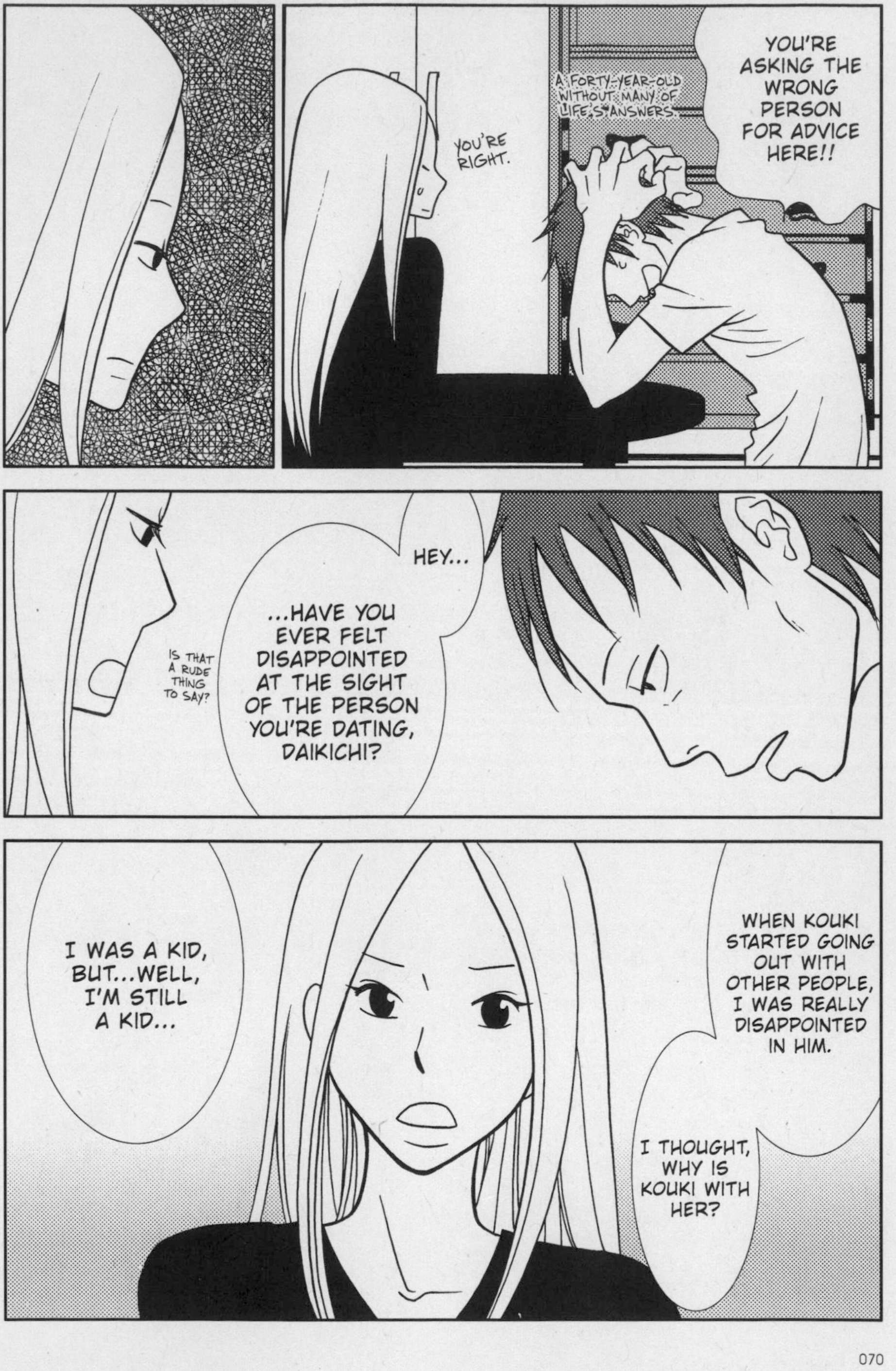
YOU'RE ASKING THE WRONG PERSON FOR ADVICE HERE!!
A FORTY-YEAR-OLD WITHOUT MANY OF LIFE'S ANSWERS
YOU'RE RIGHT.
HEY...
...HAVE YOU EVER FELT DISAPPOINTED AT THE SIGHT OF THE PERSON YOU'RE DATING, DAIKICHI?
IS THAT A RUDE THING TO SAY?
WHEN KOUKI STARTED GOING OUT WITH OTHER PEOPLE, I WAS REALLY DISAPPOINTED IN HIM.
I THOUGHT, WHY IS KOUKI WITH HER?
I WAS A KID, BUT...WELL, I'M STILL A KID...

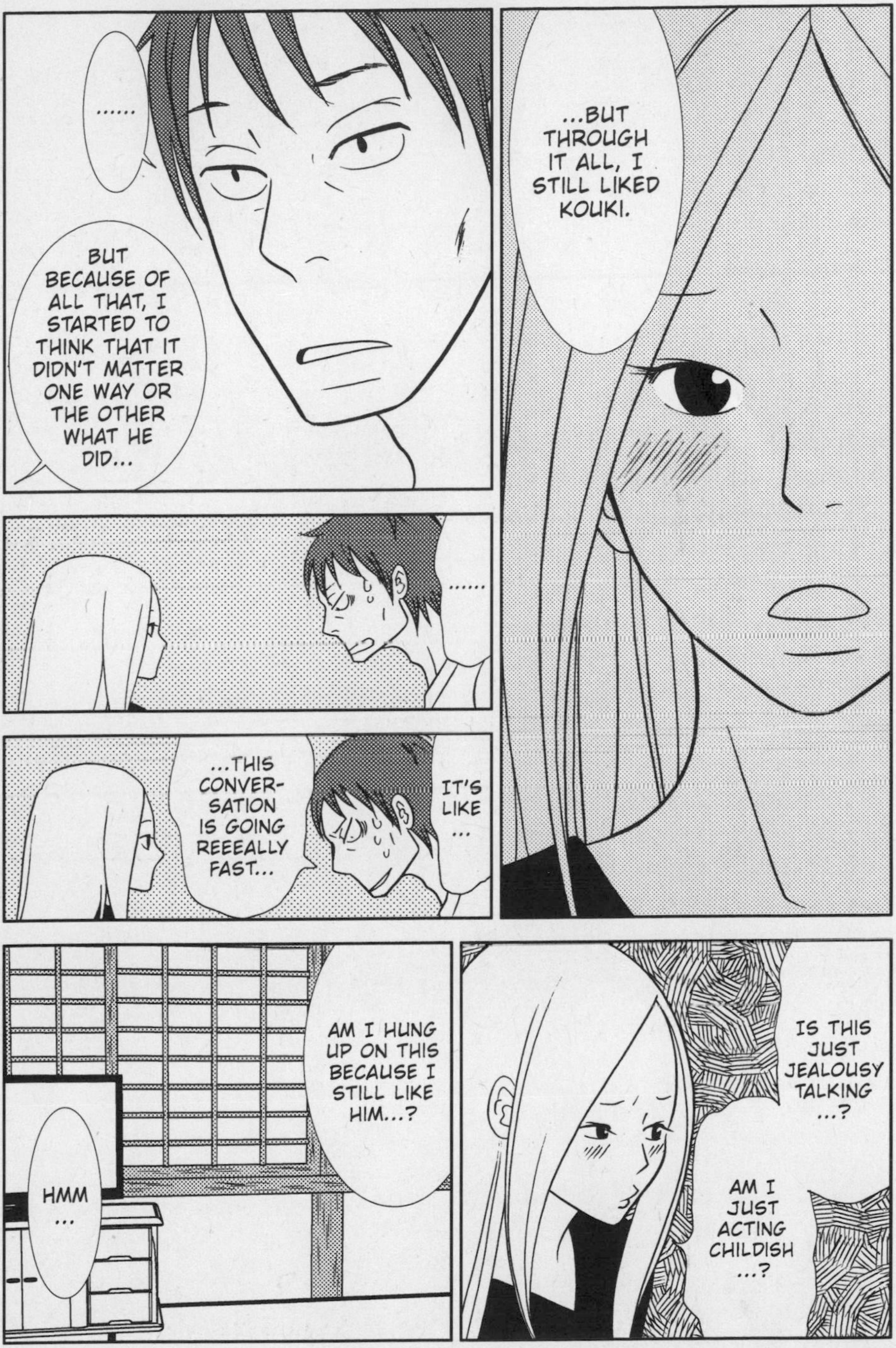
...BUT THROUGH IT ALL, I STILL LIKED KOUKI.
......
BUT BECAUSE OF ALL THAT, I STARTED TO THINK THAT IT DIDN'T MATTER ONE WAY OR THE OTHER WHAT HE DID...
......
IT'S LIKE...
...THIS CONVER-SATION IS GOING REEEALLY FAST...
IS THIS JUST JEALOUSY TALKING...?
AM I JUST ACTING CHILDISH...?
AM I HUNG UP ON THIS BECAUSE I STILL LIKE HIM...?
HMM...

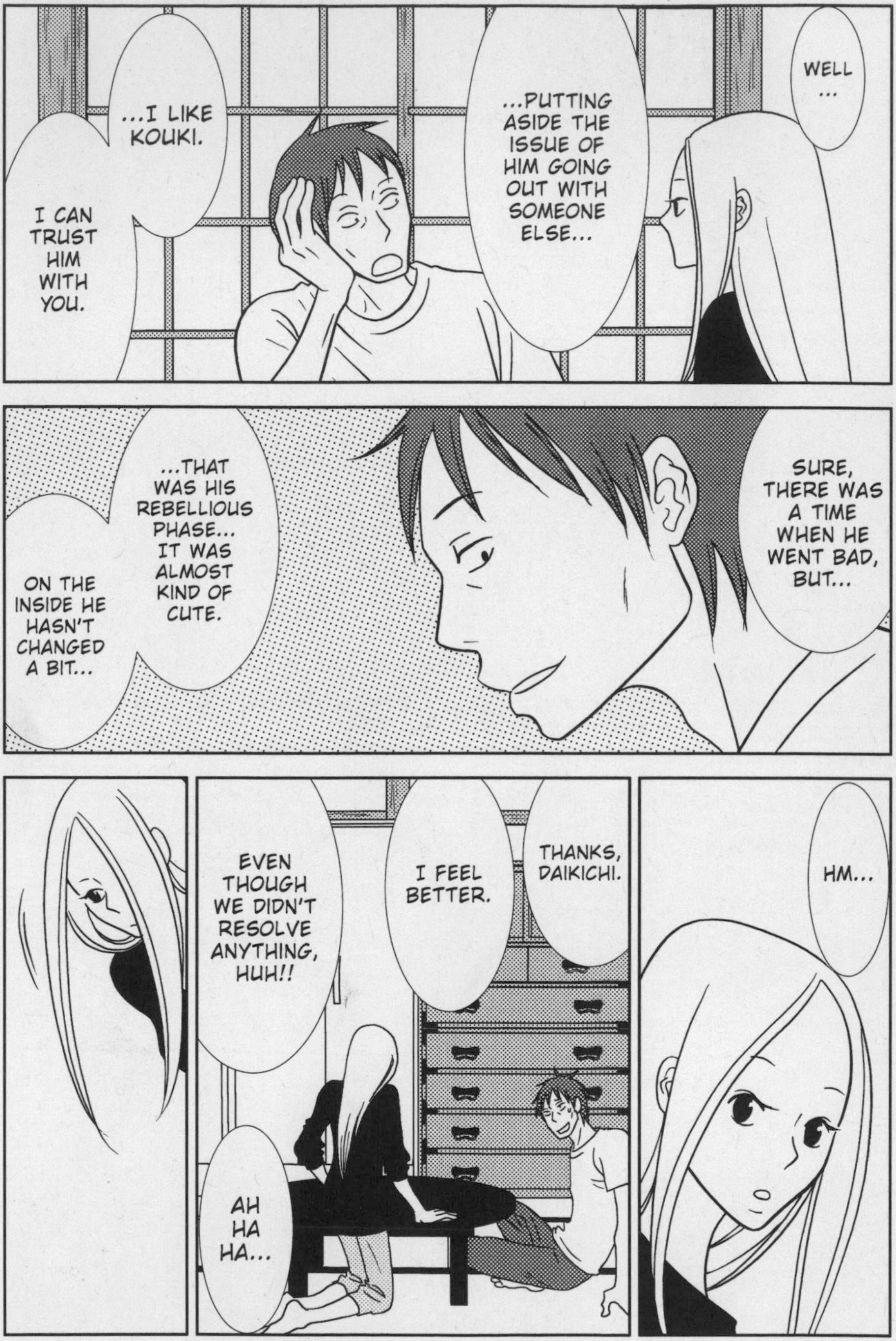
WELL ...
...PUTTING ASIDE THE ISSUE OF HIM GOING OUT WITH SOMEONE ELSE...
...I LIKE KOUKI.
I CAN TRUST HIM WITH YOU.
SURE, THERE WAS A TIME WHEN HE WENT BAD, BUT...
...THAT WAS HIS REBELLIOUS PHASE... IT WAS ALMOST KIND OF CUTE.
ON THE INSIDE HE HASN'T CHANGED A BIT...
HM...
THANKS, DAIKICHI.
I FEEL BETTER.
EVEN THOUGH WE DIDN'T RESOLVE ANYTHING, HUH!!
AH HA HA...

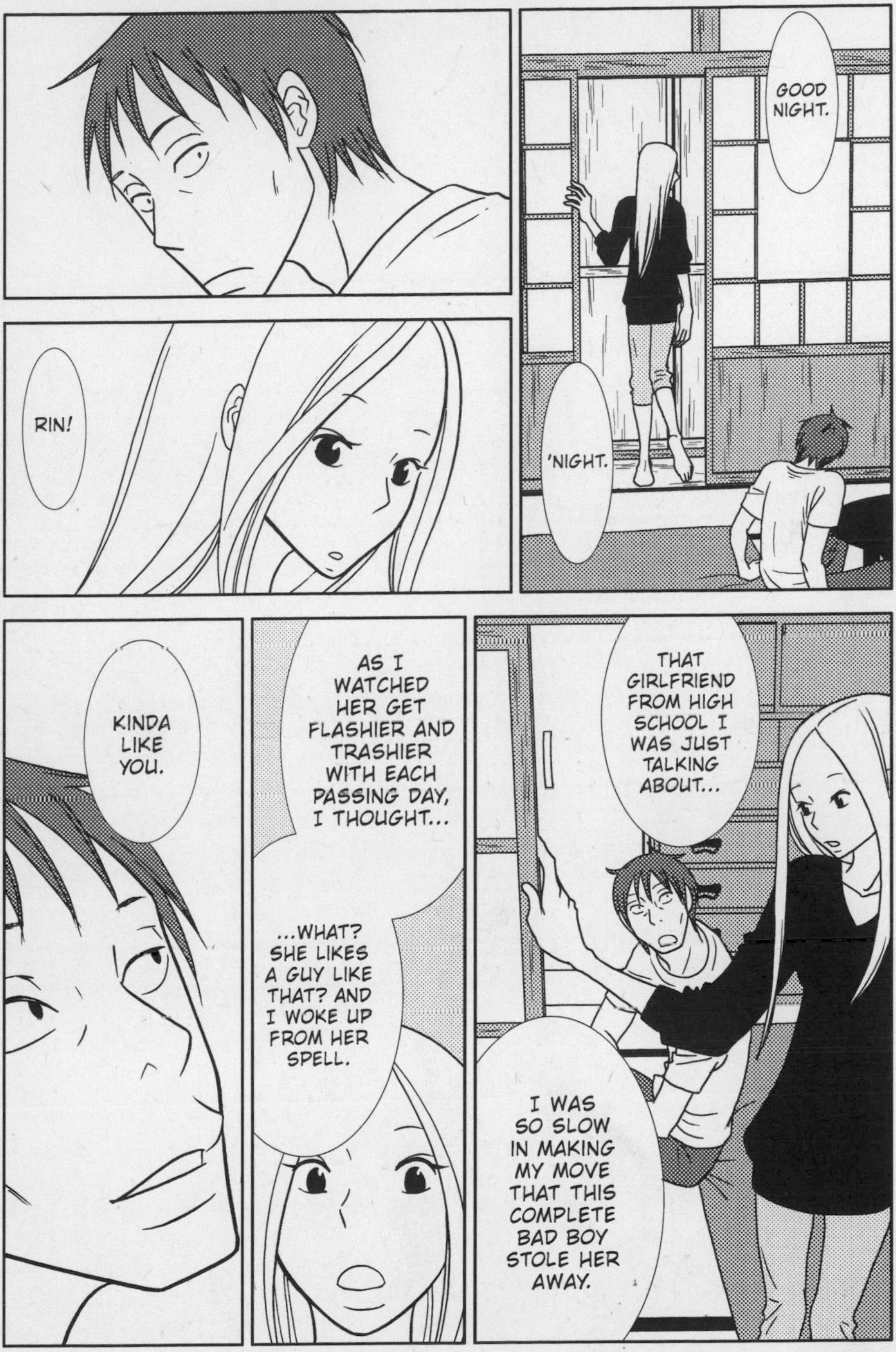
GOOD NIGHT.
'NIGHT.
RIN!
THAT GIRLFRIEND FROM HIGH SCHOOL I WAS JUST TALKING ABOUT...
I WAS SO SLOW IN MAKING MY MOVE THAT THIS COMPLETE BAD BOY STOLE HER AWAY.
AS I WATCHED HER GET FLASHIER AND TRASHIER WITH EACH PASSING DAY, I THOUGHT...
...WHAT? SHE LIKES A GUY LIKE THAT? AND I WOKE UP FROM HER SPELL.
KINDA LIKE YOU.

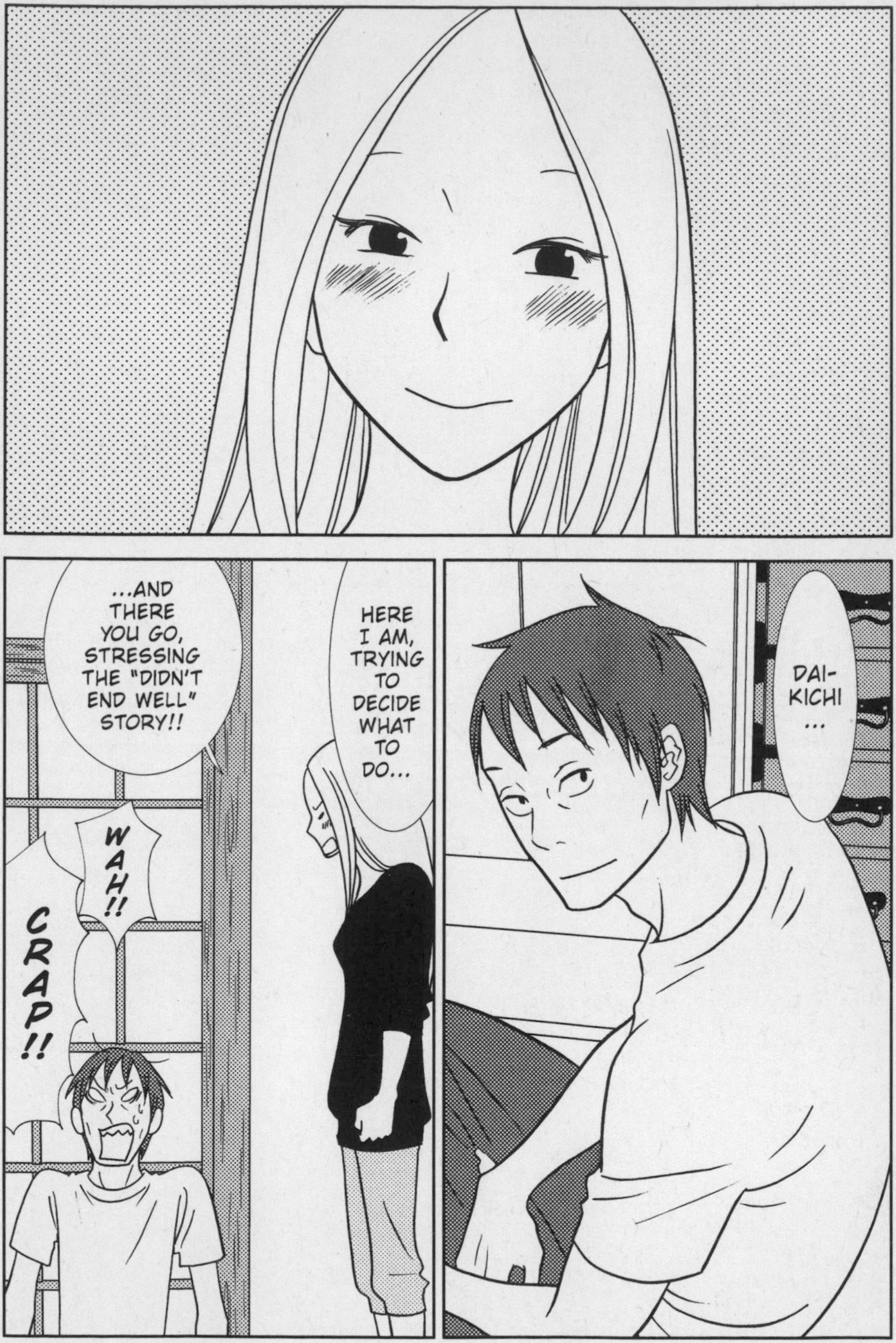
DAI-KICHI ...
HERE I AM, TRYING TO DECIDE WHAT TO DO...
...AND THERE YOU GO, STRESSING THE "DIDN'T END WELL" STORY!!
WAH!!
CRAP!!

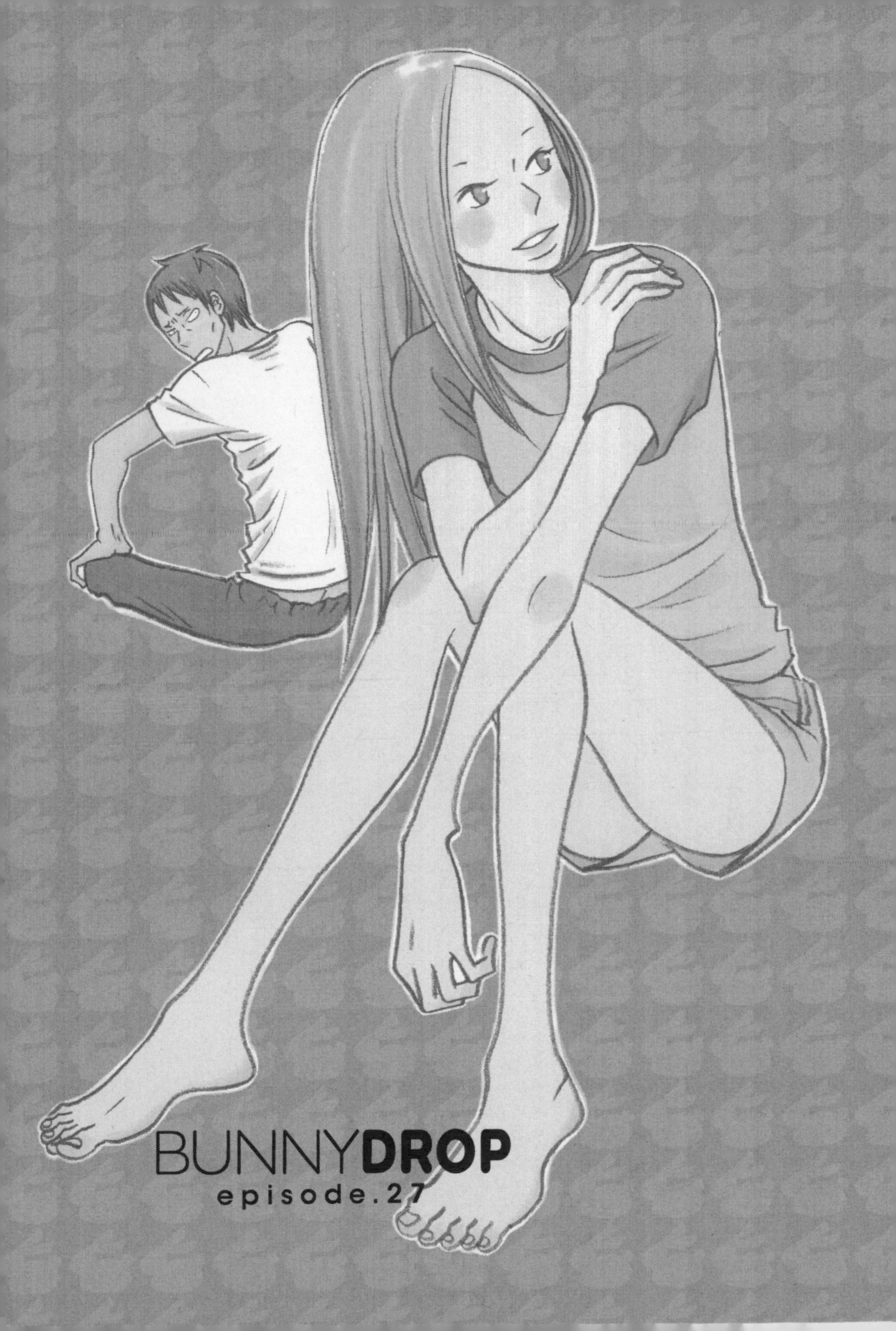
BUNNYDROP
episode.27

BUNNY**DROP**

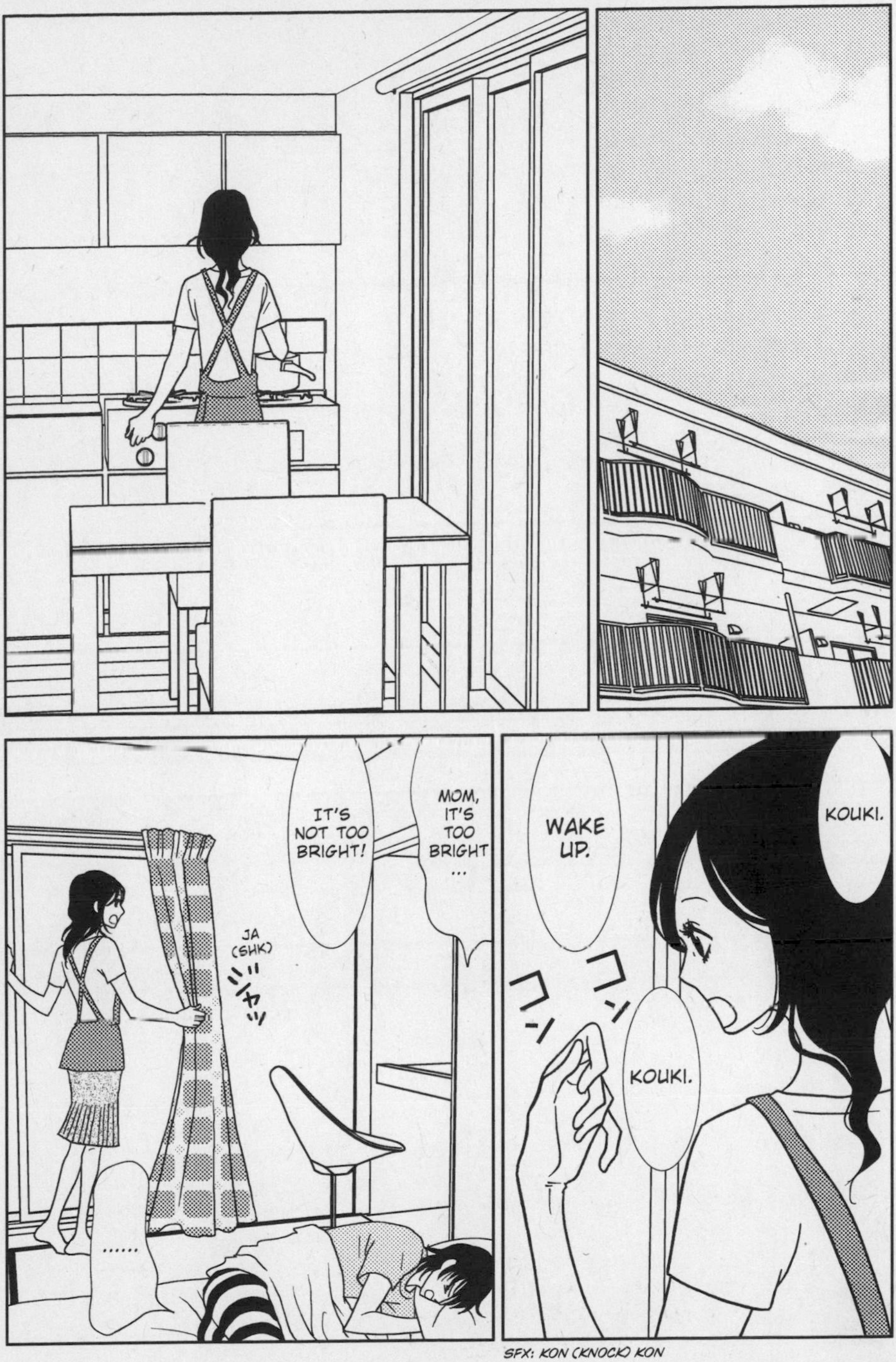
KOUKI.
WAKE UP.
KOUKI.
MOM, IT'S TOO BRIGHT...
IT'S NOT TOO BRIGHT!
JA (SHK)
......

SFX: KON (KNOCK) KON

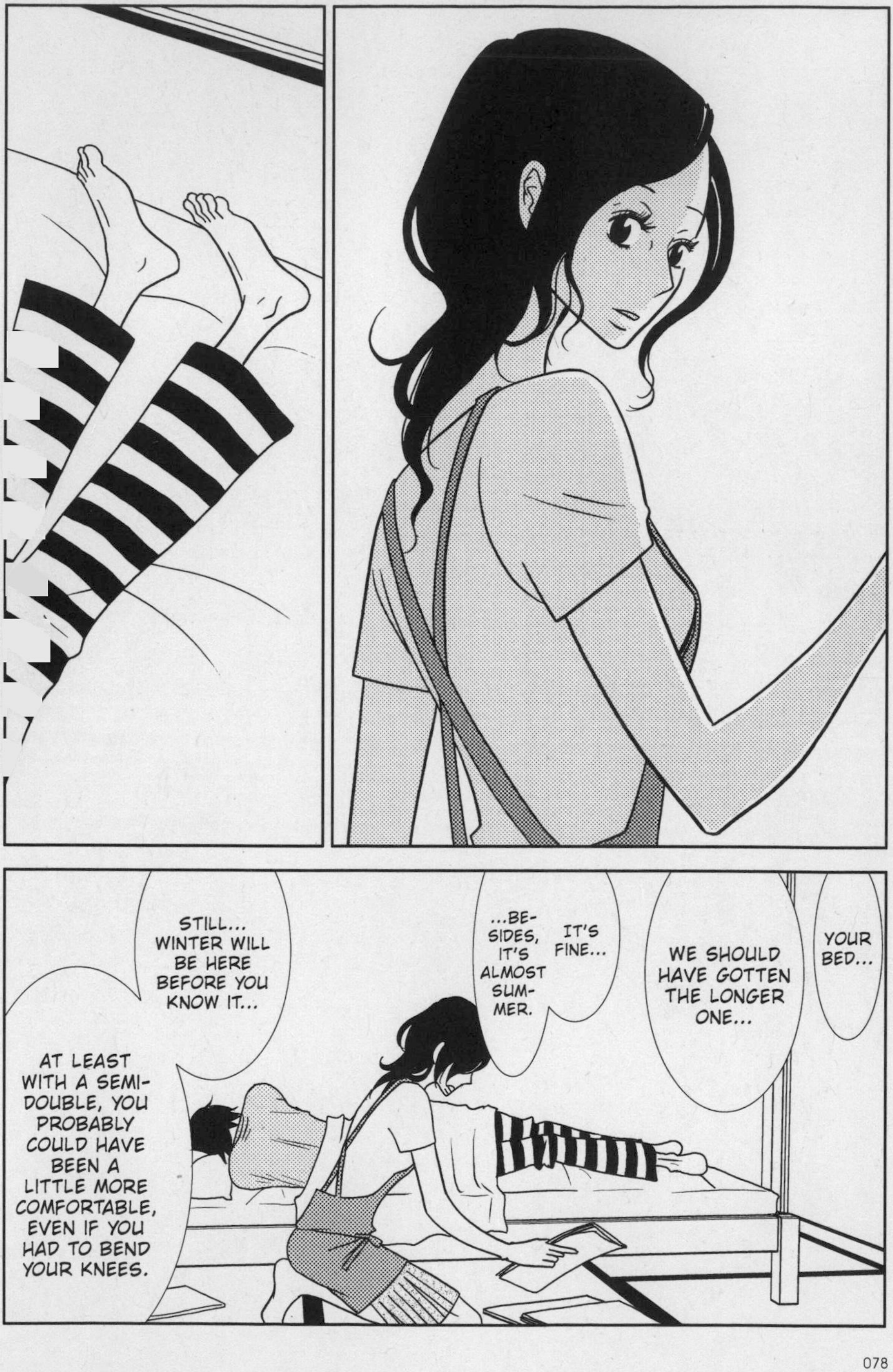
YOUR BED...
WE SHOULD HAVE GOTTEN THE LONGER ONE...
IT'S FINE...
...BE-SIDES, IT'S ALMOST SUM-MER.
STILL... WINTER WILL BE HERE BEFORE YOU KNOW IT...
AT LEAST WITH A SEMI-DOUBLE, YOU PROBABLY COULD HAVE BEEN A LITTLE MORE COMFORTABLE, EVEN IF YOU HAD TO BEND YOUR KNEES.

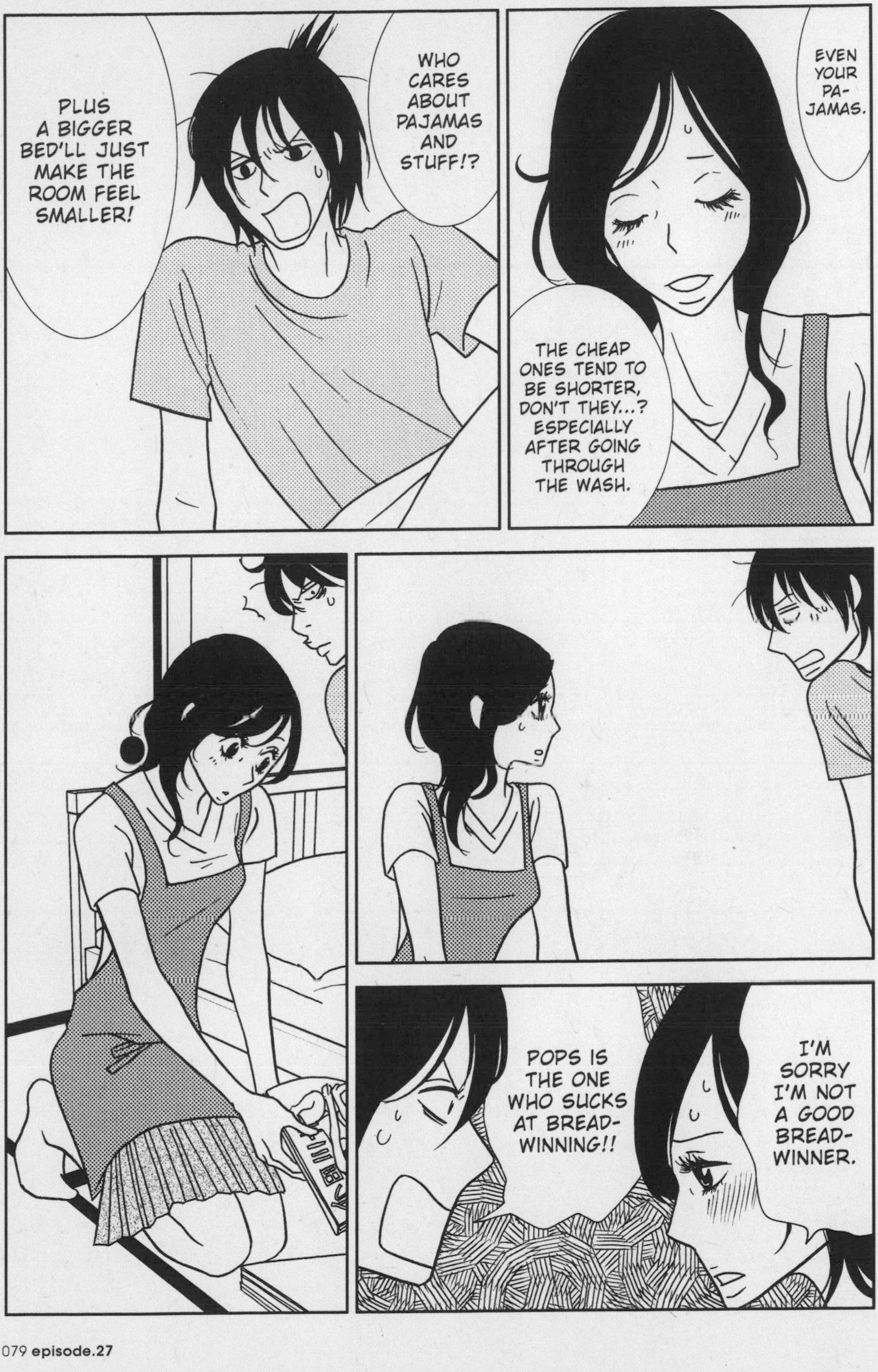
EVEN YOUR PAJAMAS.
THE CHEAP ONES TEND TO BE SHORTER, DON'T THEY...? ESPECIALLY AFTER GOING THROUGH THE WASH.
WHO CARES ABOUT PAJAMAS AND STUFF!?
PLUS A BIGGER BED'LL JUST MAKE THE ROOM FEEL SMALLER!
I'M SORRY I'M NOT A GOOD BREAD-WINNER.
POPS IS THE ONE WHO SUCKS AT BREAD-WINNING!!

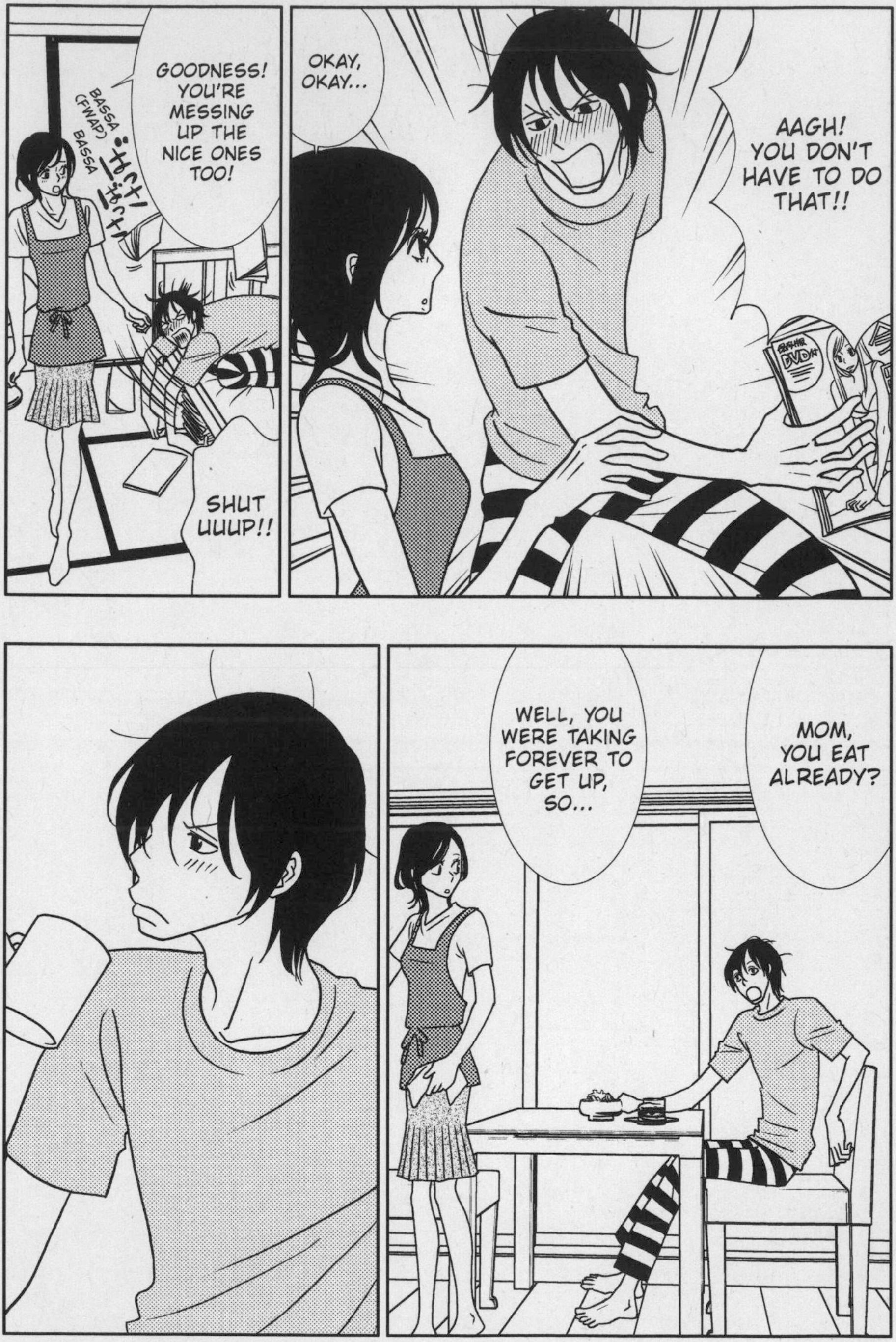
AAGH! YOU DON'T HAVE TO DO THAT!!
OKAY, OKAY...
GOODNESS! YOU'RE MESSING UP THE NICE ONES TOO!
BASSA (FWAP) BASSA
SHUT UUUP!!
MOM, YOU EAT ALREADY?
WELL, YOU WERE TAKING FOREVER TO GET UP, SO...

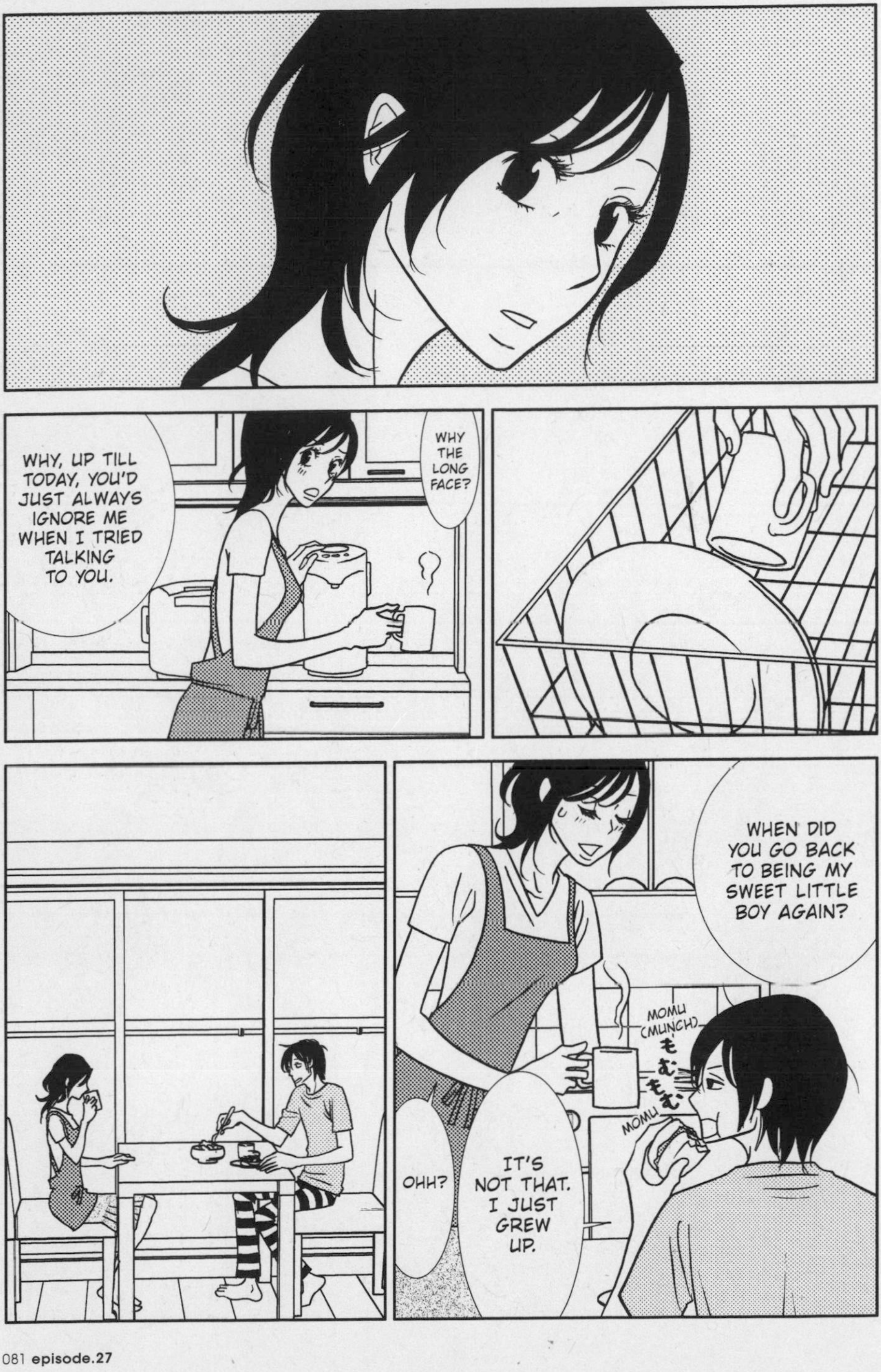
WHY THE LONG FACE?
WHY, UP TILL TODAY, YOU'D JUST ALWAYS IGNORE ME WHEN I TRIED TALKING TO YOU.
WHEN DID YOU GO BACK TO BEING MY SWEET LITTLE BOY AGAIN?
MOMU (MUNCH)
もむもむ
MOMU
IT'S NOT THAT. I JUST GREW UP.
OHH?

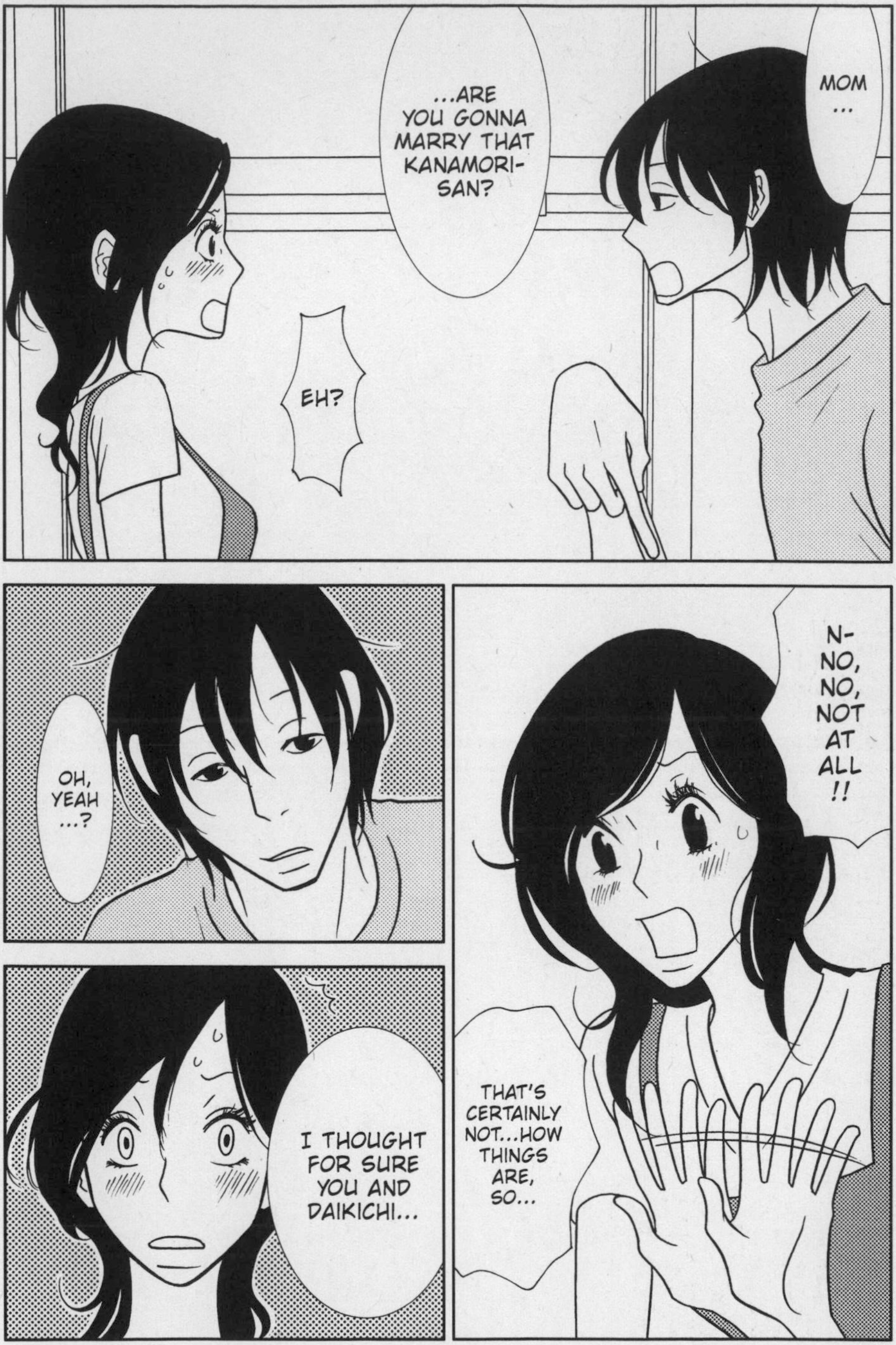
MOM ...
...ARE YOU GONNA MARRY THAT KANAMORI-SAN?
EH?
N-NO, NO, NOT AT ALL!!
THAT'S CERTAINLY NOT...HOW THINGS ARE, SO...
OH, YEAH ...?
I THOUGHT FOR SURE YOU AND DAIKICHI...

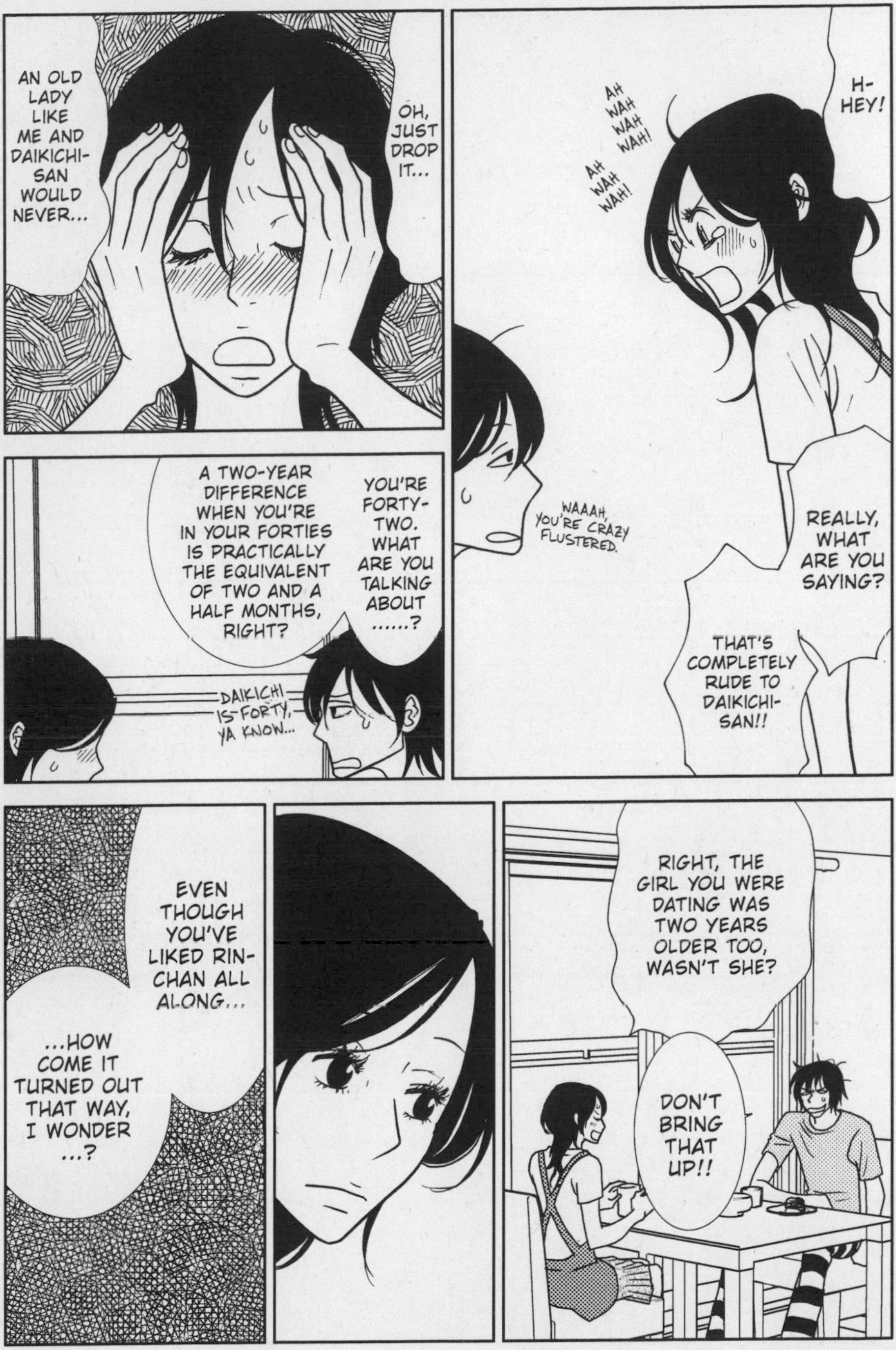
H- HEY!
AH WAH WAH WAH!
AH WAH WAH!
WAAAH, YOU'RE CRAZY FLUSTERED.
REALLY, WHAT ARE YOU SAYING?
THAT'S COMPLETELY RUDE TO DAIKICHI-SAN!!
OH, JUST DROP IT...
AN OLD LADY LIKE ME AND DAIKICHI-SAN WOULD NEVER...
YOU'RE FORTY-TWO. WHAT ARE YOU TALKING ABOUT ......?
A TWO-YEAR DIFFERENCE WHEN YOU'RE IN YOUR FORTIES IS PRACTICALLY THE EQUIVALENT OF TWO AND A HALF MONTHS, RIGHT?
DAIKICHI IS FORTY, YA KNOW...
RIGHT, THE GIRL YOU WERE DATING WAS TWO YEARS OLDER TOO, WASN'T SHE?
DON'T BRING THAT UP!!
EVEN THOUGH YOU'VE LIKED RIN-CHAN ALL ALONG...
...HOW COME IT TURNED OUT THAT WAY, I WONDER ...?

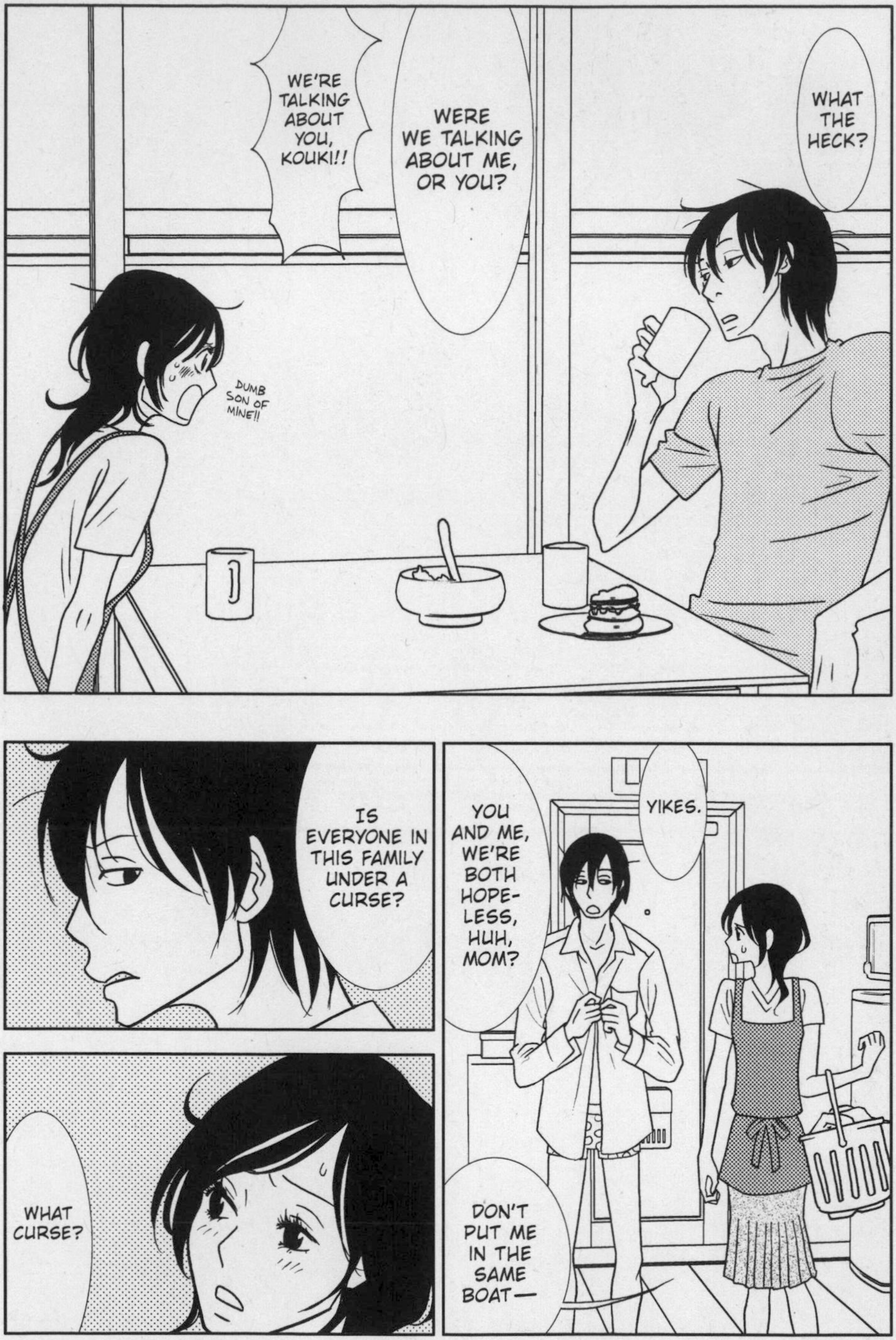
WHAT THE HECK?
WERE WE TALKING ABOUT ME, OR YOU?
WE'RE TALKING ABOUT YOU, KOUKI!!
DUMB SON OF MINE!!
YIKES.
YOU AND ME, WE'RE BOTH HOPE-LESS, HUH, MOM?
DON'T PUT ME IN THE SAME BOAT—
IS EVERYONE IN THIS FAMILY UNDER A CURSE?
WHAT CURSE?

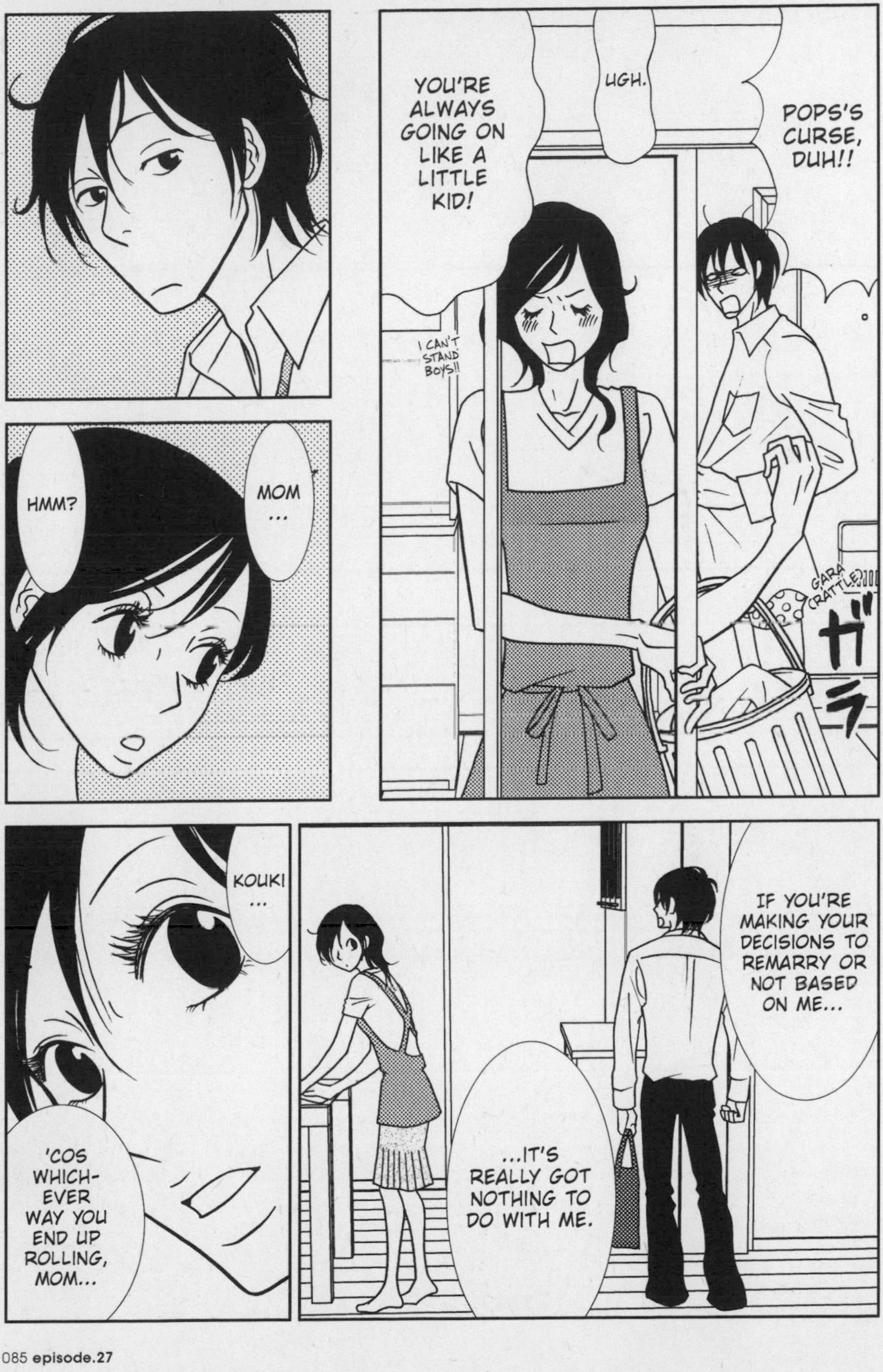
POPS'S CURSE, DUH!!
UGH.
YOU'RE ALWAYS GOING ON LIKE A LITTLE KID!
I CAN'T STAND BOYS!!
GARA (RATTLE)
MOM ...
HMM?
IF YOU'RE MAKING YOUR DECISIONS TO REMARRY OR NOT BASED ON ME...
...IT'S REALLY GOT NOTHING TO DO WITH ME.
KOUKI ...
'COS WHICH-EVER WAY YOU END UP ROLLING, MOM...

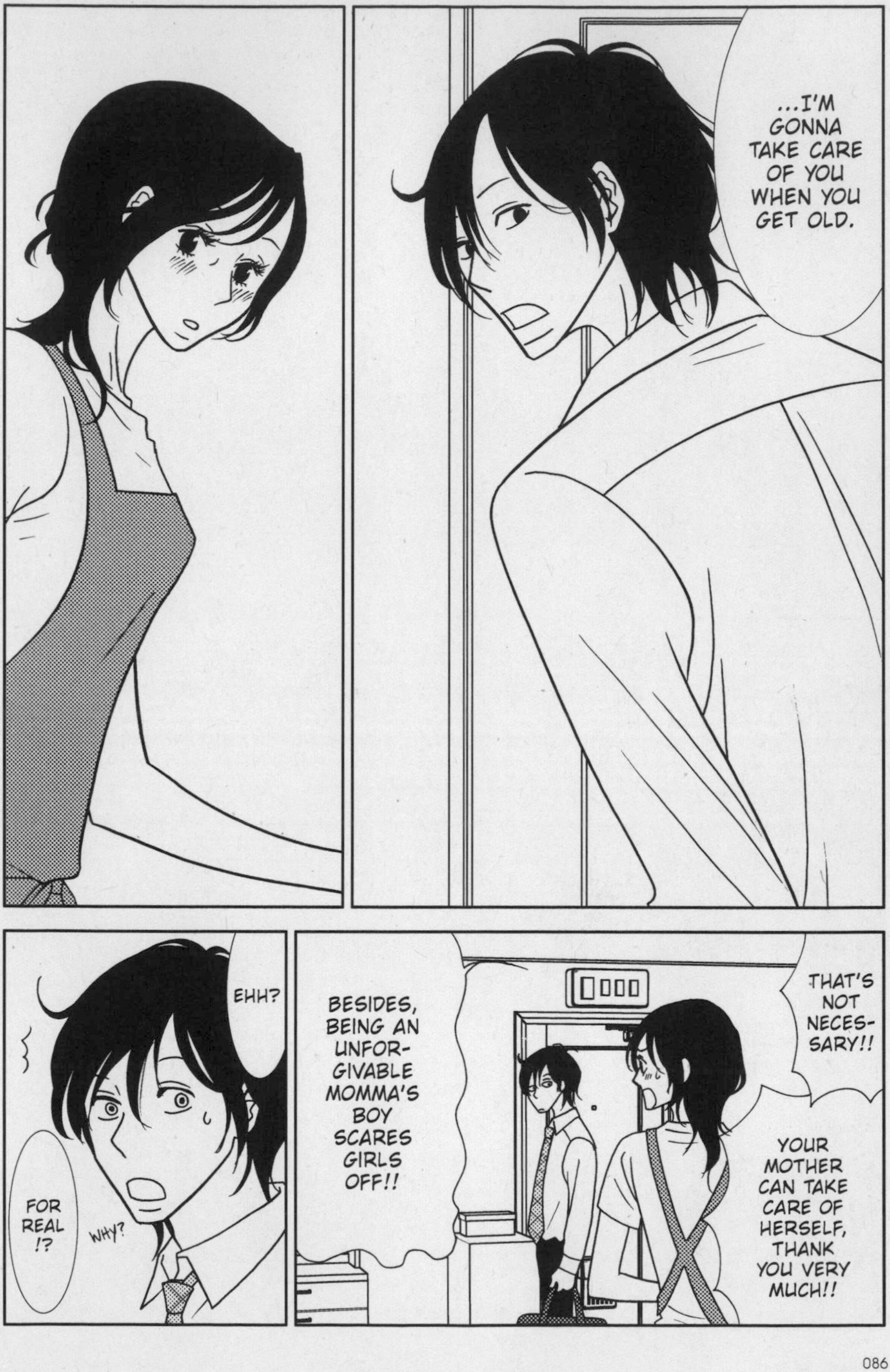
...I'M GONNA TAKE CARE OF YOU WHEN YOU GET OLD.
THAT'S NOT NECES-SARY!!
YOUR MOTHER CAN TAKE CARE OF HERSELF, THANK YOU VERY MUCH!!
BESIDES, BEING AN UNFORGIVABLE MOMMA'S BOY SCARES GIRLS OFF!!
EHH?
WHY?
FOR REAL !?

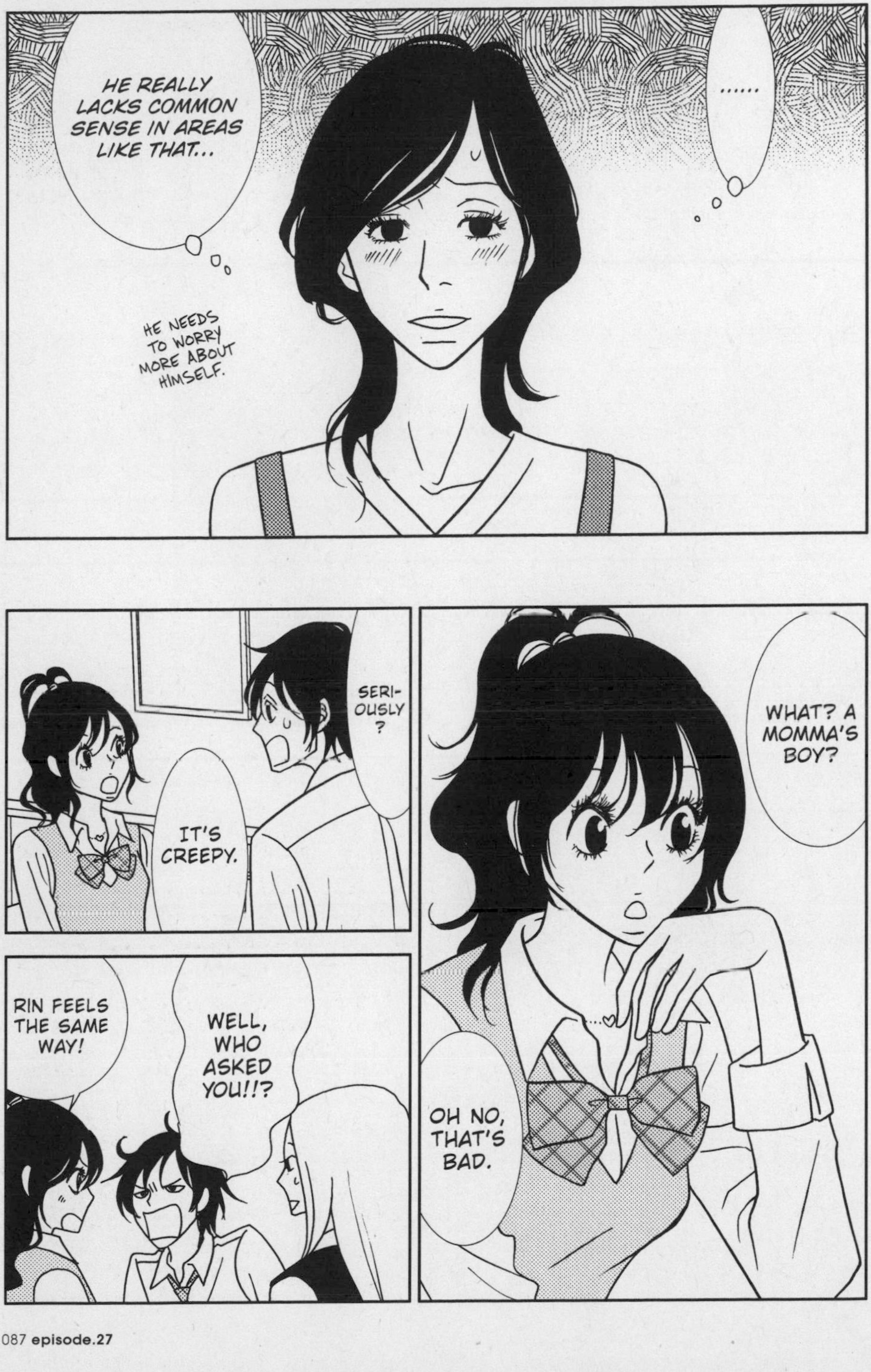
......
HE REALLY LACKS COMMON SENSE IN AREAS LIKE THAT...
HE NEEDS TO WORRY MORE ABOUT HIMSELF.
WHAT? A MOMMA'S BOY?
OH NO, THAT'S BAD.
SERI-OUSLY?
IT'S CREEPY.
WELL, WHO ASKED YOU!!?
RIN FEELS THE SAME WAY!

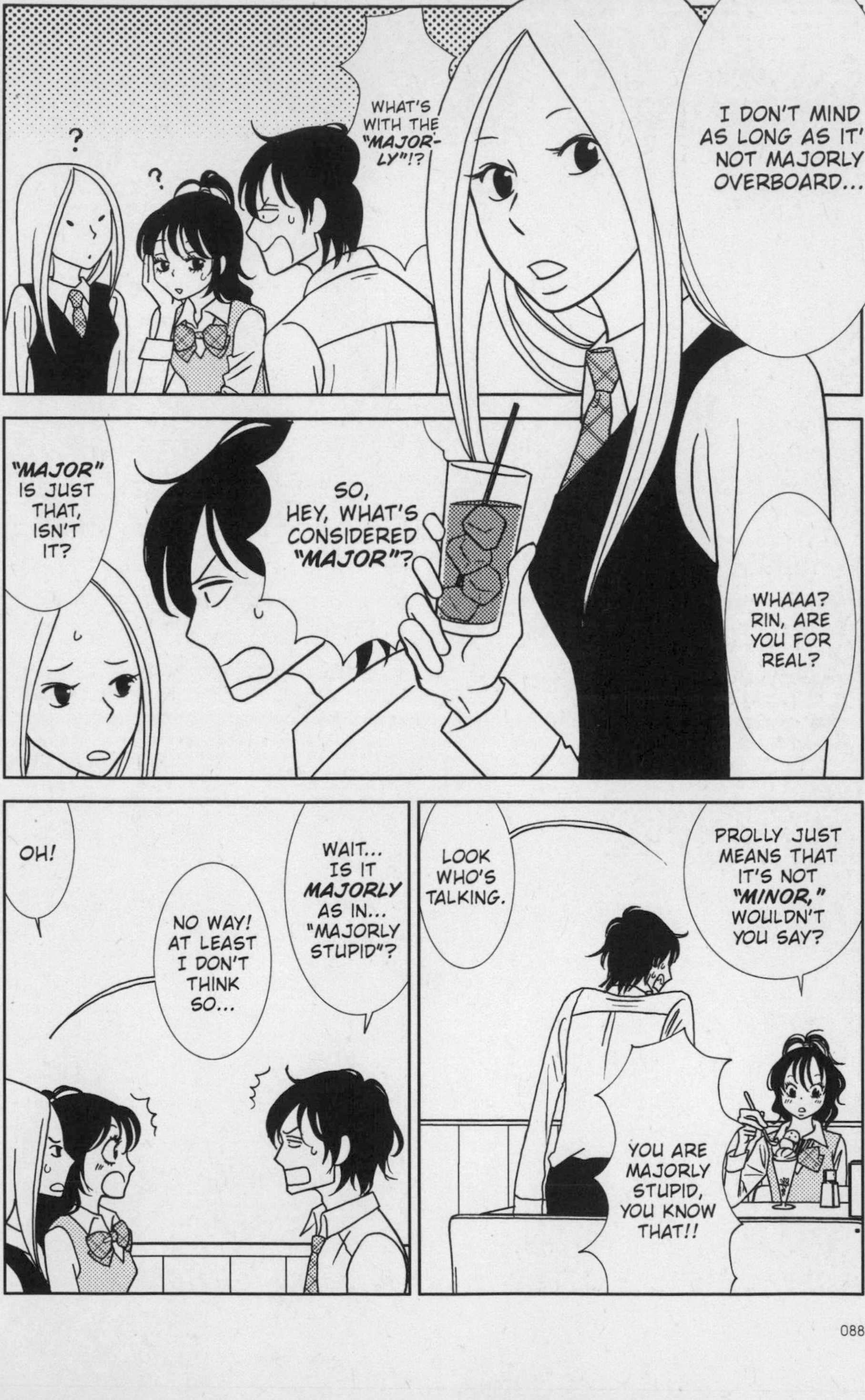
I DON'T MIND AS LONG AS IT'S NOT MAJORLY OVERBOARD...
WHAT'S WITH THE "MAJOR-LY"!?
?
?
WHAAA? RIN, ARE YOU FOR REAL?
SO, HEY, WHAT'S CONSIDERED "MAJOR"?
"MAJOR" IS JUST THAT, ISN'T IT?
PROLLY JUST MEANS THAT IT'S NOT "MINOR," WOULDN'T YOU SAY?
LOOK WHO'S TALKING.
YOU ARE MAJORLY STUPID, YOU KNOW THAT!!
WAIT... IS IT MAJORLY AS IN... "MAJORLY STUPID"?
NO WAY! AT LEAST I DON'T THINK SO...
OH!

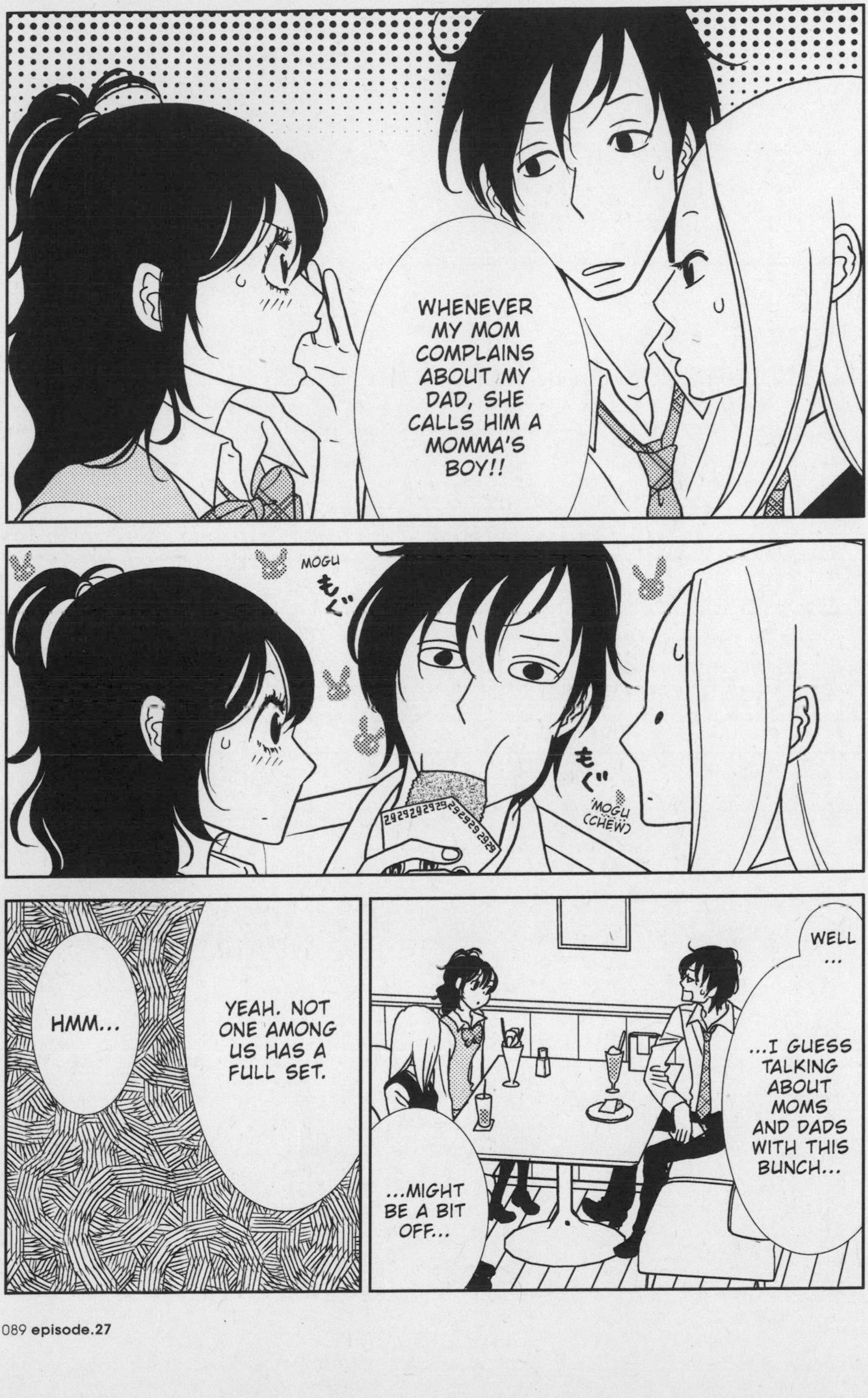
WHENEVER MY MOM COMPLAINS ABOUT MY DAD, SHE CALLS HIM A MOMMA'S BOY!!
もぐ MOGU (CHEW)
MOGU もぐ
WELL ...
...I GUESS TALKING ABOUT MOMS AND DADS WITH THIS BUNCH...
...MIGHT BE A BIT OFF...
YEAH. NOT ONE AMONG US HAS A FULL SET.
HMM...

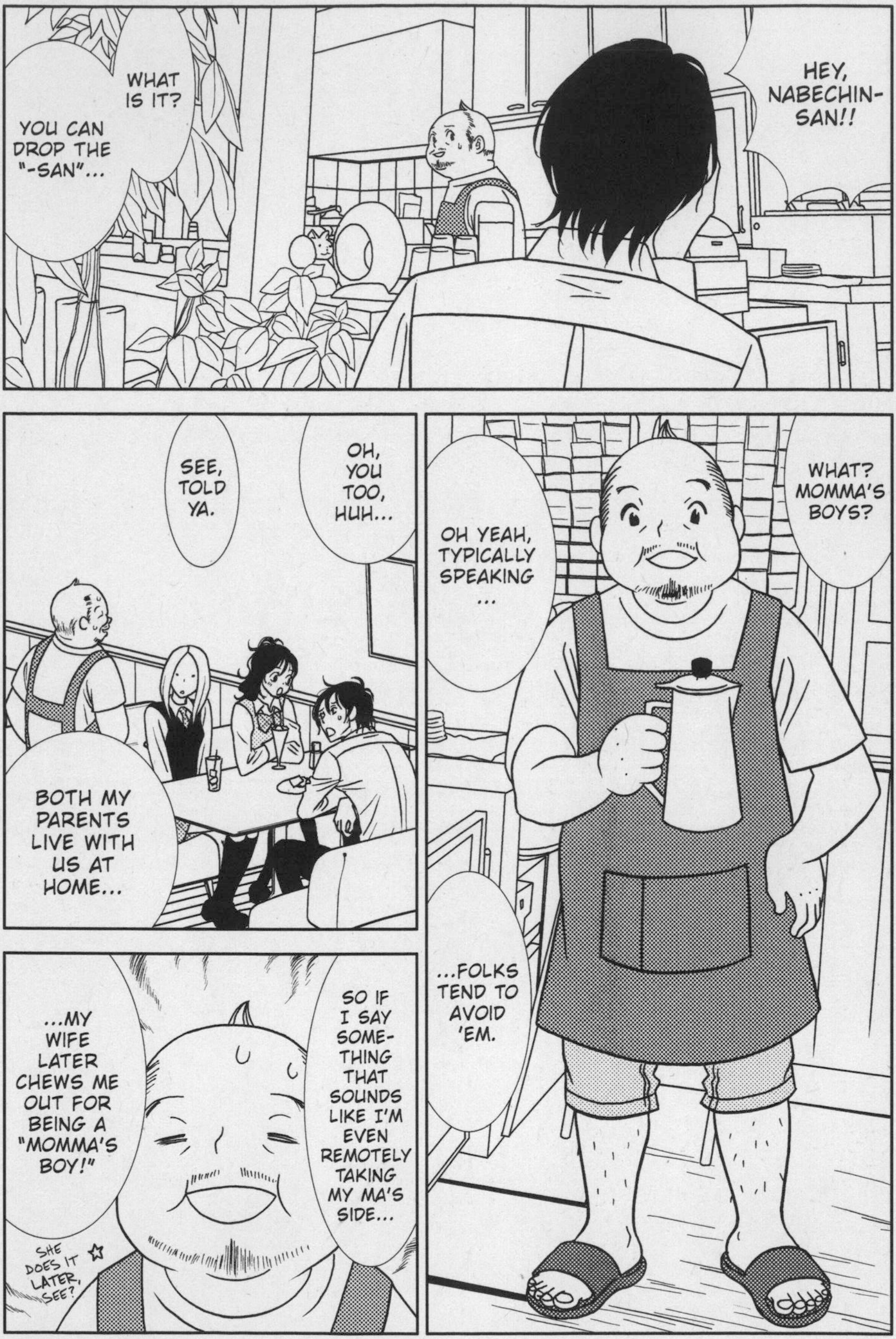
HEY, NABECHIN-SAN!!
WHAT IS IT?
YOU CAN DROP THE "-SAN"...
WHAT? MOMMA'S BOYS?
OH YEAH, TYPICALLY SPEAKING ...
...FOLKS TEND TO AVOID 'EM.
OH, YOU TOO, HUH...
SEE, TOLD YA.
BOTH MY PARENTS LIVE WITH US AT HOME...
SO IF I SAY SOME-THING THAT SOUNDS LIKE I'M EVEN REMOTELY TAKING MY MA'S SIDE...
...MY WIFE LATER CHEWS ME OUT FOR BEING A "MOMMA'S BOY!"
SHE DOES IT LATER, SEE? ☆

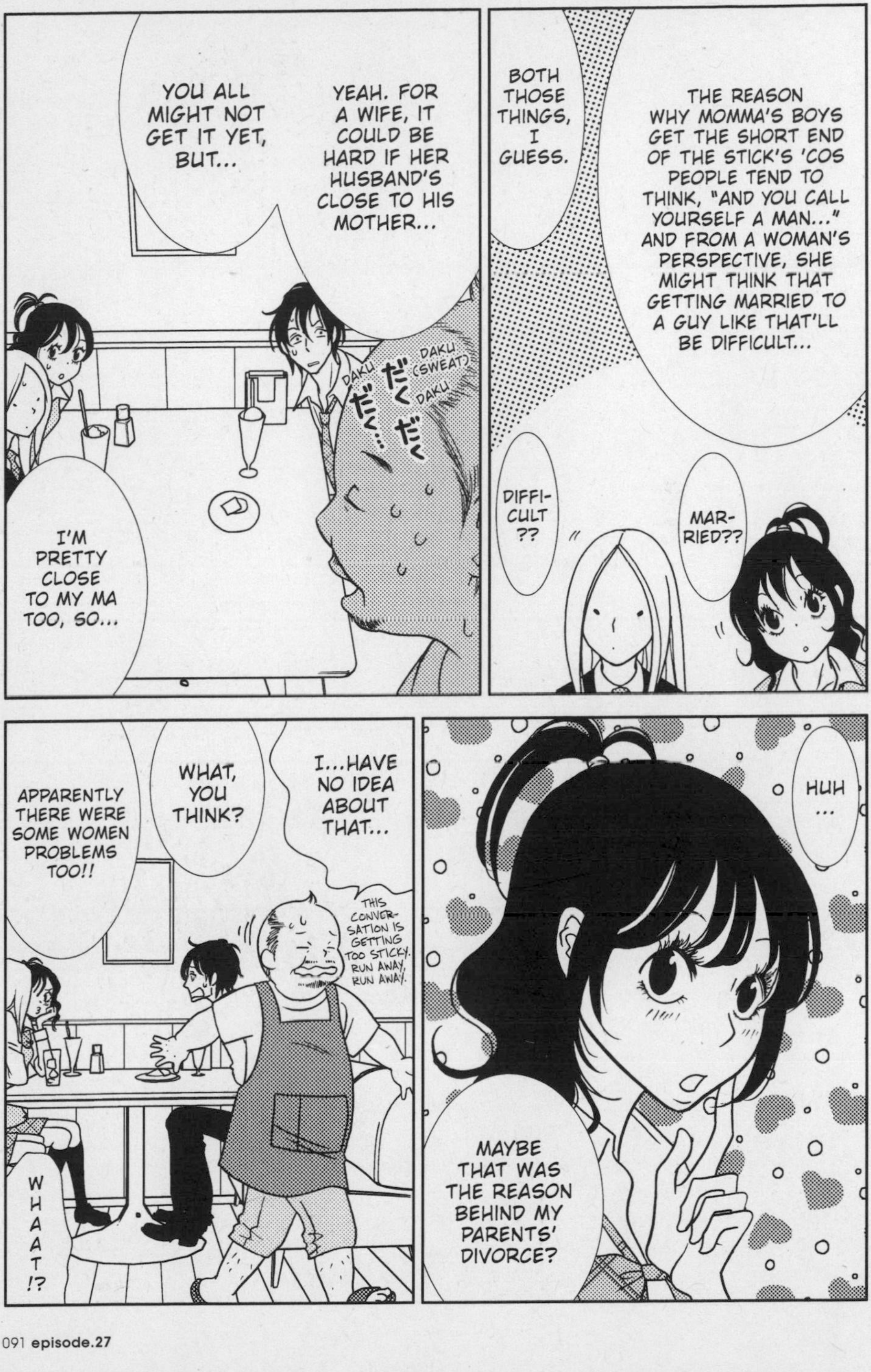
THE REASON WHY MOMMA'S BOYS GET THE SHORT END OF THE STICK'S 'COS PEOPLE TEND TO THINK, "AND YOU CALL YOURSELF A MAN..." AND FROM A WOMAN'S PERSPECTIVE, SHE MIGHT THINK THAT GETTING MARRIED TO A GUY LIKE THAT'LL BE DIFFICULT...
BOTH THOSE THINGS, I GUESS.
MAR-RIED??
DIFFI-CULT??
YEAH. FOR A WIFE, IT COULD BE HARD IF HER HUSBAND'S CLOSE TO HIS MOTHER...
YOU ALL MIGHT NOT GET IT YET, BUT...
DAKU DAKU (SWEAT) DAKU DAKU
だく だく だく だく...
I'M PRETTY CLOSE TO MY MA TOO, SO...
HUH...
MAYBE THAT WAS THE REASON BEHIND MY PARENTS' DIVORCE?
I...HAVE NO IDEA ABOUT THAT...
WHAT, YOU THINK?
APPARENTLY THERE WERE SOME WOMEN PROBLEMS TOO!!
THIS CONVER-SATION IS GETTING TOO STICKY. RUN AWAY, RUN AWAY.
WHAAAT!?

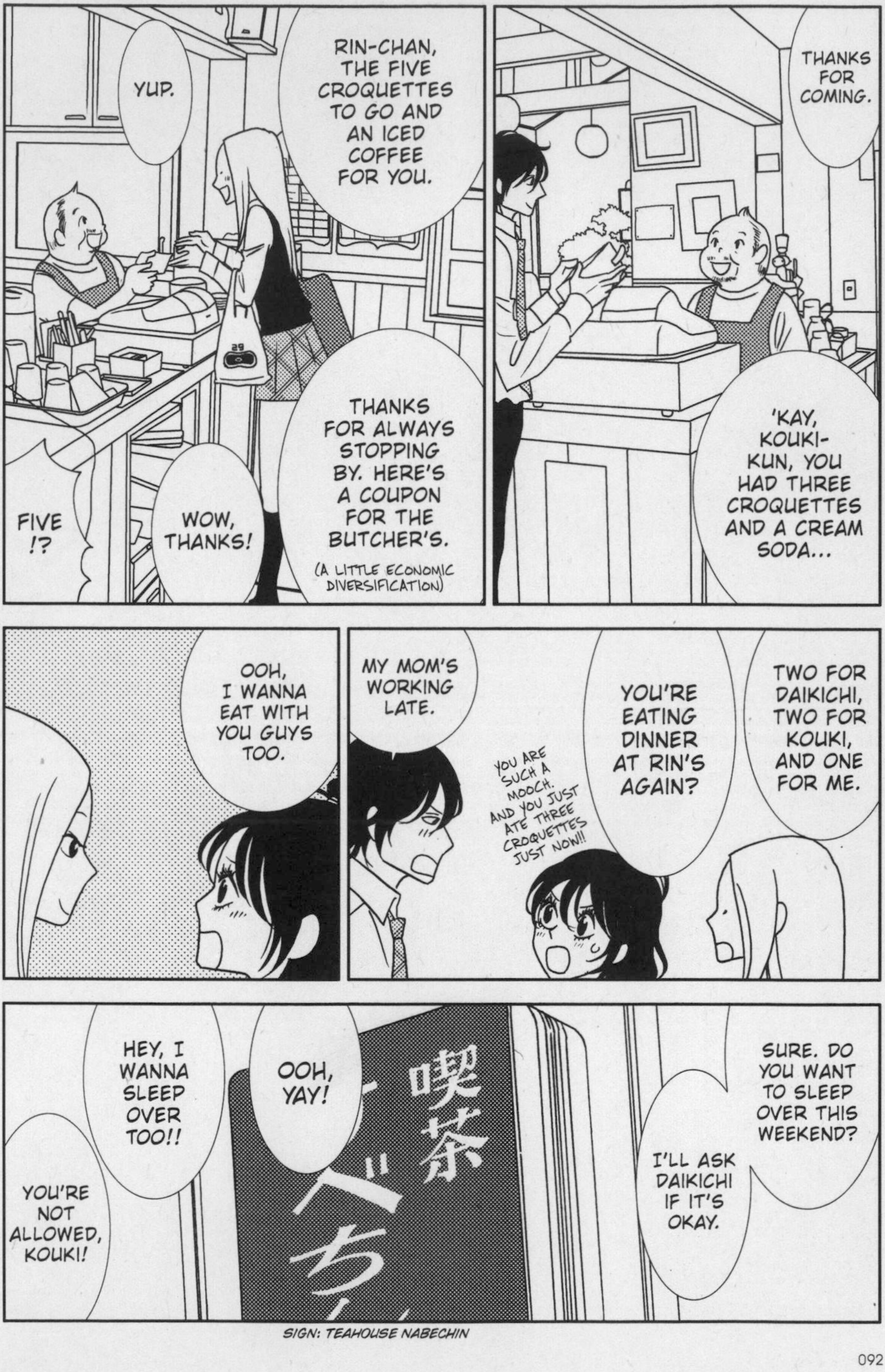
THANKS FOR COMING.
'KAY, KOUKI-KUN, YOU HAD THREE CROQUETTES AND A CREAM SODA...
RIN-CHAN, THE FIVE CROQUETTES TO GO AND AN ICED COFFEE FOR YOU.
YUP.
THANKS FOR ALWAYS STOPPING BY. HERE'S A COUPON FOR THE BUTCHER'S.
(A LITTLE ECONOMIC DIVERSIFICATION)
WOW, THANKS!
FIVE !?
TWO FOR DAIKICHI, TWO FOR KOUKI, AND ONE FOR ME.
YOU'RE EATING DINNER AT RIN'S AGAIN?
YOU ARE SUCH A MOOCH. AND YOU JUST ATE THREE CROQUETTES JUST NOW!!
MY MOM'S WORKING LATE.
OOH, I WANNA EAT WITH YOU GUYS TOO.
SURE. DO YOU WANT TO SLEEP OVER THIS WEEKEND?
I'LL ASK DAIKICHI IF IT'S OKAY.
喫茶
OOH, YAY!
HEY, I WANNA SLEEP OVER TOO!!
YOU'RE NOT ALLOWED, KOUKI!

SIGN: TEAHOUSE NABECHIN

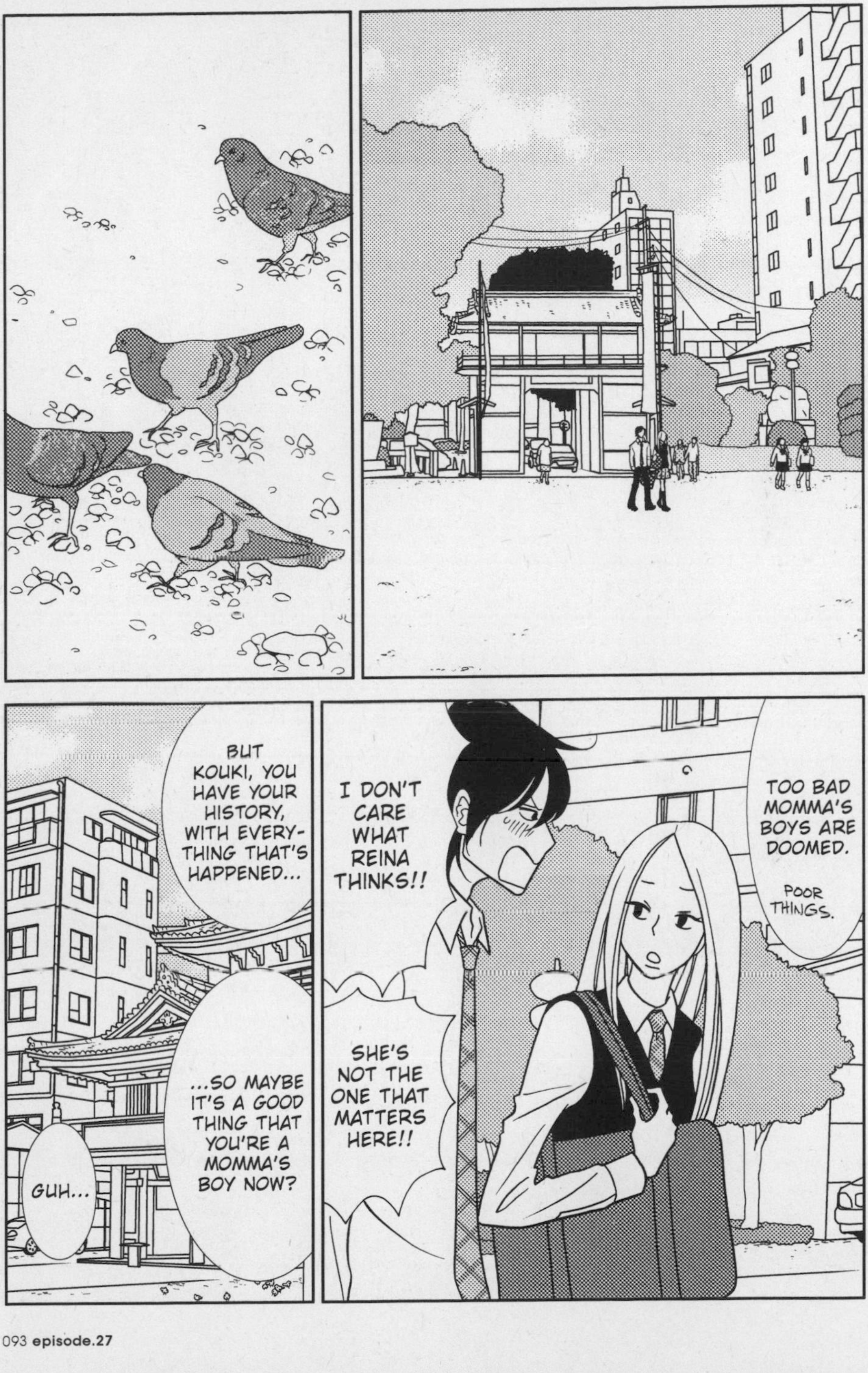
TOO BAD MOMMA'S BOYS ARE DOOMED.
POOR THINGS.
I DON'T CARE WHAT REINA THINKS!!
SHE'S NOT THE ONE THAT MATTERS HERE!!
BUT KOUKI, YOU HAVE YOUR HISTORY, WITH EVERYTHING THAT'S HAPPENED...
...SO MAYBE IT'S A GOOD THING THAT YOU'RE A MOMMA'S BOY NOW?
GUH...

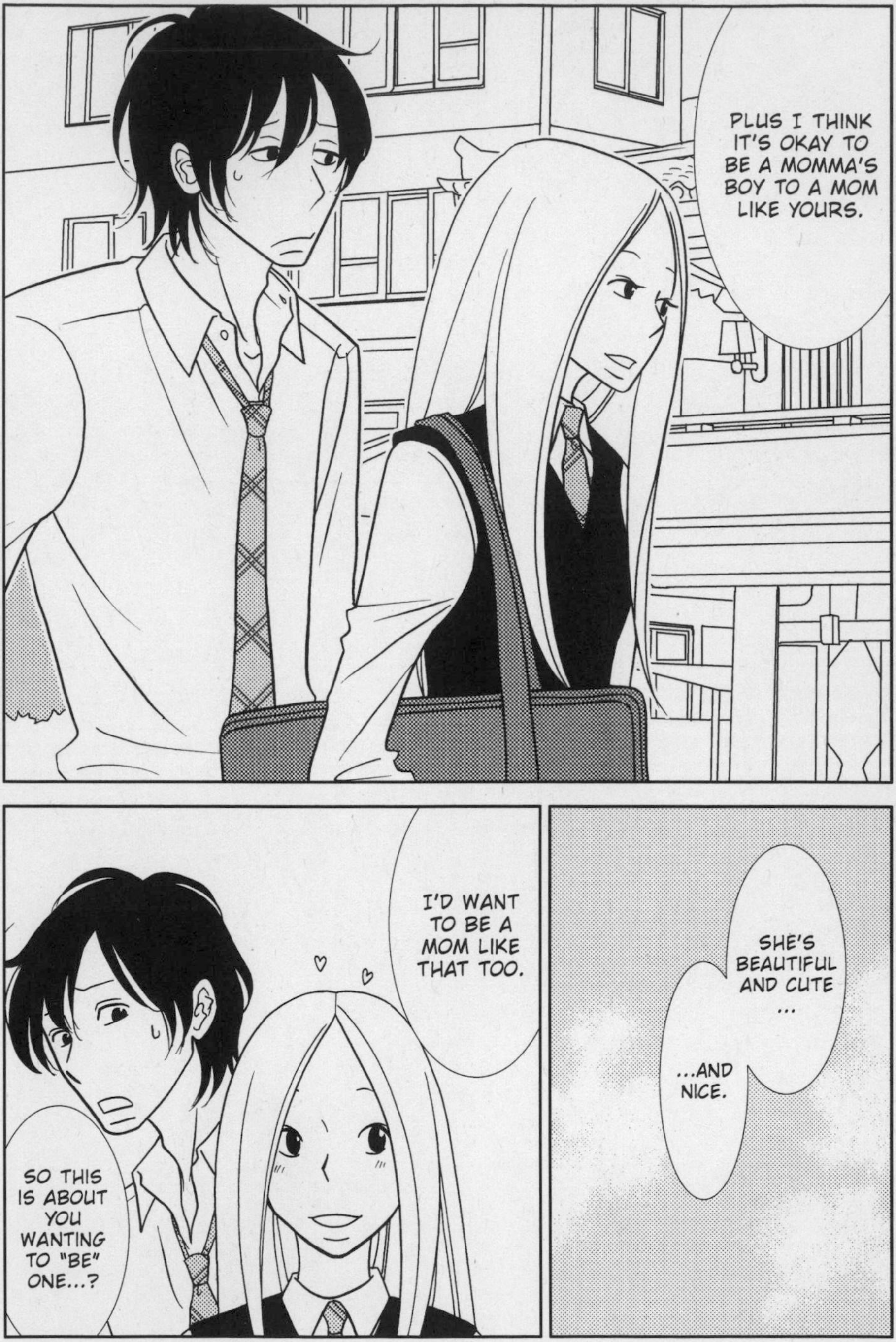
PLUS I THINK IT'S OKAY TO BE A MOMMA'S BOY TO A MOM LIKE YOURS.
SHE'S BEAUTIFUL AND CUTE ...
...AND NICE.
I'D WANT TO BE A MOM LIKE THAT TOO.
SO THIS IS ABOUT YOU WANTING TO "BE" ONE...?

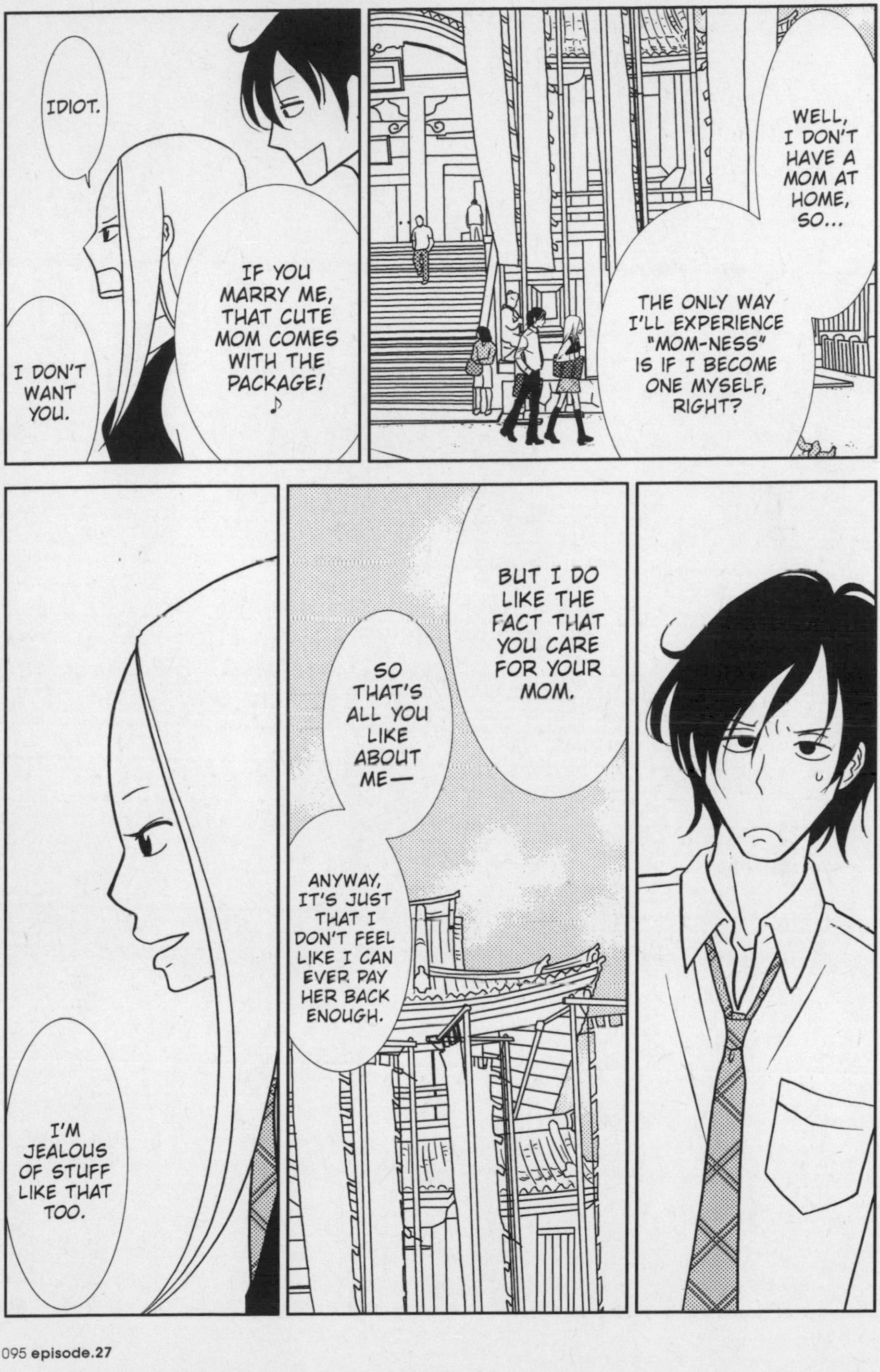
WELL, I DON'T HAVE A MOM AT HOME, SO...
THE ONLY WAY I'LL EXPERIENCE "MOM-NESS" IS IF I BECOME ONE MYSELF, RIGHT?
IF YOU MARRY ME, THAT CUTE MOM COMES WITH THE PACKAGE! ♪
IDIOT.
I DON'T WANT YOU.
BUT I DO LIKE THE FACT THAT YOU CARE FOR YOUR MOM.
SO THAT'S ALL YOU LIKE ABOUT ME—
ANYWAY, IT'S JUST THAT I DON'T FEEL LIKE I CAN EVER PAY HER BACK ENOUGH.
I'M JEALOUS OF STUFF LIKE THAT TOO.

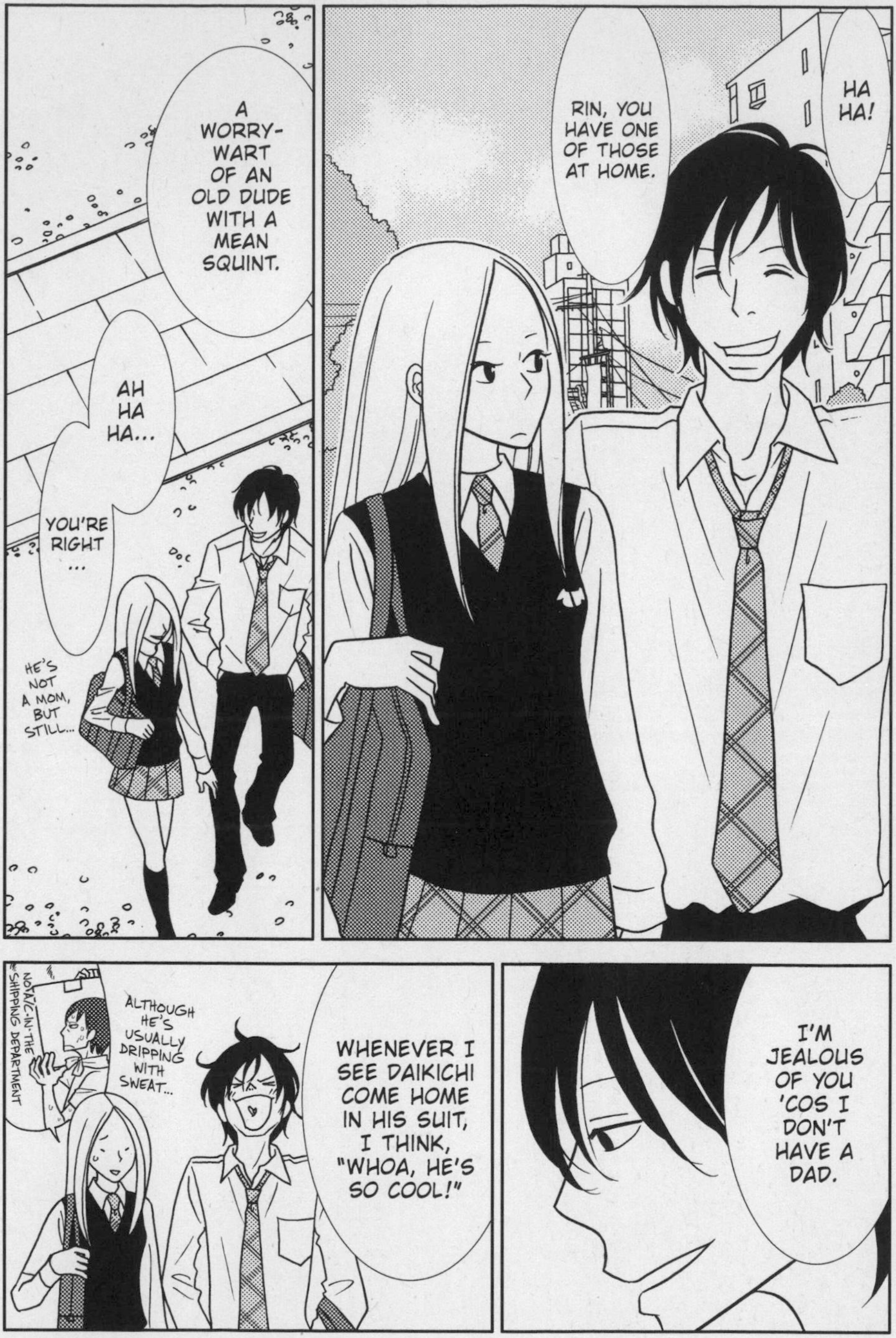
HA HA!
RIN, YOU HAVE ONE OF THOSE AT HOME.
A WORRY-WART OF AN OLD DUDE WITH A MEAN SQUINT.
AH HA HA...
YOU'RE RIGHT...
HE'S NOT A MOM, BUT STILL...
I'M JEALOUS OF YOU 'COS I DON'T HAVE A DAD.
WHENEVER I SEE DAIKICHI COME HOME IN HIS SUIT, I THINK, "WHOA, HE'S SO COOL!"
ALTHOUGH HE'S USUALLY DRIPPING WITH SWEAT...
NO A/C IN THE SHIPPING DEPARTMENT

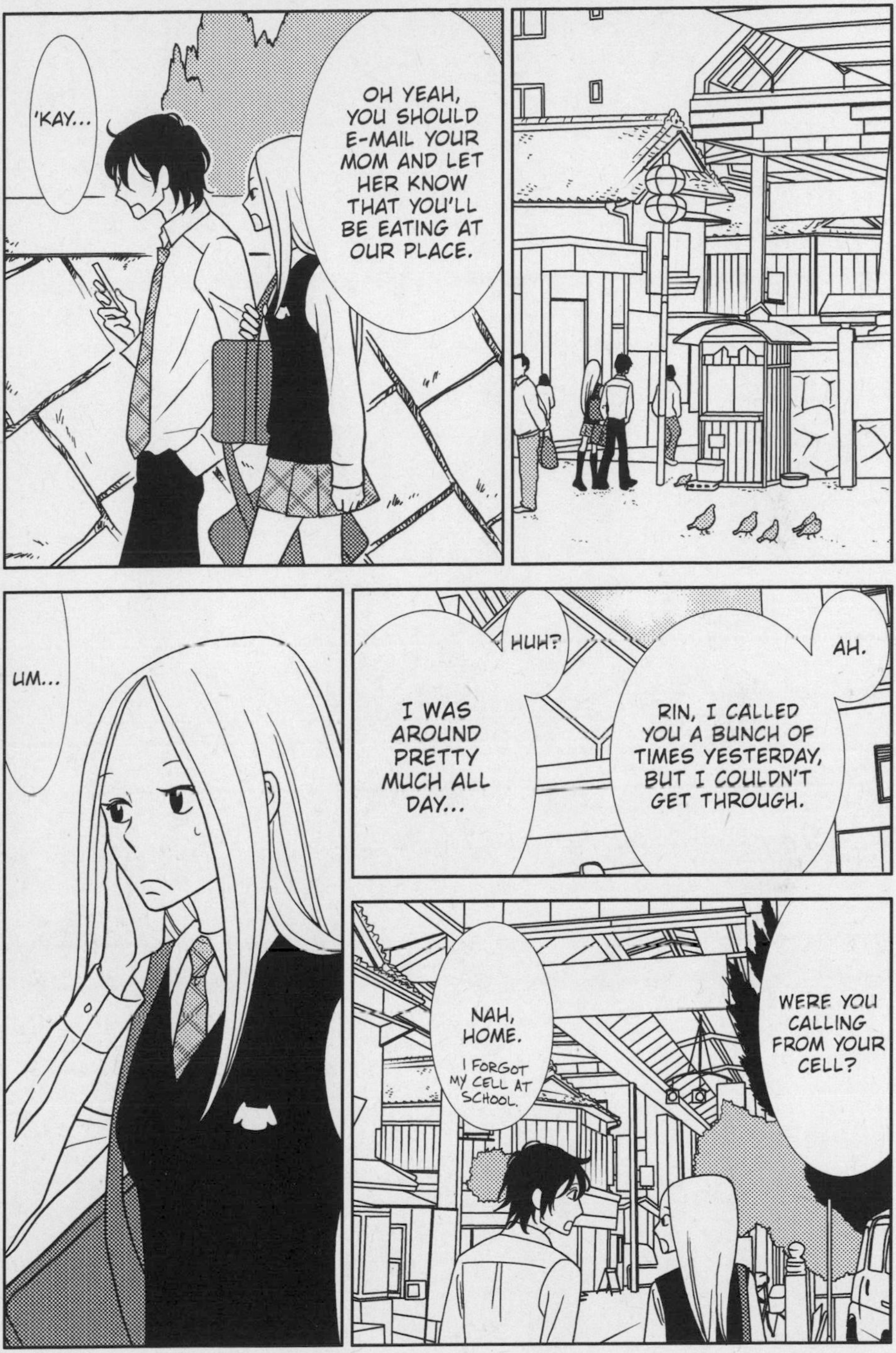
OH YEAH, YOU SHOULD E-MAIL YOUR MOM AND LET HER KNOW THAT YOU'LL BE EATING AT OUR PLACE.
'KAY...
AH.
RIN, I CALLED YOU A BUNCH OF TIMES YESTERDAY, BUT I COULDN'T GET THROUGH.
HUH?
I WAS AROUND PRETTY MUCH ALL DAY...
WERE YOU CALLING FROM YOUR CELL?
NAH, HOME.
I FORGOT MY CELL AT SCHOOL.
UM...

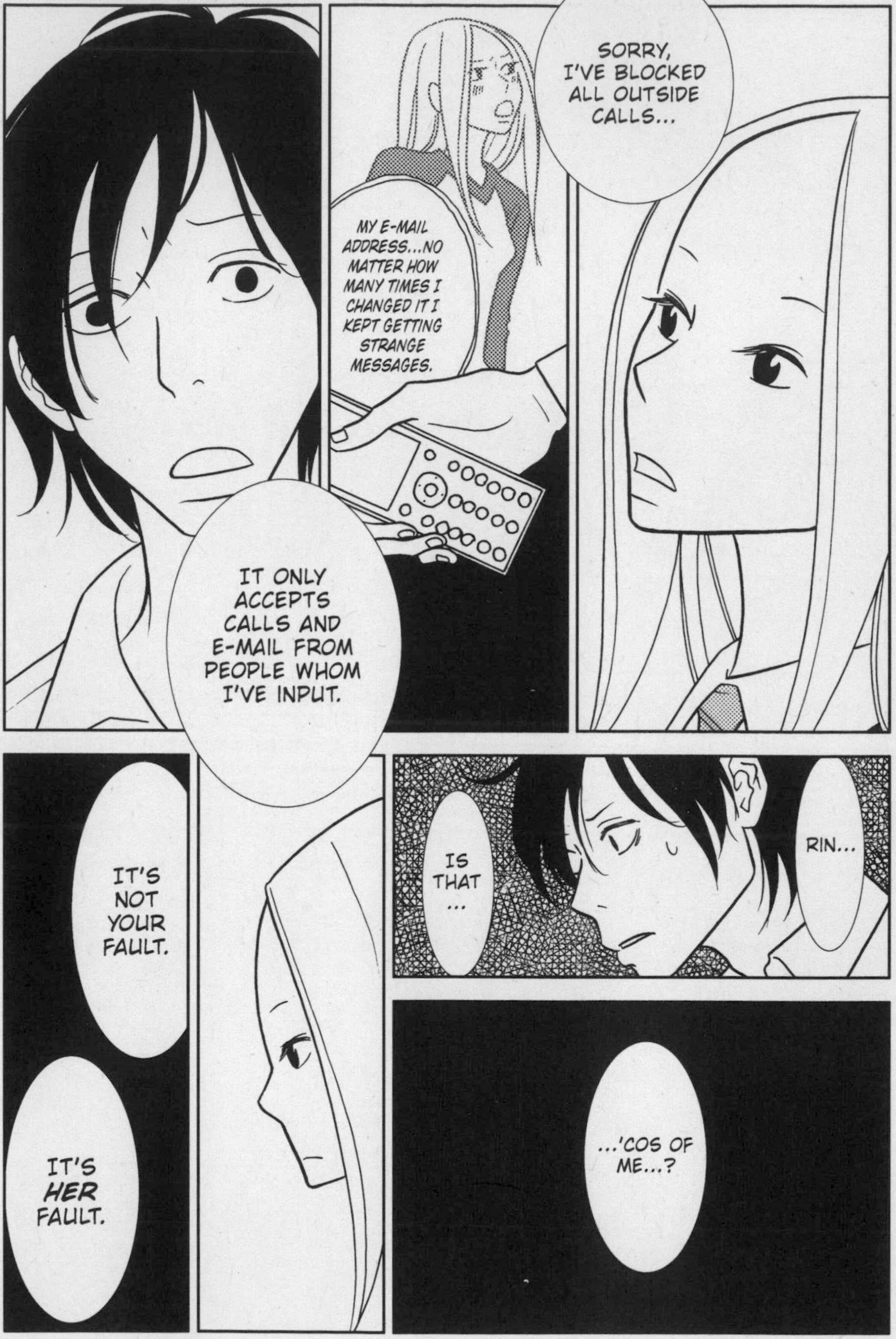
SORRY, I'VE BLOCKED ALL OUTSIDE CALLS...
MY E-MAIL ADDRESS...NO MATTER HOW MANY TIMES I CHANGED IT I KEPT GETTING STRANGE MESSAGES.
IT ONLY ACCEPTS CALLS AND E-MAIL FROM PEOPLE WHOM I'VE INPUT.
RIN...
IS THAT ...
...'COS OF ME...?
IT'S NOT YOUR FAULT.
IT'S *HER* FAULT.

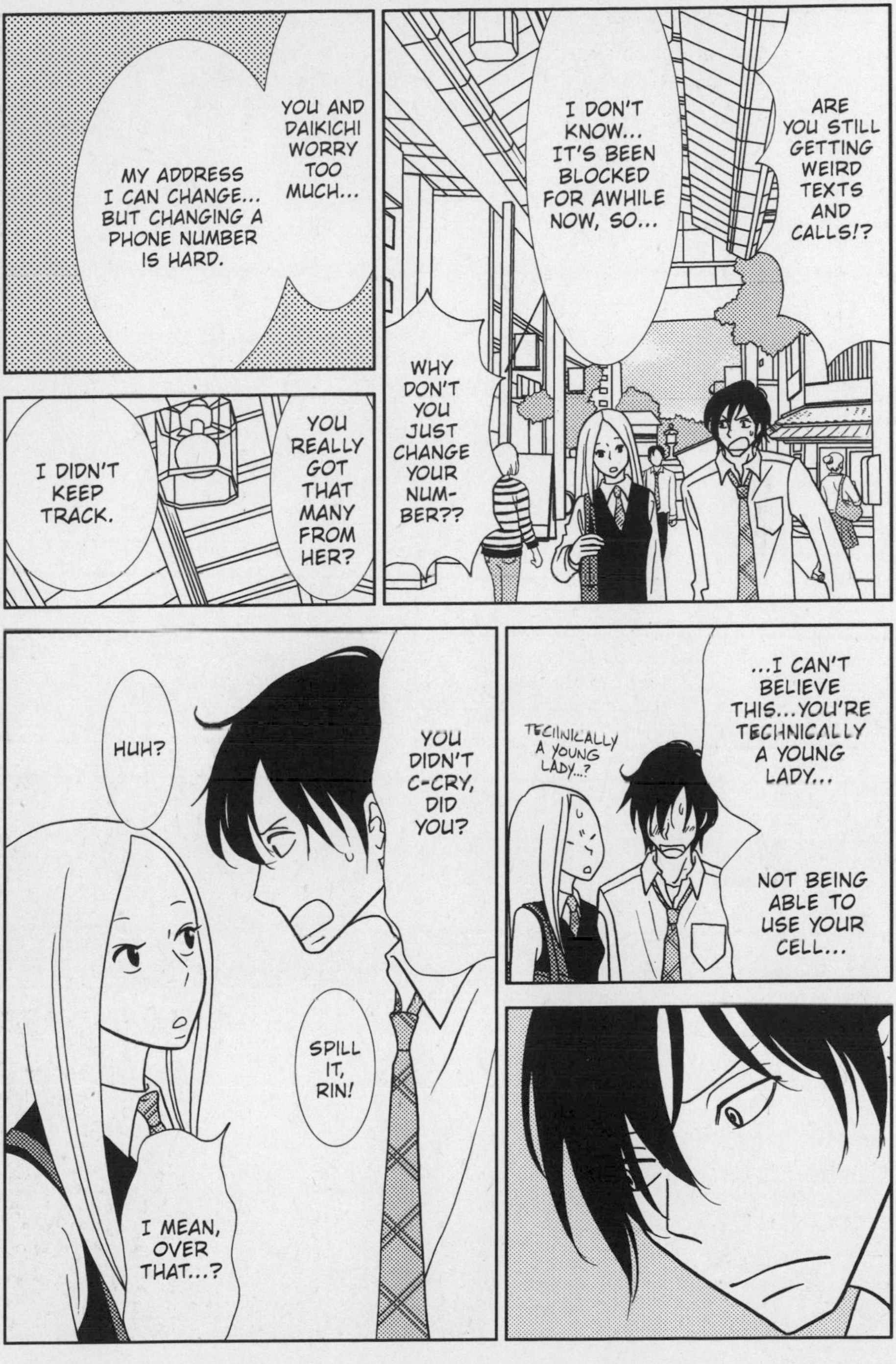
ARE YOU STILL GETTING WEIRD TEXTS AND CALLS!?
I DON'T KNOW... IT'S BEEN BLOCKED FOR AWHILE NOW, SO...
WHY DON'T YOU JUST CHANGE YOUR NUM-BER??
YOU AND DAIKICHI WORRY TOO MUCH...
MY ADDRESS I CAN CHANGE... BUT CHANGING A PHONE NUMBER IS HARD.
YOU REALLY GOT THAT MANY FROM HER?
I DIDN'T KEEP TRACK.
...I CAN'T BELIEVE THIS...YOU'RE TECHNICALLY A YOUNG LADY...
TECHNICALLY A YOUNG LADY...?
NOT BEING ABLE TO USE YOUR CELL...
YOU DIDN'T C-CRY, DID YOU?
HUH?
SPILL IT, RIN!
I MEAN, OVER THAT...?

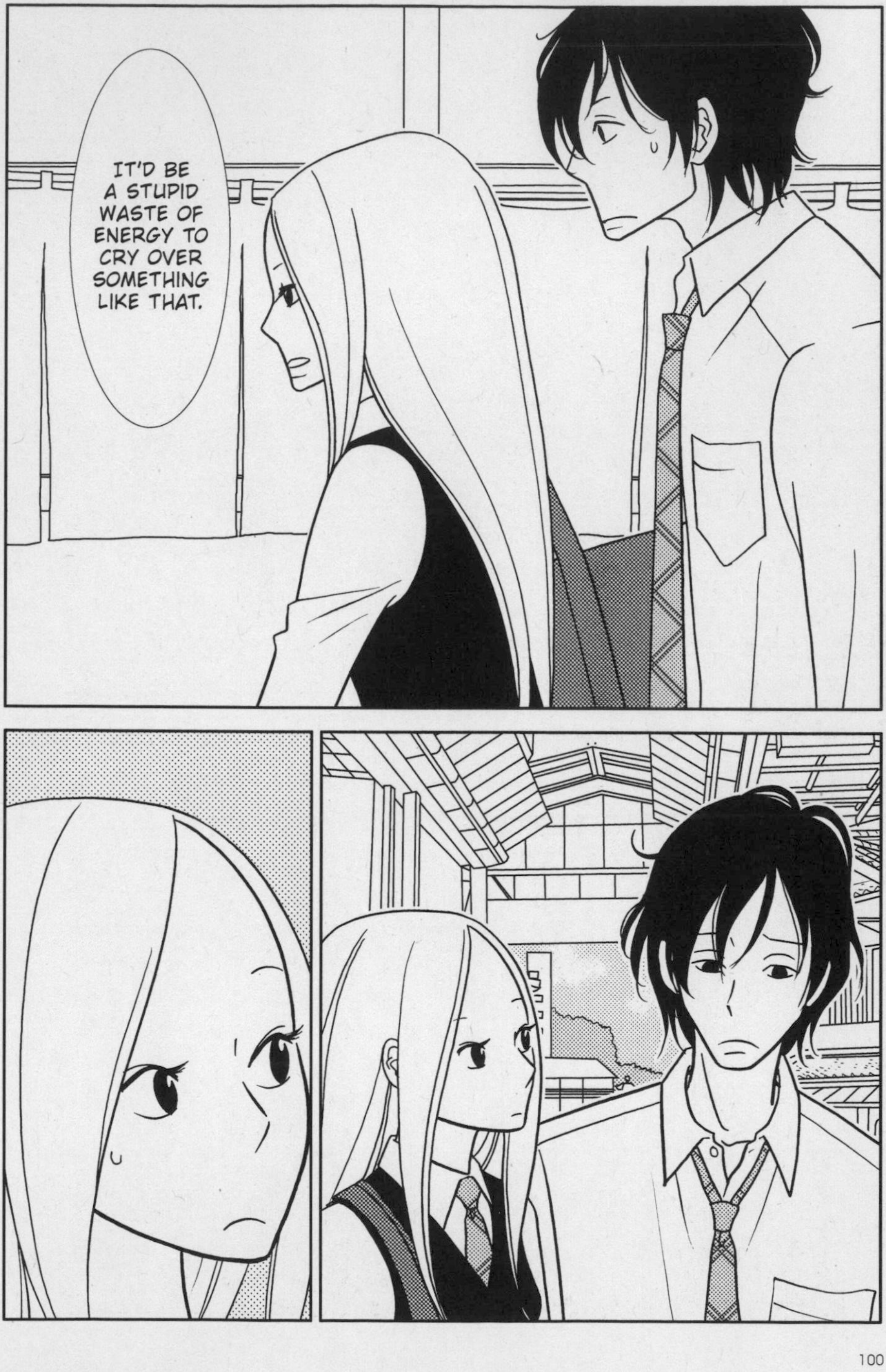
IT'D BE A STUPID WASTE OF ENERGY TO CRY OVER SOMETHING LIKE THAT.

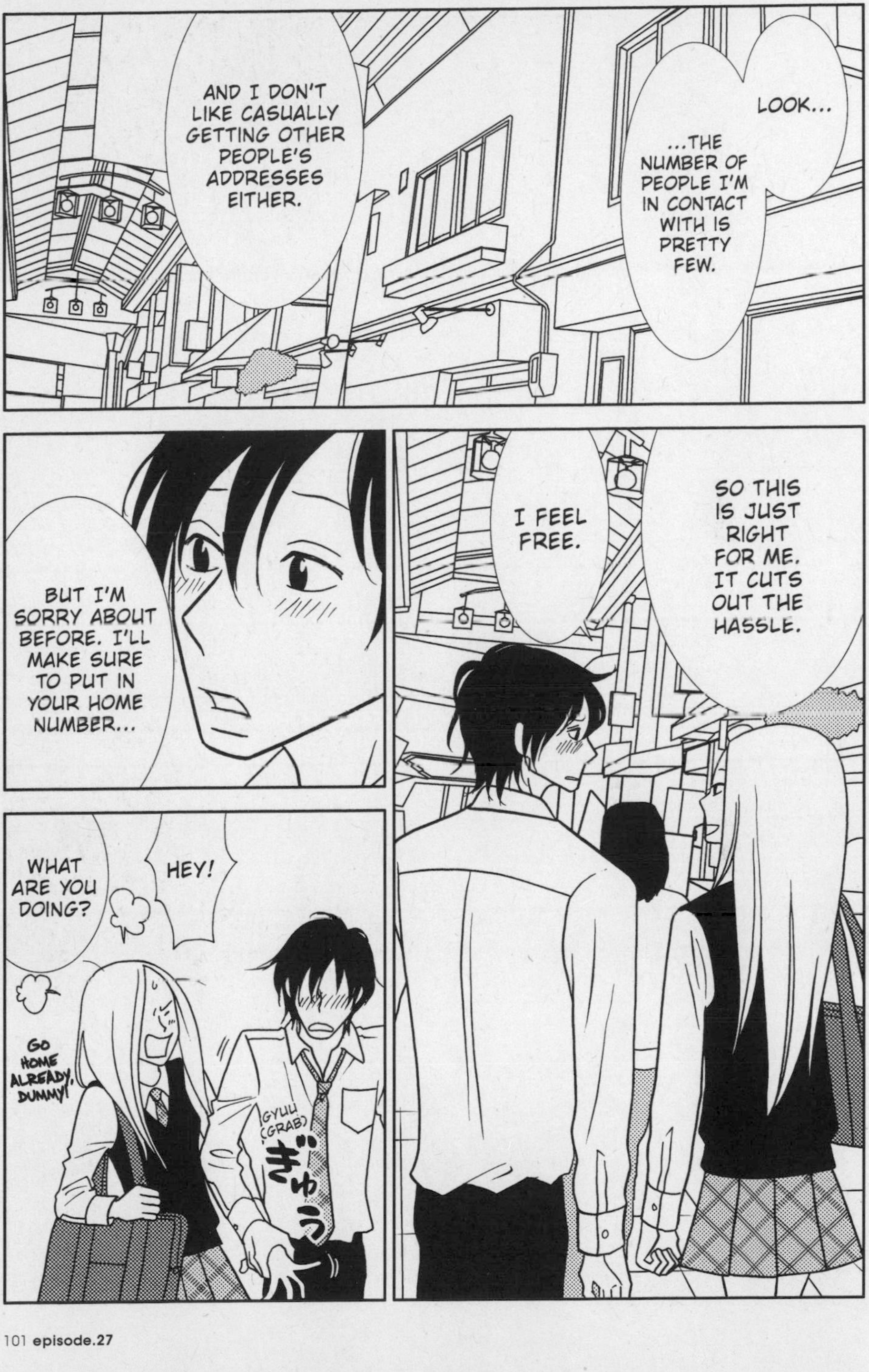
LOOK...
...THE NUMBER OF PEOPLE I'M IN CONTACT WITH IS PRETTY FEW.
AND I DON'T LIKE CASUALLY GETTING OTHER PEOPLE'S ADDRESSES EITHER.
SO THIS IS JUST RIGHT FOR ME. IT CUTS OUT THE HASSLE.
I FEEL FREE.
BUT I'M SORRY ABOUT BEFORE. I'LL MAKE SURE TO PUT IN YOUR HOME NUMBER...
HEY!
WHAT ARE YOU DOING?
GO HOME ALREADY, DUMMY!
GYUU (GRAB)
ぎゅう

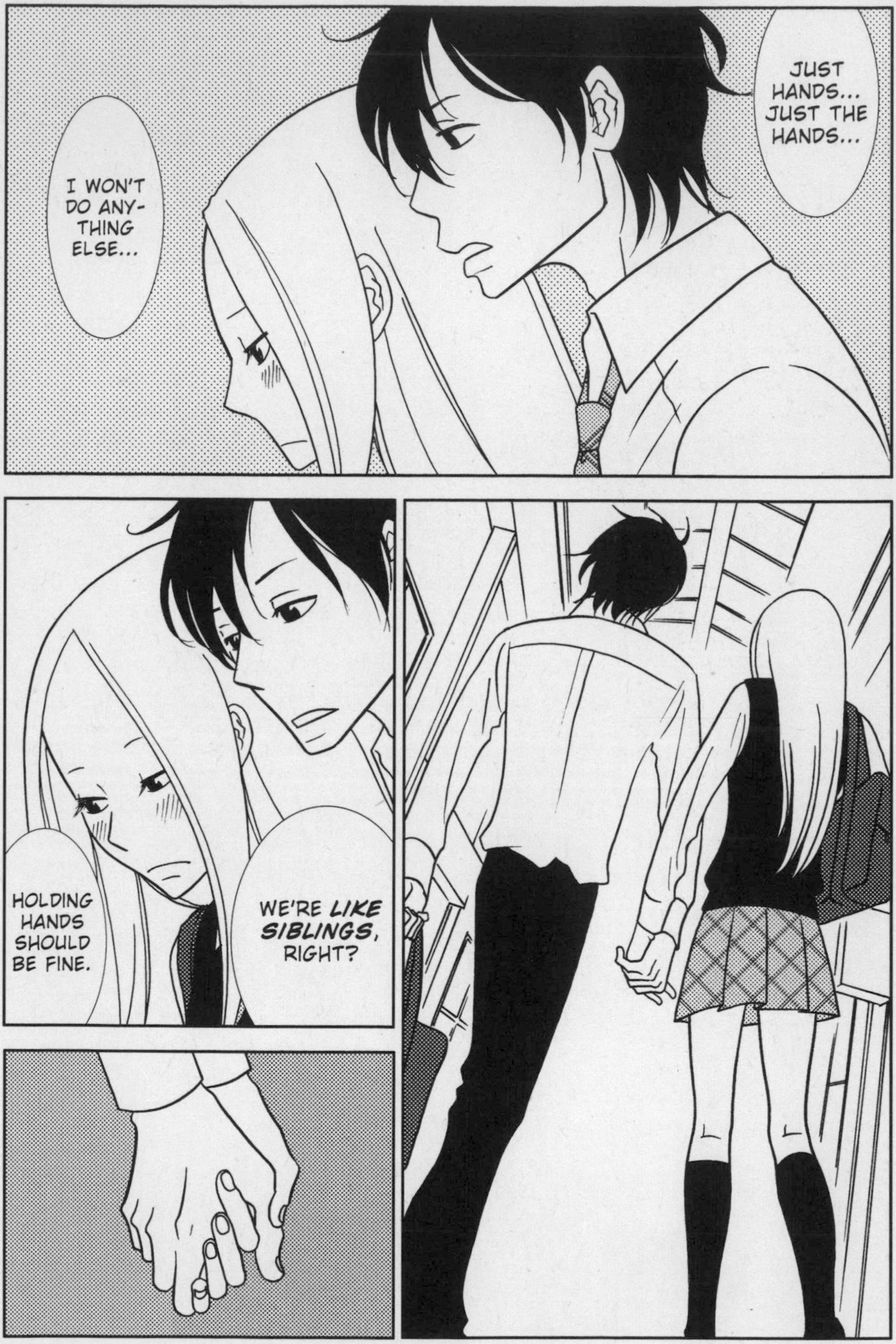
JUST HANDS... JUST THE HANDS...
I WON'T DO ANY-THING ELSE...
WE'RE *LIKE SIBLINGS*, RIGHT?
HOLDING HANDS SHOULD BE FINE.

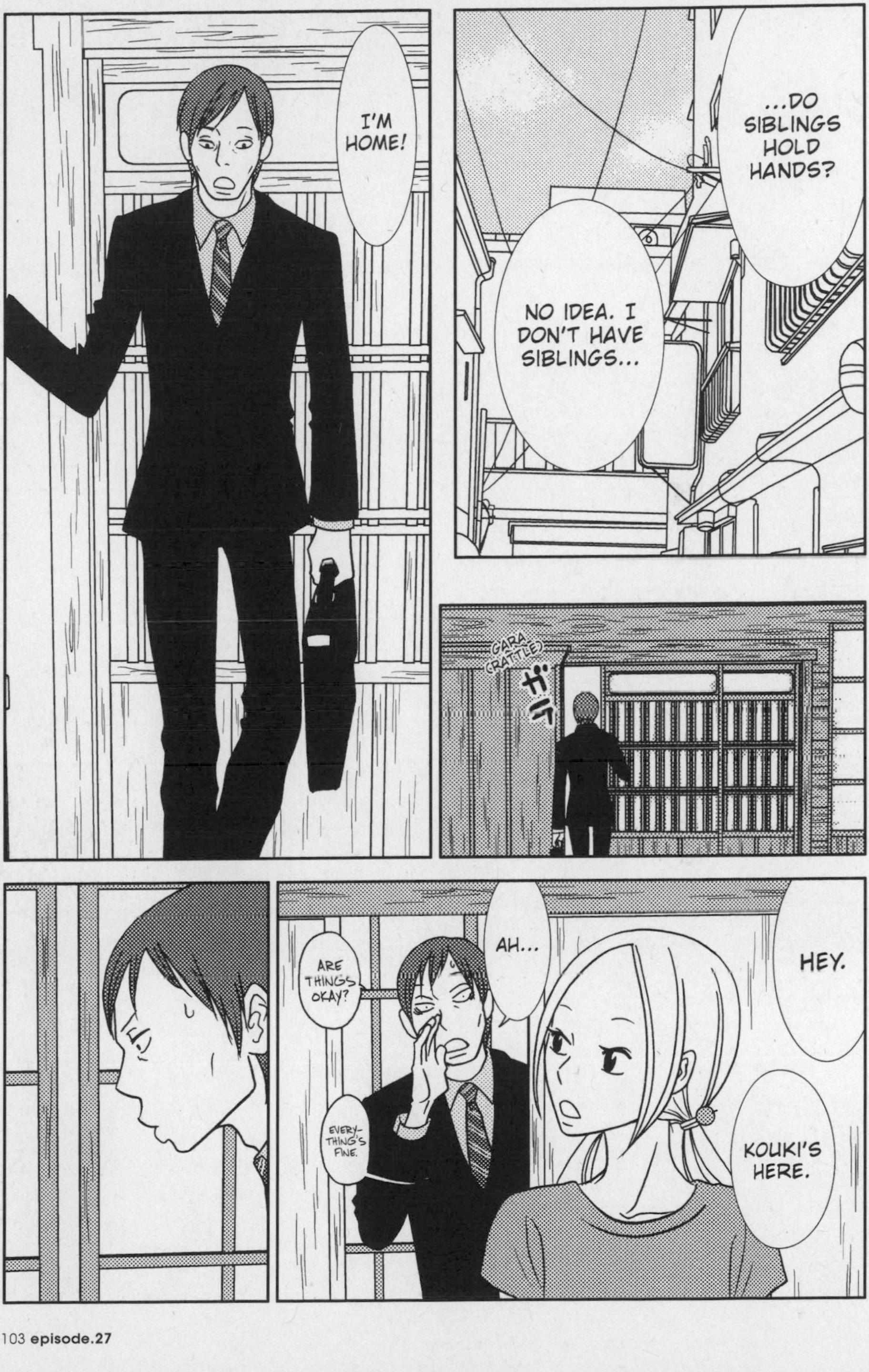
...DO SIBLINGS HOLD HANDS?
NO IDEA. I DON'T HAVE SIBLINGS...
GARA (RATTLE)
ガラ
I'M HOME!
HEY.
KOUKI'S HERE.
AH...
ARE THINGS OKAY?
EVERYTHING'S FINE.

GOOD TO SEE YA.

WELCOME BACK HOME, DAIKICHI.

RIN REJECTED ME.

...AH.

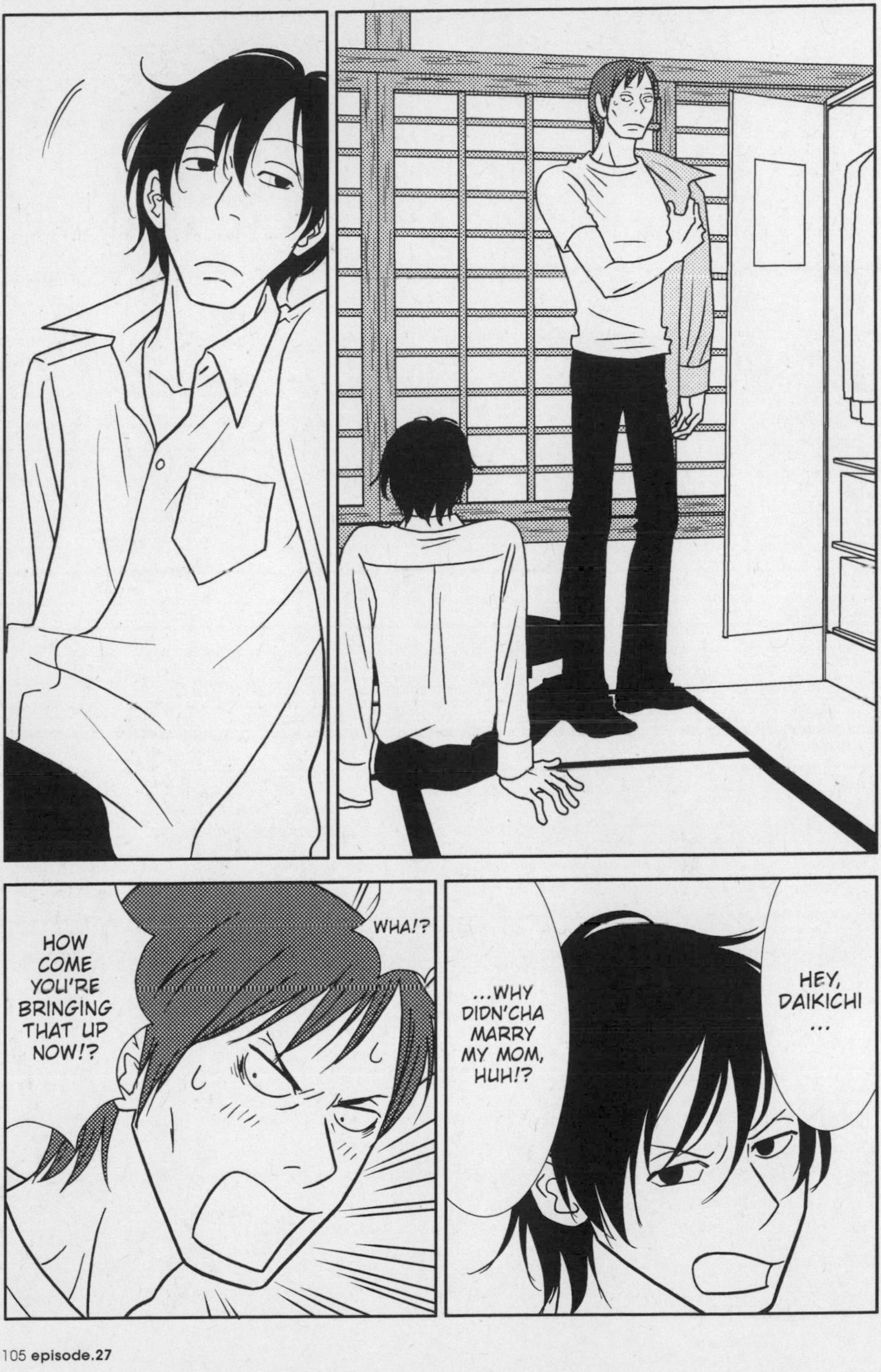
HEY, DAIKICHI ...
...WHY DIDN'CHA MARRY MY MOM, HUH!?
WHA!?
HOW COME YOU'RE BRINGING THAT UP NOW!?

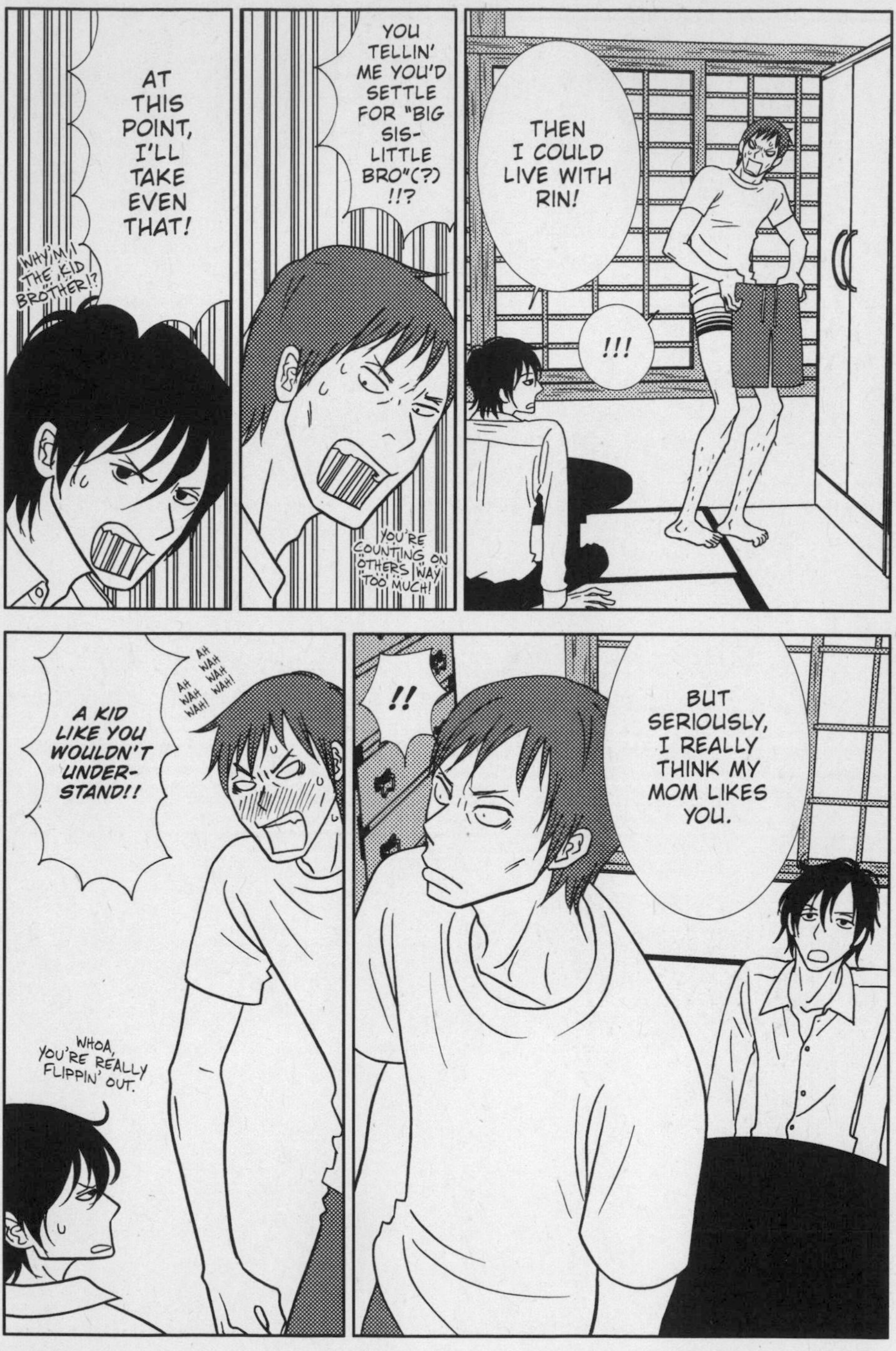
THEN I COULD LIVE WITH RIN!
!!!
YOU TELLIN' ME YOU'D SETTLE FOR "BIG SIS-LITTLE BRO"(?) !!?
YOU'RE COUNTING ON OTHERS WAY TOO MUCH!
AT THIS POINT, I'LL TAKE EVEN THAT!
WHY'M I THE KID BROTHER!?
BUT SERIOUSLY, I REALLY THINK MY MOM LIKES YOU.
!!
AH WAH WAH WAH! AH WAH WAH!
A KID LIKE YOU WOULDN'T UNDER-STAND!!
WHOA, YOU'RE REALLY FLIPPIN' OUT.

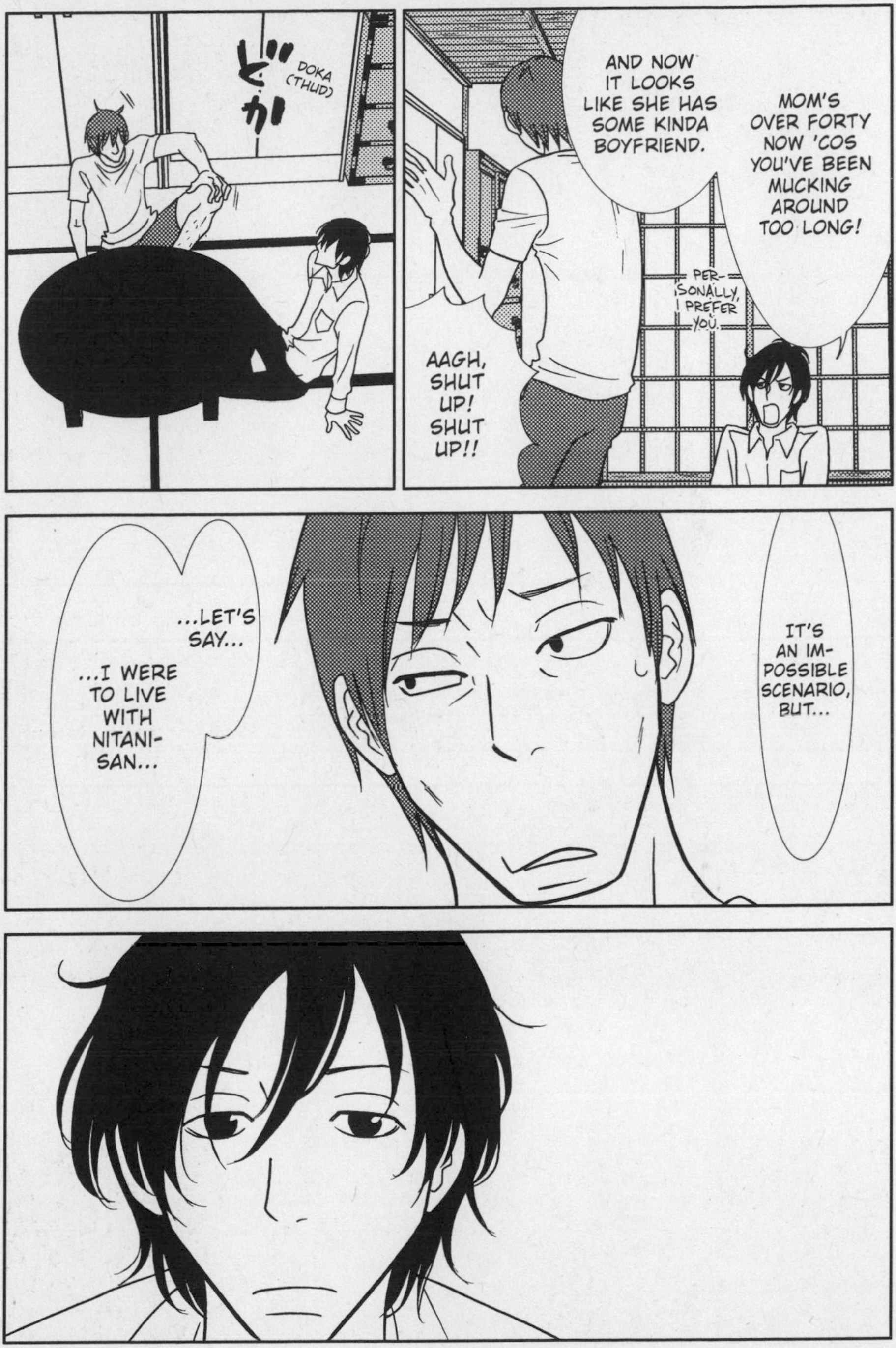
MOM'S OVER FORTY NOW 'COS YOU'VE BEEN MUCKING AROUND TOO LONG!
AND NOW IT LOOKS LIKE SHE HAS SOME KINDA BOYFRIEND.
PER-SONALLY, I PREFER YOU.
AAGH, SHUT UP! SHUT UP!!
どか
DOKA (THUD)
IT'S AN IM-POSSIBLE SCENARIO, BUT...
...LET'S SAY...
...I WERE TO LIVE WITH NITANI-SAN...

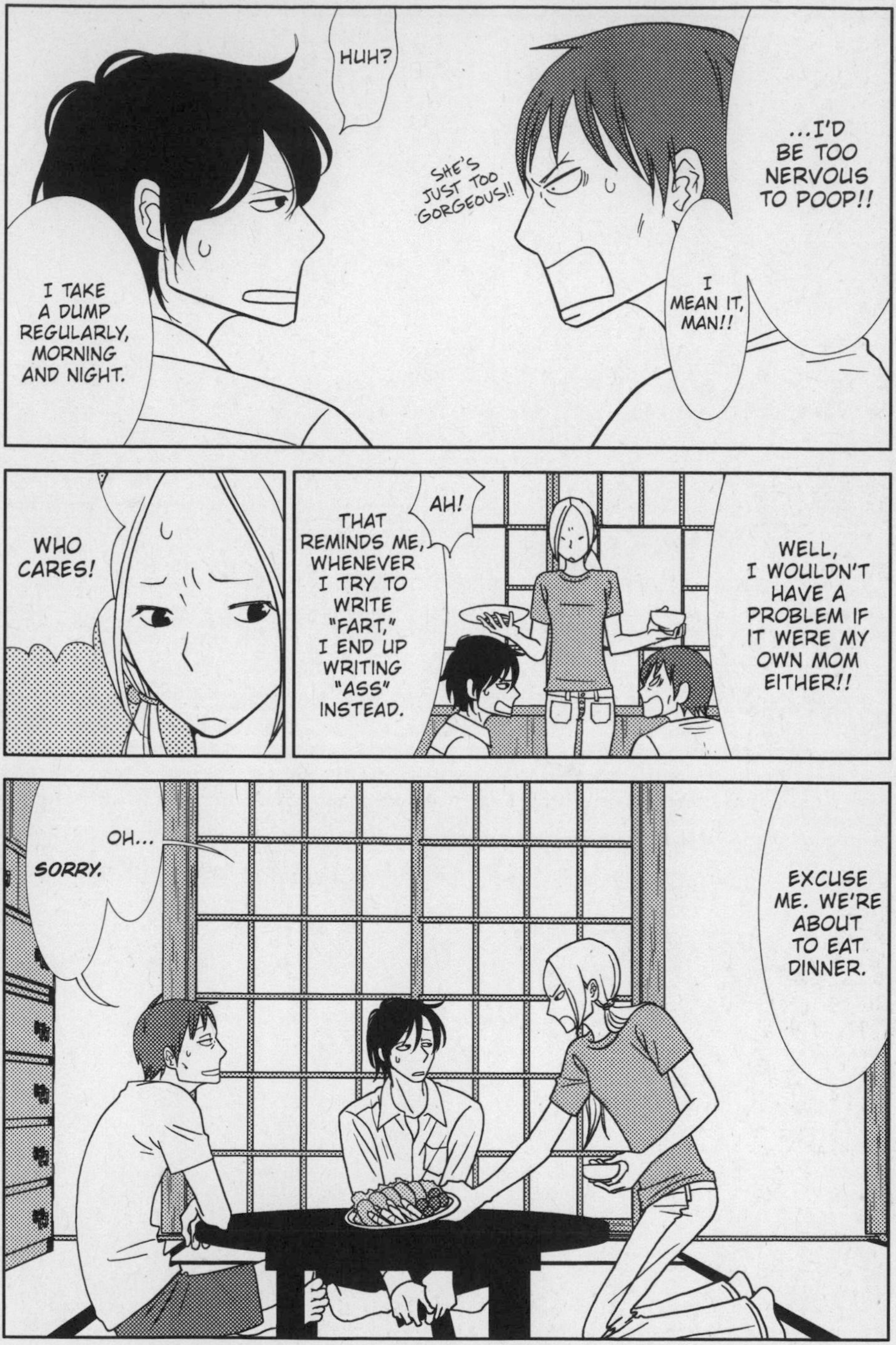
...I'D BE TOO NERVOUS TO POOP!!
I MEAN IT, MAN!!
SHE'S JUST TOO GORGEOUS!!
HUH?
I TAKE A DUMP REGULARLY, MORNING AND NIGHT.
WELL, I WOULDN'T HAVE A PROBLEM IF IT WERE MY OWN MOM EITHER!!
AH!
THAT REMINDS ME, WHENEVER I TRY TO WRITE "FART," I END UP WRITING "ASS" INSTEAD.
WHO CARES!
EXCUSE ME. WE'RE ABOUT TO EAT DINNER.
OH...
SORRY.

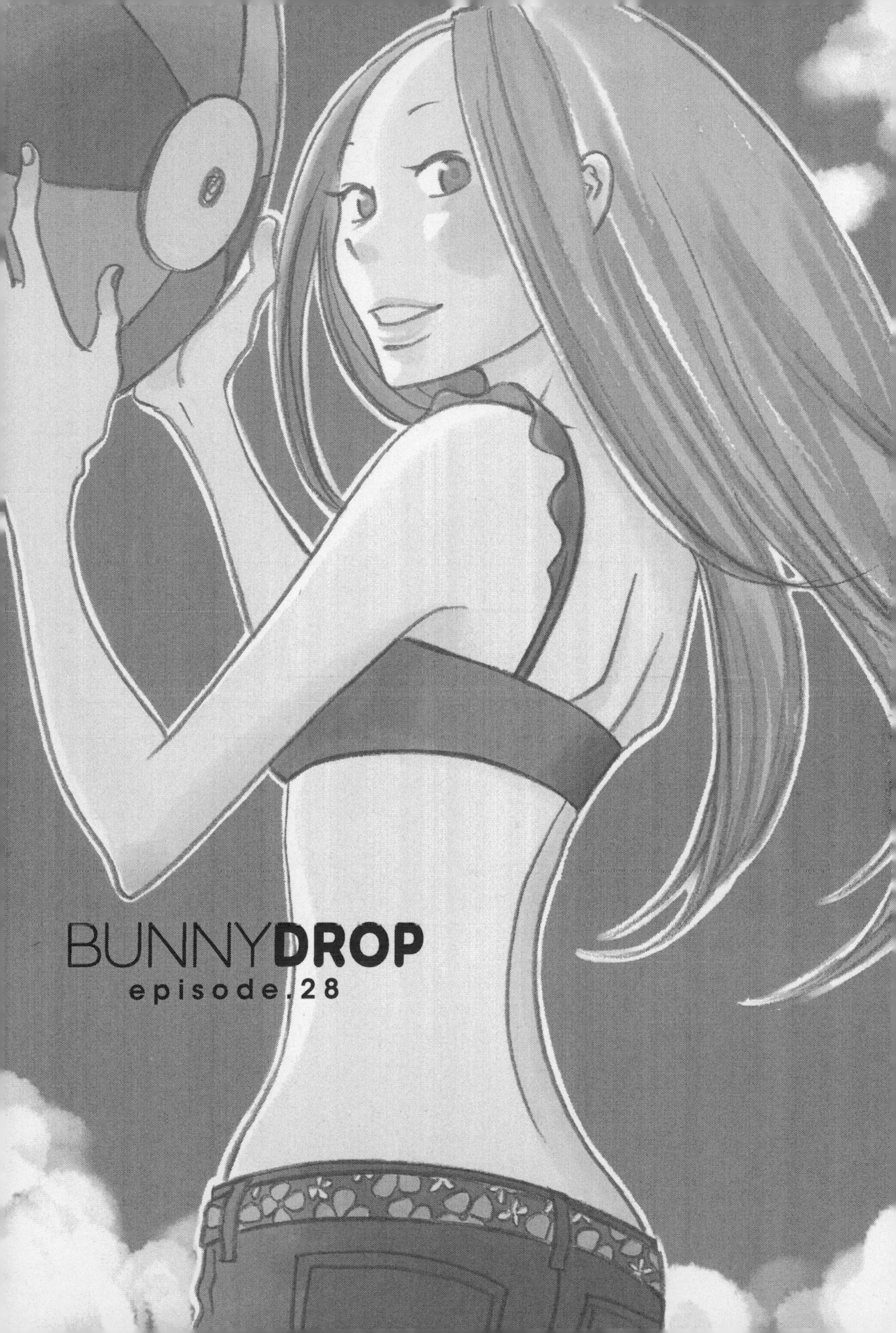

BUNNY DROP
episode.28

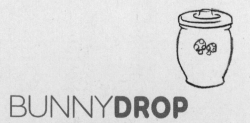

BUNNY**DROP**

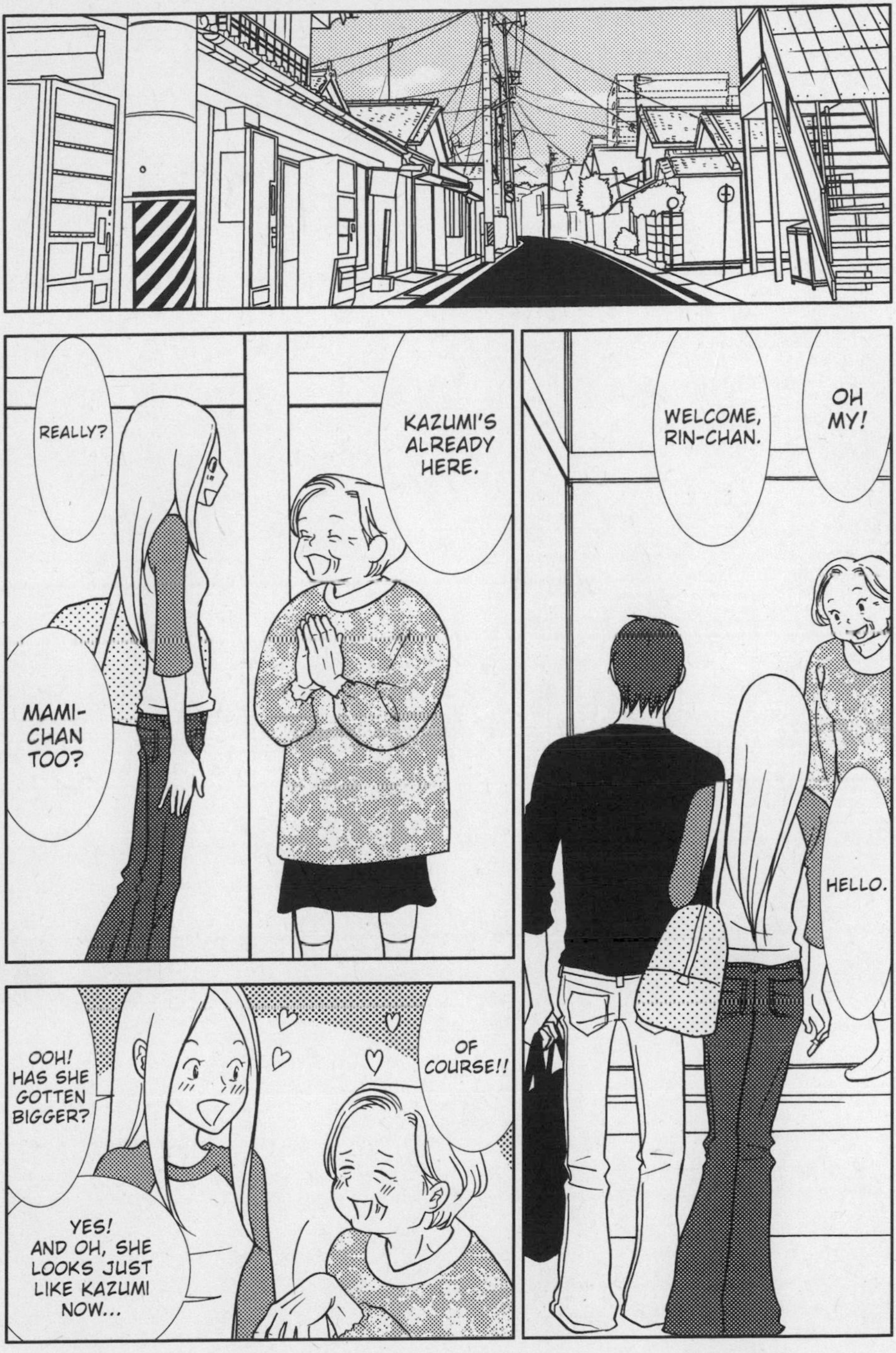
OH MY!
WELCOME, RIN-CHAN.
HELLO.
KAZUMI'S ALREADY HERE.
REALLY?
MAMI-CHAN TOO?
OF COURSE!!
OOH! HAS SHE GOTTEN BIGGER?
YES! AND OH, SHE LOOKS JUST LIKE KAZUMI NOW...

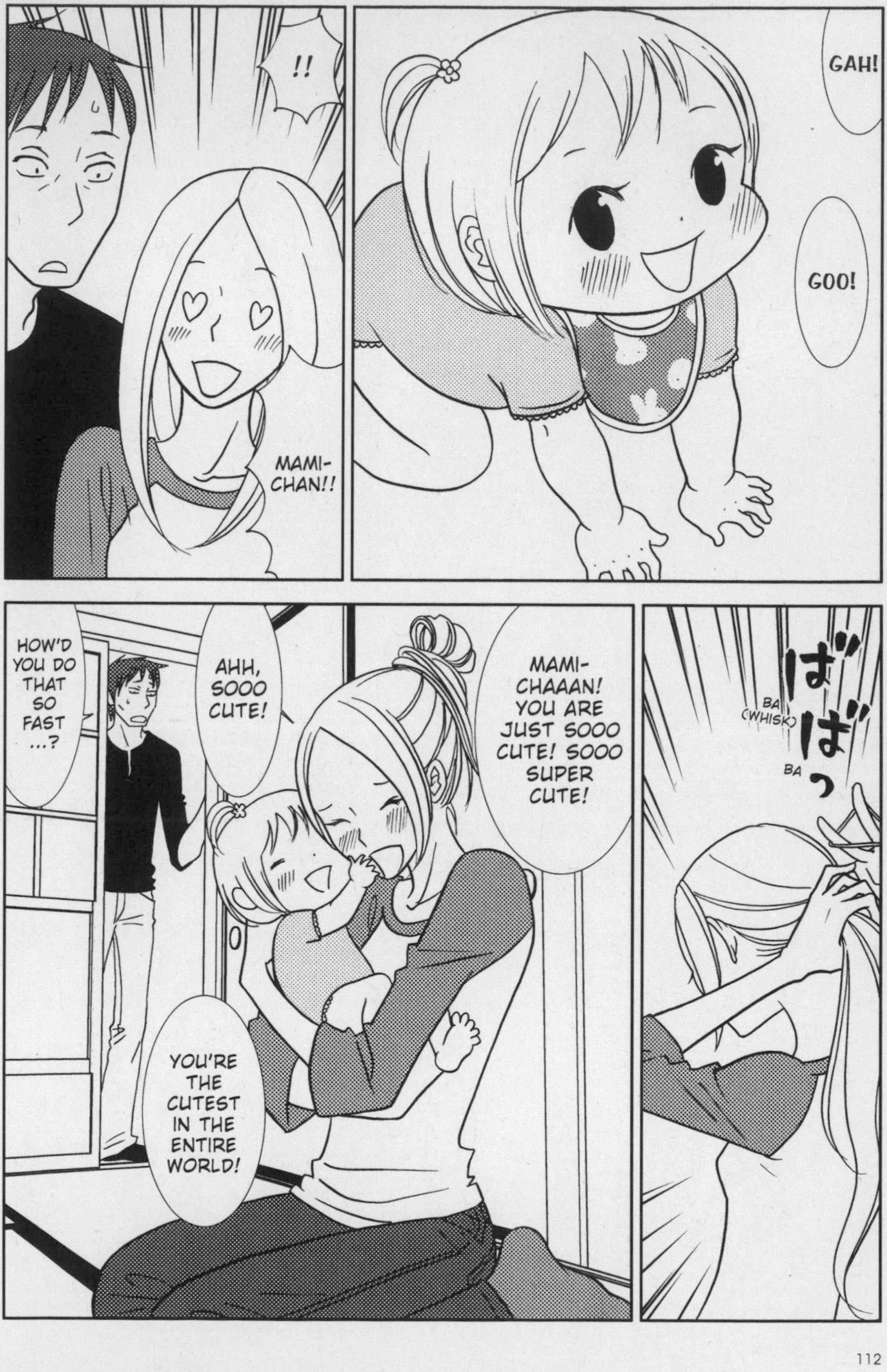
GAH!
GOO!
!!
MAMI-CHAN!!
ばばっ
BA (WHISK)
BA
MAMI-CHAAAN! YOU ARE JUST SOOO CUTE! SOOO SUPER CUTE!
AHH, SOOO CUTE!
HOW'D YOU DO THAT SO FAST ...?
YOU'RE THE CUTEST IN THE ENTIRE WORLD!

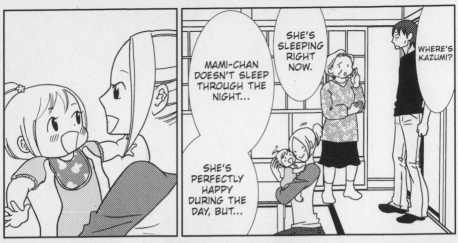

WHERE'S KAZUMI?
SHE'S SLEEPING RIGHT NOW.
MAMI-CHAN DOESN'T SLEEP THROUGH THE NIGHT...
SHE'S PERFECTLY HAPPY DURING THE DAY, BUT...
WAS KAZUMI THAT CUTE WHEN SHE WAS A BABY?
OR DOES MAMI-CHAN TAKE AFTER HER DAD?
OR DOES SHE LOOK CUTE 'COS I'M GETTING OLD?
WHAT ARE YOU TALKING ABOUT!! SHE'S JUST LIKE KAZUMI! SPITTING IMAGE!!
KAZUMI WAS CUTE AS A BUTTON WHEN SHE WAS A BABY!
ABUUU BABUUU!
HERE, OVER HERE.

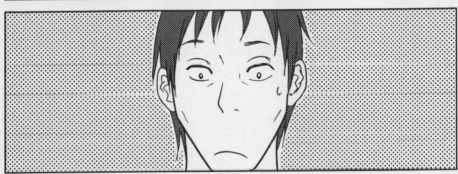

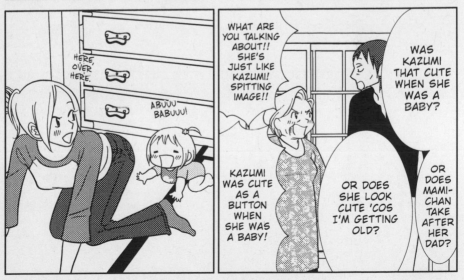

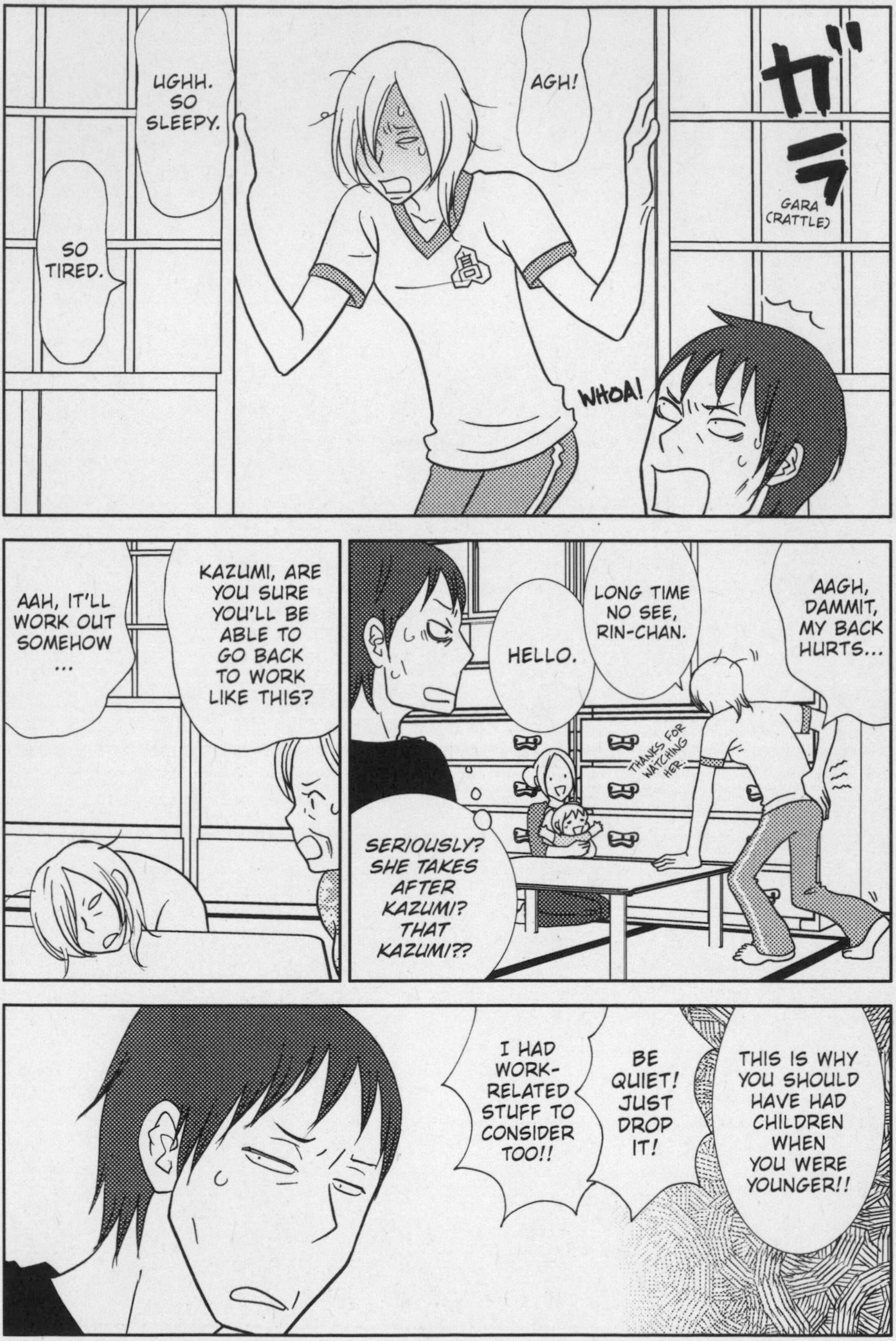
ガラ
GARA (RATTLE)
AGH!
UGHH. SO SLEEPY.
WHOA!
SO TIRED.
AAGH, DAMMIT, MY BACK HURTS...
LONG TIME NO SEE, RIN-CHAN.
THANKS FOR WATCHING HER.
HELLO.
SERIOUSLY? SHE TAKES AFTER KAZUMI? THAT KAZUMI??
KAZUMI, ARE YOU SURE YOU'LL BE ABLE TO GO BACK TO WORK LIKE THIS?
AAH, IT'LL WORK OUT SOMEHOW ...
THIS IS WHY YOU SHOULD HAVE HAD CHILDREN WHEN YOU WERE YOUNGER!!
BE QUIET! JUST DROP IT!
I HAD WORK-RELATED STUFF TO CONSIDER TOO!!

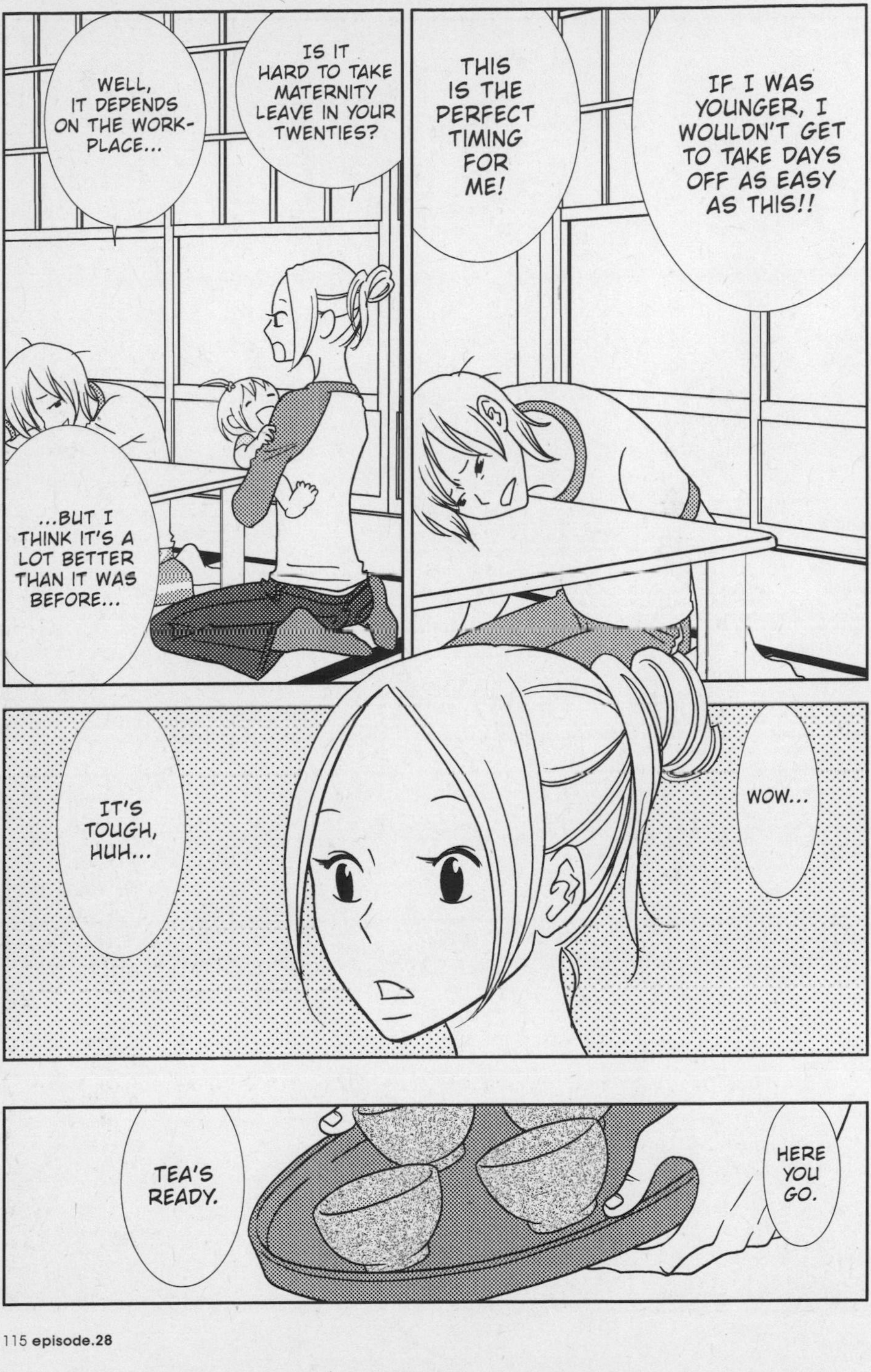
IF I WAS YOUNGER, I WOULDN'T GET TO TAKE DAYS OFF AS EASY AS THIS!!
THIS IS THE PERFECT TIMING FOR ME!
IS IT HARD TO TAKE MATERNITY LEAVE IN YOUR TWENTIES?
WELL, IT DEPENDS ON THE WORK-PLACE...
...BUT I THINK IT'S A LOT BETTER THAN IT WAS BEFORE...
WOW...
IT'S TOUGH, HUH...
HERE YOU GO.
TEA'S READY.

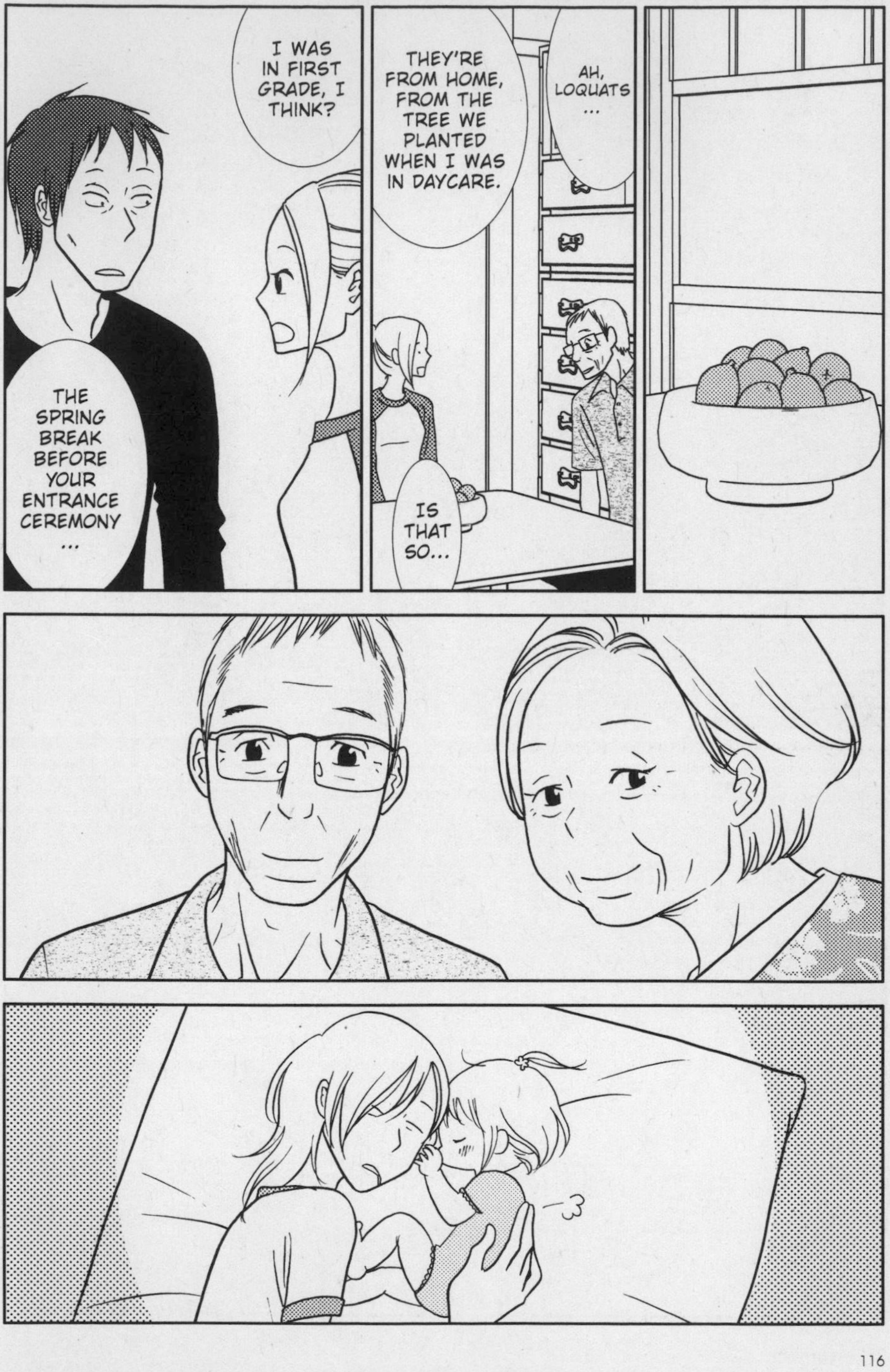
AH, LOQUATS ...
THEY'RE FROM HOME, FROM THE TREE WE PLANTED WHEN I WAS IN DAYCARE.
IS THAT SO...
I WAS IN FIRST GRADE, I THINK?
THE SPRING BREAK BEFORE YOUR ENTRANCE CEREMONY ...

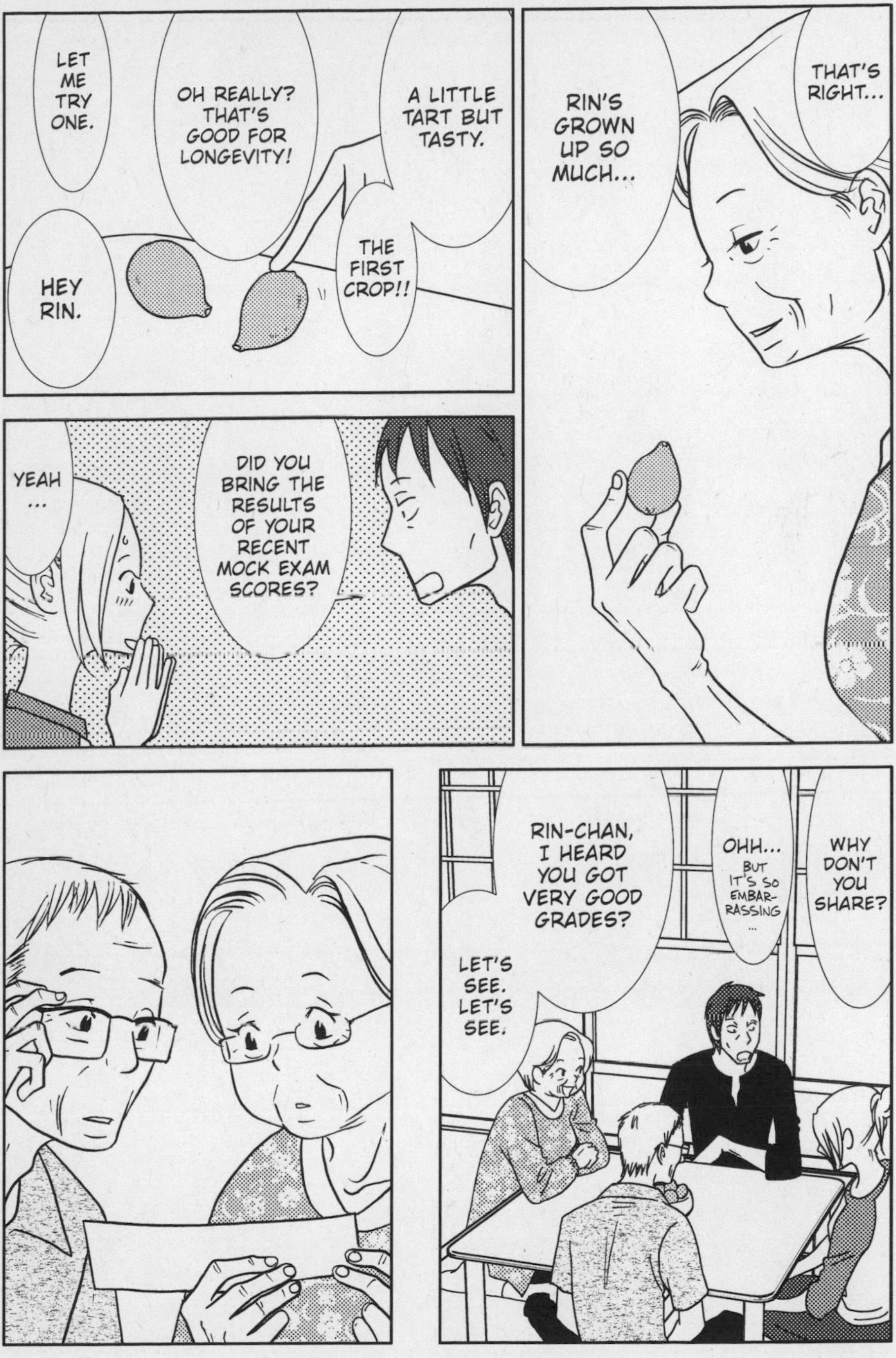
THAT'S RIGHT...
RIN'S GROWN UP SO MUCH...
A LITTLE TART BUT TASTY.
THE FIRST CROP!!
OH REALLY? THAT'S GOOD FOR LONGEVITY!
LET ME TRY ONE.
HEY RIN.
DID YOU BRING THE RESULTS OF YOUR RECENT MOCK EXAM SCORES?
YEAH ...
WHY DON'T YOU SHARE?
OHH... BUT IT'S SO EMBARRASSING ...
RIN-CHAN, I HEARD YOU GOT VERY GOOD GRADES?
LET'S SEE. LET'S SEE.

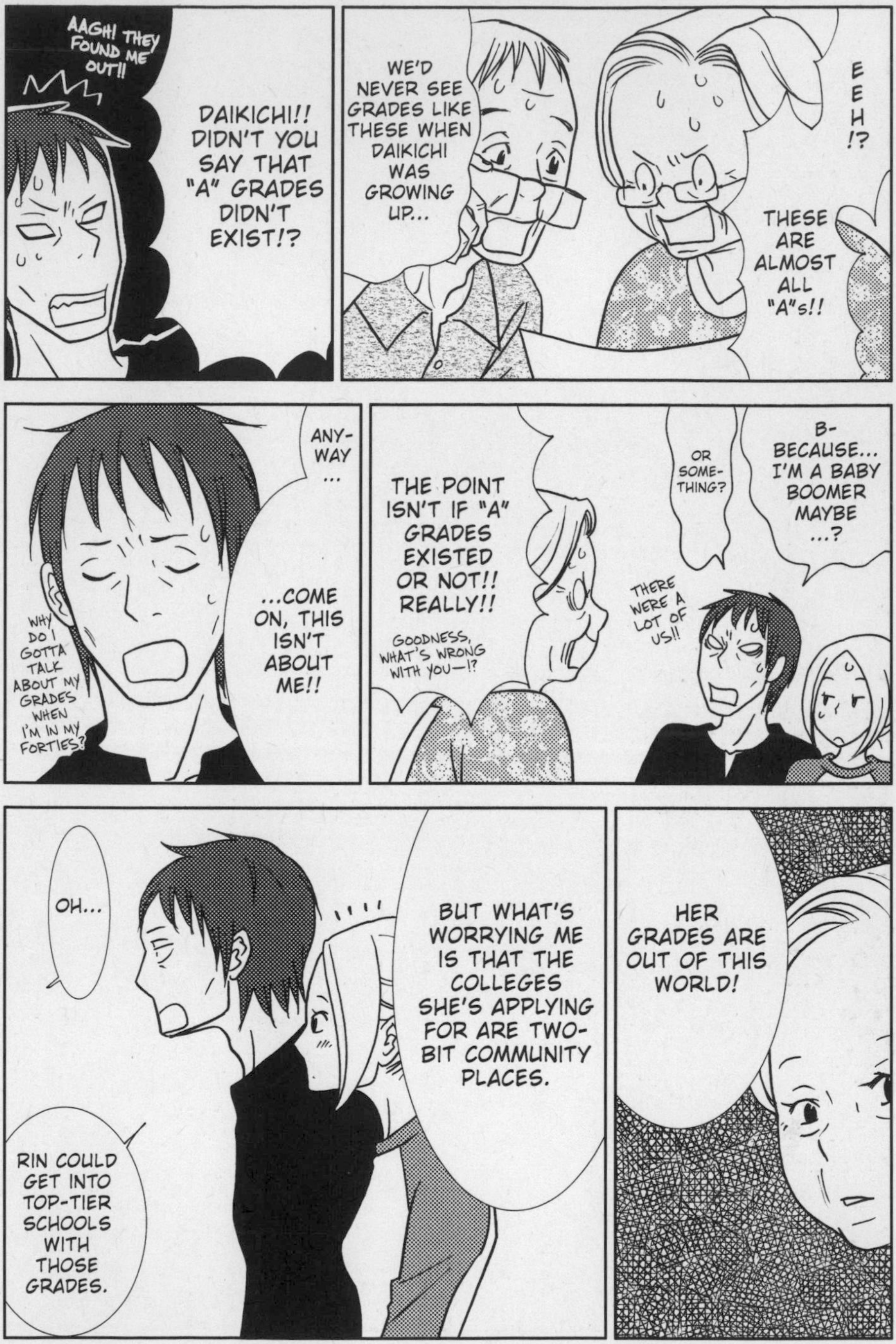
EEH!?
THESE ARE ALMOST ALL "A"s!!
WE'D NEVER SEE GRADES LIKE THESE WHEN DAIKICHI WAS GROWING UP...
DAIKICHI!! DIDN'T YOU SAY THAT "A" GRADES DIDN'T EXIST!?
AAGH! THEY FOUND ME OUT!!
B- BECAUSE... I'M A BABY BOOMER MAYBE ...?
OR SOMETHING?
THERE WERE A LOT OF US!!
THE POINT ISN'T IF "A" GRADES EXISTED OR NOT!! REALLY!!
GOODNESS, WHAT'S WRONG WITH YOU—!?
ANY-WAY ...
...COME ON, THIS ISN'T ABOUT ME!!
WHY DO I GOTTA TALK ABOUT MY GRADES WHEN I'M IN MY FORTIES?
HER GRADES ARE OUT OF THIS WORLD!
BUT WHAT'S WORRYING ME IS THAT THE COLLEGES SHE'S APPLYING FOR ARE TWO-BIT COMMUNITY PLACES.
OH...
RIN COULD GET INTO TOP-TIER SCHOOLS WITH THOSE GRADES.

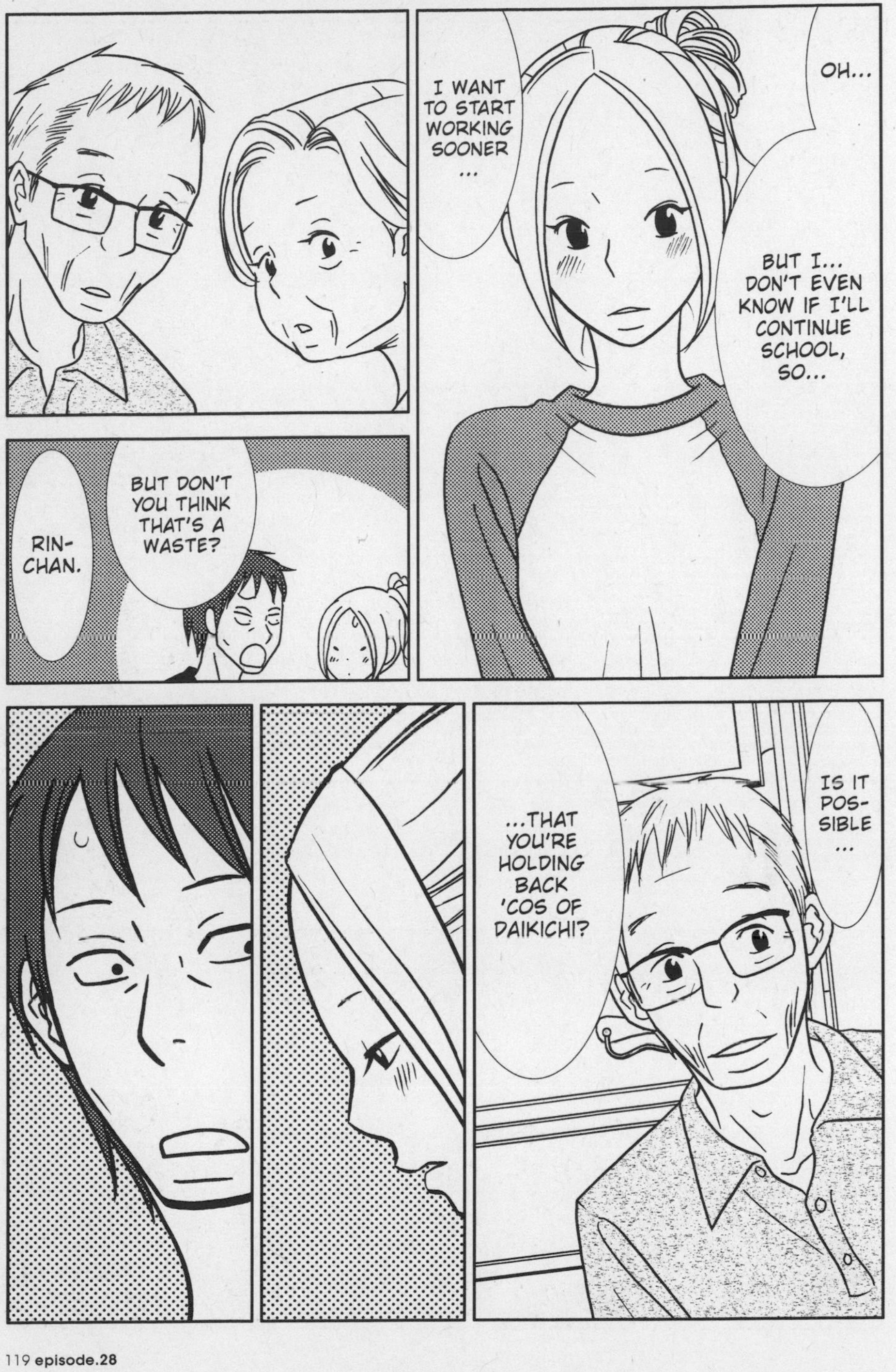
OH...
I WANT TO START WORKING SOONER ...
BUT I... DON'T EVEN KNOW IF I'LL CONTINUE SCHOOL, SO...
BUT DON'T YOU THINK THAT'S A WASTE?
RIN-CHAN.
IS IT POSSIBLE ...
...THAT YOU'RE HOLDING BACK 'COS OF DAIKICHI?

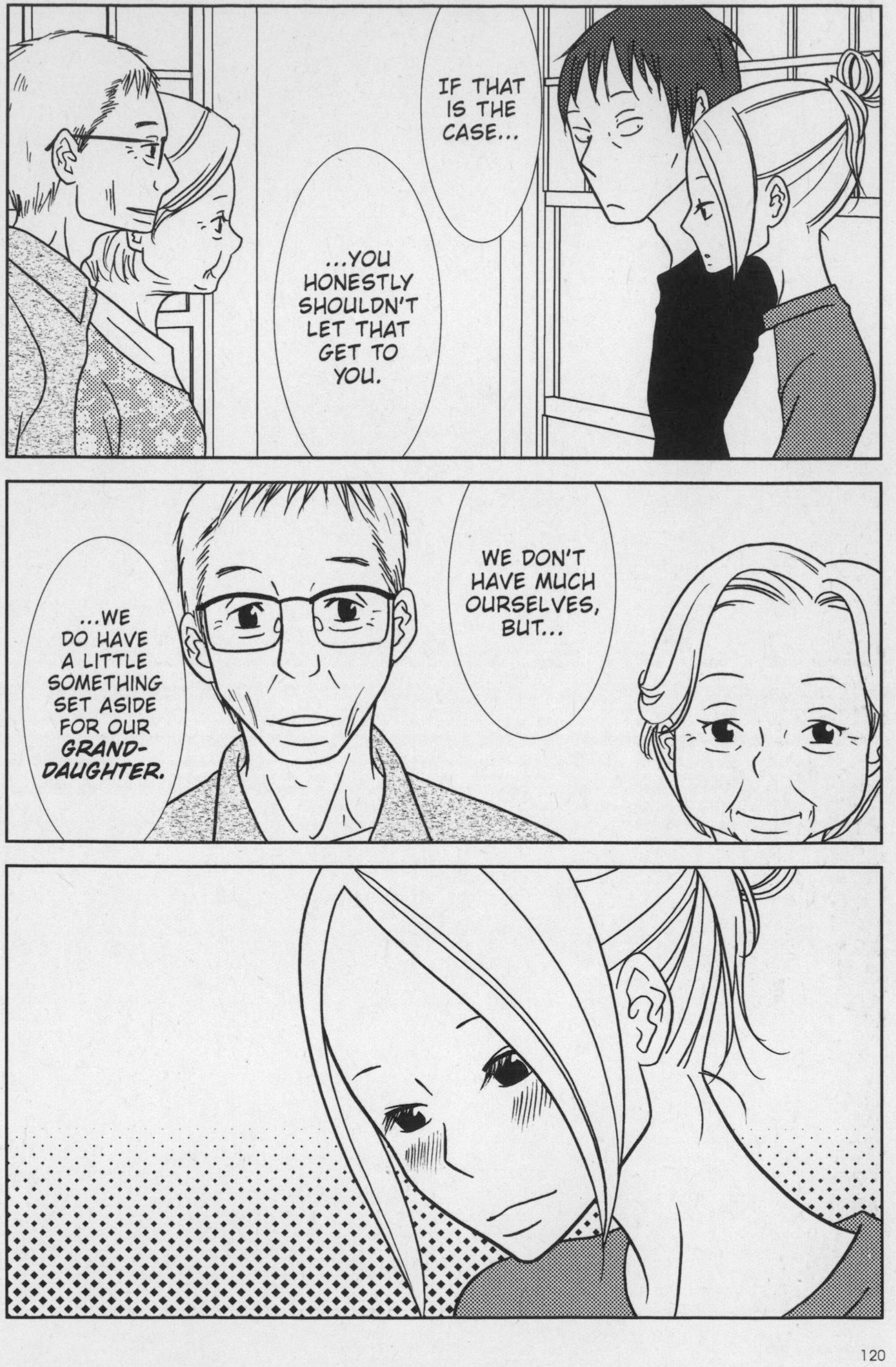
IF THAT IS THE CASE...
...YOU HONESTLY SHOULDN'T LET THAT GET TO YOU.
WE DON'T HAVE MUCH OURSELVES, BUT...
...WE DO HAVE A LITTLE SOMETHING SET ASIDE FOR OUR ***GRAND-DAUGHTER.***

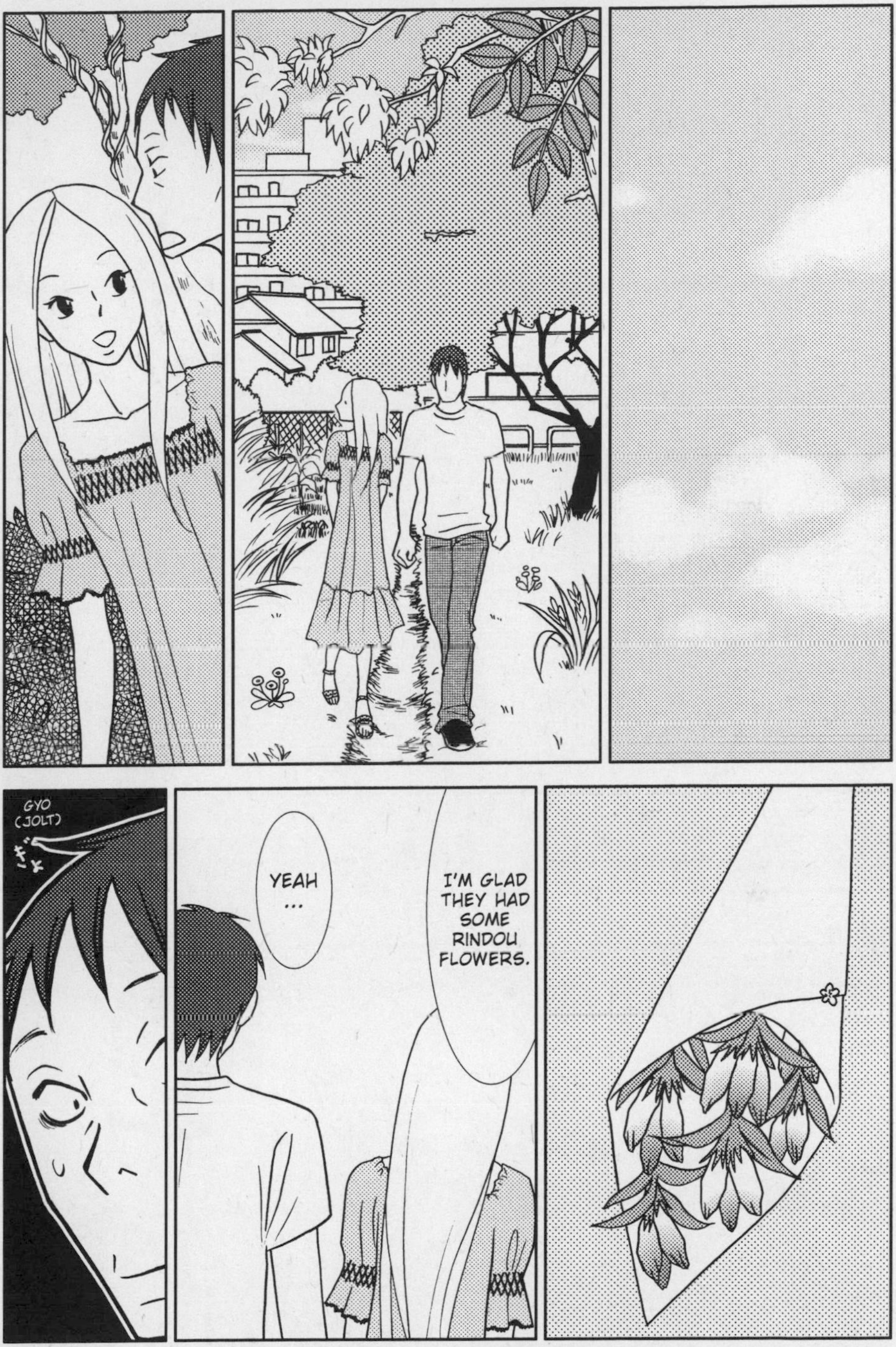
I'M GLAD THEY HAD SOME RINDOU FLOWERS.
YEAH ...
GYO (JOLT)

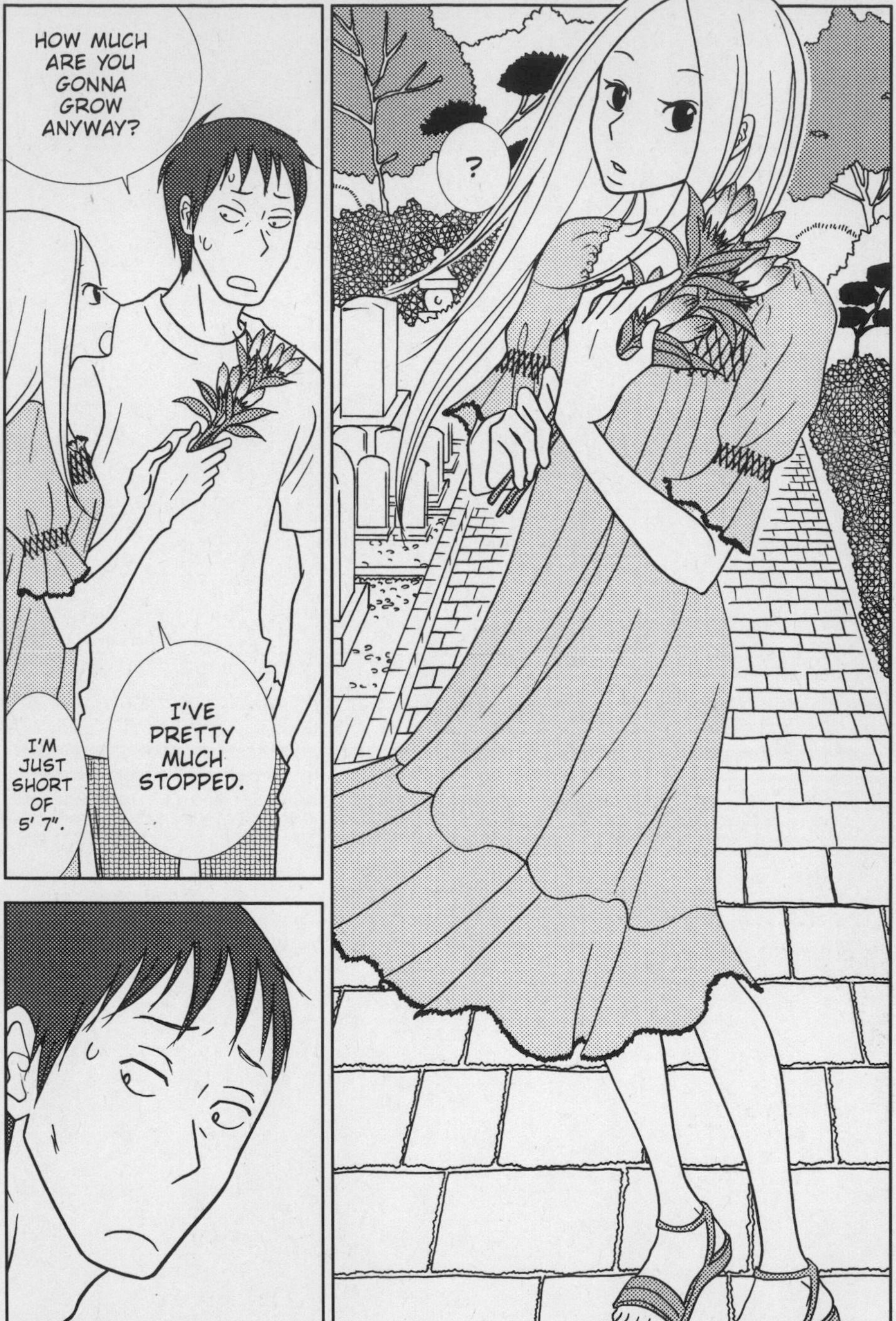
?
HOW MUCH ARE YOU GONNA GROW ANYWAY?
I'VE PRETTY MUCH STOPPED.
I'M JUST SHORT OF 5' 7".

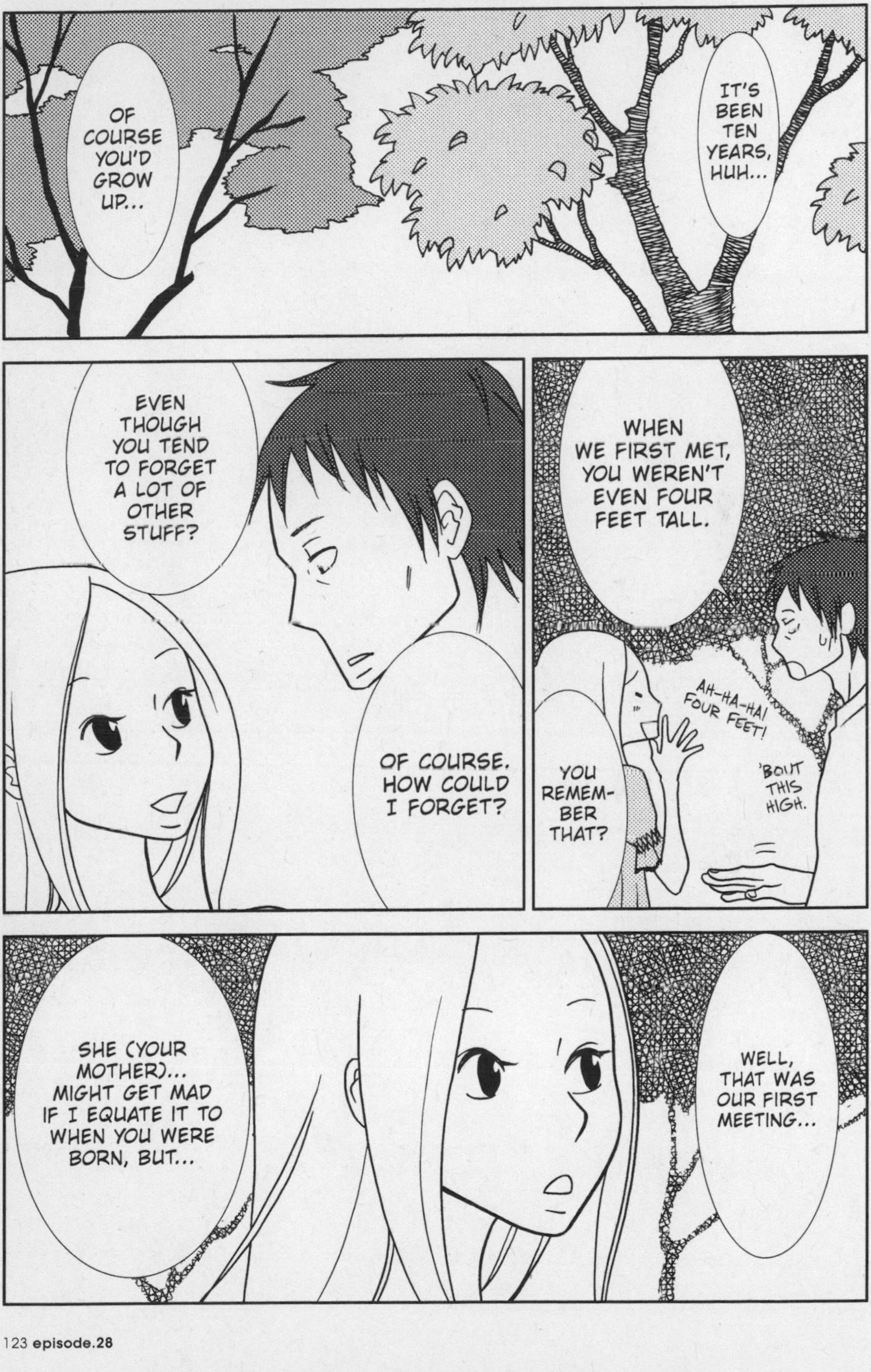
IT'S BEEN TEN YEARS, HUH...
OF COURSE YOU'D GROW UP...
WHEN WE FIRST MET, YOU WEREN'T EVEN FOUR FEET TALL.
'BOUT THIS HIGH.
AH-HA-HA! FOUR FEET!
YOU REMEMBER THAT?
OF COURSE. HOW COULD I FORGET?
EVEN THOUGH YOU TEND TO FORGET A LOT OF OTHER STUFF?
WELL, THAT WAS OUR FIRST MEETING...
SHE (YOUR MOTHER)... MIGHT GET MAD IF I EQUATE IT TO WHEN YOU WERE BORN, BUT...

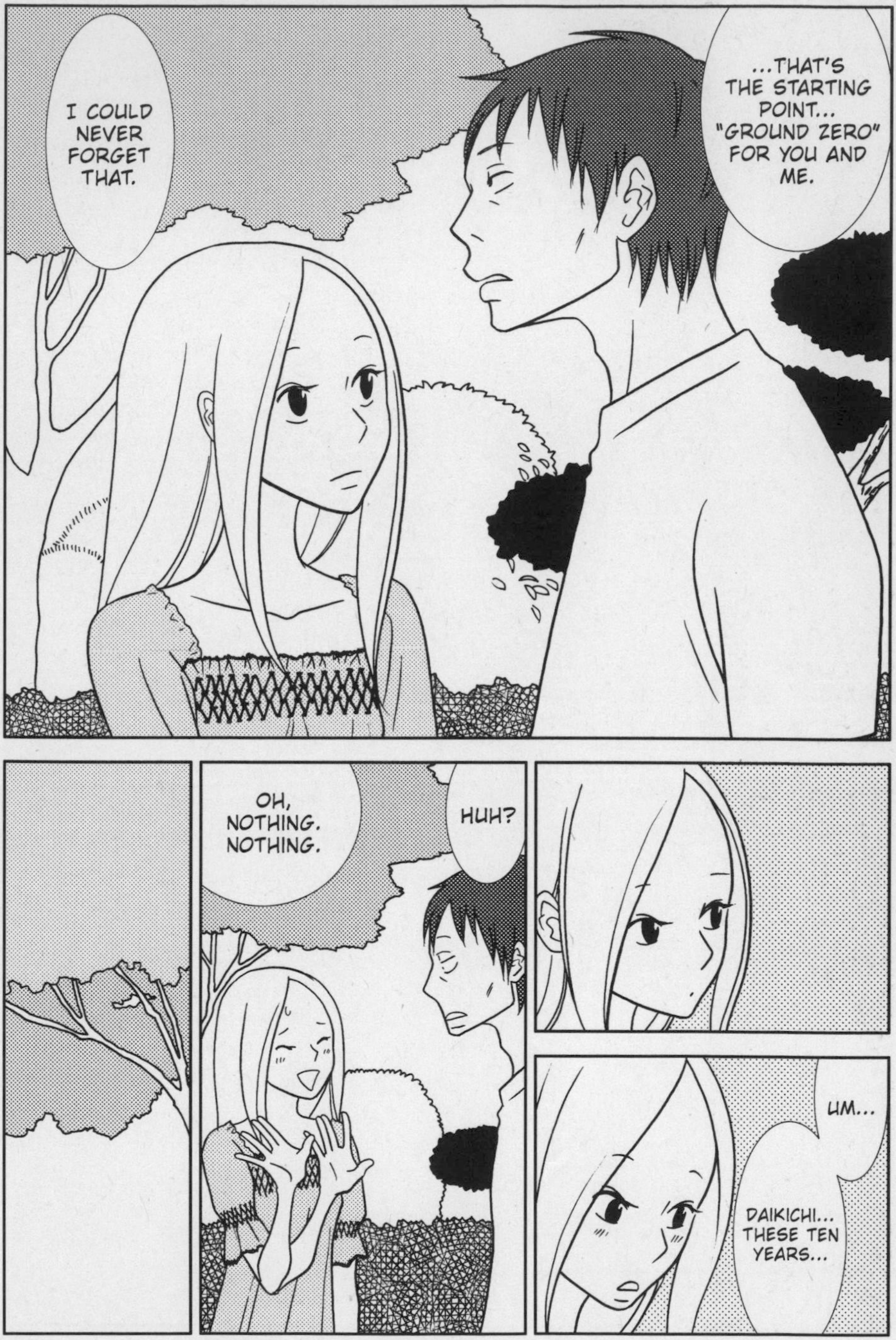
...THAT'S THE STARTING POINT... "GROUND ZERO" FOR YOU AND ME.
I COULD NEVER FORGET THAT.
UM...
DAIKICHI... THESE TEN YEARS...
HUH?
OH, NOTHING. NOTHING.

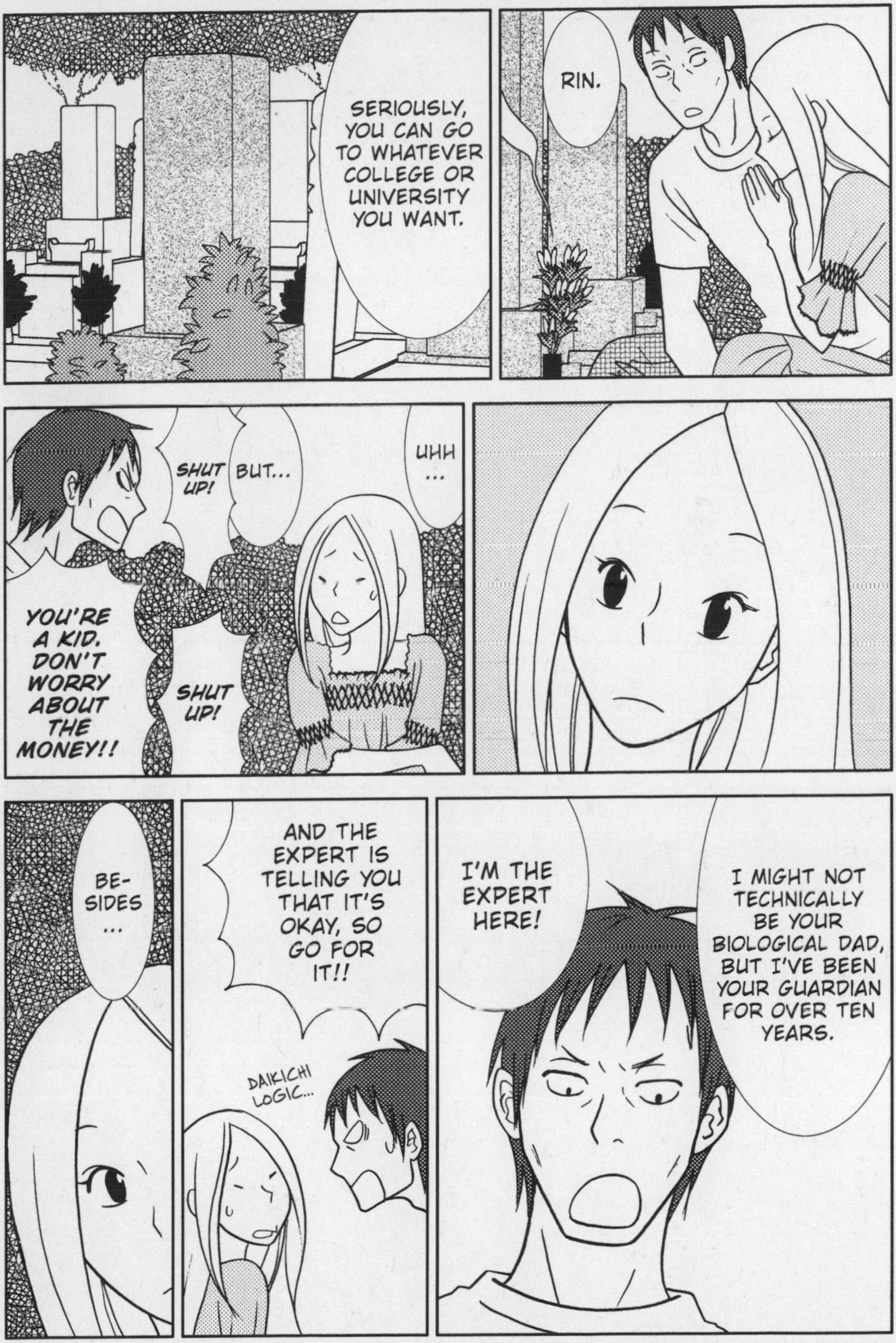
RIN.
SERIOUSLY, YOU CAN GO TO WHATEVER COLLEGE OR UNIVERSITY YOU WANT.
UHH ...
BUT...
SHUT UP!
SHUT UP!
YOU'RE A KID. DON'T WORRY ABOUT THE MONEY!!
I MIGHT NOT TECHNICALLY BE YOUR BIOLOGICAL DAD, BUT I'VE BEEN YOUR GUARDIAN FOR OVER TEN YEARS.
I'M THE EXPERT HERE!
AND THE EXPERT IS TELLING YOU THAT IT'S OKAY, SO GO FOR IT!!
DAIKICHI LOGIC...
BE-SIDES ...

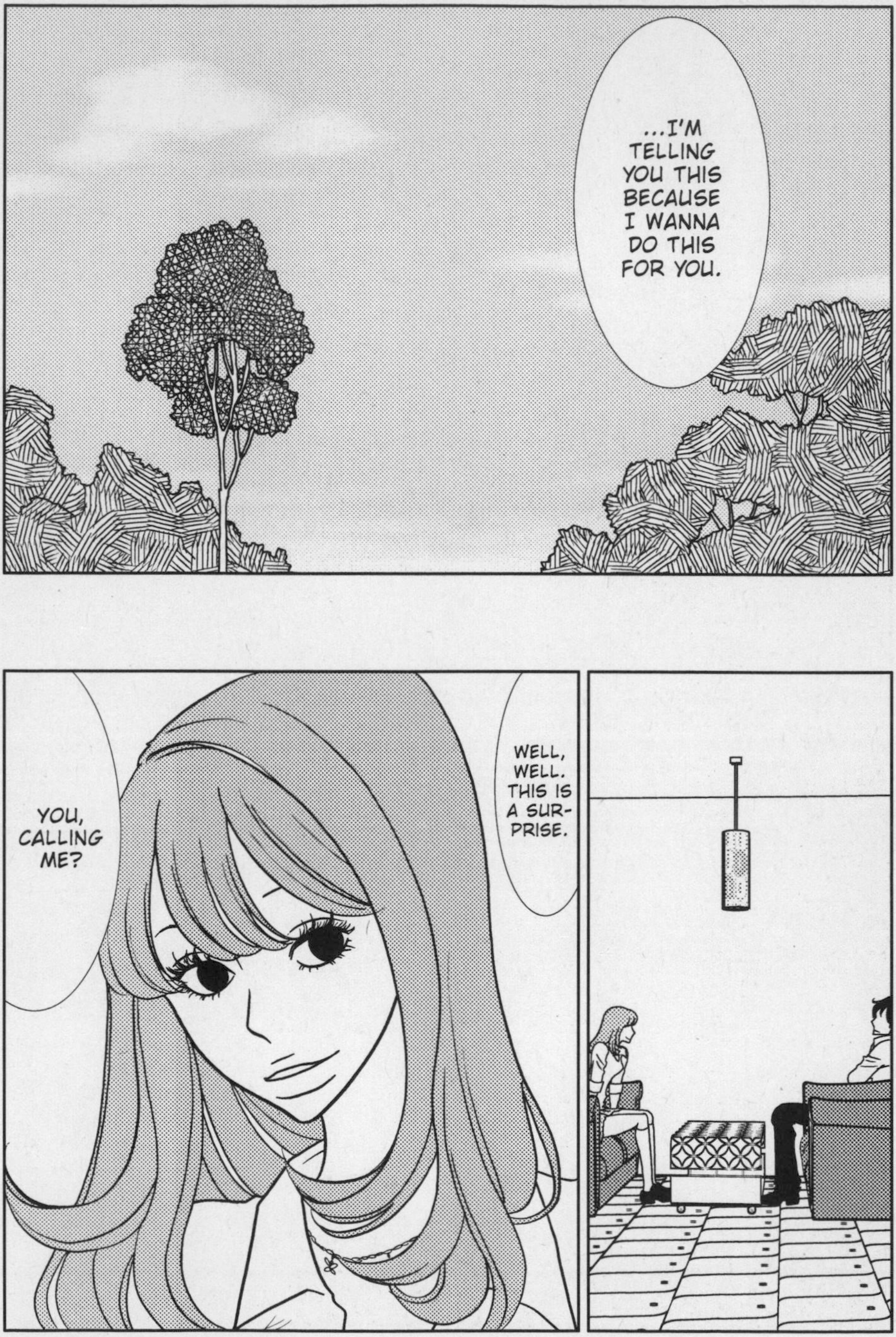
...I'M TELLING YOU THIS BECAUSE I WANNA DO THIS FOR YOU.
WELL, WELL. THIS IS A SUR-PRISE.
YOU, CALLING ME?

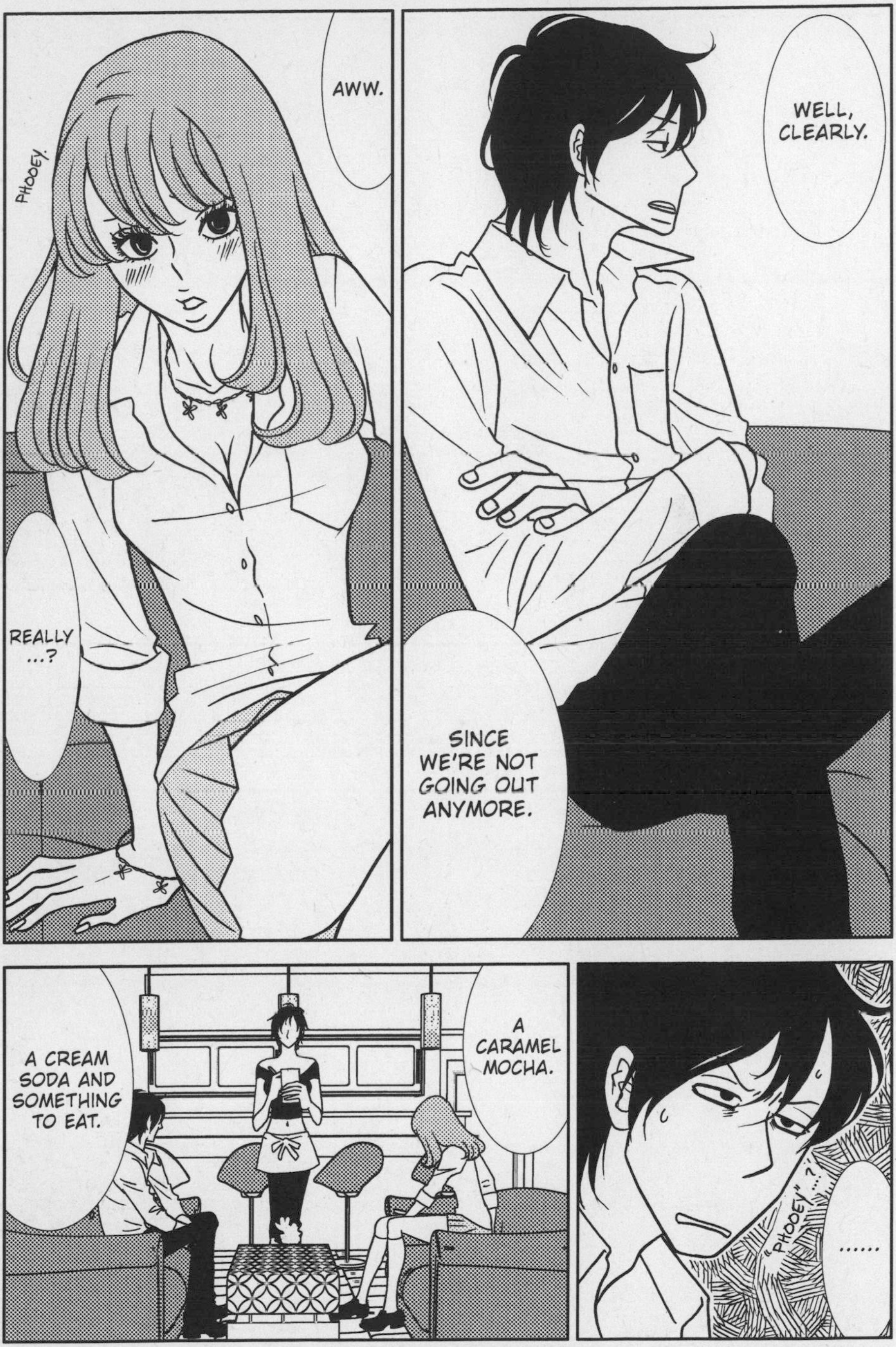
WELL, CLEARLY.
SINCE WE'RE NOT GOING OUT ANYMORE.
AWW.
PHOOEY.
REALLY ...?
......
"PHOOEY" ...?
A CARAMEL MOCHA.
A CREAM SODA AND SOMETHING TO EAT.

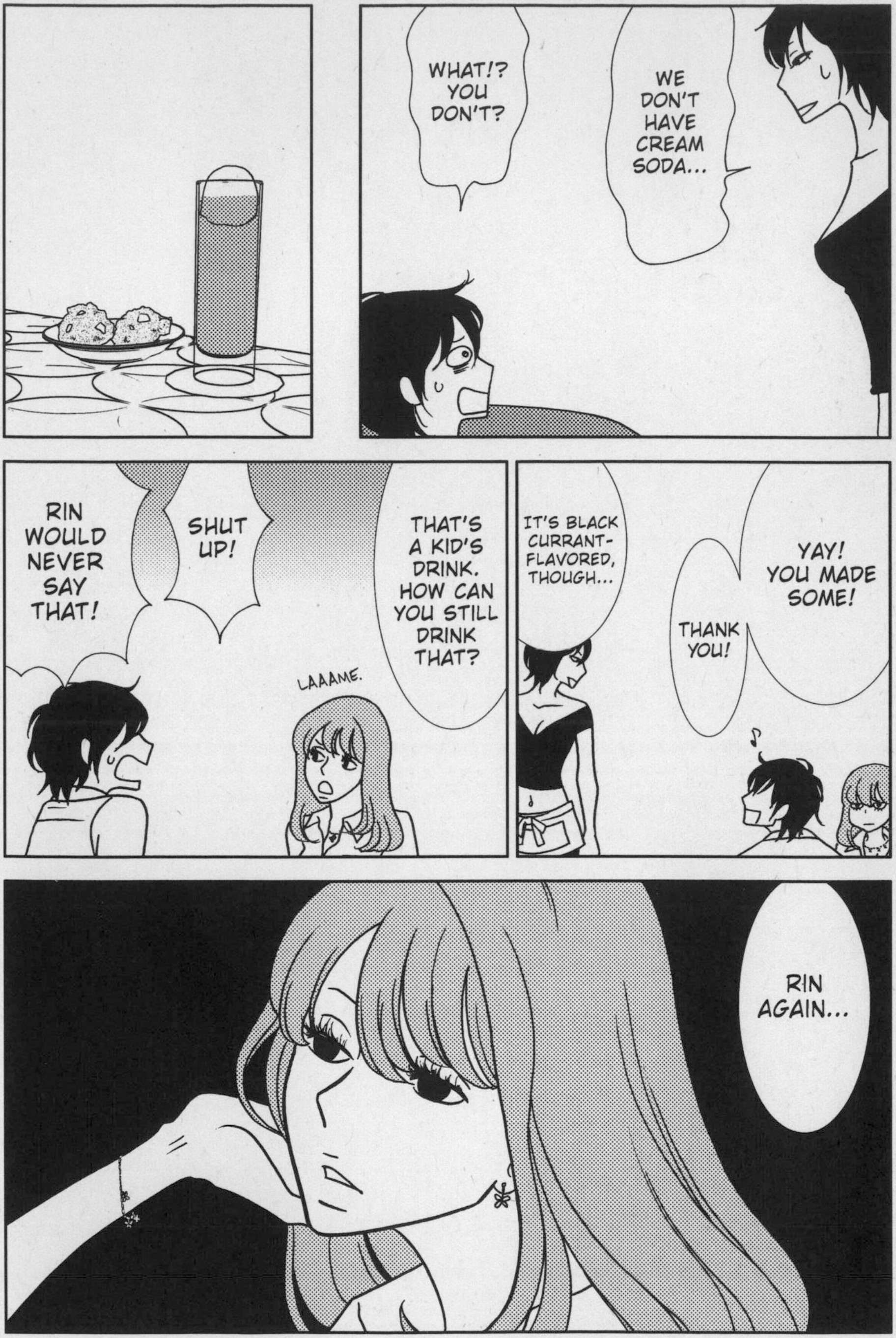
WE DON'T HAVE CREAM SODA...
WHAT!? YOU DON'T?
YAY! YOU MADE SOME!
THANK YOU!
IT'S BLACK CURRANT-FLAVORED, THOUGH...
THAT'S A KID'S DRINK. HOW CAN YOU STILL DRINK THAT?
LAAAME.
SHUT UP!
RIN WOULD NEVER SAY THAT!
RIN AGAIN...

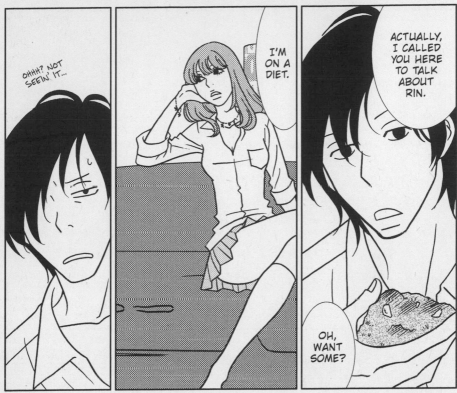

ACTUALLY, I CALLED YOU HERE TO TALK ABOUT RIN.
OH, WANT SOME?
I'M ON A DIET.
OHHH? NOT SEEIN' IT...
SO, HEY, AKARI...
...QUIT HARASSING RIN, WILL YA...?

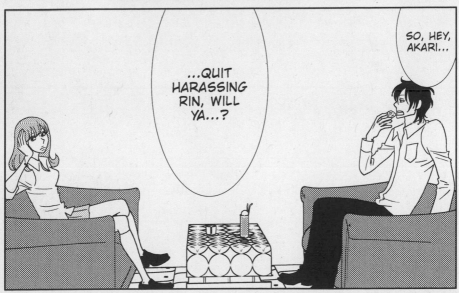

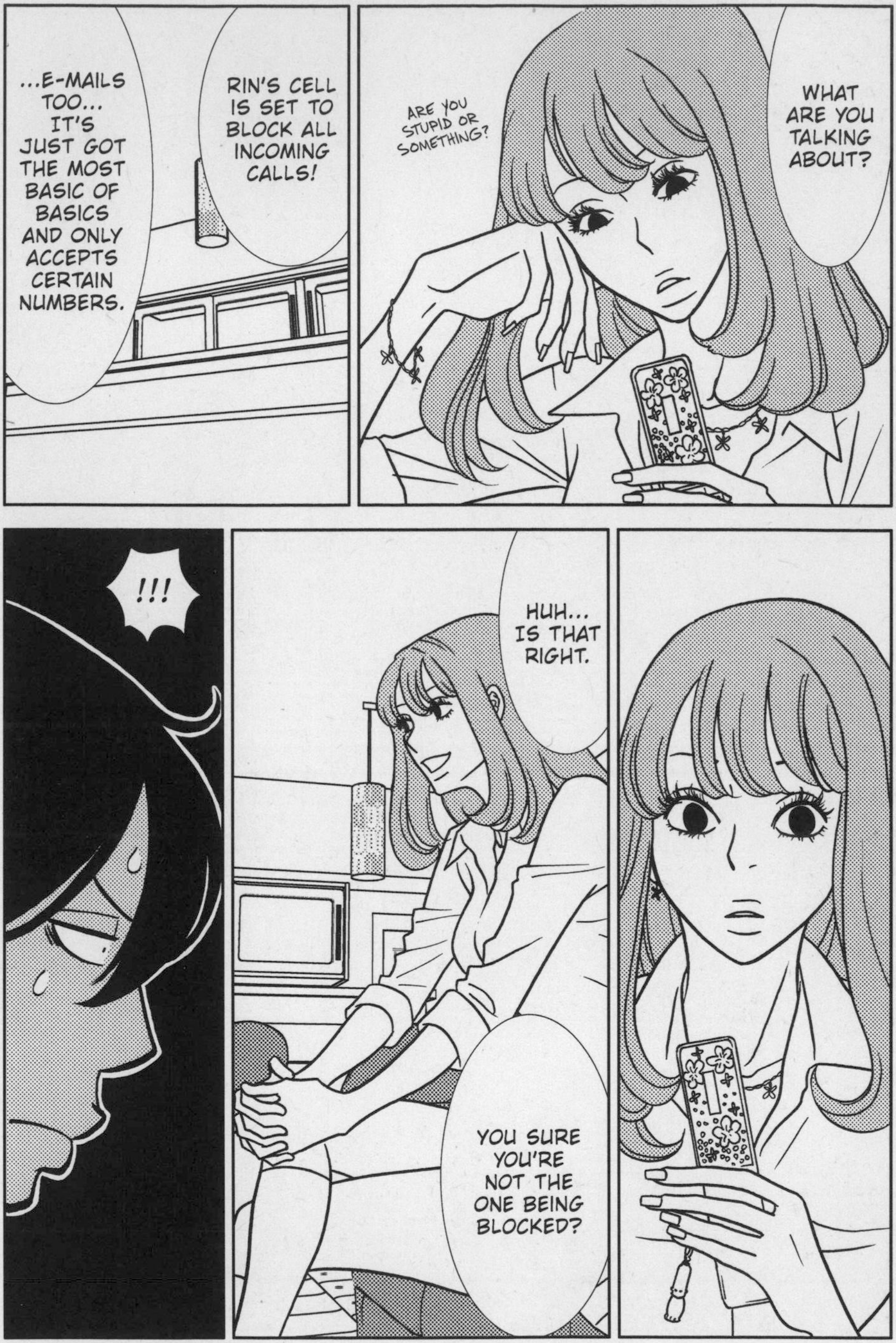
WHAT ARE YOU TALKING ABOUT?
ARE YOU STUPID OR SOMETHING?
RIN'S CELL IS SET TO BLOCK ALL INCOMING CALLS!
...E-MAILS TOO... IT'S JUST GOT THE MOST BASIC OF BASICS AND ONLY ACCEPTS CERTAIN NUMBERS.
HUH... IS THAT RIGHT.
YOU SURE YOU'RE NOT THE ONE BEING BLOCKED?
!!!

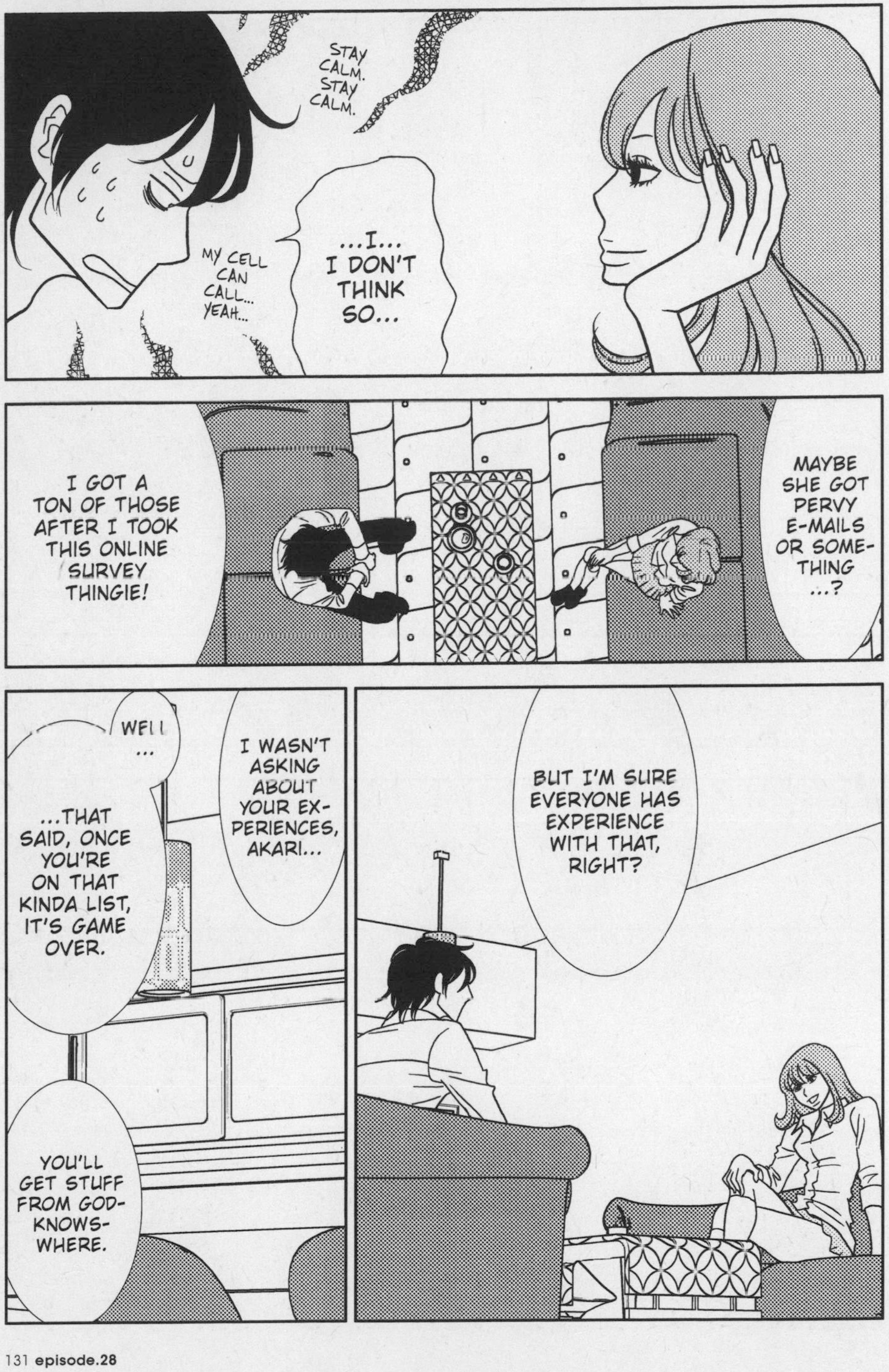
STAY CALM. STAY CALM.
...I... I DON'T THINK SO...
MY CELL CAN CALL... YEAH...
MAYBE SHE GOT PERVY E-MAILS OR SOME-THING ...?
I GOT A TON OF THOSE AFTER I TOOK THIS ONLINE SURVEY THINGIE!
BUT I'M SURE EVERYONE HAS EXPERIENCE WITH THAT, RIGHT?
I WASN'T ASKING ABOUT YOUR EX-PERIENCES, AKARI...
WELL ...
...THAT SAID, ONCE YOU'RE ON THAT KINDA LIST, IT'S GAME OVER.
YOU'LL GET STUFF FROM GOD-KNOWS-WHERE.

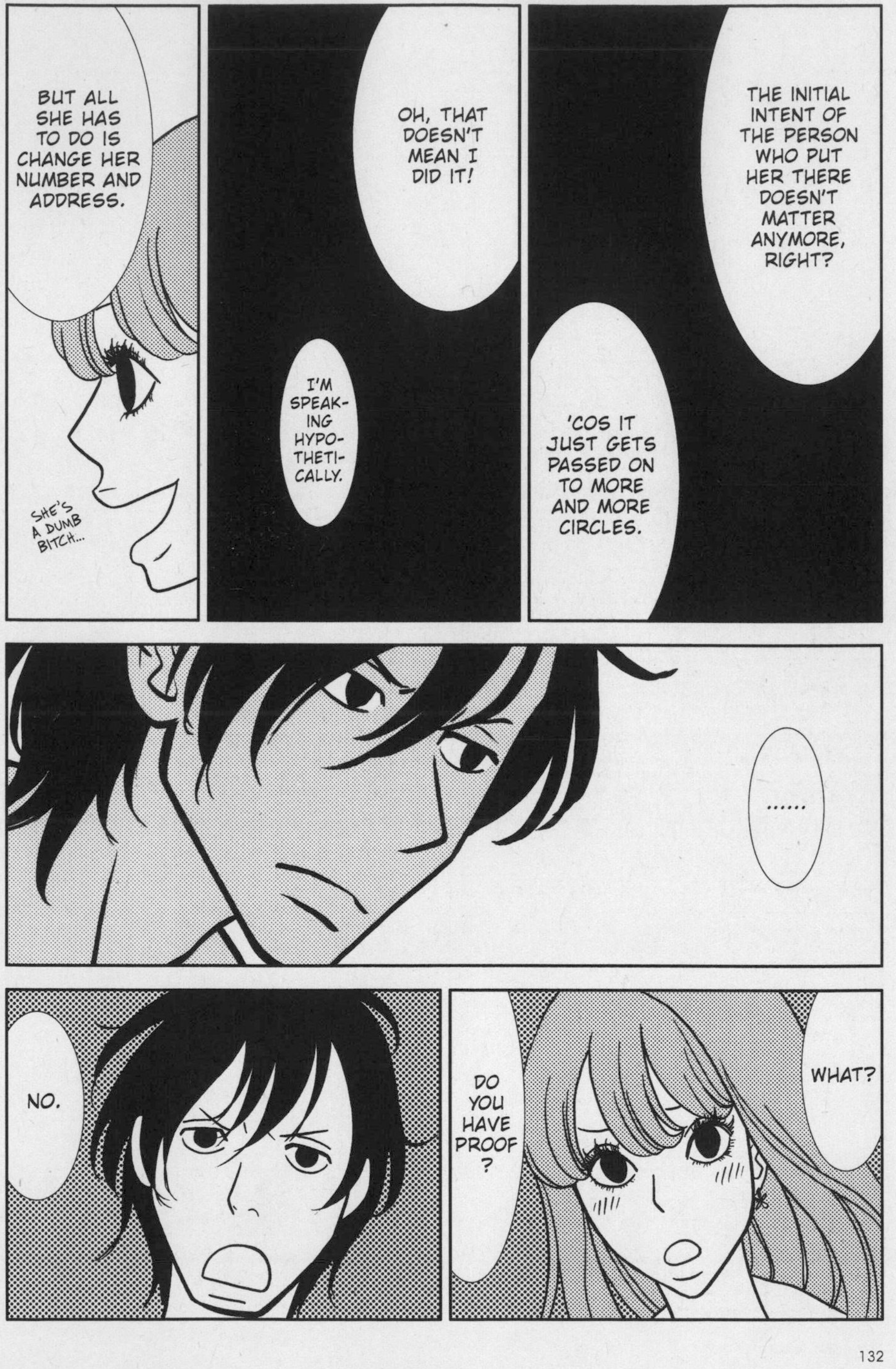
THE INITIAL INTENT OF THE PERSON WHO PUT HER THERE DOESN'T MATTER ANYMORE, RIGHT?
'COS IT JUST GETS PASSED ON TO MORE AND MORE CIRCLES.
OH, THAT DOESN'T MEAN I DID IT!
I'M SPEAK-ING HYPO-THETI-CALLY.
BUT ALL SHE HAS TO DO IS CHANGE HER NUMBER AND ADDRESS.
SHE'S A DUMB BITCH...
......
WHAT?
DO YOU HAVE PROOF ?
NO.

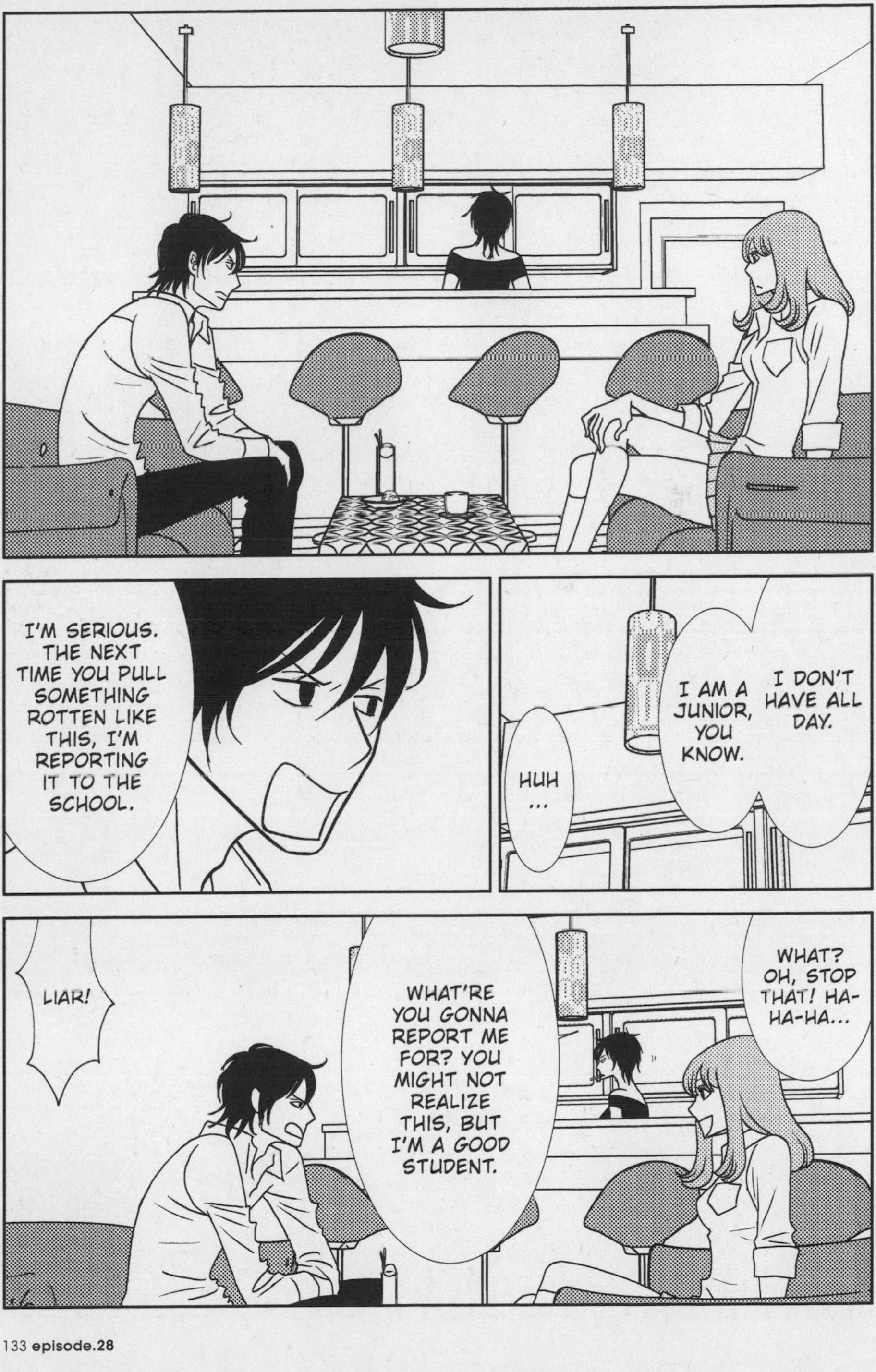
I DON'T HAVE ALL DAY.
I AM A JUNIOR, YOU KNOW.
HUH ...
I'M SERIOUS. THE NEXT TIME YOU PULL SOMETHING ROTTEN LIKE THIS, I'M REPORTING IT TO THE SCHOOL.
WHAT? OH, STOP THAT! HA-HA-HA...
WHAT'RE YOU GONNA REPORT ME FOR? YOU MIGHT NOT REALIZE THIS, BUT I'M A GOOD STUDENT.
LIAR!

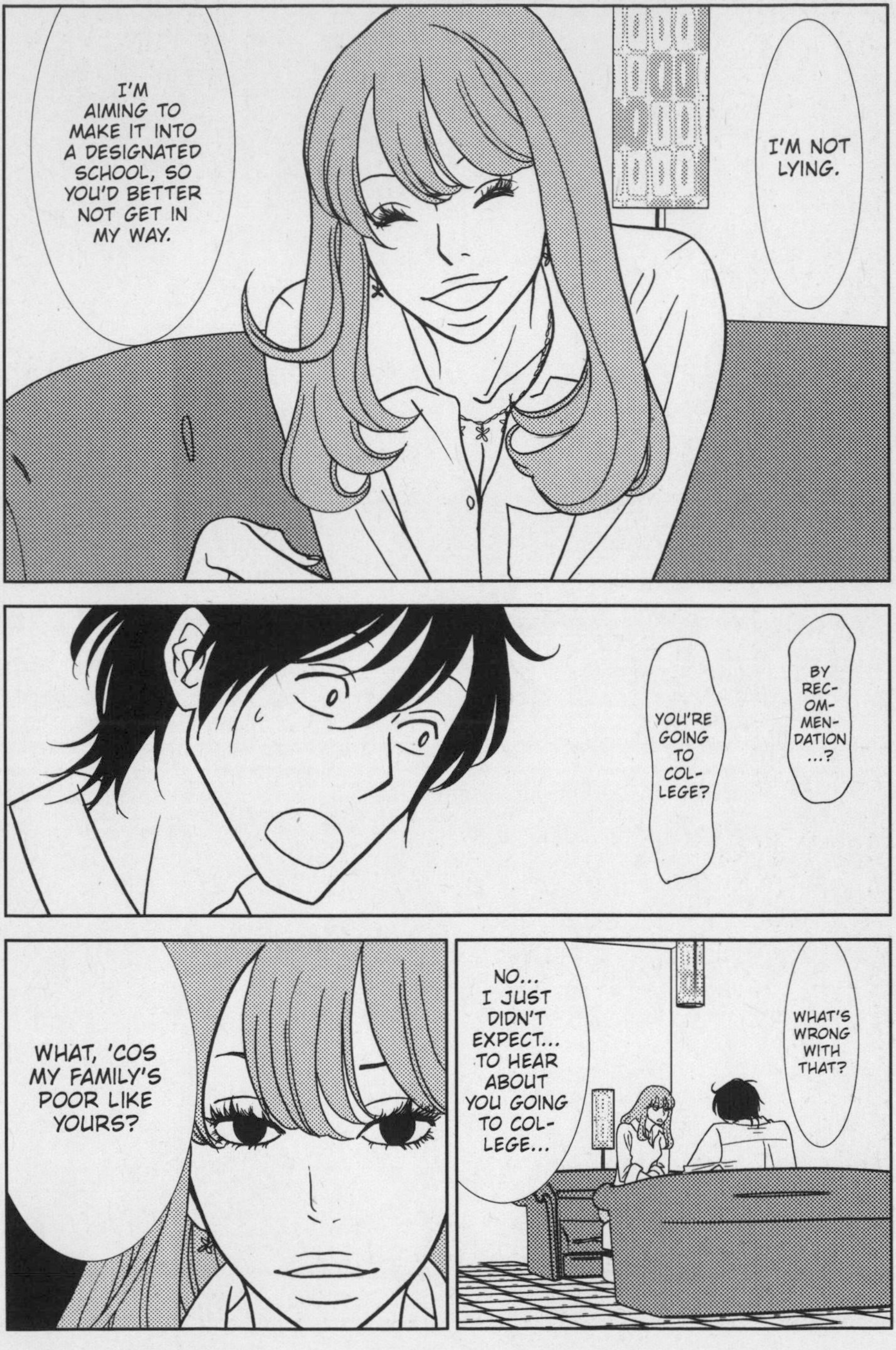
I'M NOT LYING.
I'M AIMING TO MAKE IT INTO A DESIGNATED SCHOOL, SO YOU'D BETTER NOT GET IN MY WAY.
BY RECOMMENDATION...?
YOU'RE GOING TO COLLEGE?
WHAT'S WRONG WITH THAT?
NO... I JUST DIDN'T EXPECT... TO HEAR ABOUT YOU GOING TO COLLEGE...
WHAT, 'COS MY FAMILY'S POOR LIKE YOURS?

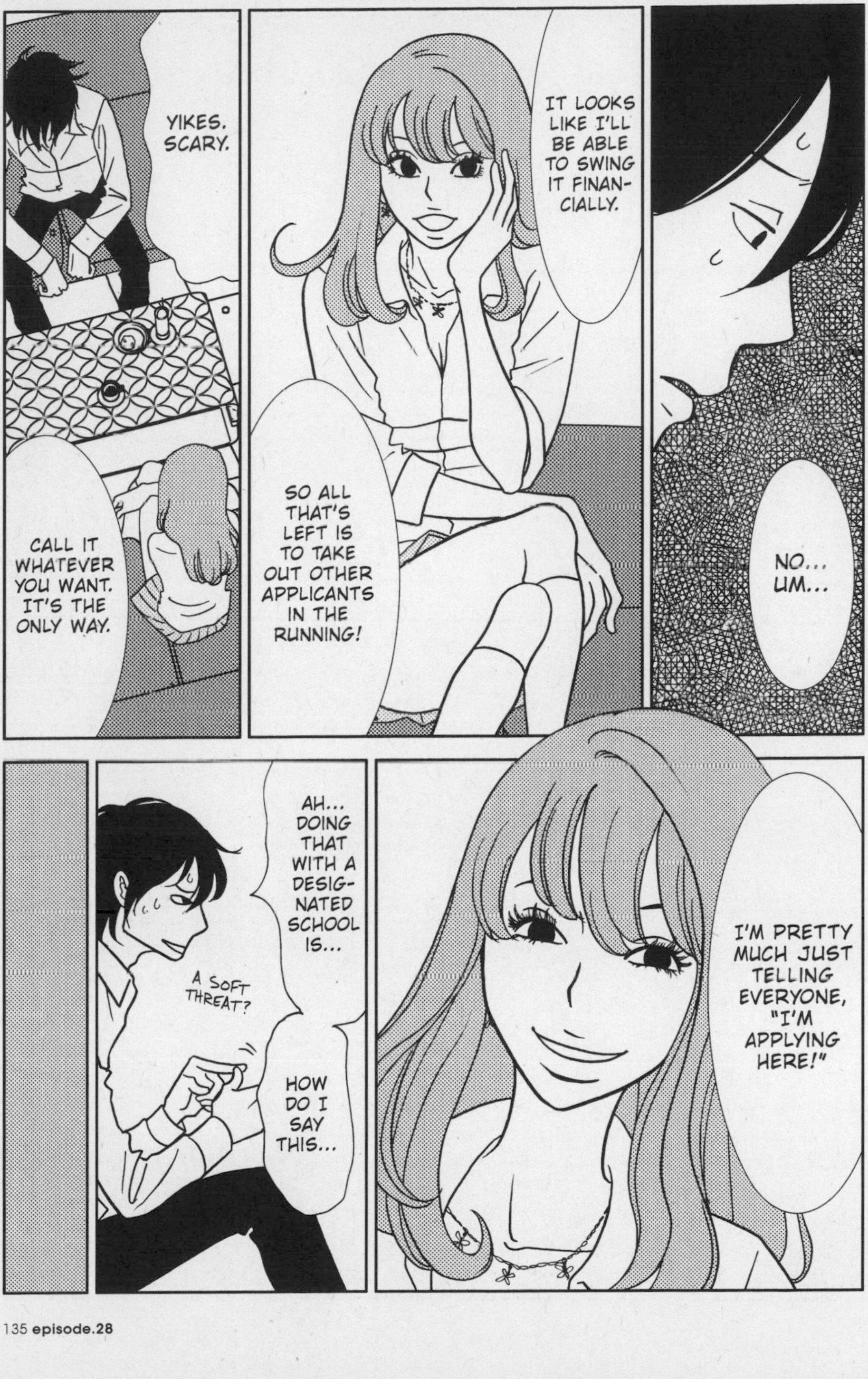
NO... UM...
IT LOOKS LIKE I'LL BE ABLE TO SWING IT FINANCIALLY.
SO ALL THAT'S LEFT IS TO TAKE OUT OTHER APPLICANTS IN THE RUNNING!
YIKES. SCARY.
CALL IT WHATEVER YOU WANT. IT'S THE ONLY WAY.
I'M PRETTY MUCH JUST TELLING EVERYONE, "I'M APPLYING HERE!"
AH... DOING THAT WITH A DESIGNATED SCHOOL IS...
A SOFT THREAT?
HOW DO I SAY THIS...

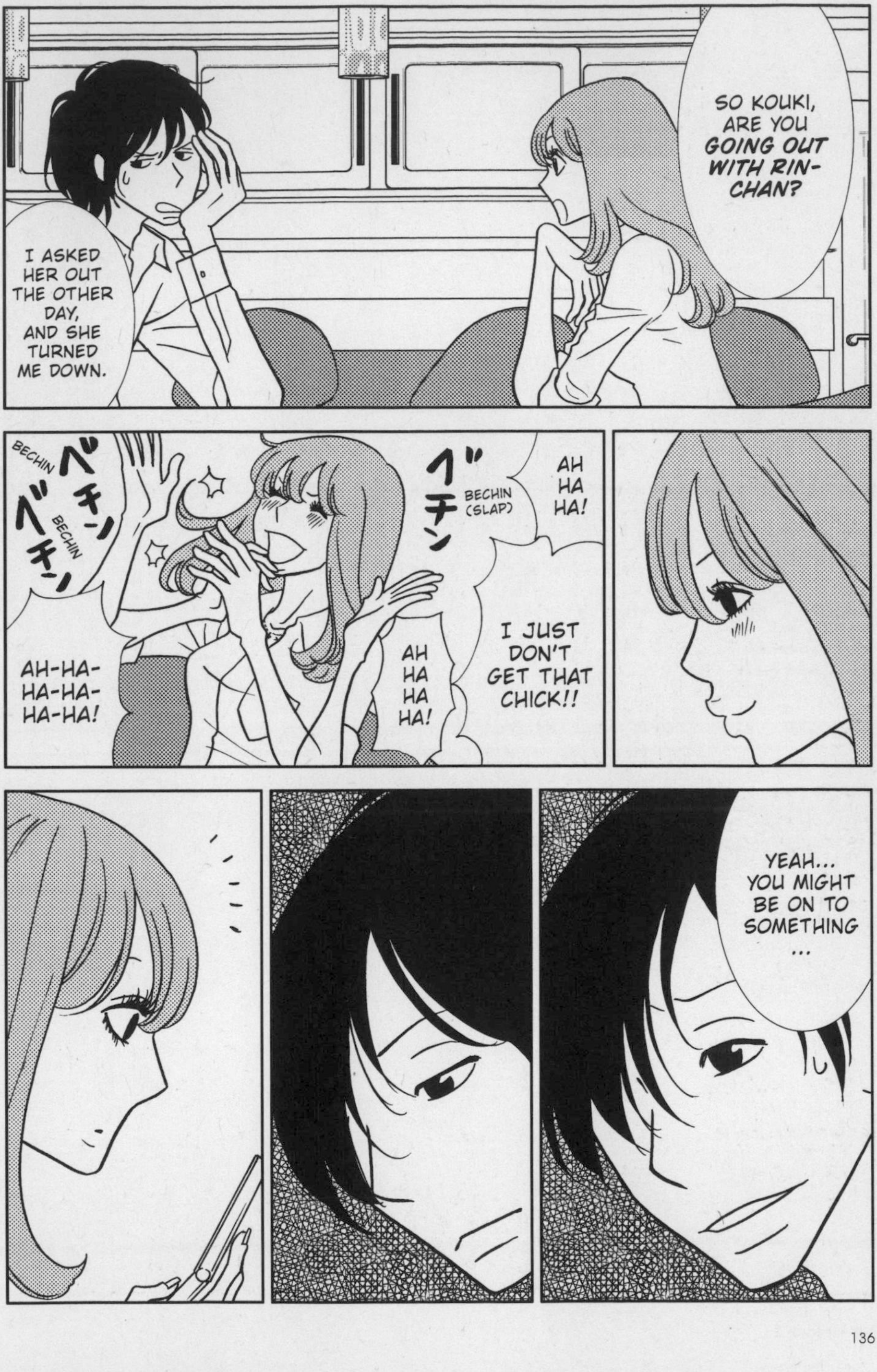
SO KOUKI, ARE YOU GOING OUT WITH RIN-CHAN?
I ASKED HER OUT THE OTHER DAY, AND SHE TURNED ME DOWN.
AH HA HA!
ベチン
BECHIN (SLAP)
I JUST DON'T GET THAT CHICK!!
AH HA HA HA!
ベチン
BECHIN
ベチン
BECHIN
AH-HA-HA-HA-HA-HA!
YEAH... YOU MIGHT BE ON TO SOMETHING ...

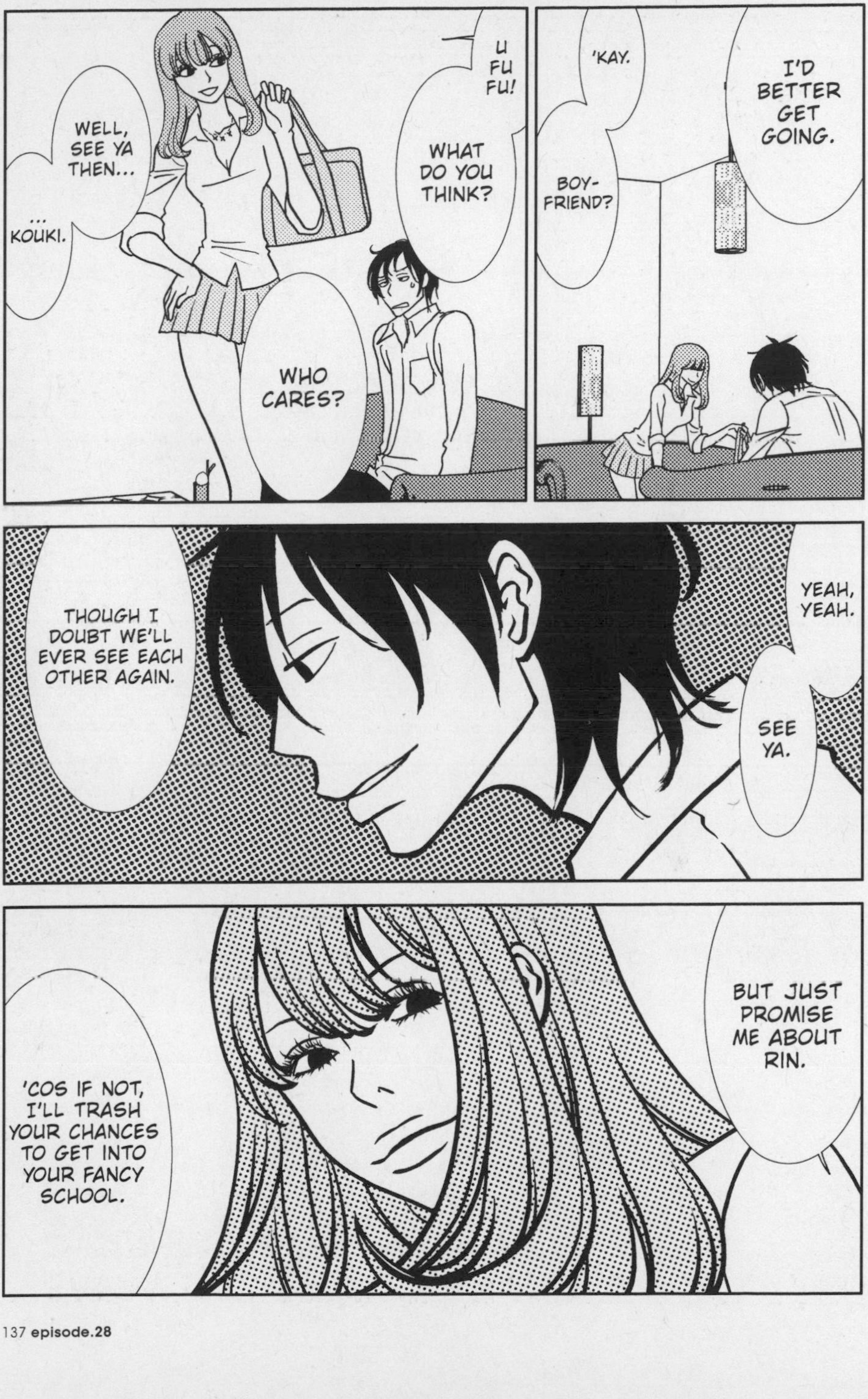
I'D BETTER GET GOING.
'KAY.
BOY-FRIEND?
U FU FU!
WHAT DO YOU THINK?
WELL, SEE YA THEN...
... KOUKI.
WHO CARES?
YEAH, YEAH.
SEE YA.
THOUGH I DOUBT WE'LL EVER SEE EACH OTHER AGAIN.
BUT JUST PROMISE ME ABOUT RIN.
'COS IF NOT, I'LL TRASH YOUR CHANCES TO GET INTO YOUR FANCY SCHOOL.

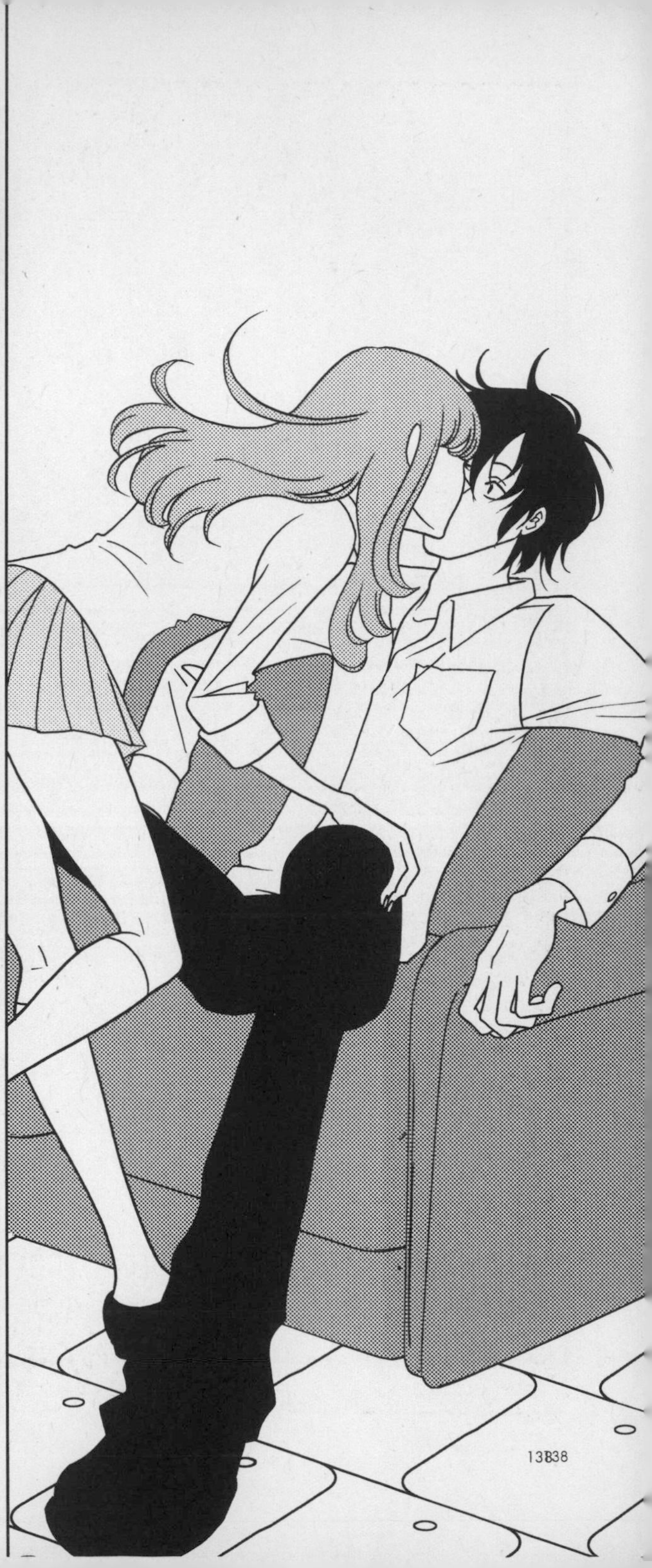

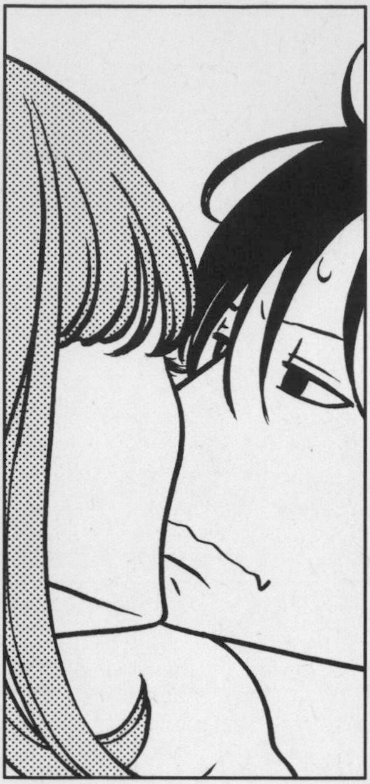

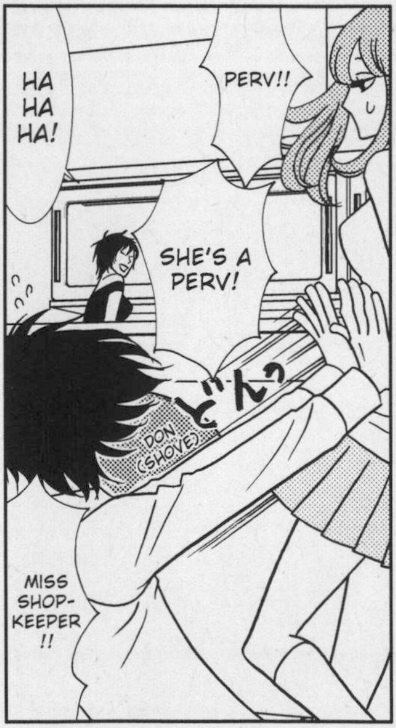
PERV!!
HA HA HA!
SHE'S A PERV!
どんっ
DON (SHOVE)
MISS SHOP-KEEPER!!

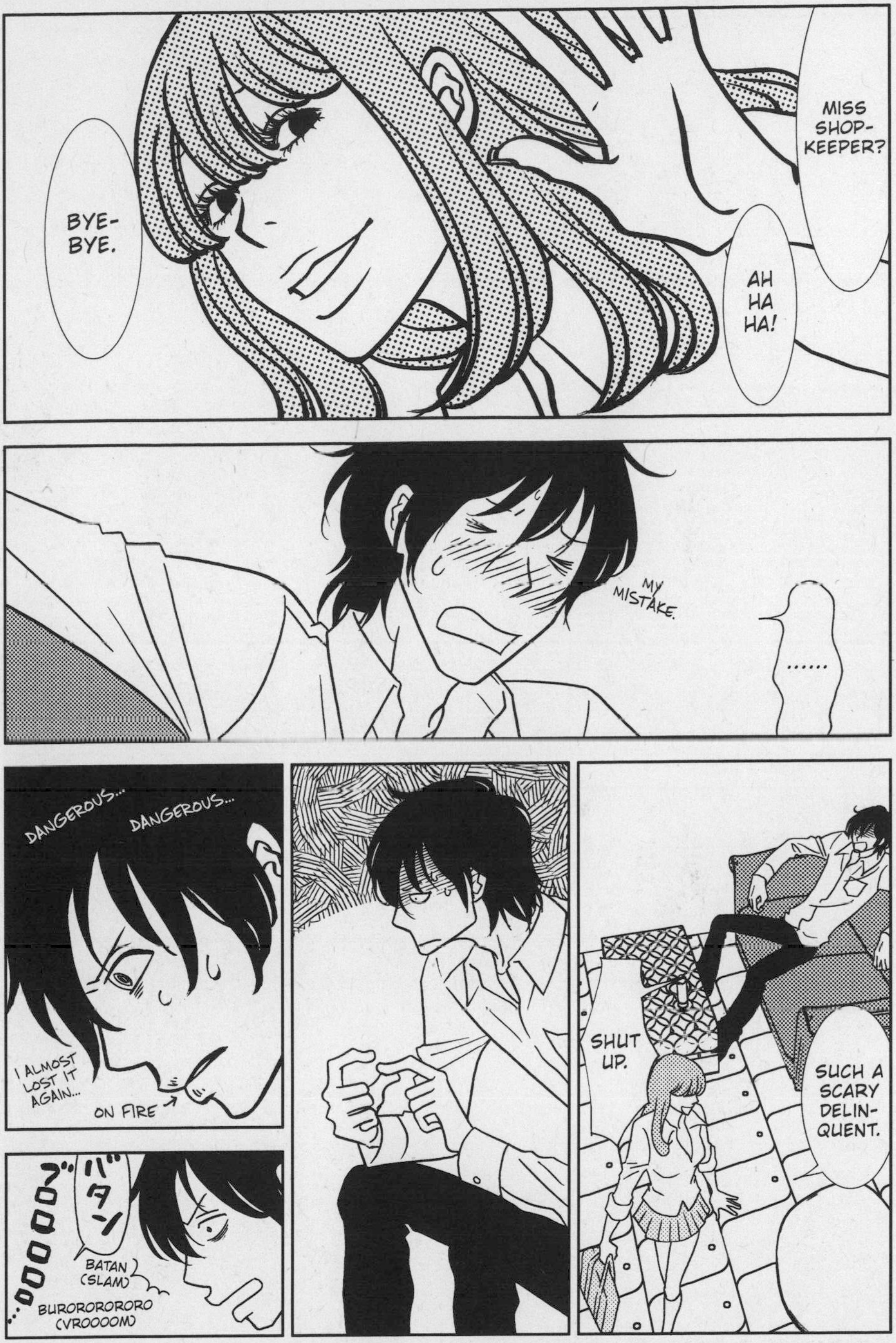
MISS SHOP-KEEPER?
AH HA HA!
BYE-BYE.
......
MY MISTAKE.
SUCH A SCARY DELIN-QUENT.
SHUT UP.
DANGEROUS...
DANGEROUS...
I ALMOST LOST IT AGAIN...
ON FIRE
バタン
ブロロロロロロ...
BATAN (SLAM)
BURORORORORO (VROOOOM)

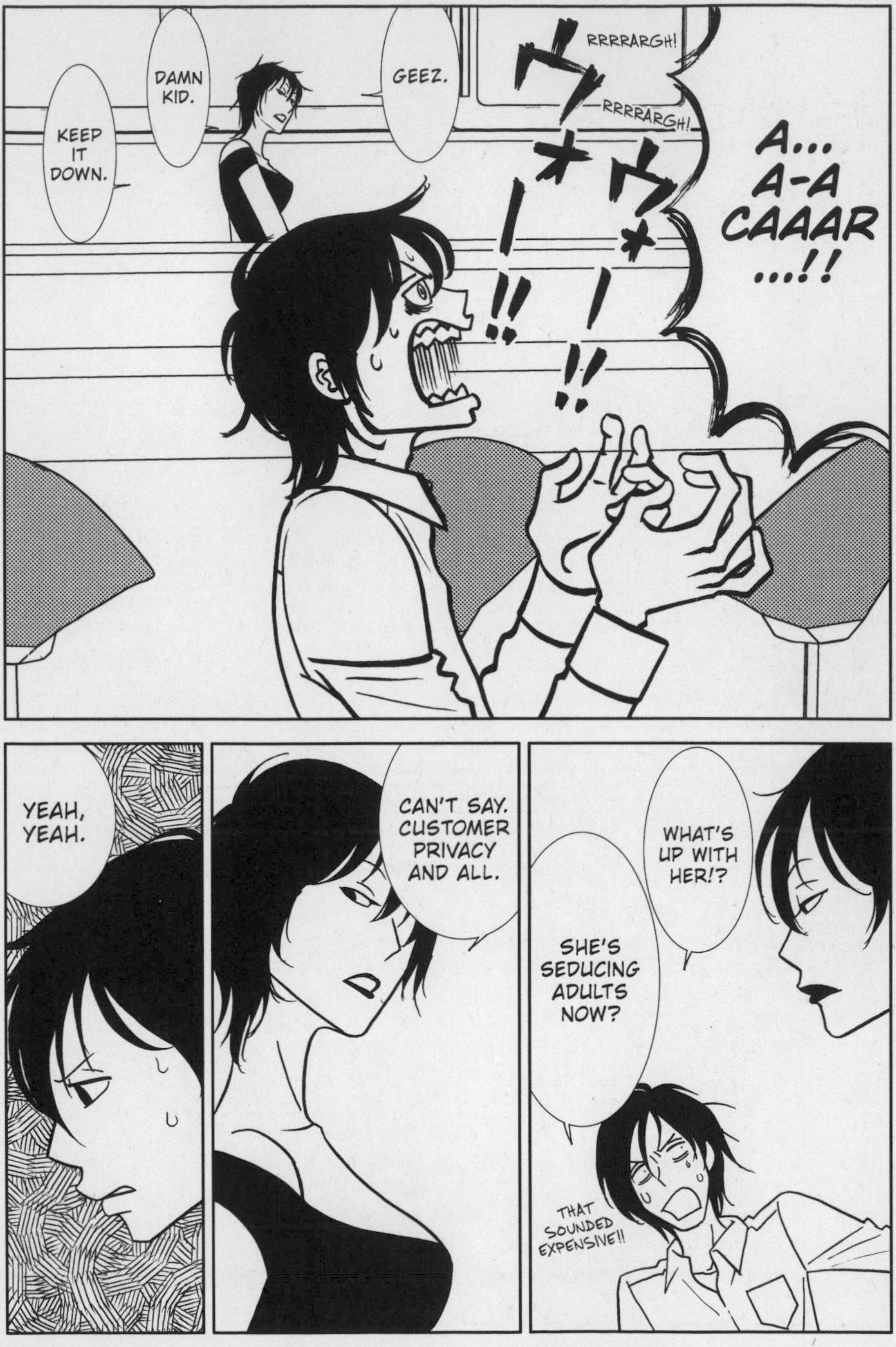
A... A-A CAAAR...!!
ウォー!!
RRRRARGH!
ウォー!!
RRRRARGH!
GEEZ.
DAMN KID.
KEEP IT DOWN.
WHAT'S UP WITH HER!?
SHE'S SEDUCING ADULTS NOW?
THAT SOUNDED EXPENSIVE!!
CAN'T SAY. CUSTOMER PRIVACY AND ALL.
YEAH, YEAH.

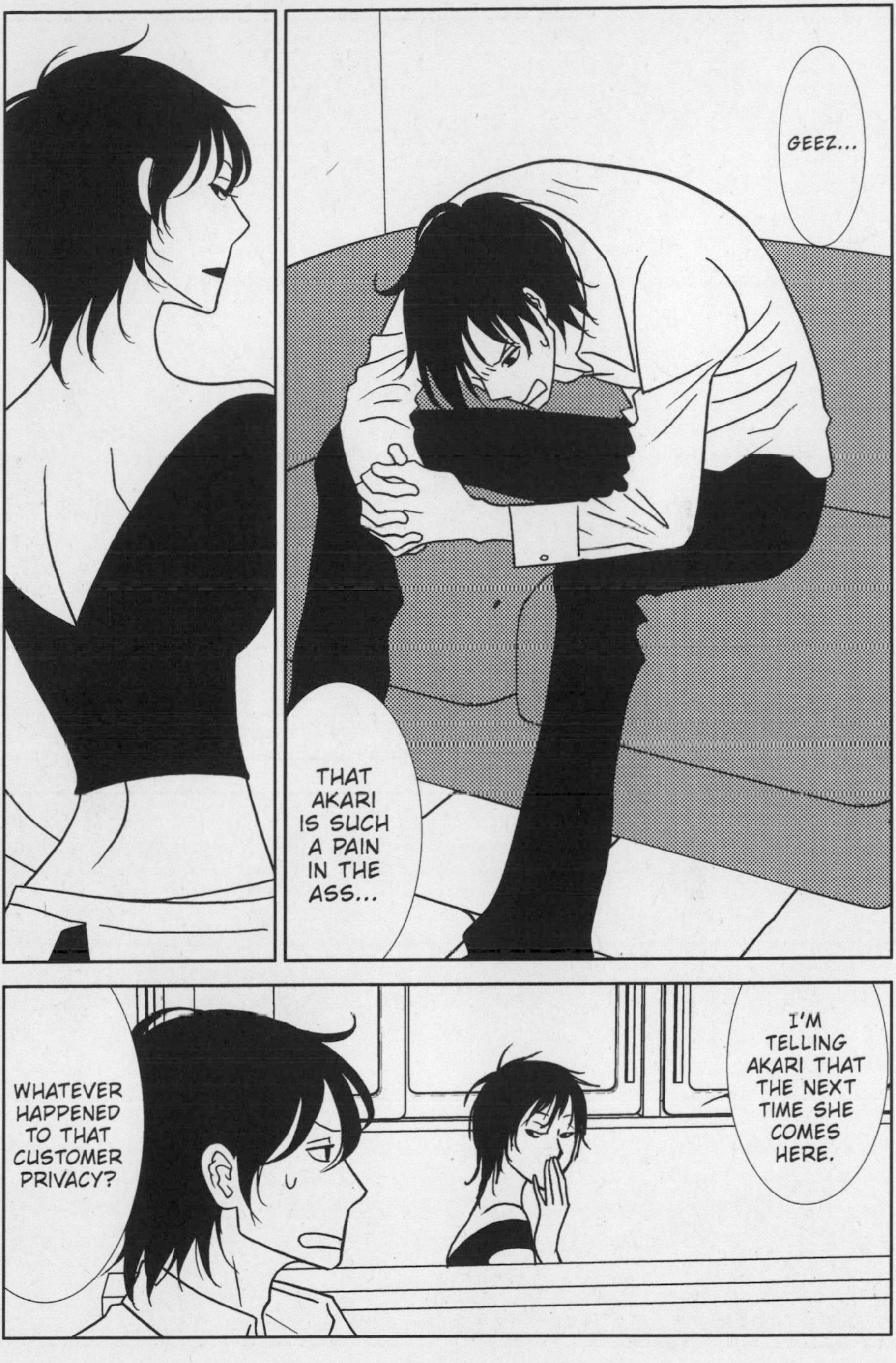
GEEZ...
THAT AKARI IS SUCH A PAIN IN THE ASS...
I'M TELLING AKARI THAT THE NEXT TIME SHE COMES HERE.
WHATEVER HAPPENED TO THAT CUSTOMER PRIVACY?

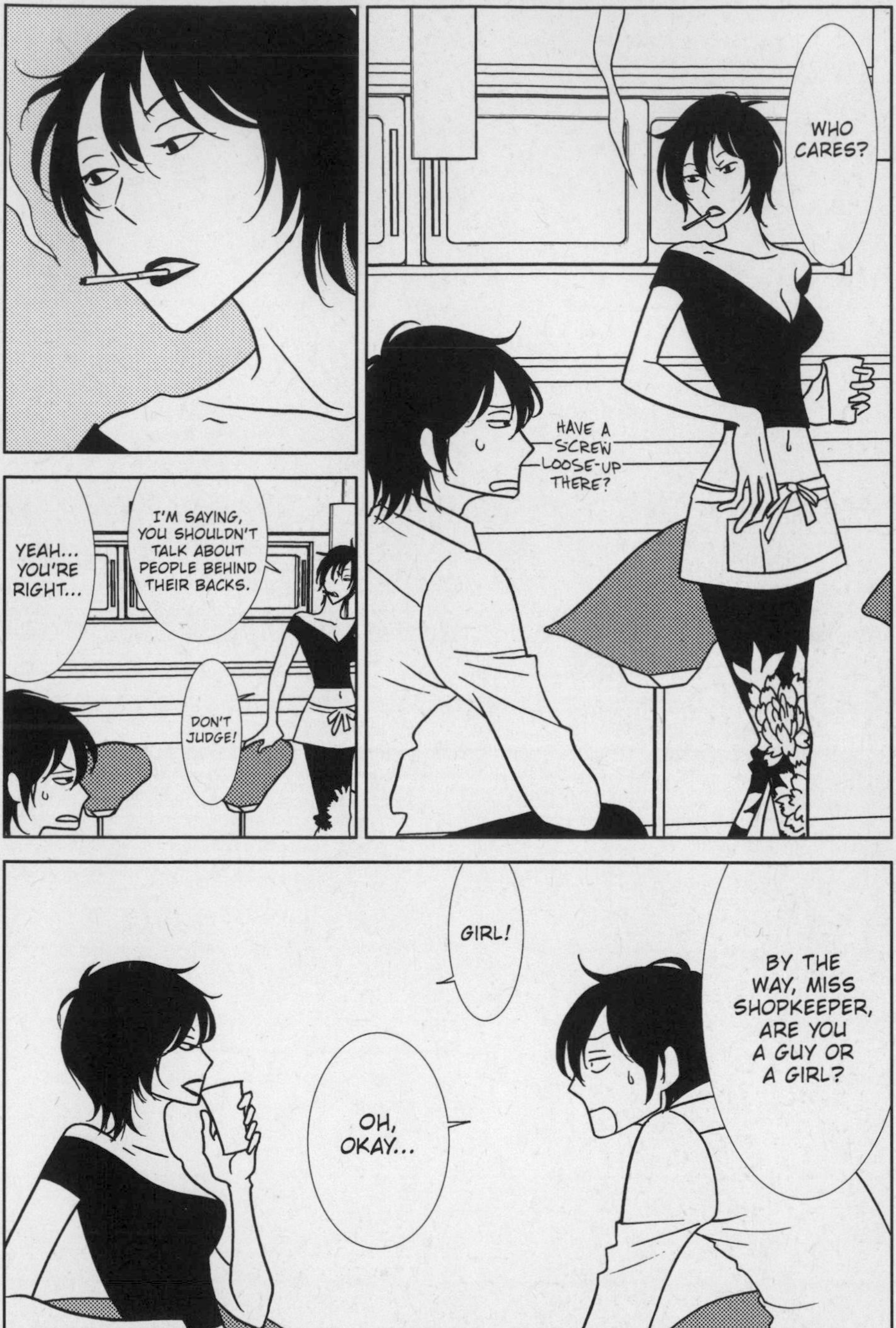
WHO CARES?
HAVE A SCREW LOOSE-UP THERE?
I'M SAYING, YOU SHOULDN'T TALK ABOUT PEOPLE BEHIND THEIR BACKS.
YEAH... YOU'RE RIGHT...
DON'T JUDGE!
BY THE WAY, MISS SHOPKEEPER, ARE YOU A GUY OR A GIRL?
GIRL!
OH, OKAY...

BUNNY DROP
episode.29

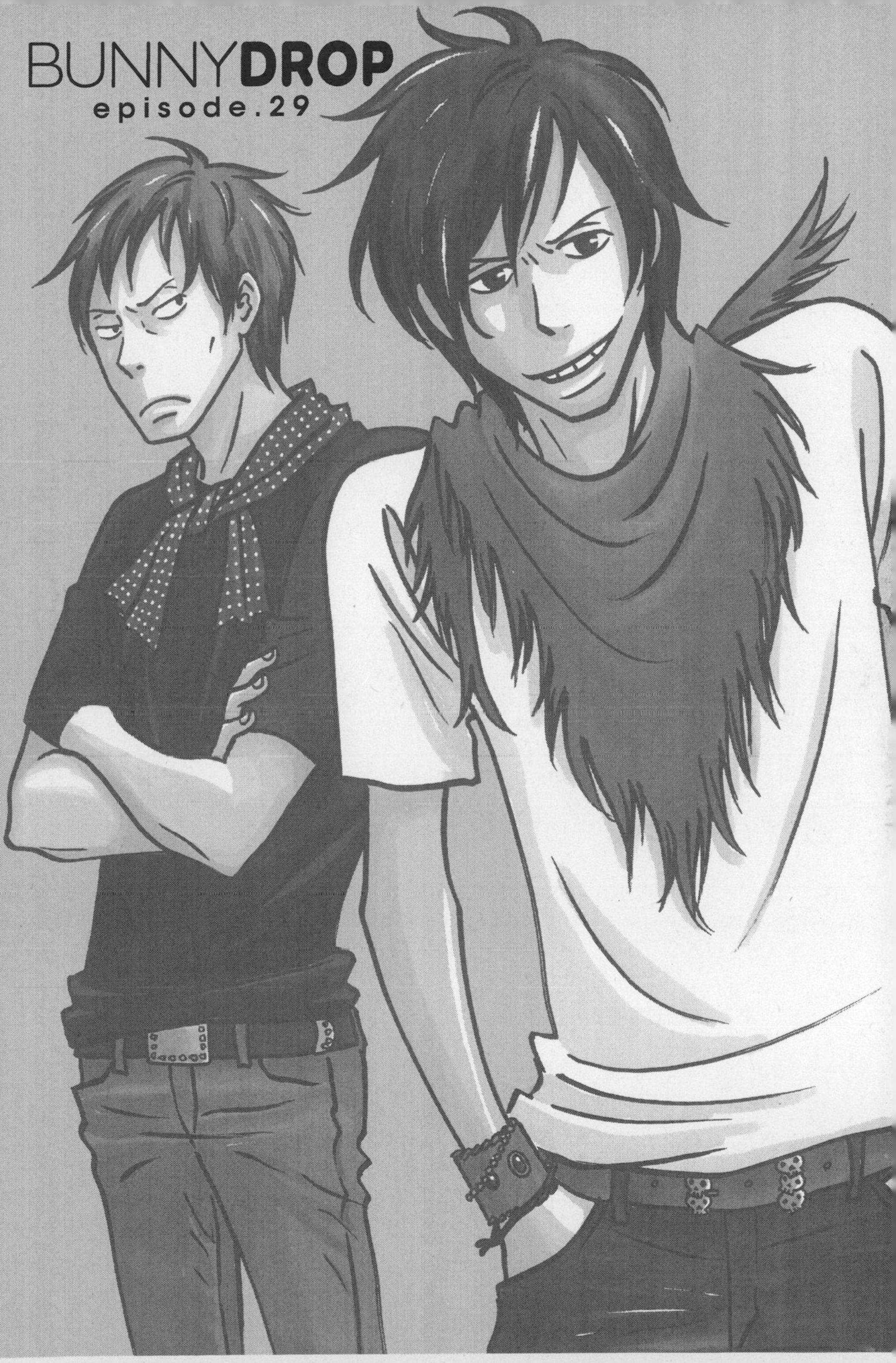

BUNNY**DROP**

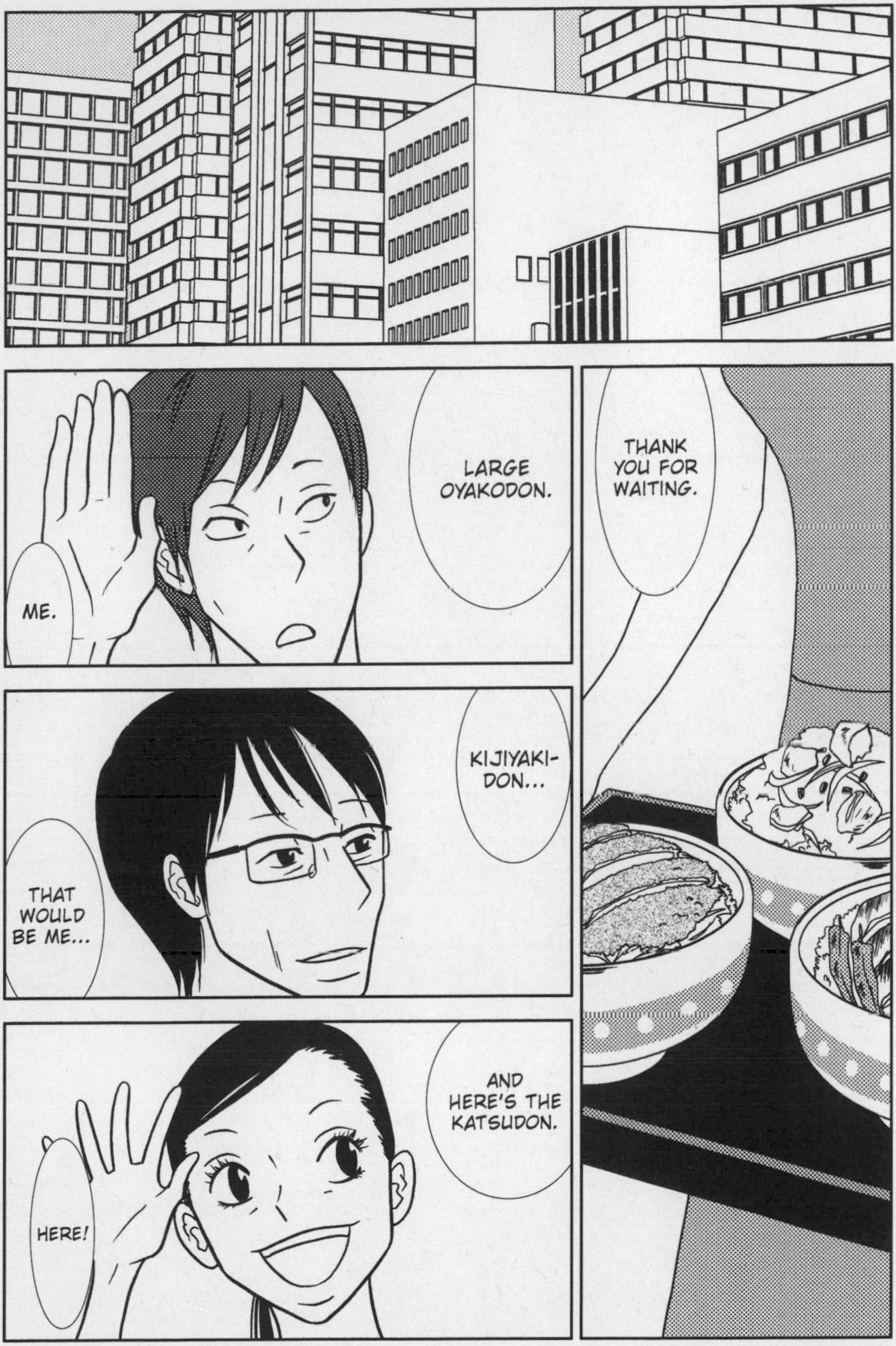
THANK YOU FOR WAITING.
LARGE OYAKODON.
ME.
KIJIYAKI-DON...
THAT WOULD BE ME...
AND HERE'S THE KATSUDON.
HERE!

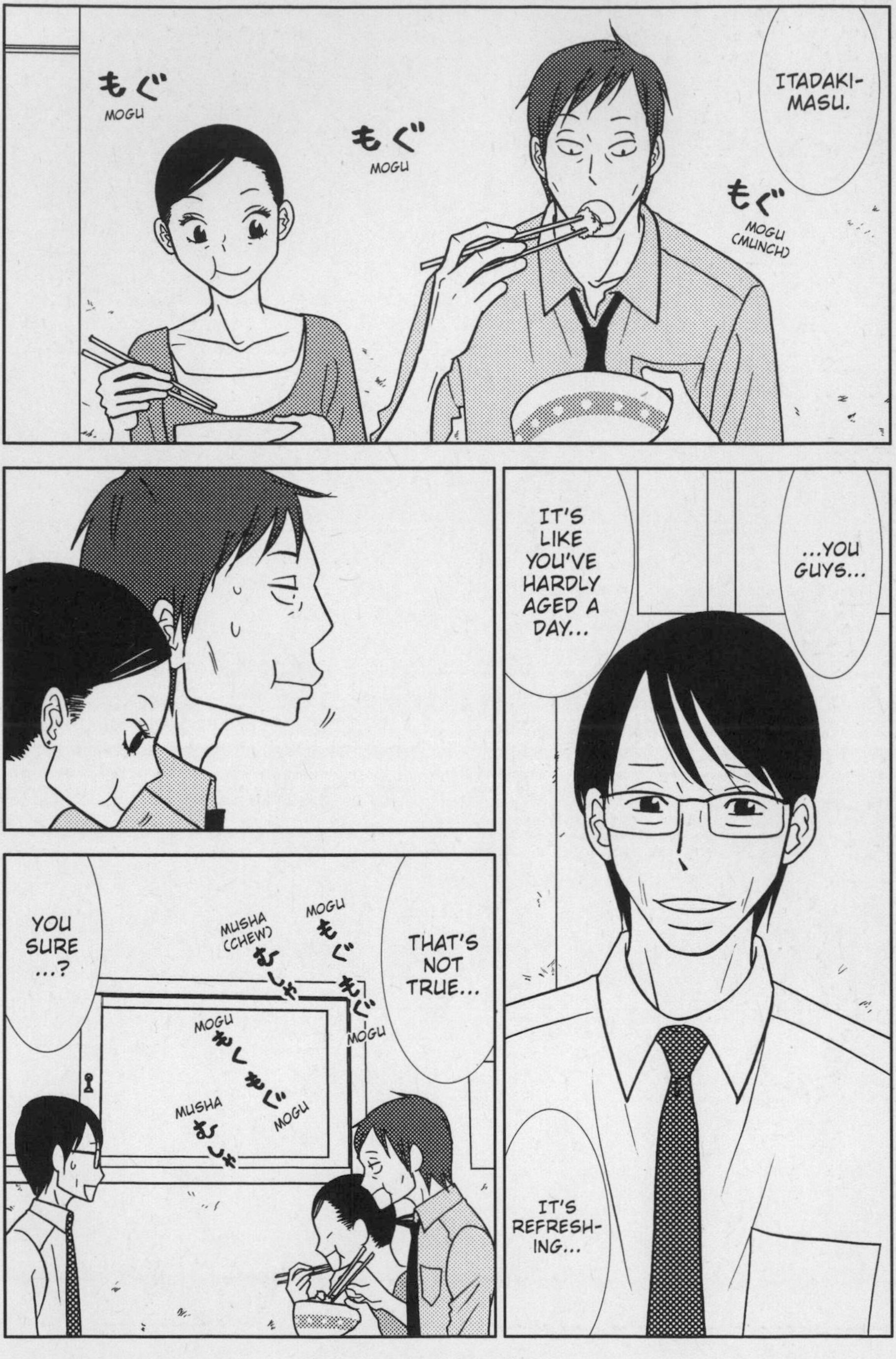
ITADAKI-MASU.
もぐ MOGU (MUNCH)
もぐ MOGU
もぐ MOGU
...YOU GUYS...
IT'S LIKE YOU'VE HARDLY AGED A DAY...
IT'S REFRESHING...
THAT'S NOT TRUE...
もぐもぐ MOGU MOGU
むしゃ MUSHA (CHEW)
もぐもぐ MOGU MOGU
むしゃ MUSHA
YOU SURE ...?

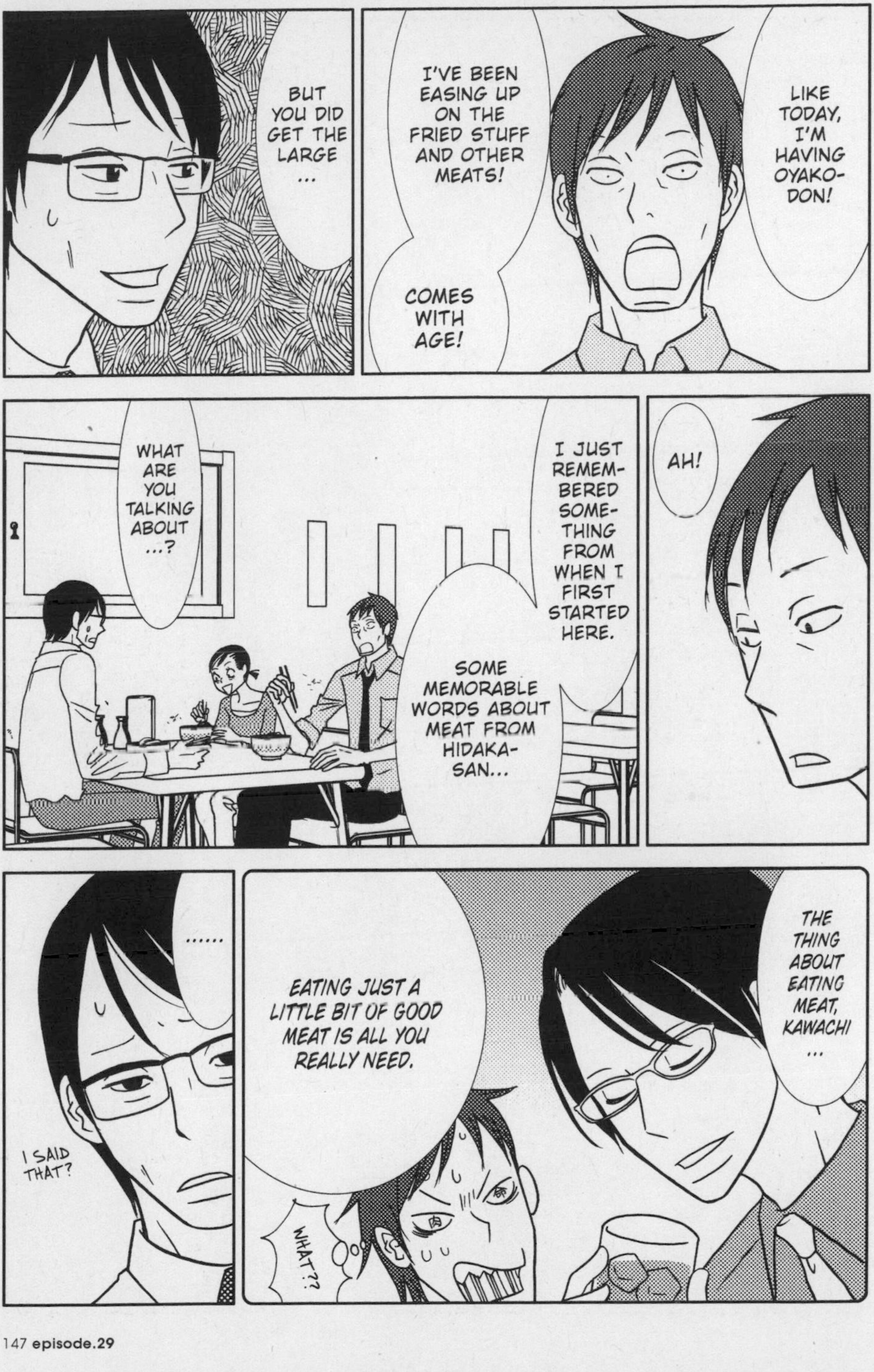

LIKE TODAY, I'M HAVING OYAKO-DON!
I'VE BEEN EASING UP ON THE FRIED STUFF AND OTHER MEATS!
COMES WITH AGE!
BUT YOU DID GET THE LARGE ...
AH!
I JUST REMEM-BERED SOME-THING FROM WHEN I FIRST STARTED HERE.
SOME MEMORABLE WORDS ABOUT MEAT FROM HIDAKA-SAN...
WHAT ARE YOU TALKING ABOUT ...?
THE THING ABOUT EATING MEAT, KAWACHI ...
EATING JUST A LITTLE BIT OF GOOD MEAT IS ALL YOU REALLY NEED.
WHAT??
......
I SAID THAT?

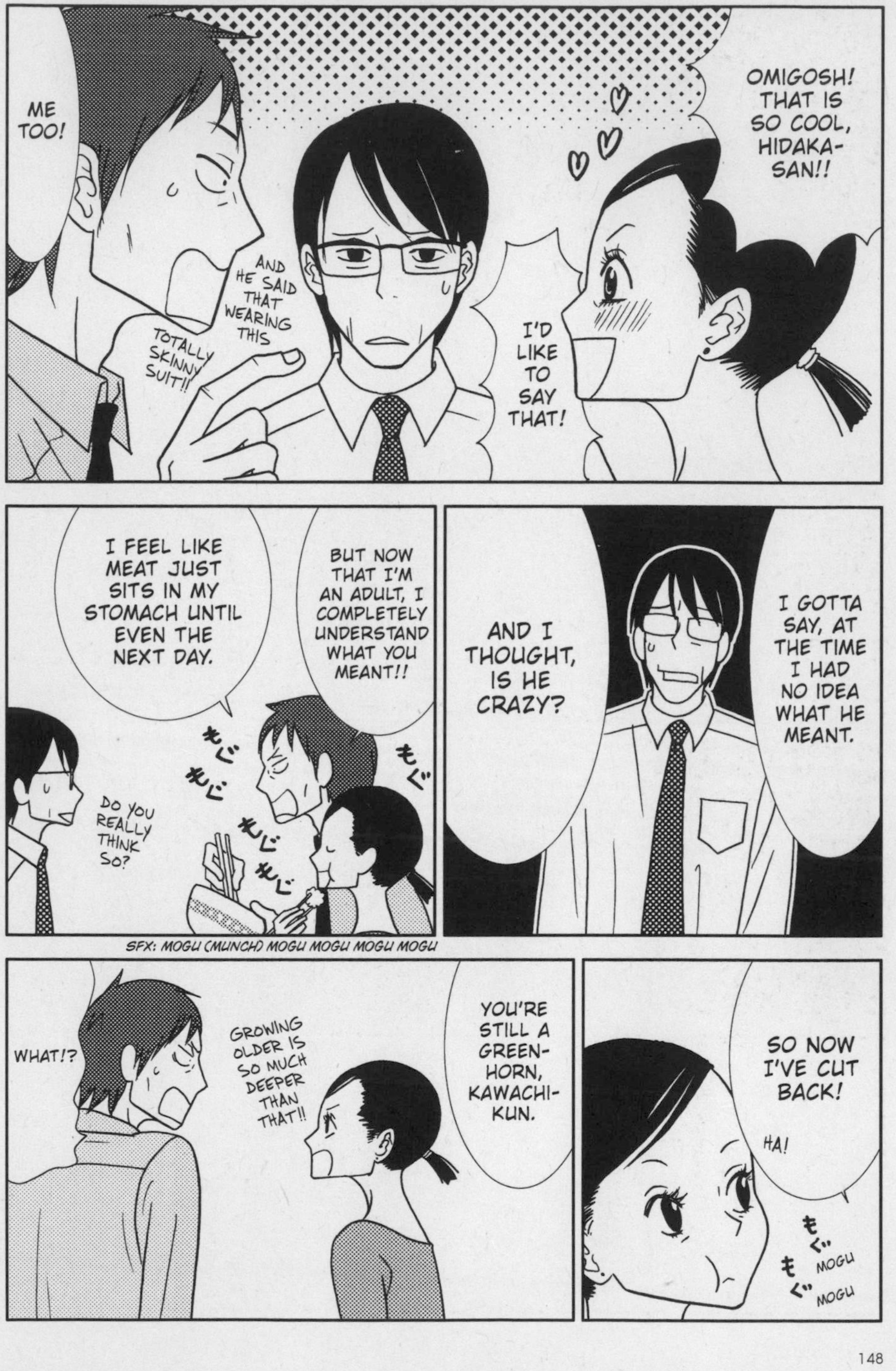
OMIGOSH! THAT IS SO COOL, HIDAKA-SAN!!
I'D LIKE TO SAY THAT!
ME TOO!
AND HE SAID THAT WEARING THIS
TOTALLY SKINNY SUIT!!
I GOTTA SAY, AT THE TIME I HAD NO IDEA WHAT HE MEANT.
AND I THOUGHT, IS HE CRAZY?
BUT NOW THAT I'M AN ADULT, I COMPLETELY UNDERSTAND WHAT YOU MEANT!!
I FEEL LIKE MEAT JUST SITS IN MY STOMACH UNTIL EVEN THE NEXT DAY.
もぐ
もじ もじ
もじ もじ
DO YOU REALLY THINK SO?
SFX: MOGU (MUNCH) MOGU MOGU MOGU MOGU
SO NOW I'VE CUT BACK!
HA!
もぐ MOGU
もぐ MOGU
YOU'RE STILL A GREENHORN, KAWACHI-KUN.
GROWING OLDER IS SO MUCH DEEPER THAN THAT!!
WHAT!?

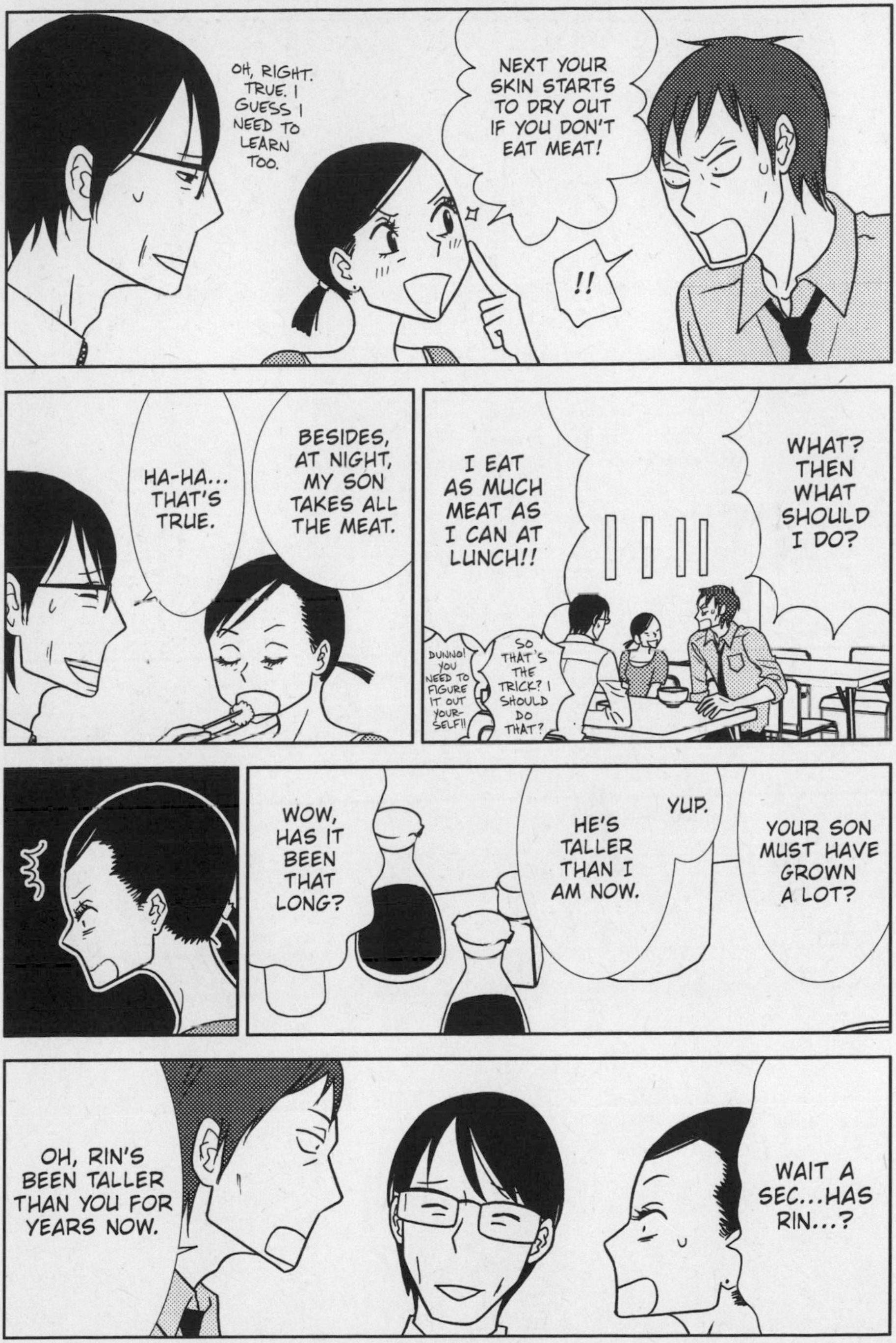
NEXT YOUR SKIN STARTS TO DRY OUT IF YOU DON'T EAT MEAT!
!!
OH, RIGHT. TRUE. I GUESS I NEED TO LEARN TOO.
WHAT? THEN WHAT SHOULD I DO?
I EAT AS MUCH MEAT AS I CAN AT LUNCH!!
SO THAT'S THE TRICK? I SHOULD DO THAT?
DUNNO! YOU NEED TO FIGURE IT OUT YOURSELF!!
BESIDES, AT NIGHT, MY SON TAKES ALL THE MEAT.
HA-HA... THAT'S TRUE.
YOUR SON MUST HAVE GROWN A LOT?
YUP.
HE'S TALLER THAN I AM NOW.
WOW, HAS IT BEEN THAT LONG?
WAIT A SEC...HAS RIN...?
OH, RIN'S BEEN TALLER THAN YOU FOR YEARS NOW.

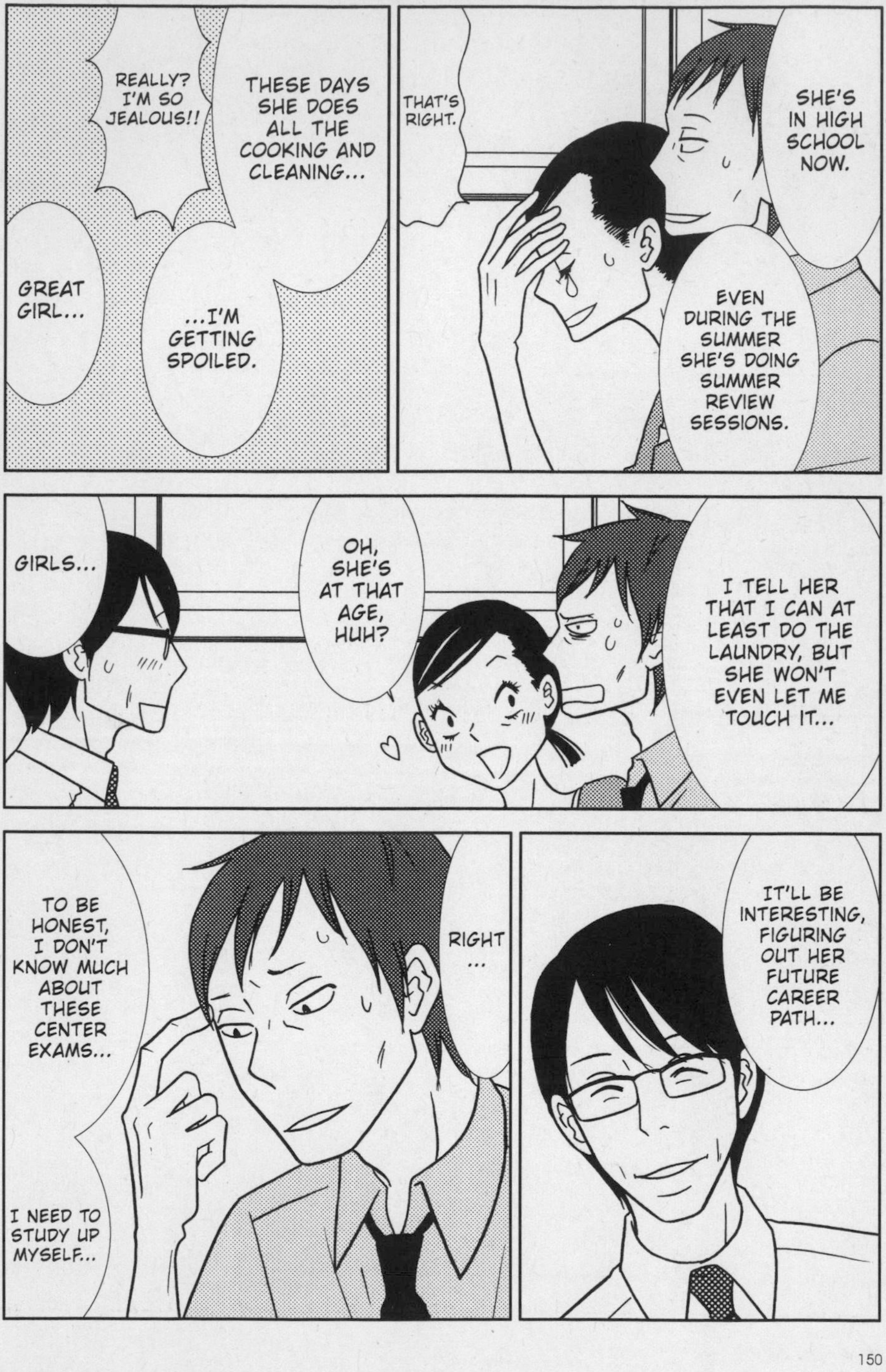
SHE'S IN HIGH SCHOOL NOW.
EVEN DURING THE SUMMER SHE'S DOING SUMMER REVIEW SESSIONS.
THAT'S RIGHT.
THESE DAYS SHE DOES ALL THE COOKING AND CLEANING...
...I'M GETTING SPOILED.
REALLY? I'M SO JEALOUS!!
GREAT GIRL...
I TELL HER THAT I CAN AT LEAST DO THE LAUNDRY, BUT SHE WON'T EVEN LET ME TOUCH IT...
OH, SHE'S AT THAT AGE, HUH?
GIRLS...
IT'LL BE INTERESTING, FIGURING OUT HER FUTURE CAREER PATH...
RIGHT ...
TO BE HONEST, I DON'T KNOW MUCH ABOUT THESE CENTER EXAMS...
I NEED TO STUDY UP MYSELF...

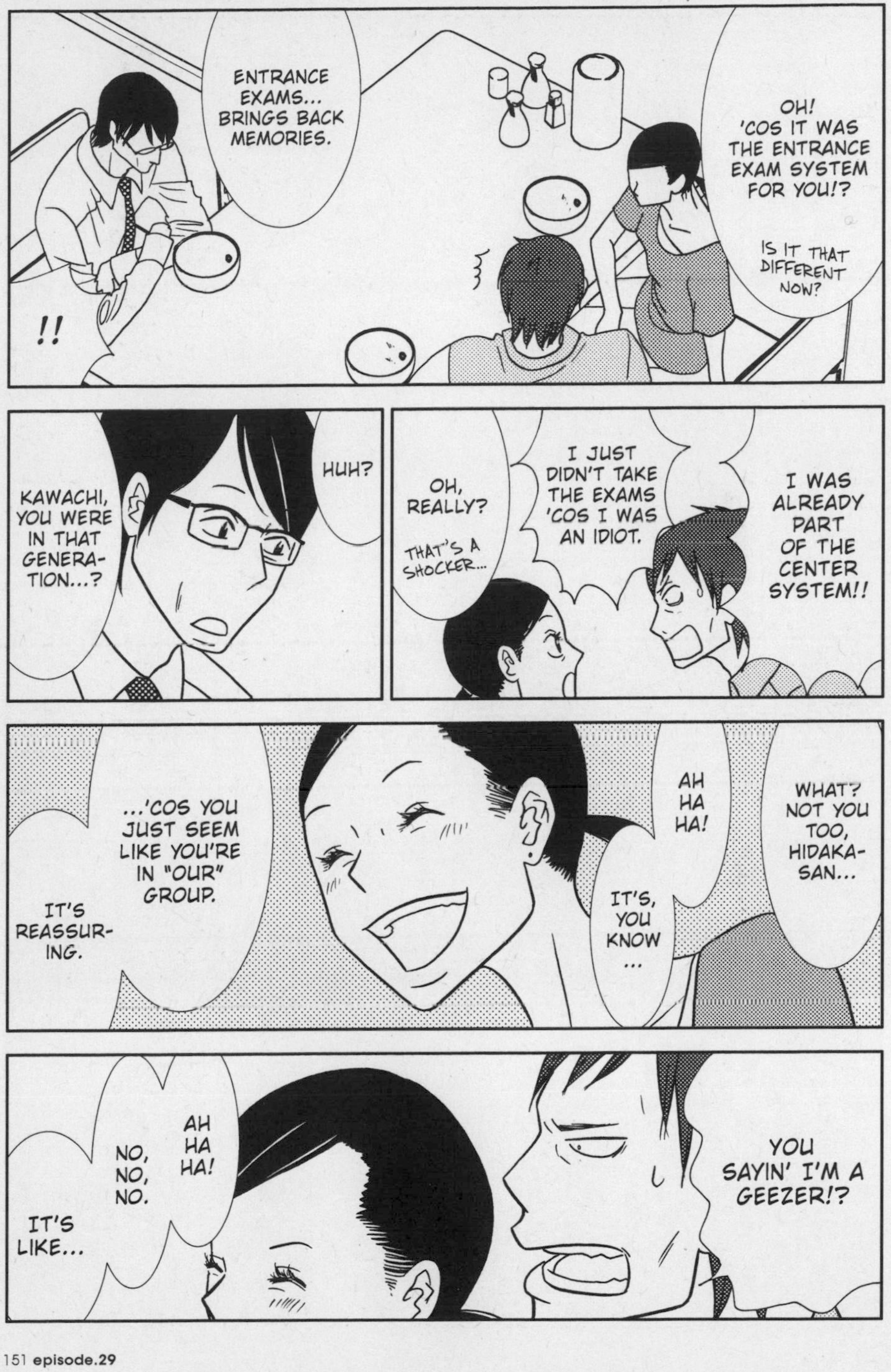
OH! 'COS IT WAS THE ENTRANCE EXAM SYSTEM FOR YOU!?
IS IT THAT DIFFERENT NOW?
ENTRANCE EXAMS... BRINGS BACK MEMORIES.
!!
I WAS ALREADY PART OF THE CENTER SYSTEM!!
I JUST DIDN'T TAKE THE EXAMS 'COS I WAS AN IDIOT.
OH, REALLY?
THAT'S A SHOCKER...
HUH?
KAWACHI, YOU WERE IN THAT GENERA-TION...?
WHAT? NOT YOU TOO, HIDAKA-SAN...
AH HA HA!
IT'S, YOU KNOW ...
...'COS YOU JUST SEEM LIKE YOU'RE IN "OUR" GROUP.
IT'S REASSUR-ING.
YOU SAYIN' I'M A GEEZER!?
AH HA HA!
NO, NO, NO.
IT'S LIKE...

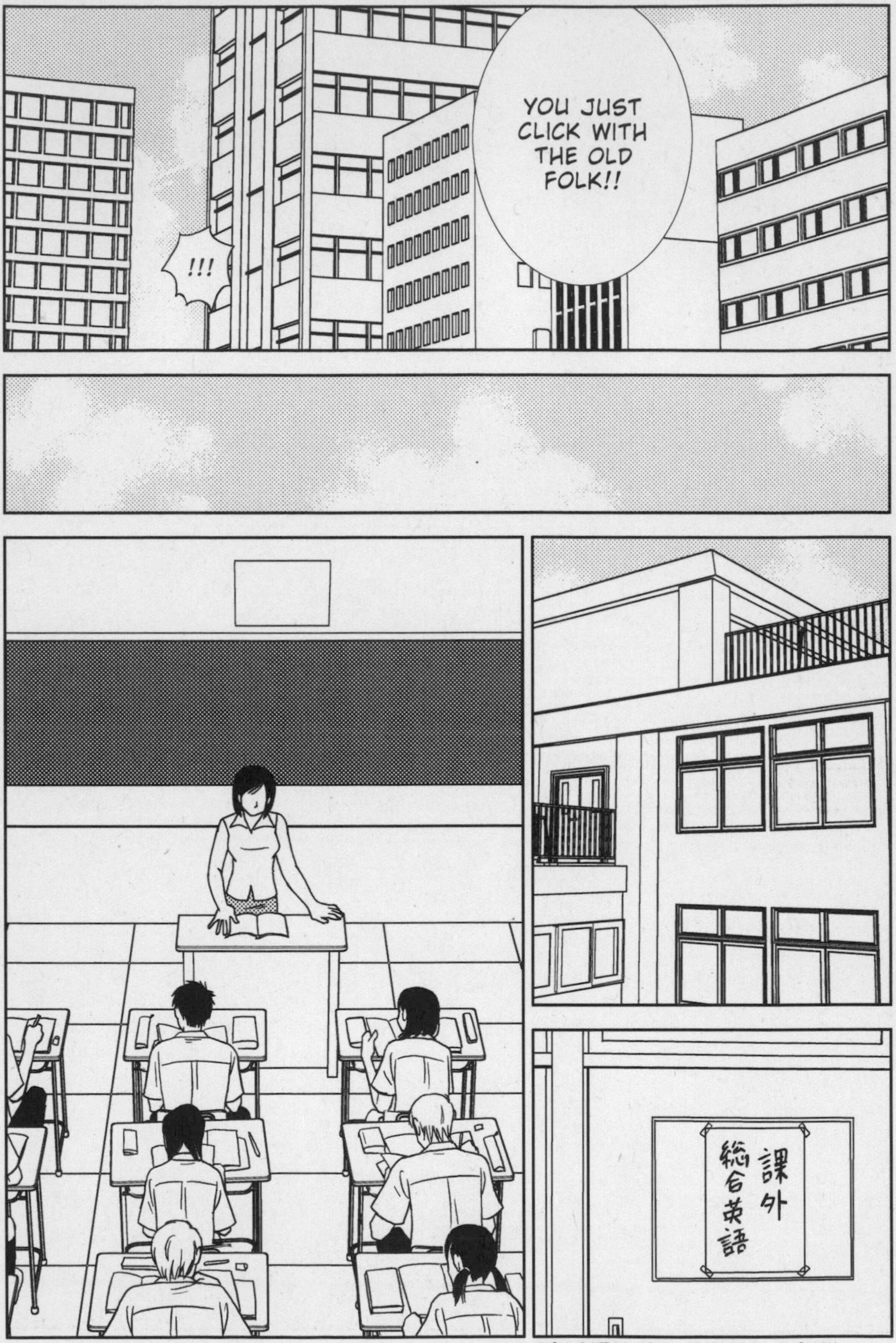
YOU JUST CLICK WITH THE OLD FOLK!!
!!!
課外
総合英語

SIGN: EXTRACURRICULAR SESSION: ENGLISH

SIGN: SUPPLEMENTARY SESSION: ANCIENT GRAMMAR

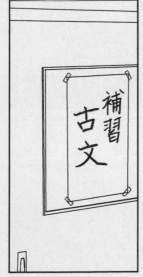

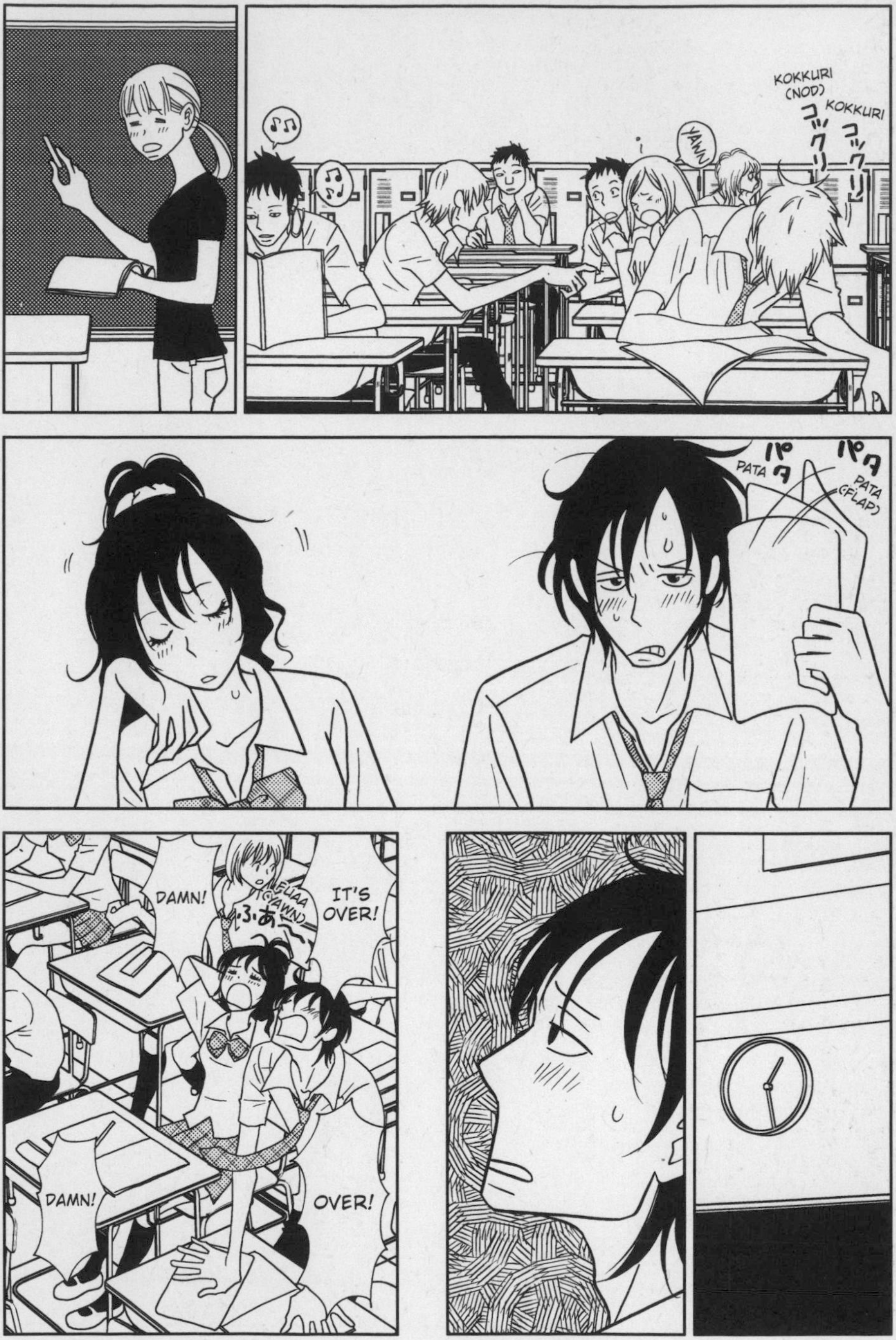
KOKKURI
コックリ
(NOD) KOKKURI
コックリ
YAWN
PATA
パタ
PATA (FLAP)
パタ
IT'S OVER!
FUAA (YAWN)
ふあ〜
DAMN!
OVER!
DAMN!

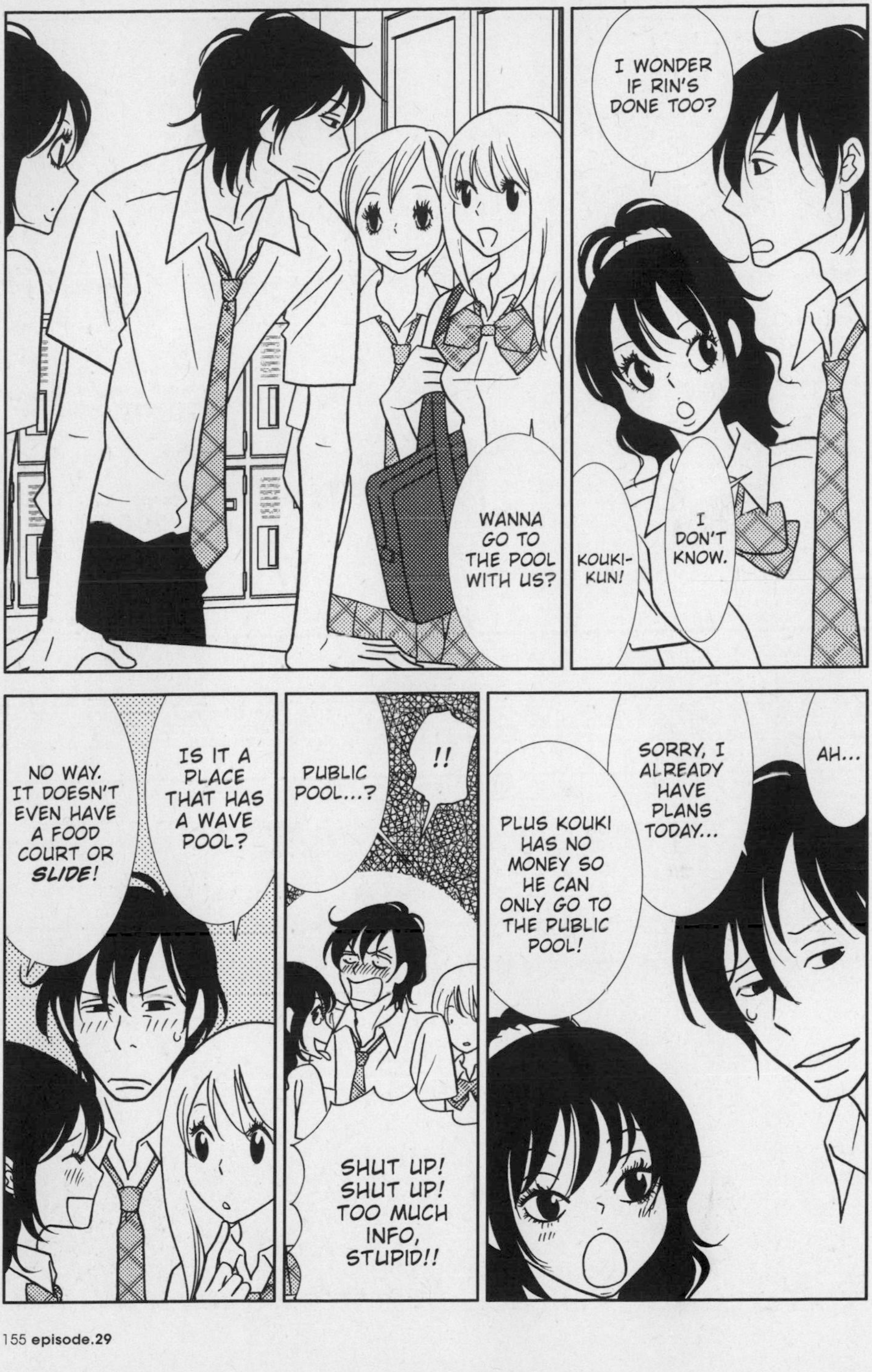
I WONDER IF RIN'S DONE TOO?
I DON'T KNOW.
KOUKI-KUN!
WANNA GO TO THE POOL WITH US?
AH...
SORRY, I ALREADY HAVE PLANS TODAY...
PLUS KOUKI HAS NO MONEY SO HE CAN ONLY GO TO THE PUBLIC POOL!
!!
PUBLIC POOL...?
SHUT UP! SHUT UP! TOO MUCH INFO, STUPID!!
IS IT A PLACE THAT HAS A WAVE POOL?
NO WAY. IT DOESN'T EVEN HAVE A FOOD COURT OR *SLIDE*!

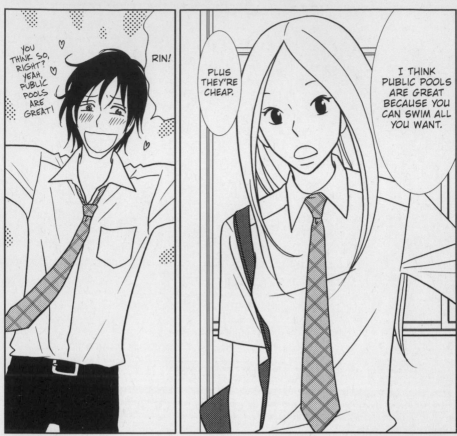

I THINK PUBLIC POOLS ARE GREAT BECAUSE YOU CAN SWIM ALL YOU WANT.
PLUS THEY'RE CHEAP.
RIN!
YOU THINK SO, RIGHT? YEAH, PUBLIC POOLS ARE GREAT!
ぎゅっ
GYU (HUG)
SURU (SLIP)
PLUS THE BULK PASSES ARE AN EVEN BETTER DISCOUNT.
OH, RIN.
AH-HA HA!
YOU'RE JUST LIKE A HOUSE-WIFE.
NINJA SLEIGHT OF HAND?
WE'RE GOING THERE LATER TODAY.
REALLY?

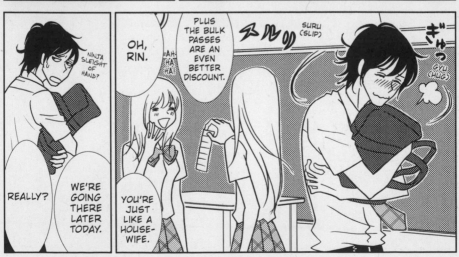

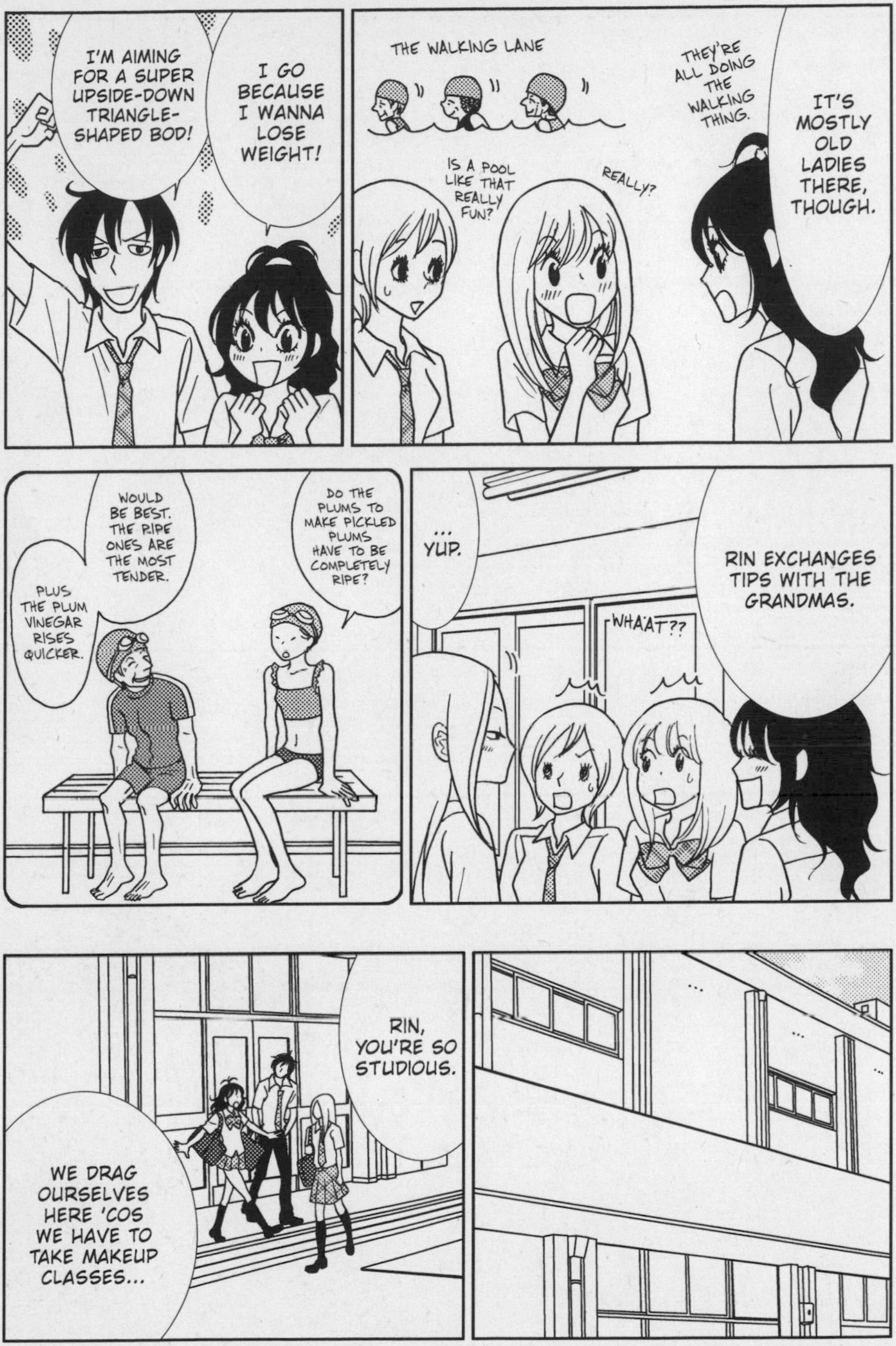
IT'S MOSTLY OLD LADIES THERE, THOUGH.
THEY'RE ALL DOING THE WALKING THING.
THE WALKING LANE
REALLY?
IS A POOL LIKE THAT REALLY FUN?
I GO BECAUSE I WANNA LOSE WEIGHT!
I'M AIMING FOR A SUPER UPSIDE-DOWN TRIANGLE-SHAPED BOD!
RIN EXCHANGES TIPS WITH THE GRANDMAS.
WHA'AT??
... YUP.
DO THE PLUMS TO MAKE PICKLED PLUMS HAVE TO BE COMPLETELY RIPE?
WOULD BE BEST. THE RIPE ONES ARE THE MOST TENDER.
PLUS THE PLUM VINEGAR RISES QUICKER.
...
...
...
RIN, YOU'RE SO STUDIOUS.
WE DRAG OURSELVES HERE 'COS WE HAVE TO TAKE MAKEUP CLASSES...

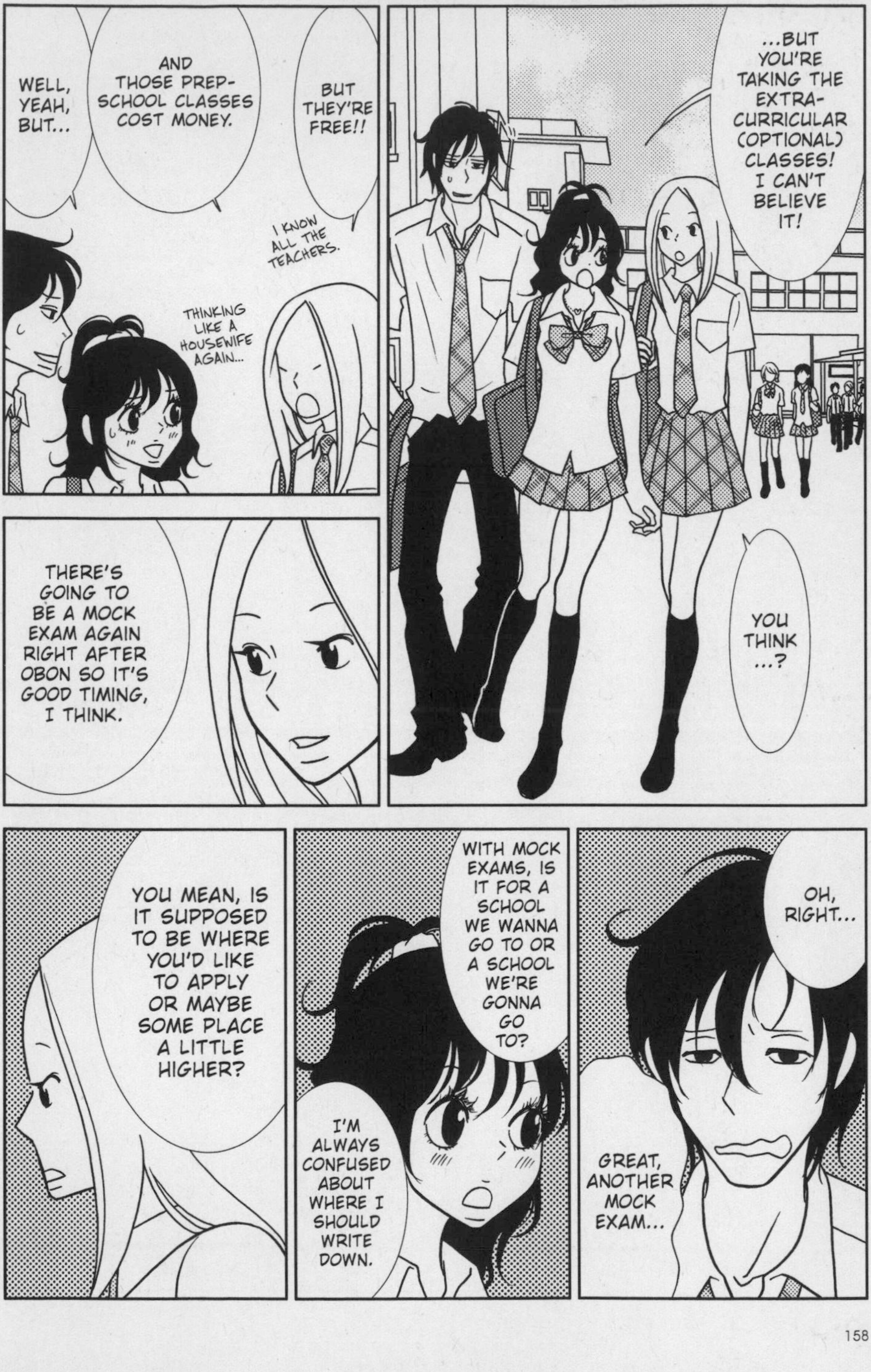
...BUT YOU'RE TAKING THE EXTRA-CURRICULAR (OPTIONAL) CLASSES! I CAN'T BELIEVE IT!
YOU THINK ...?
BUT THEY'RE FREE!!
I KNOW ALL THE TEACHERS.
AND THOSE PREP-SCHOOL CLASSES COST MONEY.
WELL, YEAH, BUT...
THINKING LIKE A HOUSEWIFE AGAIN...
THERE'S GOING TO BE A MOCK EXAM AGAIN RIGHT AFTER OBON SO IT'S GOOD TIMING, I THINK.
OH, RIGHT...
GREAT, ANOTHER MOCK EXAM...
WITH MOCK EXAMS, IS IT FOR A SCHOOL WE WANNA GO TO OR A SCHOOL WE'RE GONNA GO TO?
I'M ALWAYS CONFUSED ABOUT WHERE I SHOULD WRITE DOWN.
YOU MEAN, IS IT SUPPOSED TO BE WHERE YOU'D LIKE TO APPLY OR MAYBE SOME PLACE A LITTLE HIGHER?

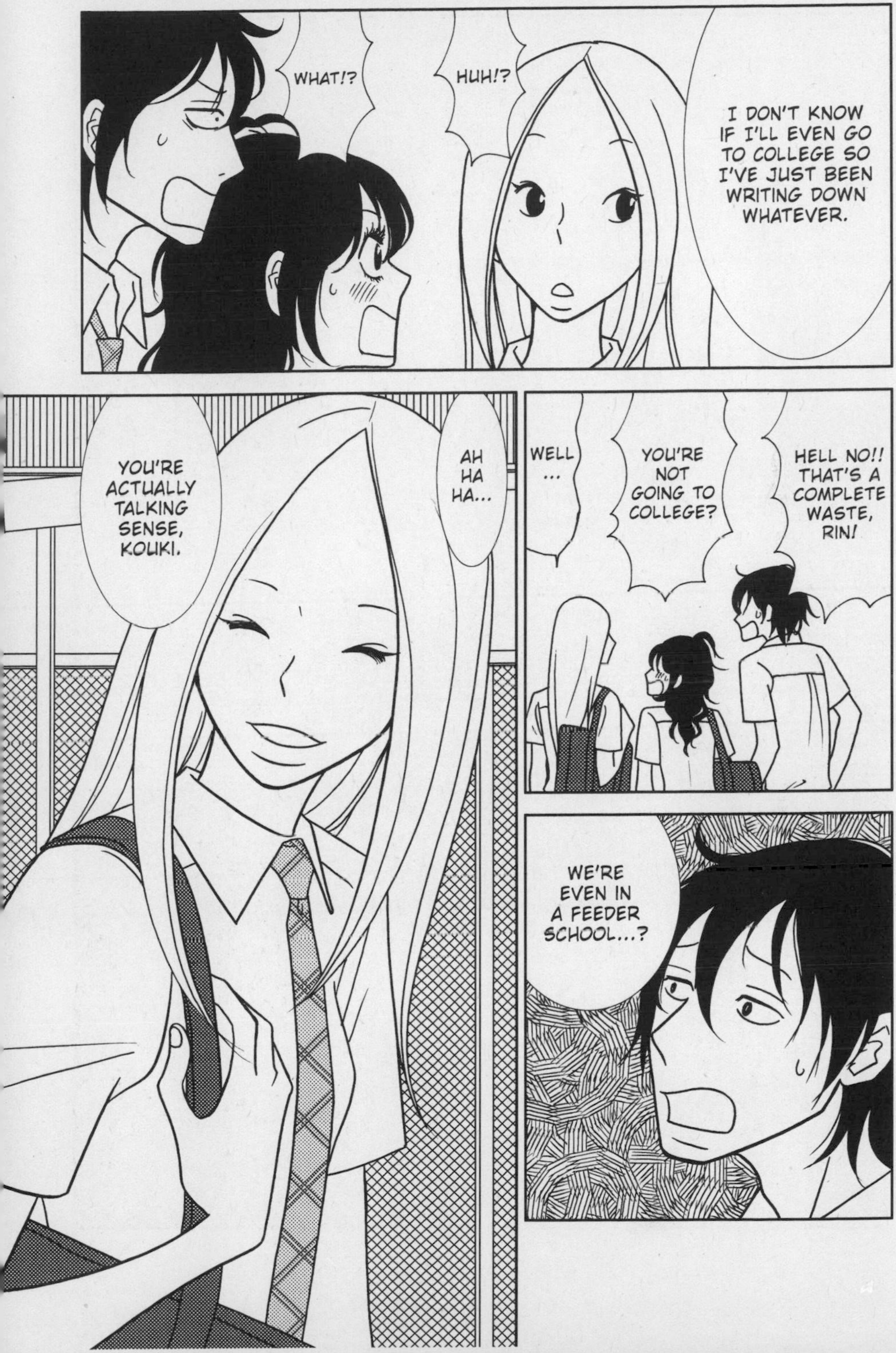
I DON'T KNOW IF I'LL EVEN GO TO COLLEGE SO I'VE JUST BEEN WRITING DOWN WHATEVER.
HUH!?
WHAT!?
HELL NO!! THAT'S A COMPLETE WASTE, RIN!
YOU'RE NOT GOING TO COLLEGE?
WELL ...
WE'RE EVEN IN A FEEDER SCHOOL...?
AH HA HA...
YOU'RE ACTUALLY TALKING SENSE, KOUKI.

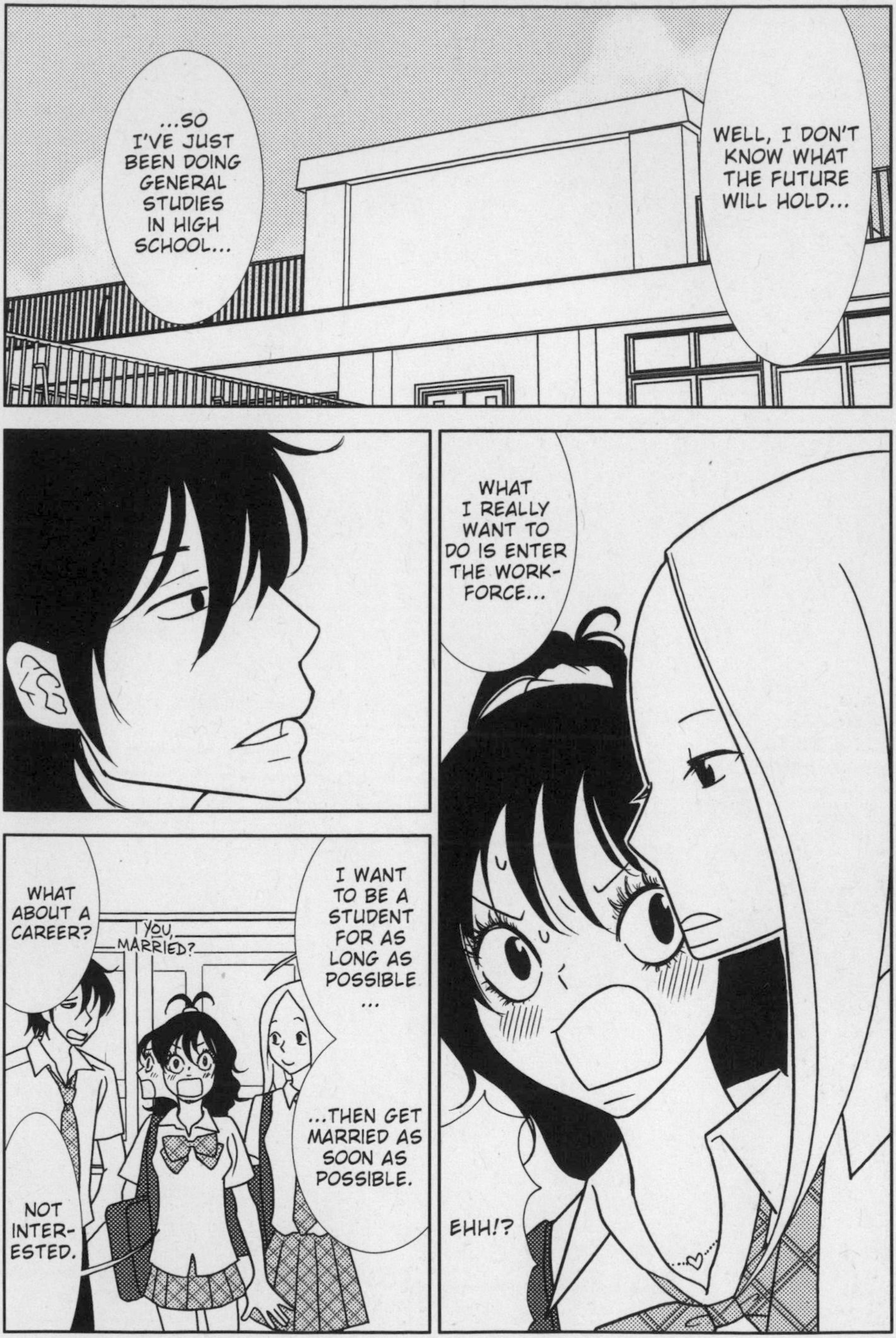

WELL, I DON'T KNOW WHAT THE FUTURE WILL HOLD...
...SO I'VE JUST BEEN DOING GENERAL STUDIES IN HIGH SCHOOL...
WHAT I REALLY WANT TO DO IS ENTER THE WORK-FORCE...
EHH!?
I WANT TO BE A STUDENT FOR AS LONG AS POSSIBLE ...
...THEN GET MARRIED AS SOON AS POSSIBLE.
YOU, MARRIED?
WHAT ABOUT A CAREER?
NOT INTER-ESTED.

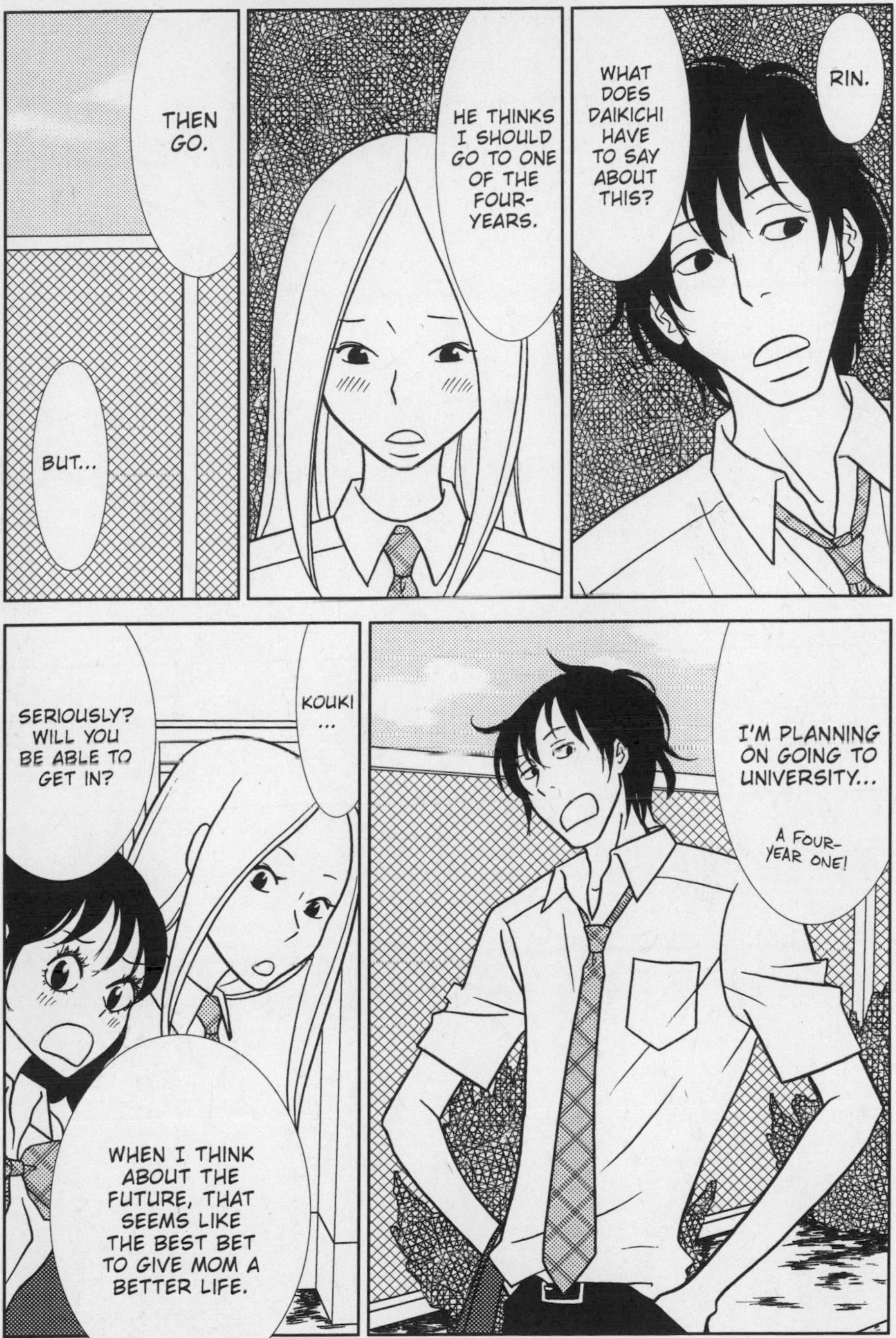
RIN.
WHAT DOES DAIKICHI HAVE TO SAY ABOUT THIS?
HE THINKS I SHOULD GO TO ONE OF THE FOUR-YEARS.
THEN GO.
BUT...
I'M PLANNING ON GOING TO UNIVERSITY...
A FOUR-YEAR ONE!
KOUKI ...
SERIOUSLY? WILL YOU BE ABLE TO GET IN?
WHEN I THINK ABOUT THE FUTURE, THAT SEEMS LIKE THE BEST BET TO GIVE MOM A BETTER LIFE.

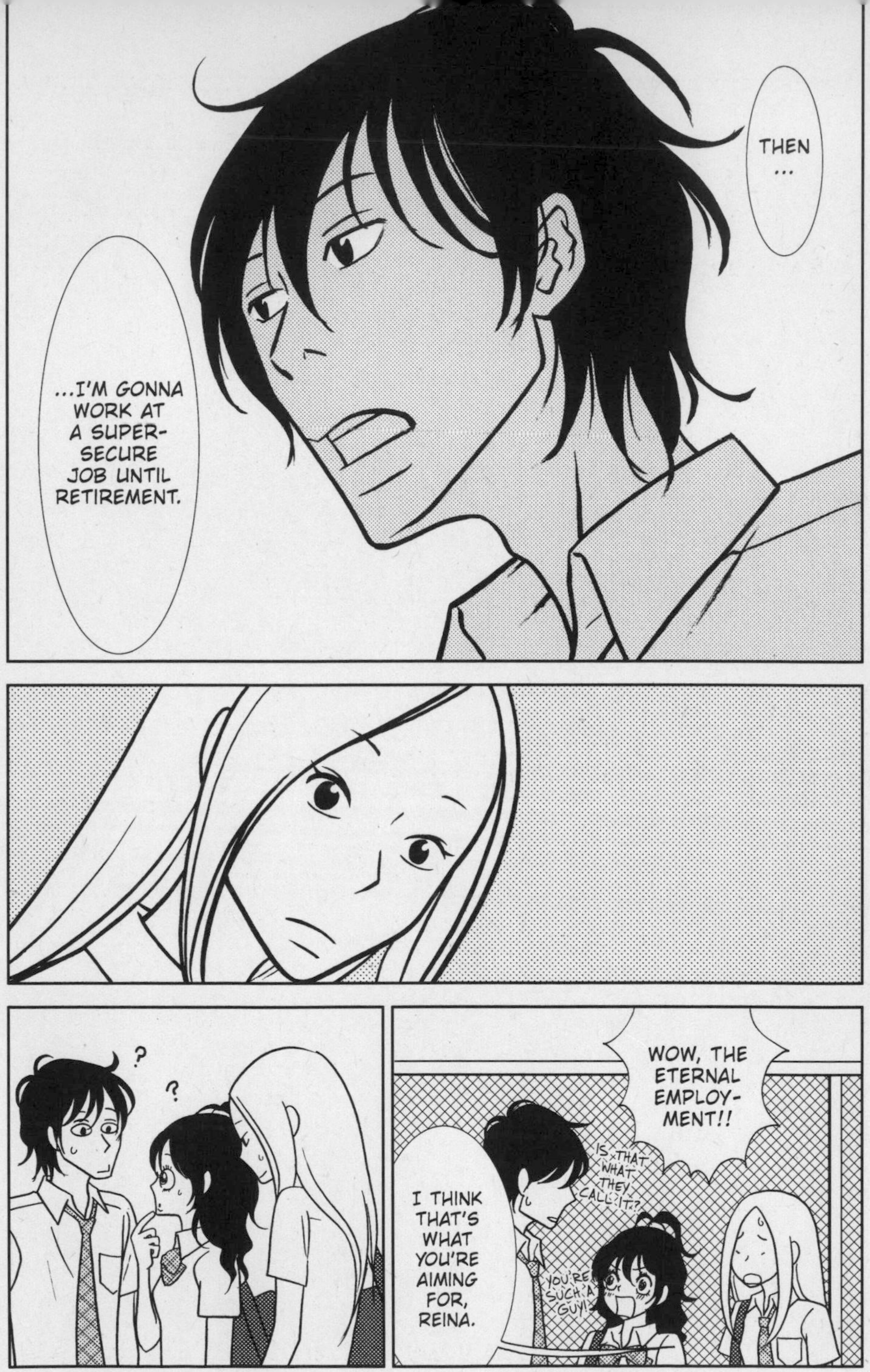
THEN...
...I'M GONNA WORK AT A SUPER-SECURE JOB UNTIL RETIREMENT.
WOW, THE ETERNAL EMPLOY-MENT!!
IS THAT WHAT THEY CALL IT?
I THINK THAT'S WHAT YOU'RE AIMING FOR, REINA.
YOU'RE SUCH A GUY!
?
?

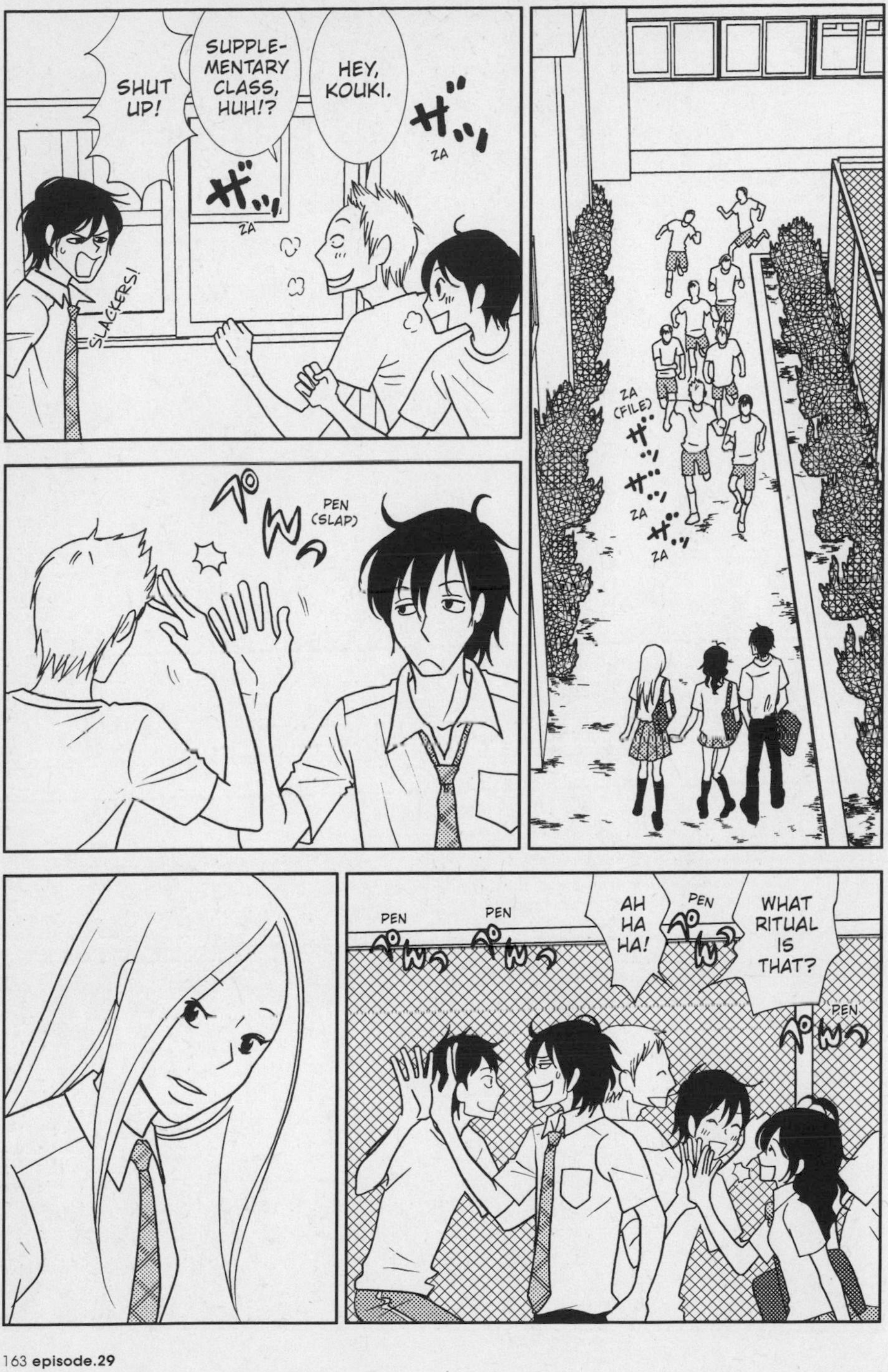
ZA (FILE)
ZA
ZA
HEY, KOUKI.
SUPPLEMENTARY CLASS, HUH!?
SHUT UP!
SLACKERS!
ZA
ZA
PEN (SLAP)
PEN
WHAT RITUAL IS THAT?
PEN
AH HA HA!
PEN
PEN

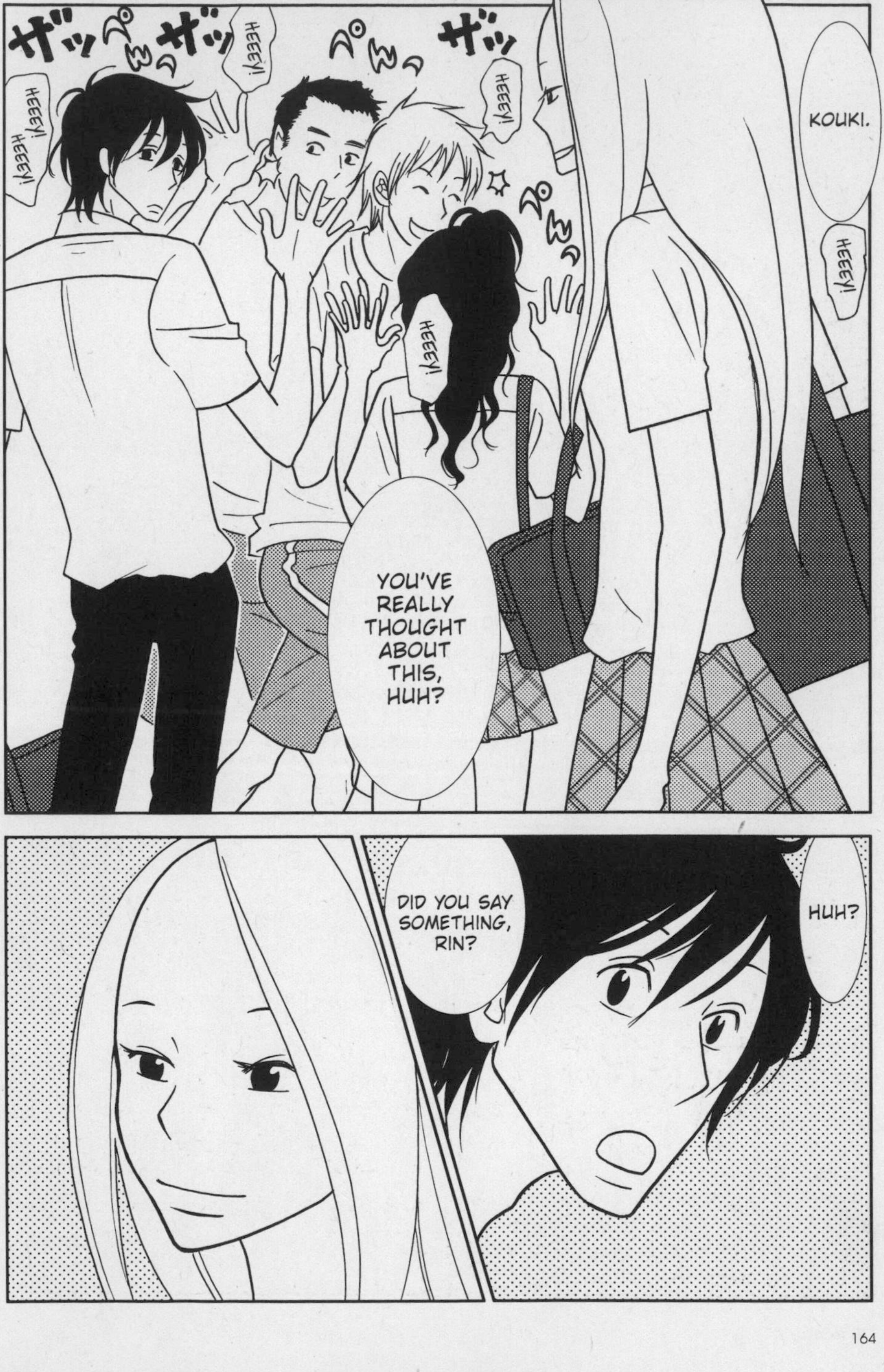
KOUKI.
HEEEY!
HEEEY!
HEEEY!
HEEEY!
HEEEY!
HEEEY!
YOU'VE REALLY THOUGHT ABOUT THIS, HUH?
HUH?
DID YOU SAY SOMETHING, RIN?

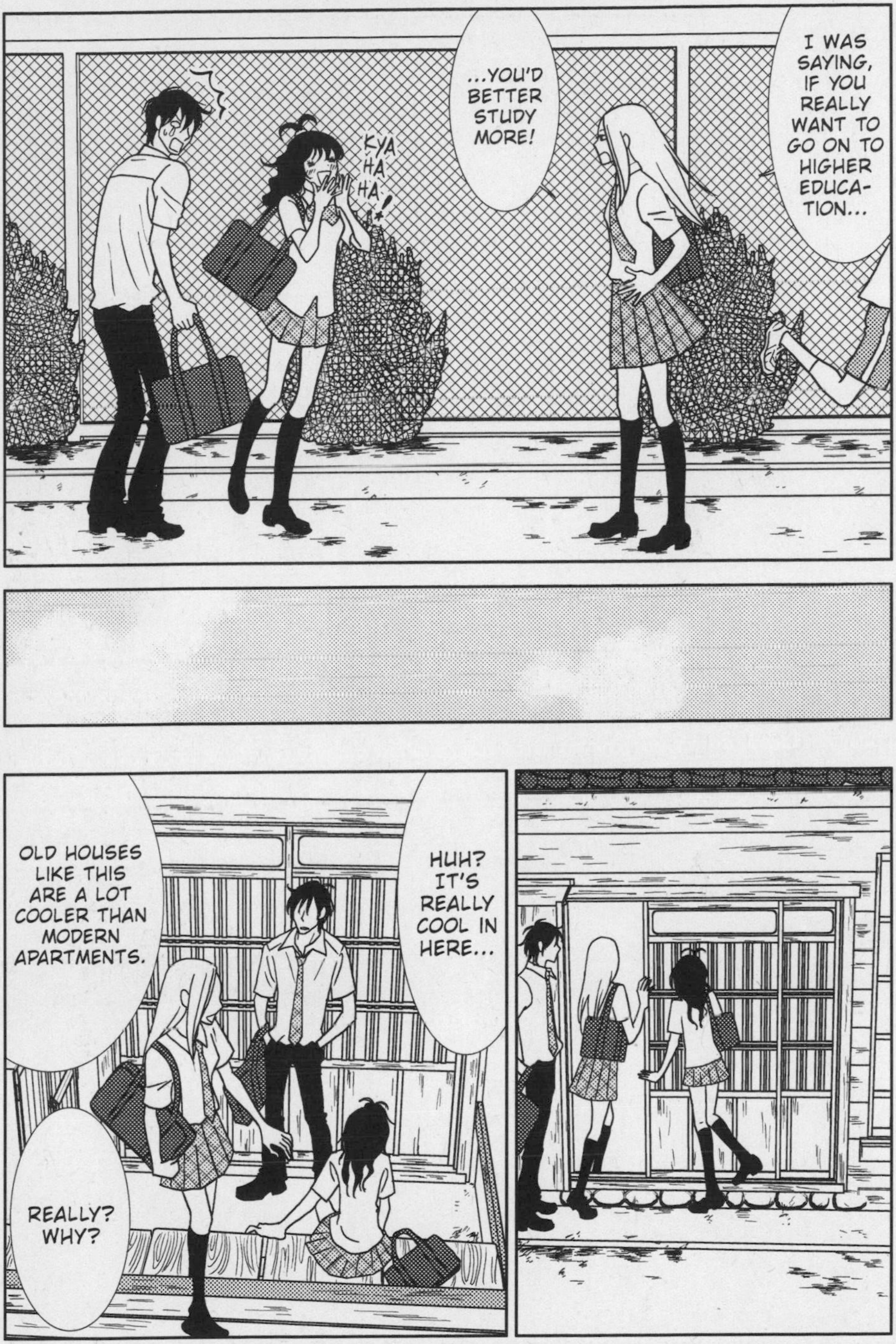
I WAS SAYING, IF YOU REALLY WANT TO GO ON TO HIGHER EDUCATION...
...YOU'D BETTER STUDY MORE!
KYA HA HA!
HUH? IT'S REALLY COOL IN HERE...
OLD HOUSES LIKE THIS ARE A LOT COOLER THAN MODERN APARTMENTS.
REALLY? WHY?

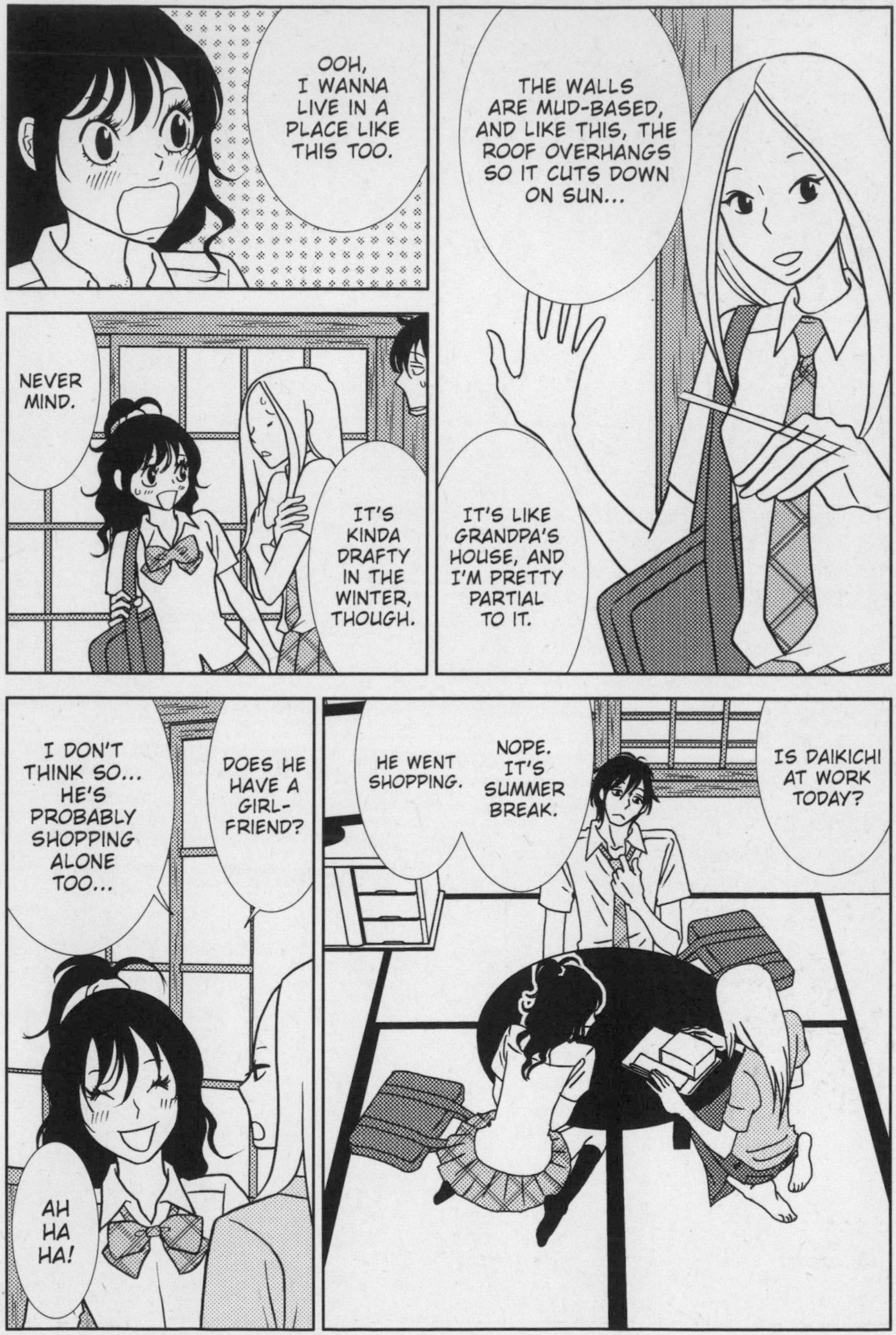
THE WALLS ARE MUD-BASED, AND LIKE THIS, THE ROOF OVERHANGS SO IT CUTS DOWN ON SUN...
IT'S LIKE GRANDPA'S HOUSE, AND I'M PRETTY PARTIAL TO IT.
OOH, I WANNA LIVE IN A PLACE LIKE THIS TOO.
IT'S KINDA DRAFTY IN THE WINTER, THOUGH.
NEVER MIND.
IS DAIKICHI AT WORK TODAY?
NOPE. IT'S SUMMER BREAK.
HE WENT SHOPPING.
DOES HE HAVE A GIRL-FRIEND?
I DON'T THINK SO... HE'S PROBABLY SHOPPING ALONE TOO...
AH HA HA!

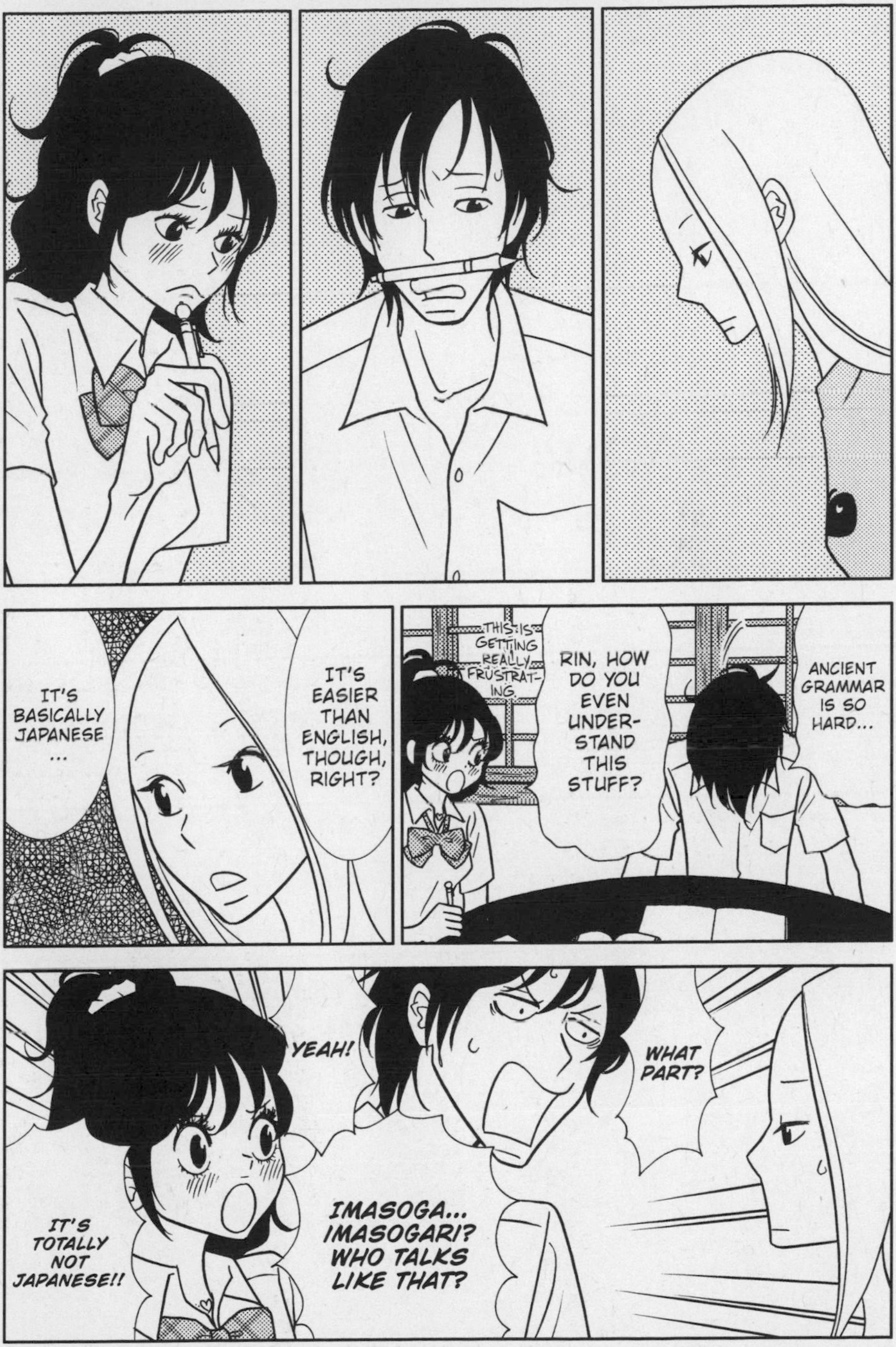
ANCIENT GRAMMAR IS SO HARD...
RIN, HOW DO YOU EVEN UNDER-STAND THIS STUFF?
THIS IS GETTING REALLY FRUSTRAT-ING.
IT'S EASIER THAN ENGLISH, THOUGH, RIGHT?
IT'S BASICALLY JAPANESE ...
WHAT PART?
YEAH!
IMASOGA... IMASOGARI? WHO TALKS LIKE THAT?
IT'S TOTALLY NOT JAPANESE!!

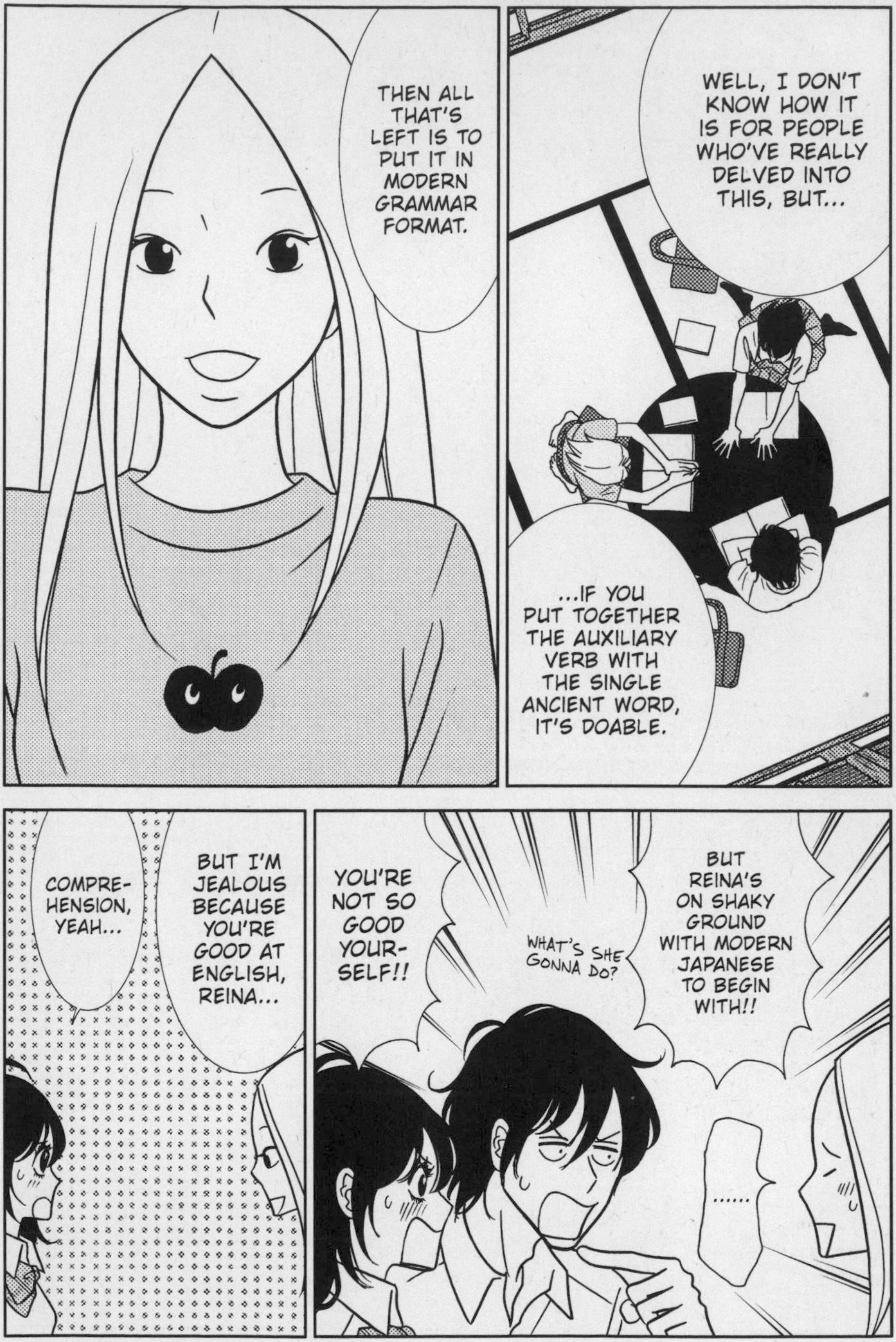
WELL, I DON'T KNOW HOW IT IS FOR PEOPLE WHO'VE REALLY DELVED INTO THIS, BUT...
...IF YOU PUT TOGETHER THE AUXILIARY VERB WITH THE SINGLE ANCIENT WORD, IT'S DOABLE.
THEN ALL THAT'S LEFT IS TO PUT IT IN MODERN GRAMMAR FORMAT.
BUT REINA'S ON SHAKY GROUND WITH MODERN JAPANESE TO BEGIN WITH!!
WHAT'S SHE GONNA DO?
YOU'RE NOT SO GOOD YOURSELF!!
......
BUT I'M JEALOUS BECAUSE YOU'RE GOOD AT ENGLISH, REINA...
COMPREHENSION, YEAH...

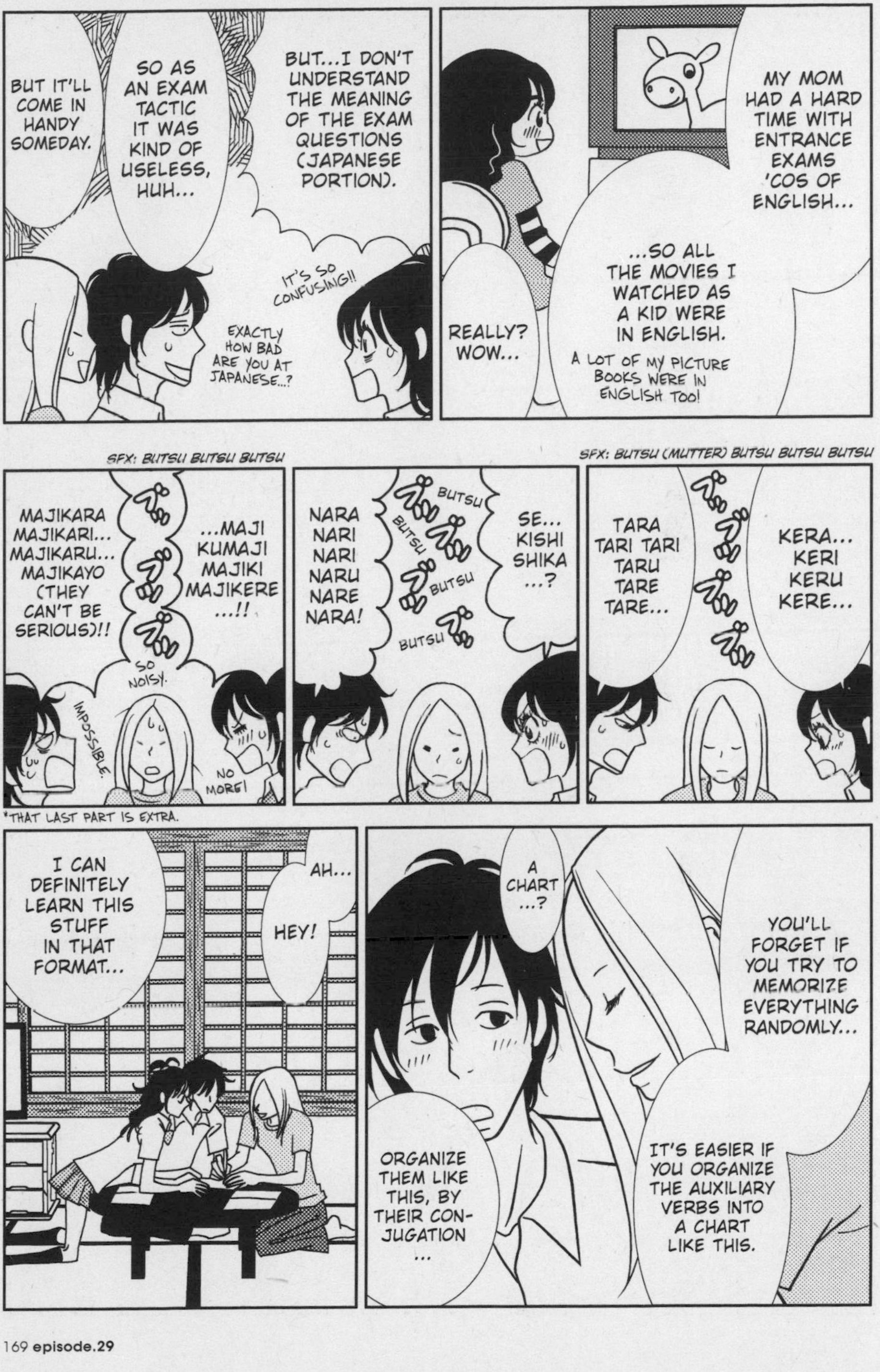
MY MOM HAD A HARD TIME WITH ENTRANCE EXAMS 'COS OF ENGLISH...
...SO ALL THE MOVIES I WATCHED AS A KID WERE IN ENGLISH.
A LOT OF MY PICTURE BOOKS WERE IN ENGLISH TOO!
REALLY? WOW...
BUT...I DON'T UNDERSTAND THE MEANING OF THE EXAM QUESTIONS (JAPANESE PORTION).
SO AS AN EXAM TACTIC IT WAS KIND OF USELESS, HUH...
BUT IT'LL COME IN HANDY SOMEDAY.
IT'S SO CONFUSING!!
EXACTLY HOW BAD ARE YOU AT JAPANESE...?
SFX: BUTSU (MUTTER) BUTSU BUTSU BUTSU
KERA... KERI KERU KERE...
TARA TARI TARI TARU TARE TARE...
SE... KISHI SHIKA ...?
BUTSU
BUTSU
BUTSU
BUTSU
NARA NARI NARI NARU NARE NARA!
SFX: BUTSU BUTSU BUTSU
...MAJI KUMAJI MAJIKI MAJIKERE ...!!
MAJIKARA MAJIKARI... MAJIKARU... MAJIKAYO (THEY CAN'T BE SERIOUS)!!
SO NOISY.
NO MORE!
IMPOSSIBLE.
*THAT LAST PART IS EXTRA.
A CHART ...?
YOU'LL FORGET IF YOU TRY TO MEMORIZE EVERYTHING RANDOMLY...
IT'S EASIER IF YOU ORGANIZE THE AUXILIARY VERBS INTO A CHART LIKE THIS.
ORGANIZE THEM LIKE THIS, BY THEIR CONJUGATION ...
AH...
HEY!
I CAN DEFINITELY LEARN THIS STUFF IN THAT FORMAT...

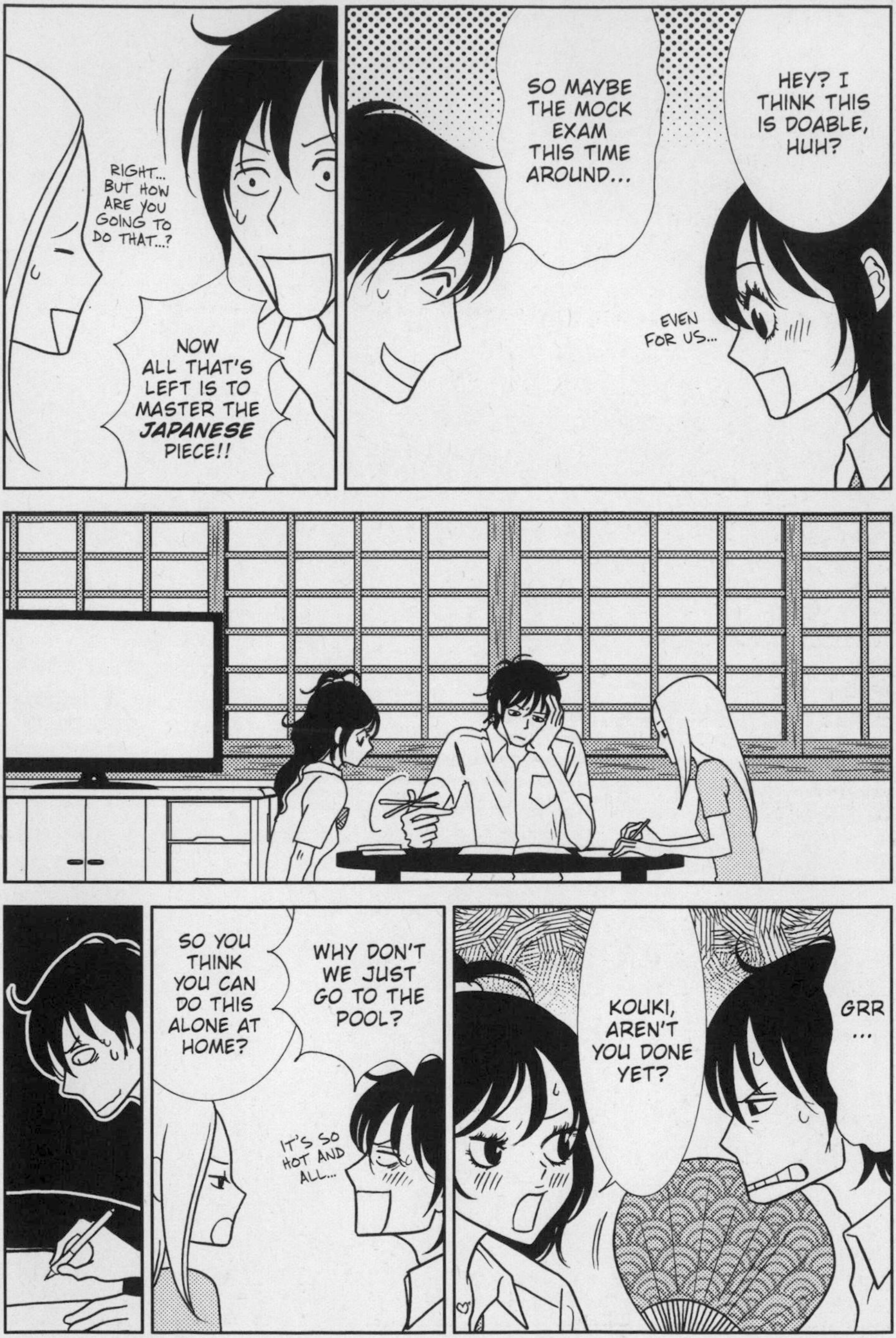
HEY? I THINK THIS IS DOABLE, HUH?
SO MAYBE THE MOCK EXAM THIS TIME AROUND...
EVEN FOR US...
NOW ALL THAT'S LEFT IS TO MASTER THE ***JAPANESE*** PIECE!!
RIGHT... BUT HOW ARE YOU GOING TO DO THAT...?
KOUKI, AREN'T YOU DONE YET?
GRR ...
WHY DON'T WE JUST GO TO THE POOL?
IT'S SO HOT AND ALL...
SO YOU THINK YOU CAN DO THIS ALONE AT HOME?

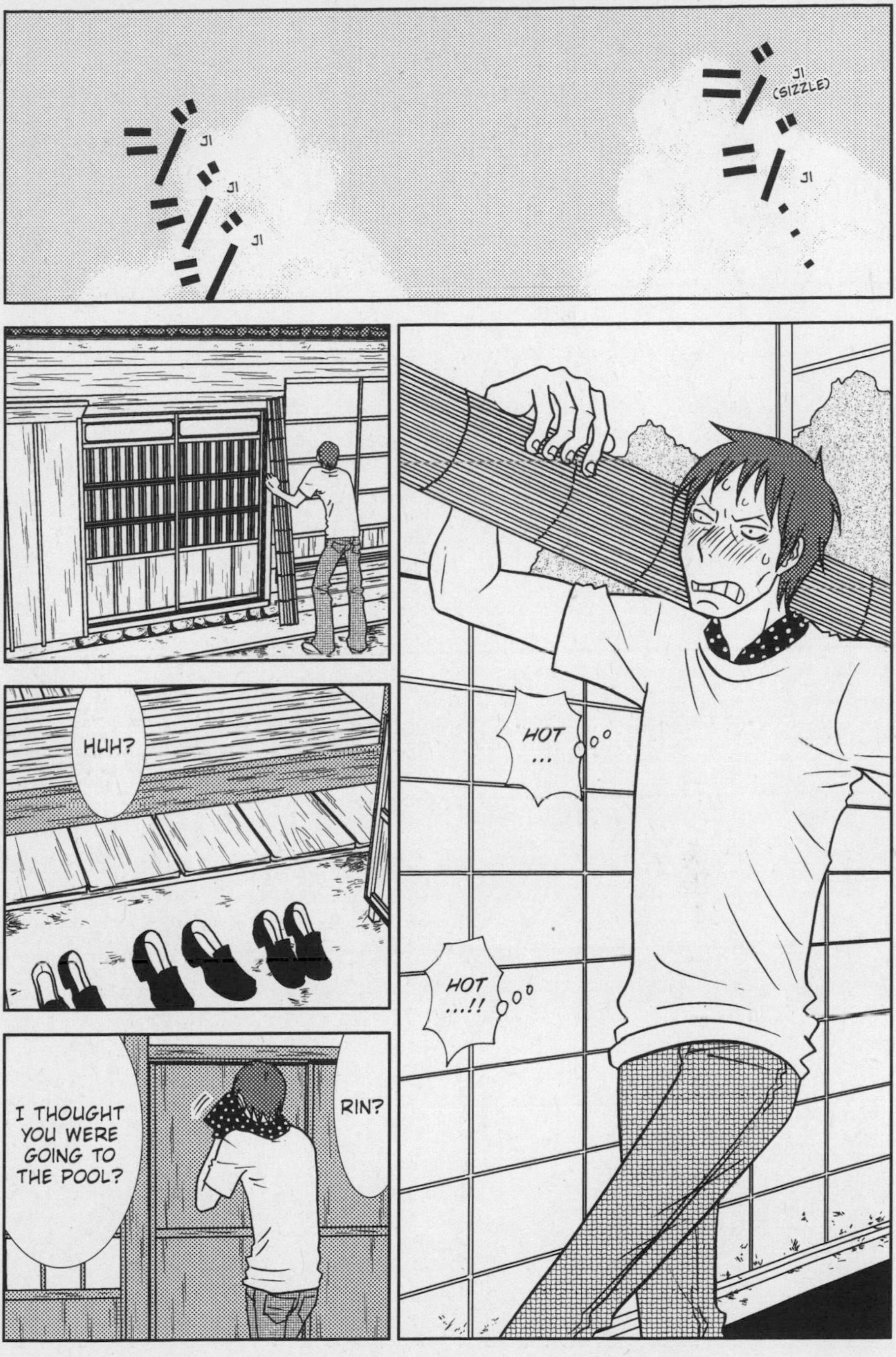
JI
(SIZZLE)
JI
JI
JI
JI
HOT ...
HOT ...!!
HUH?
RIN?
I THOUGHT YOU WERE GOING TO THE POOL?

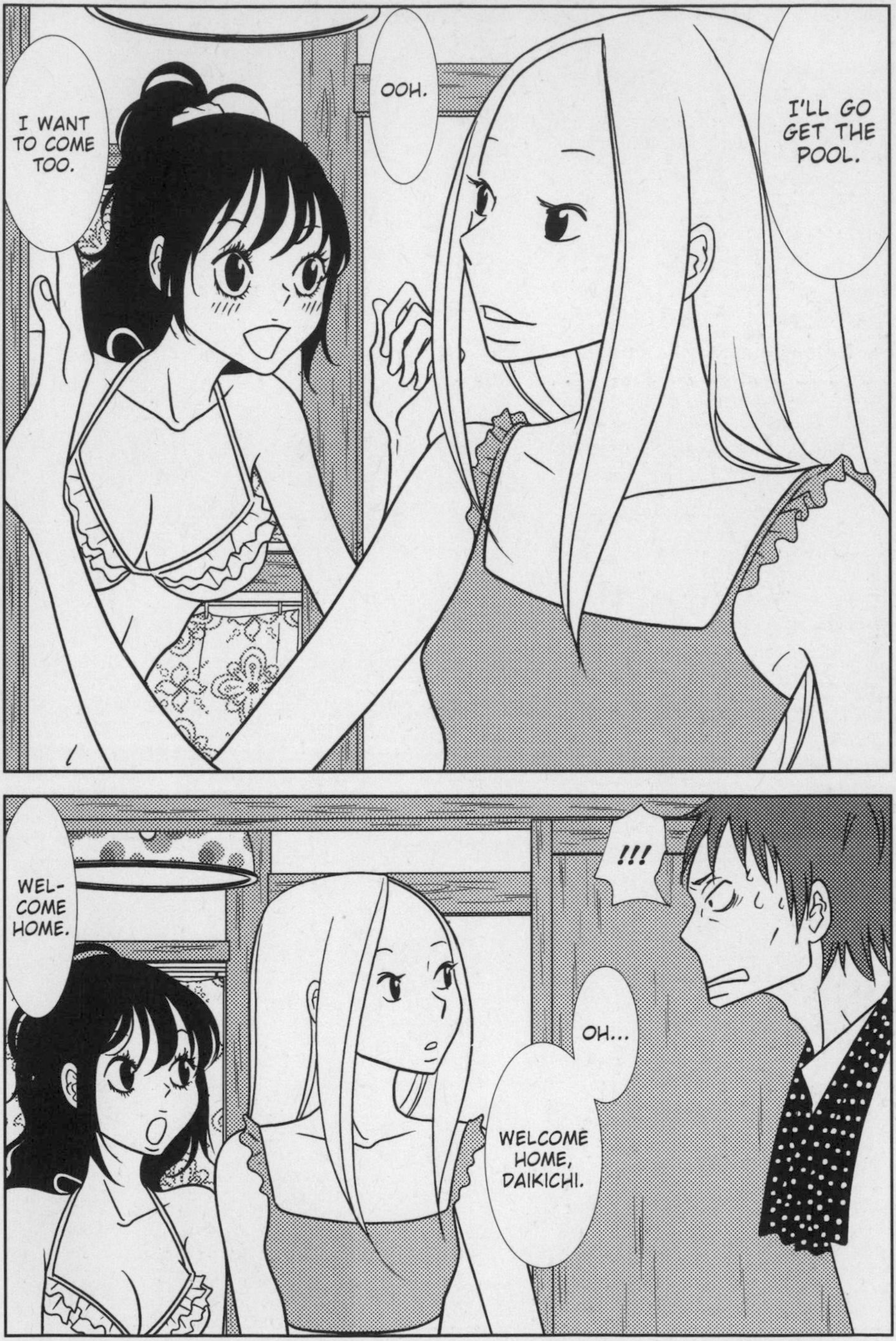
I'LL GO GET THE POOL.
OOH.
I WANT TO COME TOO.
!!!
OH...
WELCOME HOME, DAIKICHI.
WEL-COME HOME.

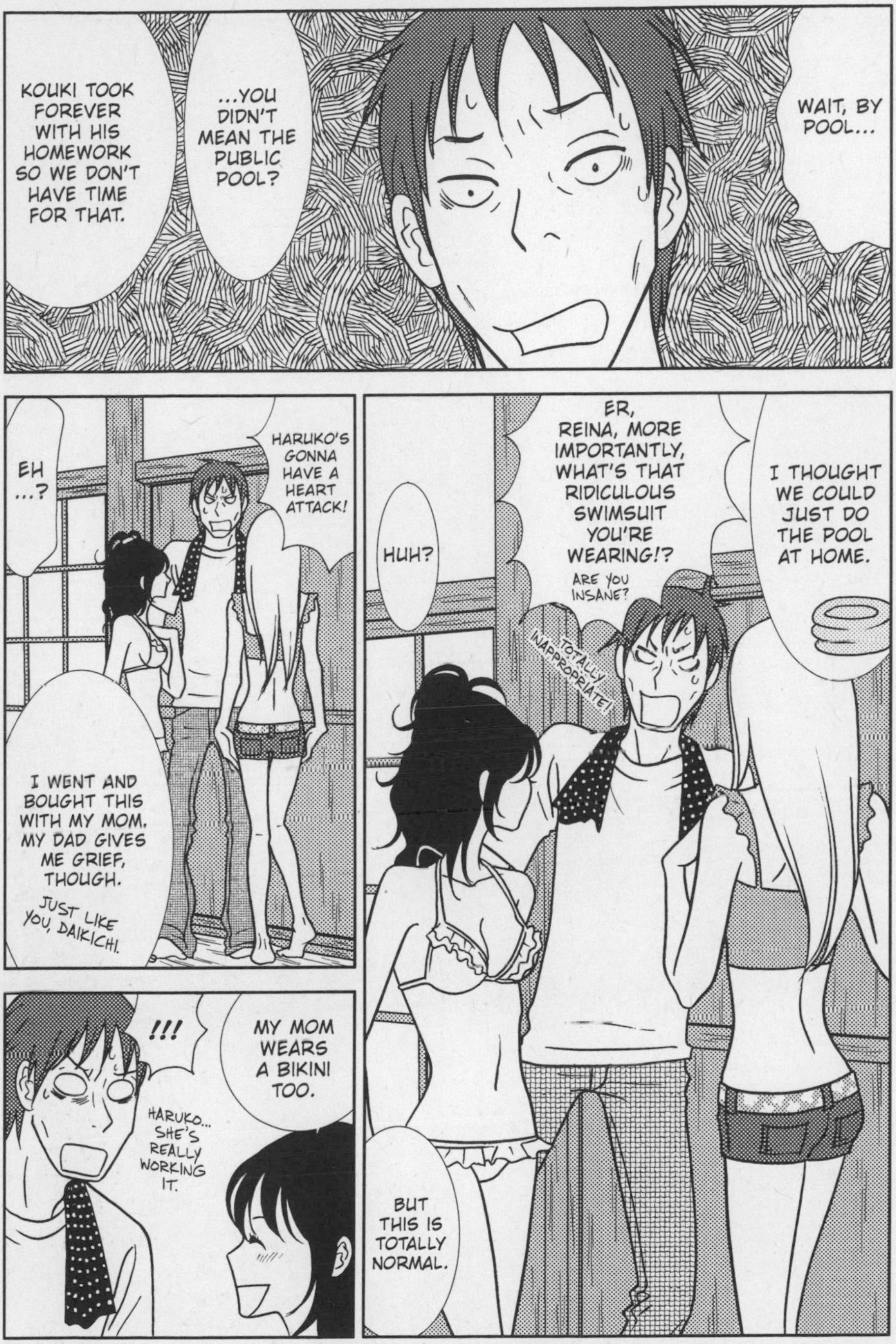
WAIT, BY POOL...
...YOU DIDN'T MEAN THE PUBLIC POOL?
KOUKI TOOK FOREVER WITH HIS HOMEWORK SO WE DON'T HAVE TIME FOR THAT.
I THOUGHT WE COULD JUST DO THE POOL AT HOME.
ER, REINA, MORE IMPORTANTLY, WHAT'S THAT RIDICULOUS SWIMSUIT YOU'RE WEARING!?
ARE YOU INSANE?
TOTALLY INAPPROPRIATE!
HUH?
BUT THIS IS TOTALLY NORMAL.
HARUKO'S GONNA HAVE A HEART ATTACK!
EH ...?
I WENT AND BOUGHT THIS WITH MY MOM. MY DAD GIVES ME GRIEF, THOUGH.
JUST LIKE YOU, DAIKICHI.
MY MOM WEARS A BIKINI TOO.
!!!
HARUKO... SHE'S REALLY WORKING IT.

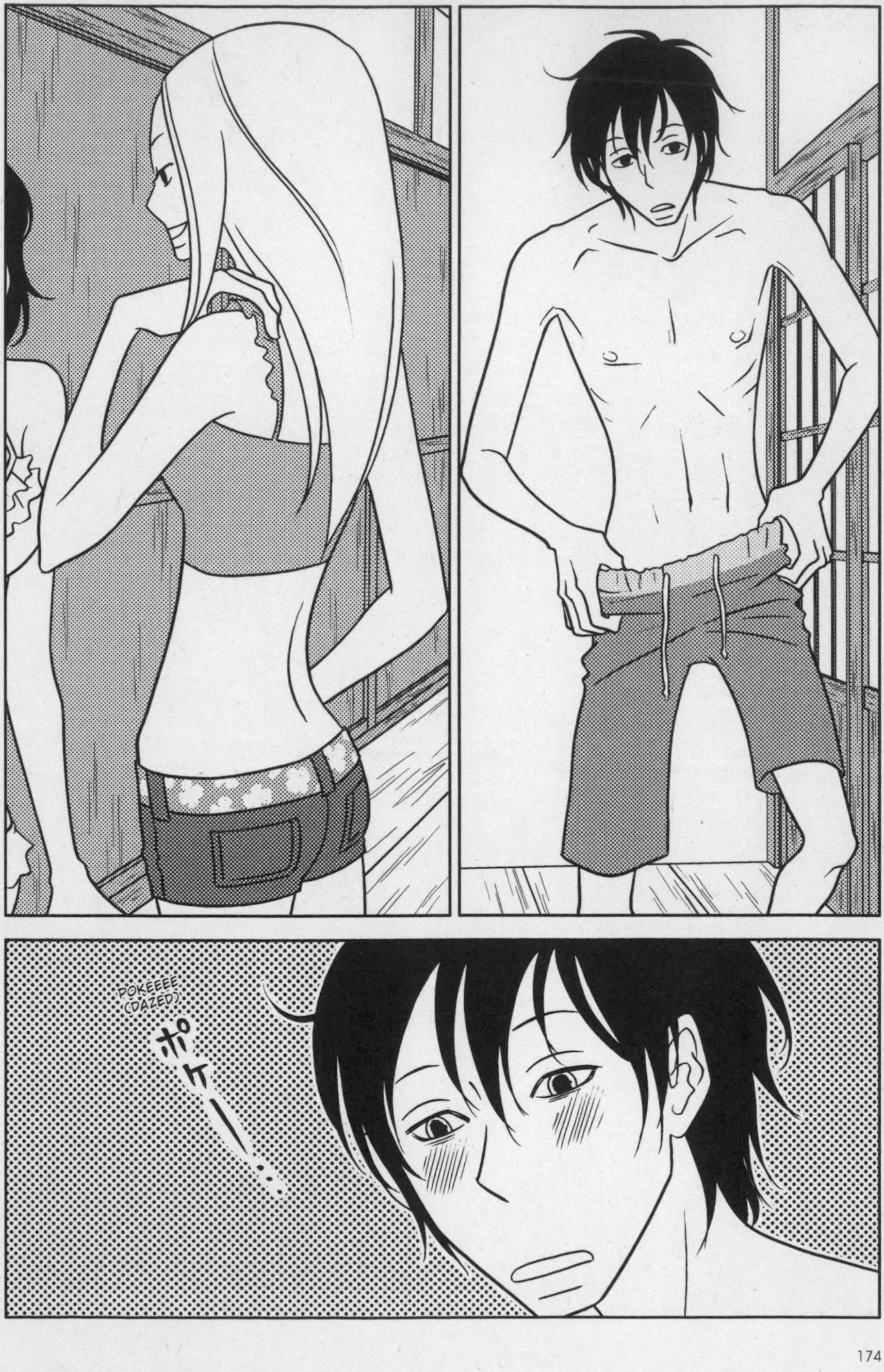
POKEEEE (DAZED)
ポケー

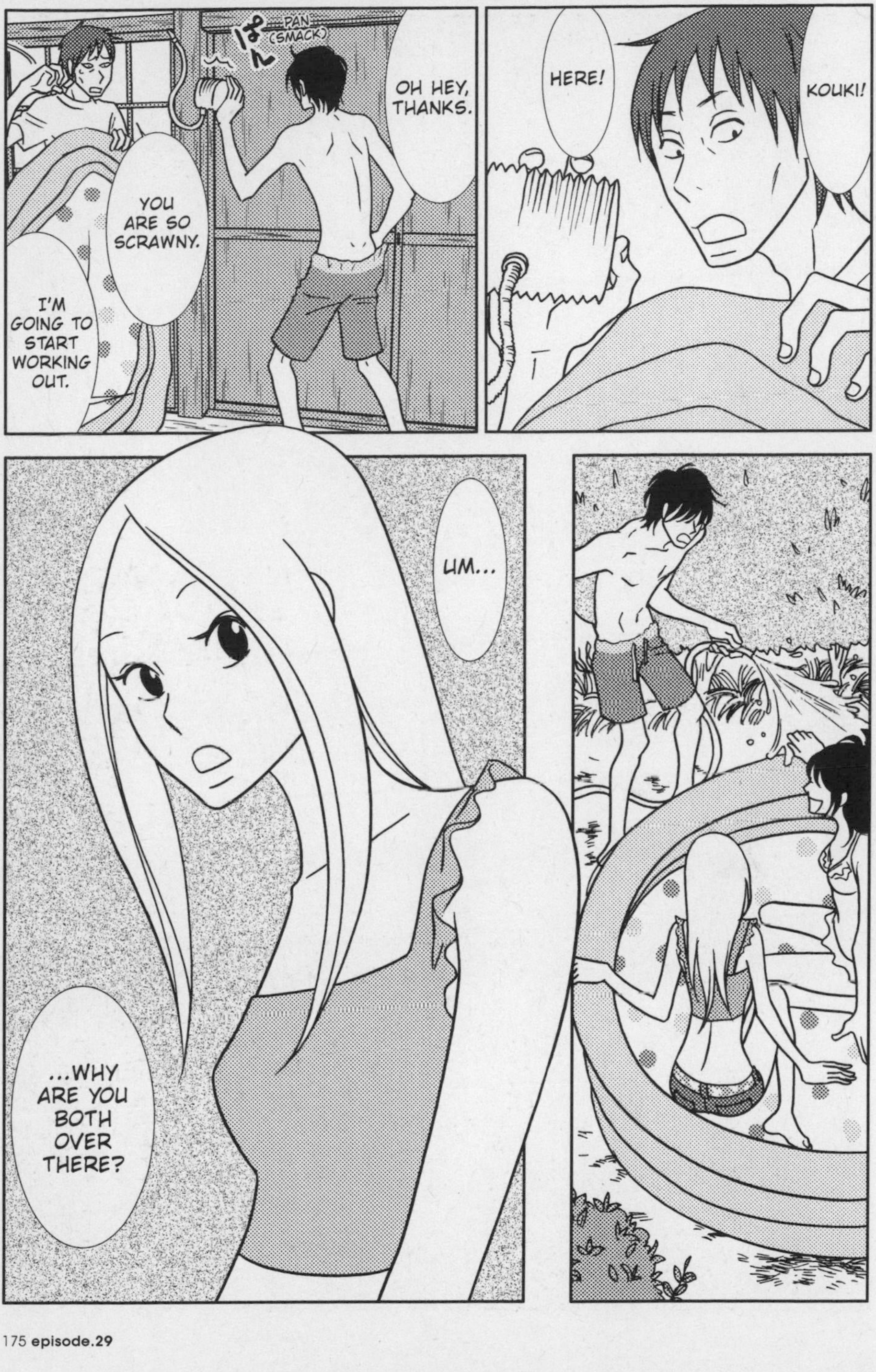
KOUKI!
HERE!
OH HEY, THANKS.
ぱん
PAN (SMACK)
YOU ARE SO SCRAWNY.
I'M GOING TO START WORKING OUT.
UM...
...WHY ARE YOU BOTH OVER THERE?

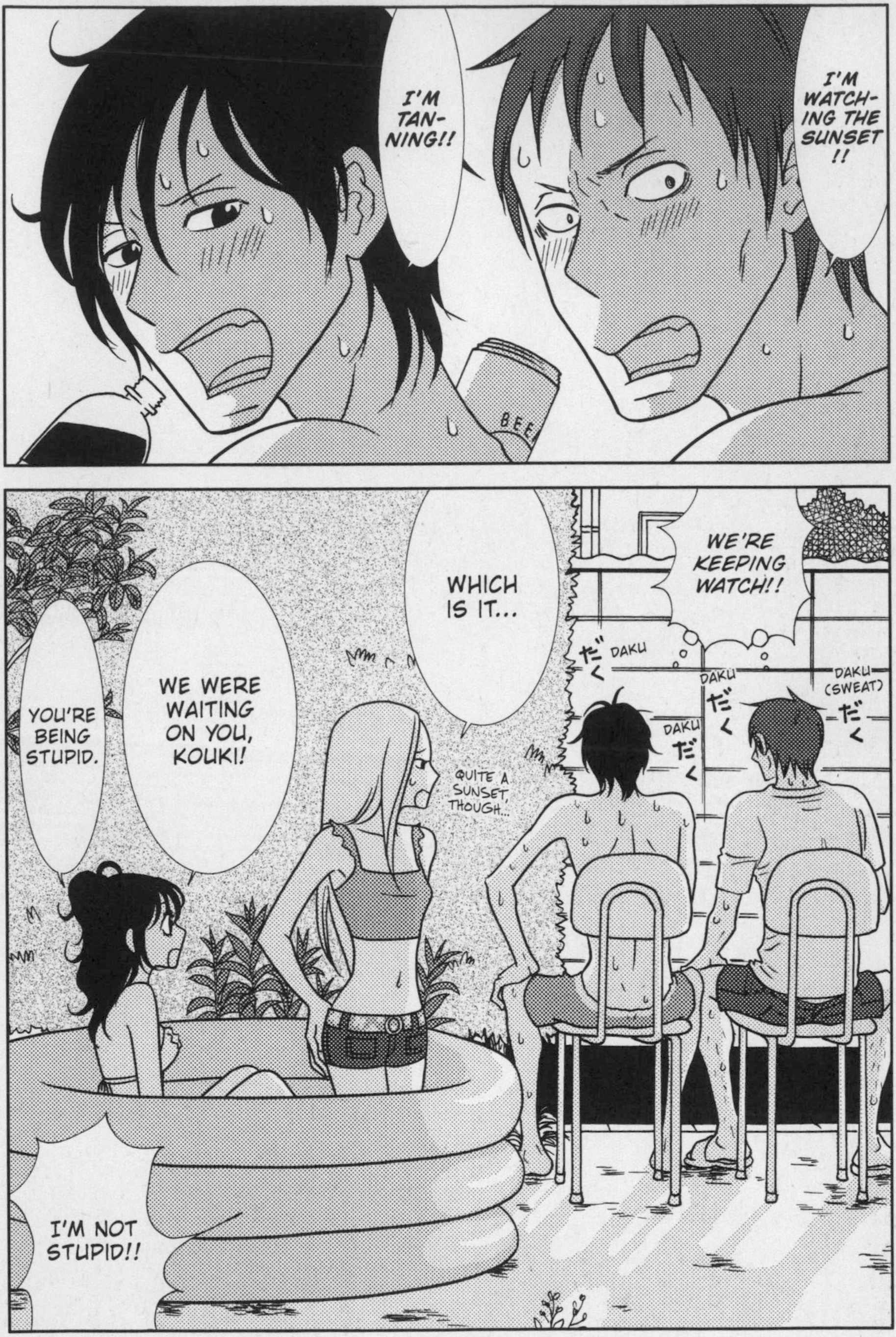
I'M WATCHING THE SUNSET!!
I'M TANNING!!
WE'RE KEEPING WATCH!!
だく DAKU (SWEAT)
だく DAKU
だく DAKU
だく DAKU
WHICH IS IT...
QUITE A SUNSET, THOUGH...
WE WERE WAITING ON YOU, KOUKI!
YOU'RE BEING STUPID.
I'M NOT STUPID!!

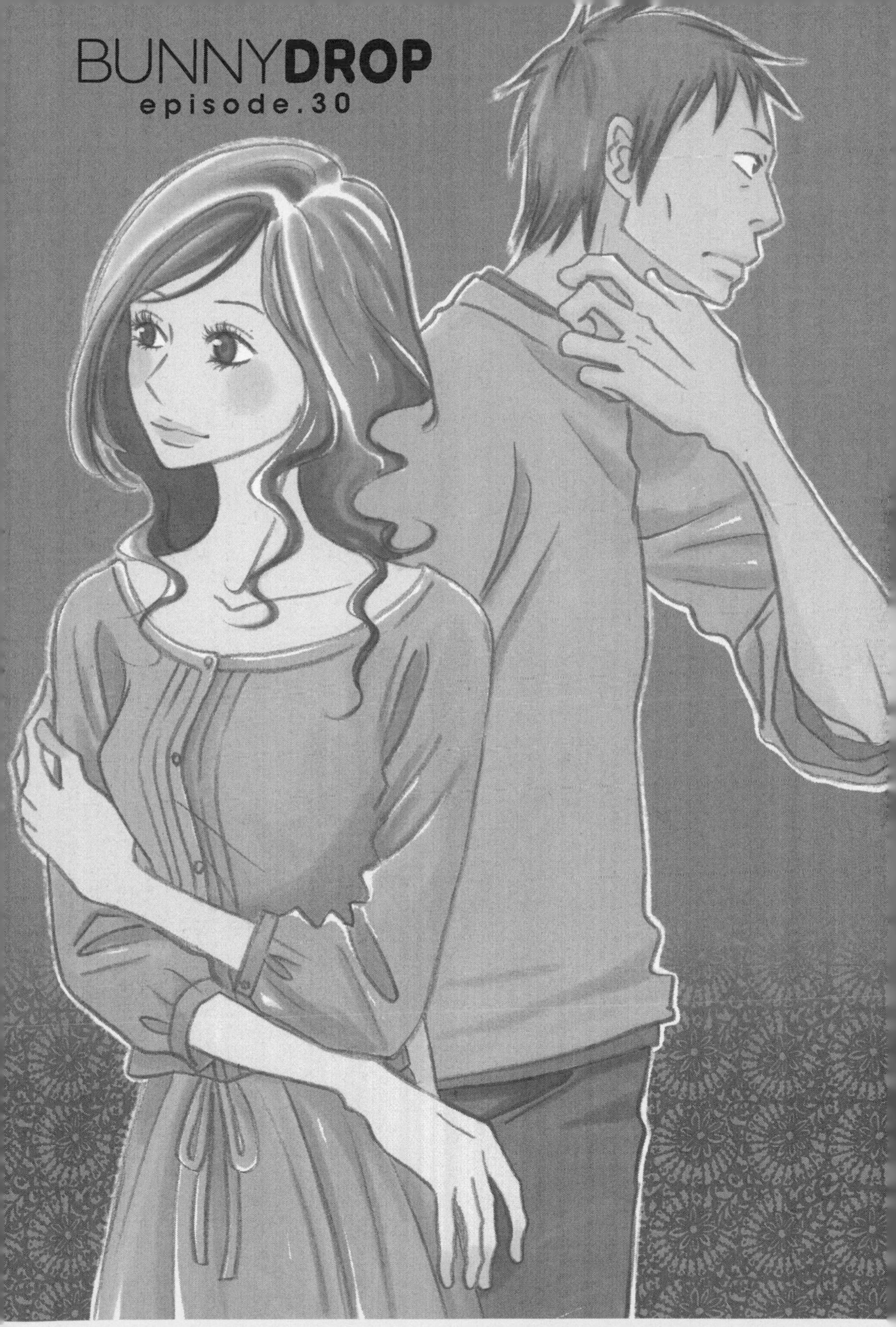
BUNNY DROP
episode.30

BUNNY**DROP**

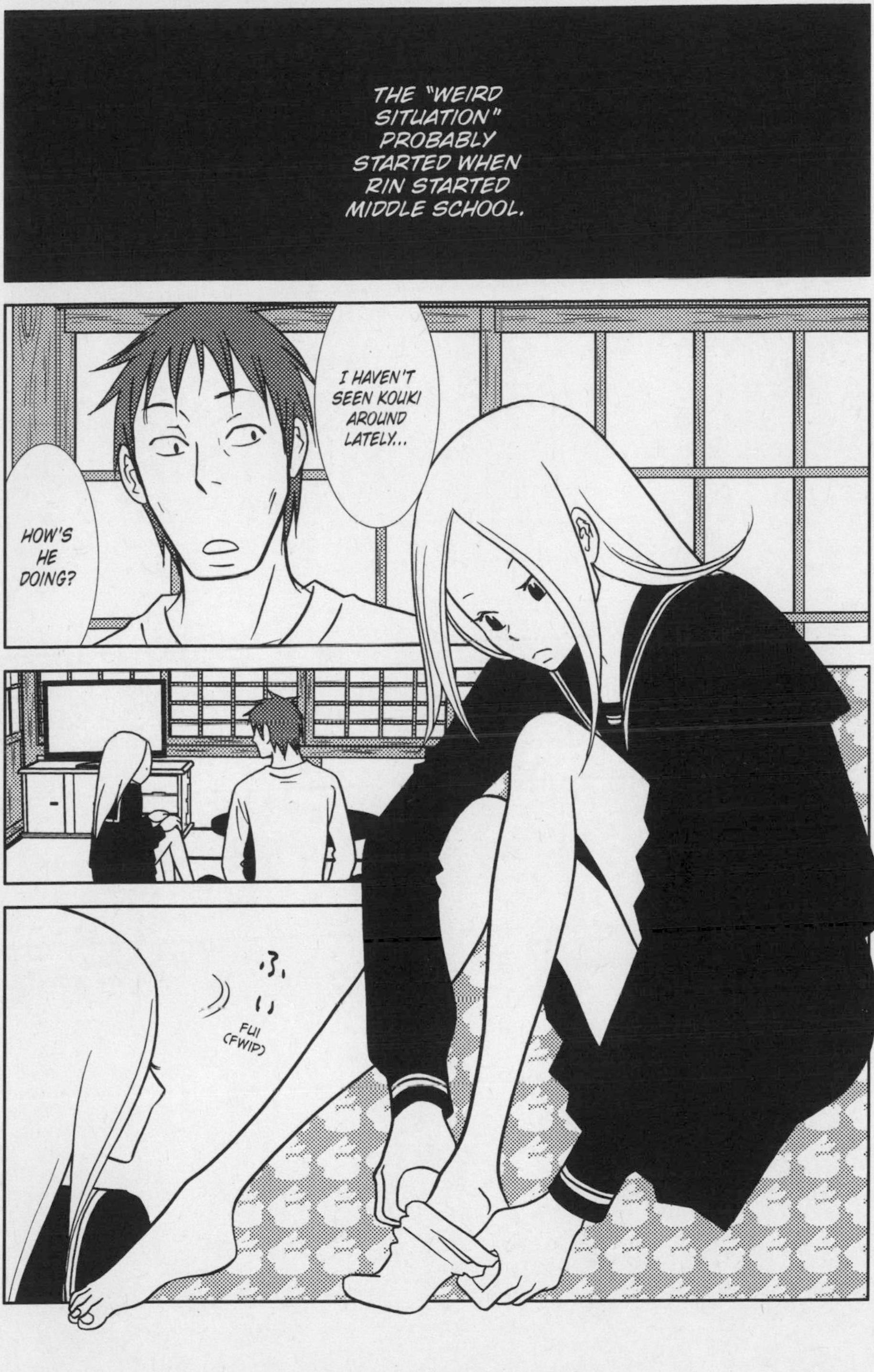
THE "WEIRD SITUATION" PROBABLY STARTED WHEN RIN STARTED MIDDLE SCHOOL.
I HAVEN'T SEEN KOUKI AROUND LATELY...
HOW'S HE DOING?
ふい
FUI (FWIP)

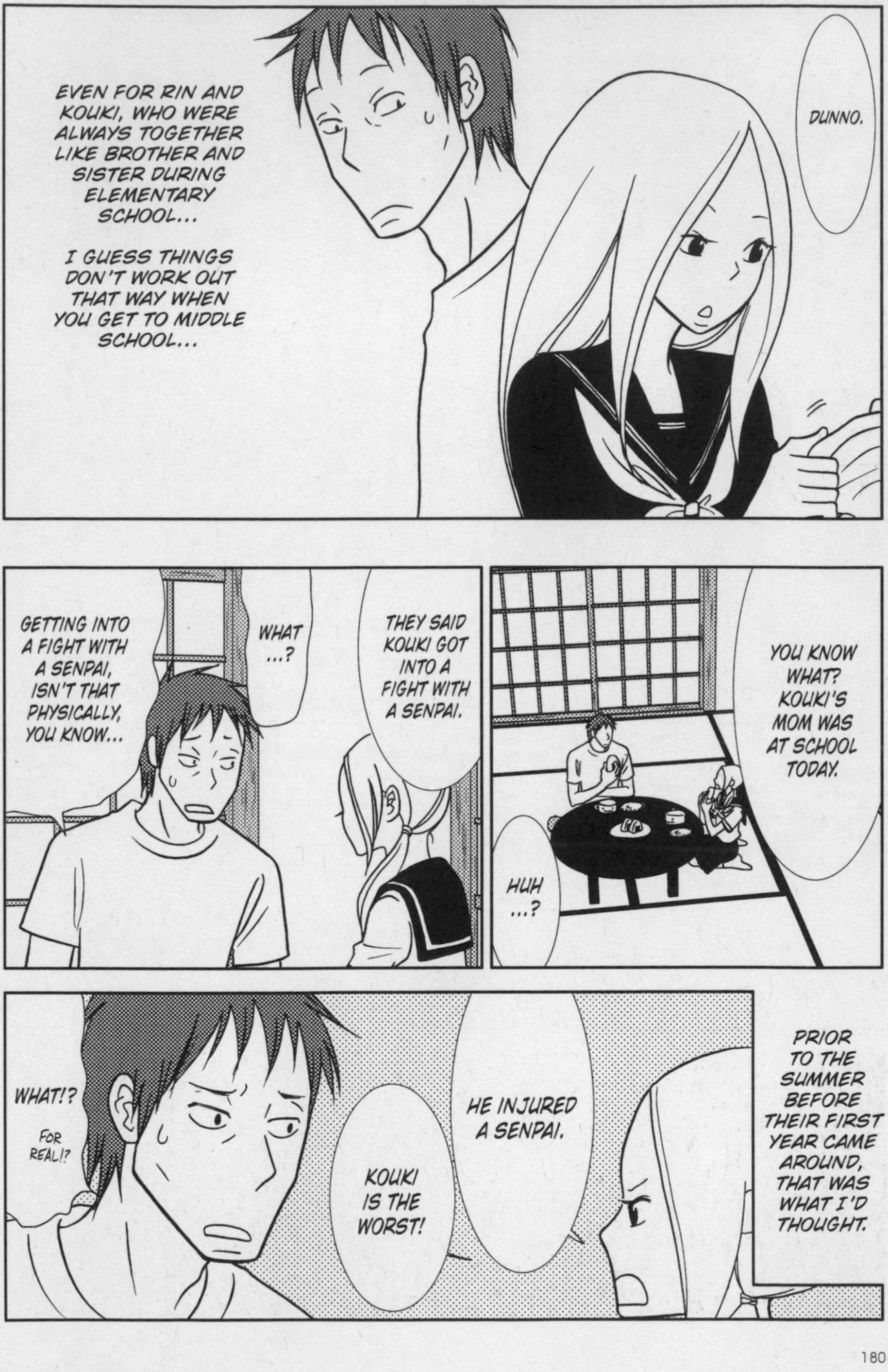
DUNNO.
EVEN FOR RIN AND KOUKI, WHO WERE ALWAYS TOGETHER LIKE BROTHER AND SISTER DURING ELEMENTARY SCHOOL...
I GUESS THINGS DON'T WORK OUT THAT WAY WHEN YOU GET TO MIDDLE SCHOOL...
YOU KNOW WHAT? KOUKI'S MOM WAS AT SCHOOL TODAY.
HUH ...?
THEY SAID KOUKI GOT INTO A FIGHT WITH A SENPAI.
WHAT ...?
GETTING INTO A FIGHT WITH A SENPAI, ISN'T THAT PHYSICALLY, YOU KNOW...
PRIOR TO THE SUMMER BEFORE THEIR FIRST YEAR CAME AROUND, THAT WAS WHAT I'D THOUGHT.
HE INJURED A SENPAI.
KOUKI IS THE WORST!
WHAT!?
FOR REAL!?

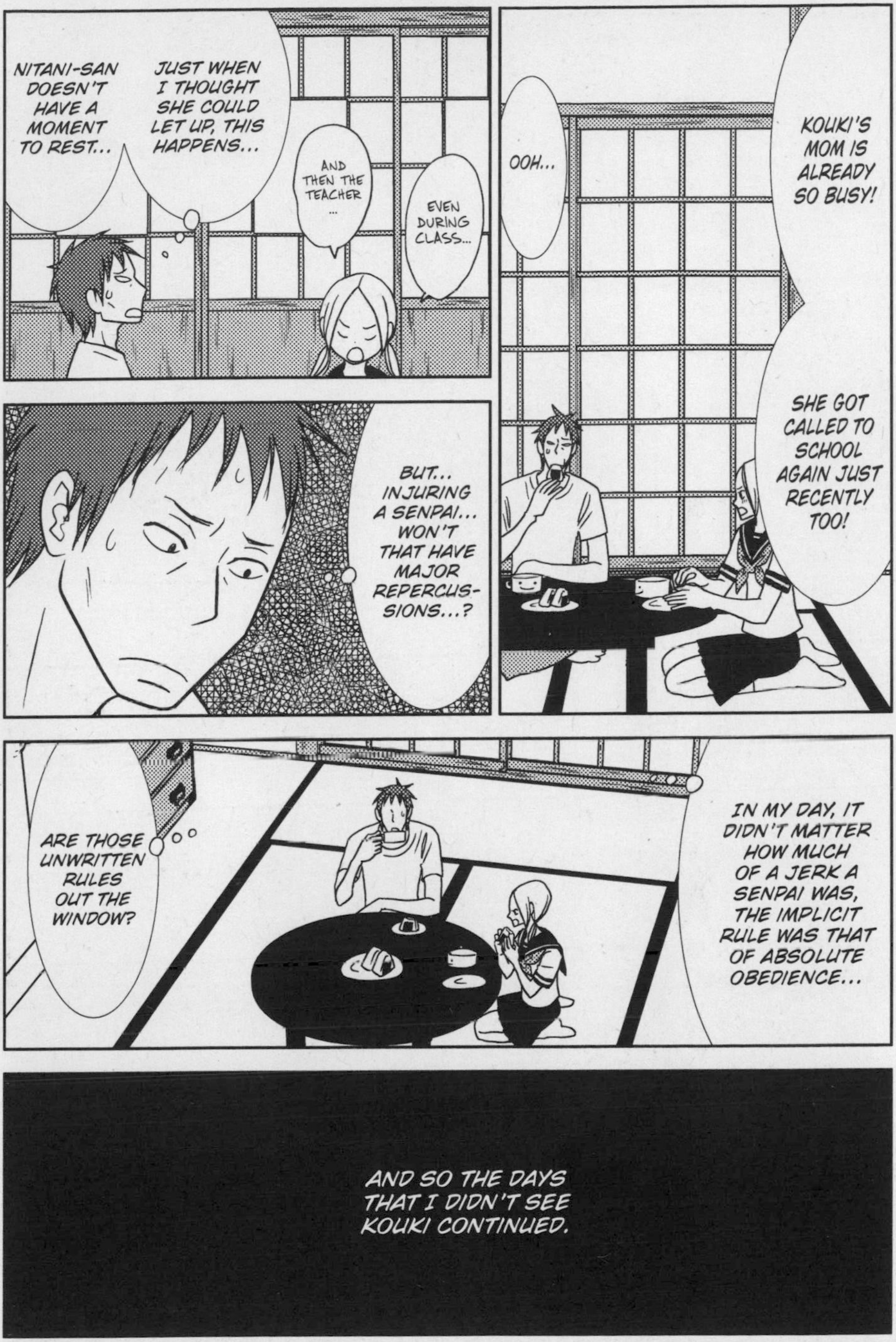

KOUKI'S MOM IS ALREADY SO BUSY!
OOH...
SHE GOT CALLED TO SCHOOL AGAIN JUST RECENTLY TOO!
JUST WHEN I THOUGHT SHE COULD LET UP, THIS HAPPENS...
NITANI-SAN DOESN'T HAVE A MOMENT TO REST...
EVEN DURING CLASS...
AND THEN THE TEACHER ...
BUT... INJURING A SENPAI... WON'T THAT HAVE MAJOR REPERCUS-SIONS...?
IN MY DAY, IT DIDN'T MATTER HOW MUCH OF A JERK A SENPAI WAS, THE IMPLICIT RULE WAS THAT OF ABSOLUTE OBEDIENCE...
ARE THOSE UNWRITTEN RULES OUT THE WINDOW?
AND SO THE DAYS THAT I DIDN'T SEE KOUKI CONTINUED.

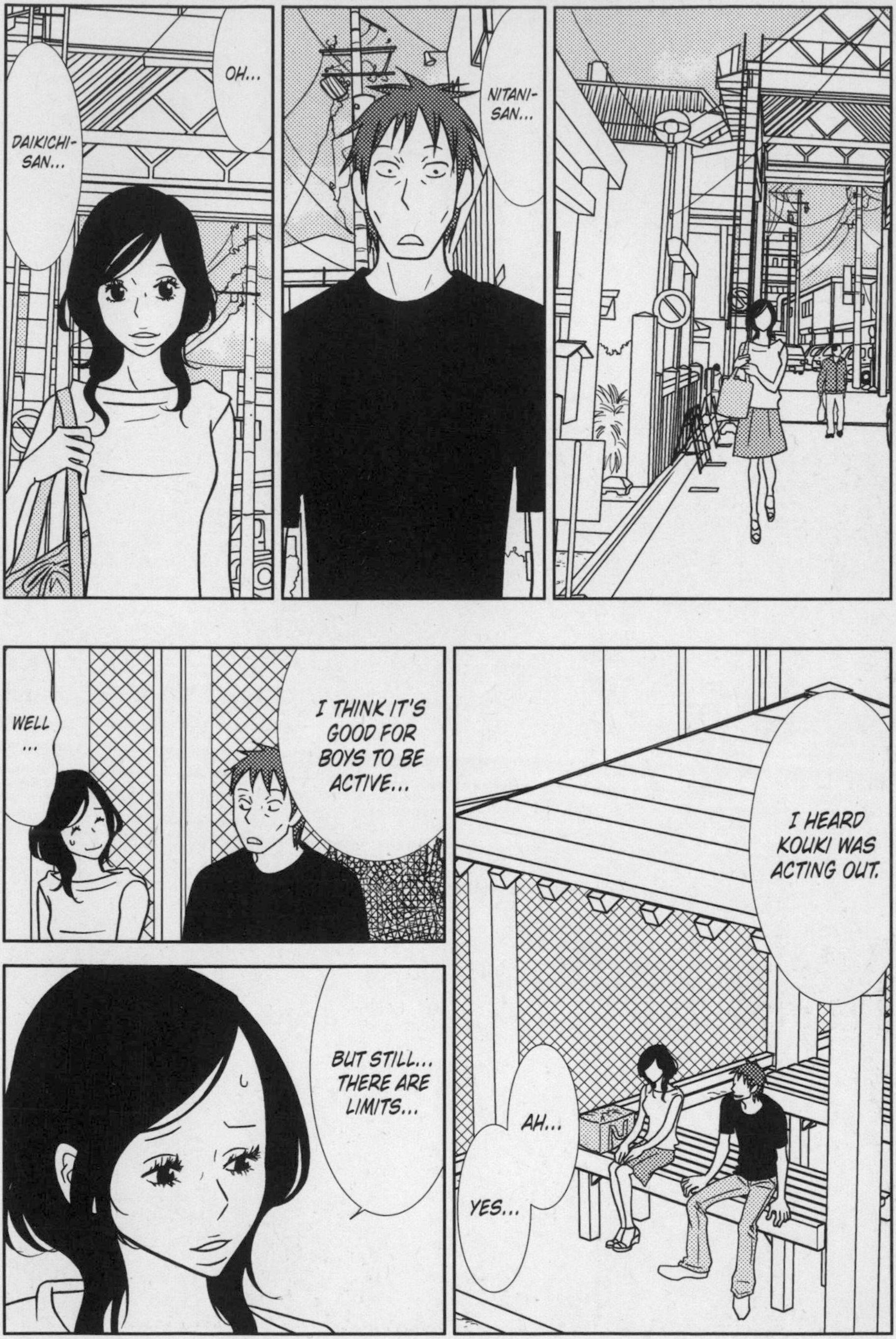
NITANI-SAN...
OH...
DAIKICHI-SAN...
I HEARD KOUKI WAS ACTING OUT.
AH...
YES...
I THINK IT'S GOOD FOR BOYS TO BE ACTIVE...
WELL...
BUT STILL... THERE ARE LIMITS...

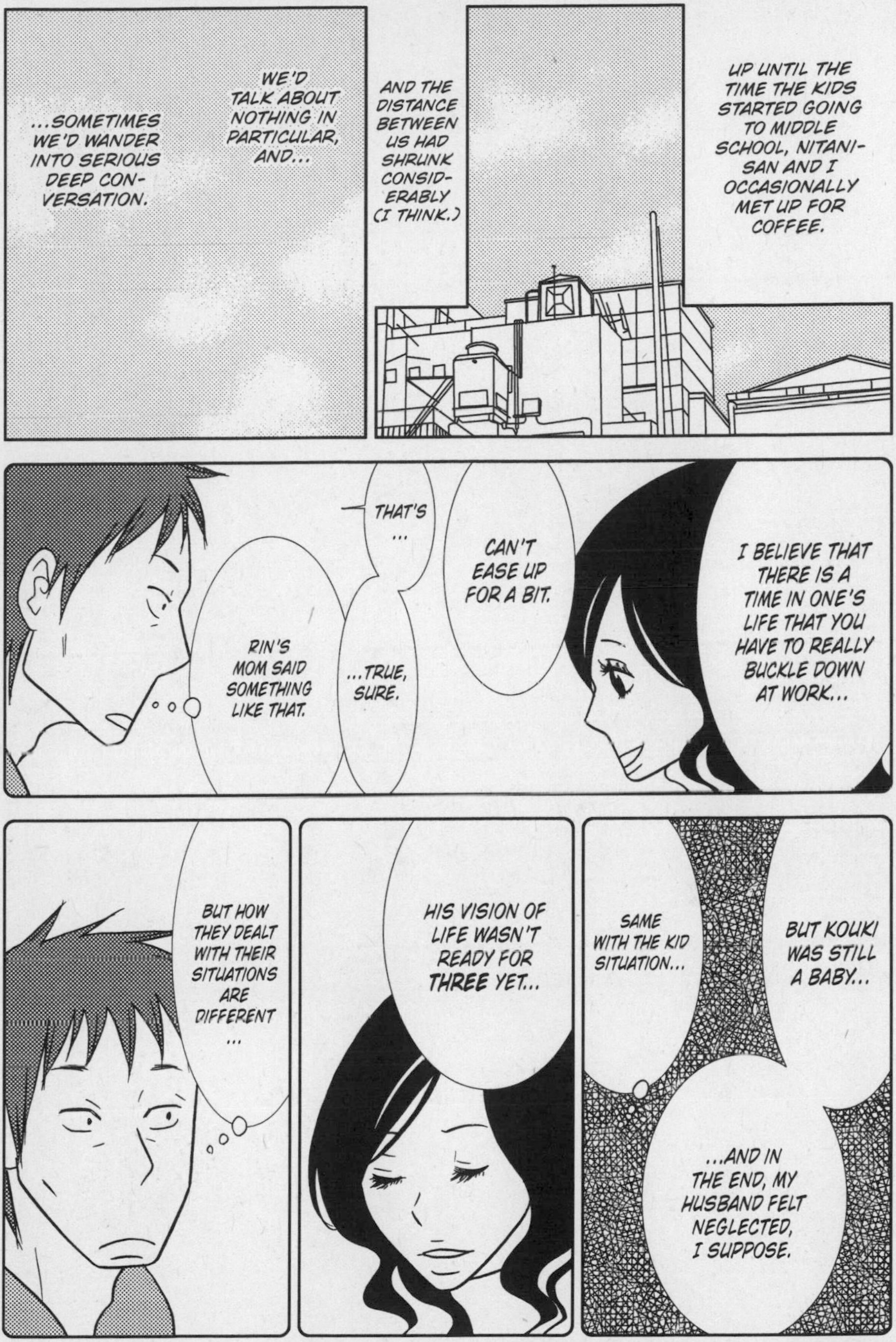
UP UNTIL THE TIME THE KIDS STARTED GOING TO MIDDLE SCHOOL, NITANI-SAN AND I OCCASIONALLY MET UP FOR COFFEE.
AND THE DISTANCE BETWEEN US HAD SHRUNK CONSID-ERABLY (I THINK.)
WE'D TALK ABOUT NOTHING IN PARTICULAR, AND...
...SOMETIMES WE'D WANDER INTO SERIOUS DEEP CON-VERSATION.
I BELIEVE THAT THERE IS A TIME IN ONE'S LIFE THAT YOU HAVE TO REALLY BUCKLE DOWN AT WORK...
CAN'T EASE UP FOR A BIT.
THAT'S ...
...TRUE, SURE.
RIN'S MOM SAID SOMETHING LIKE THAT.
BUT KOUKI WAS STILL A BABY...
SAME WITH THE KID SITUATION...
...AND IN THE END, MY HUSBAND FELT NEGLECTED, I SUPPOSE.
HIS VISION OF LIFE WASN'T READY FOR THREE YET...
BUT HOW THEY DEALT WITH THEIR SITUATIONS ARE DIFFERENT ...

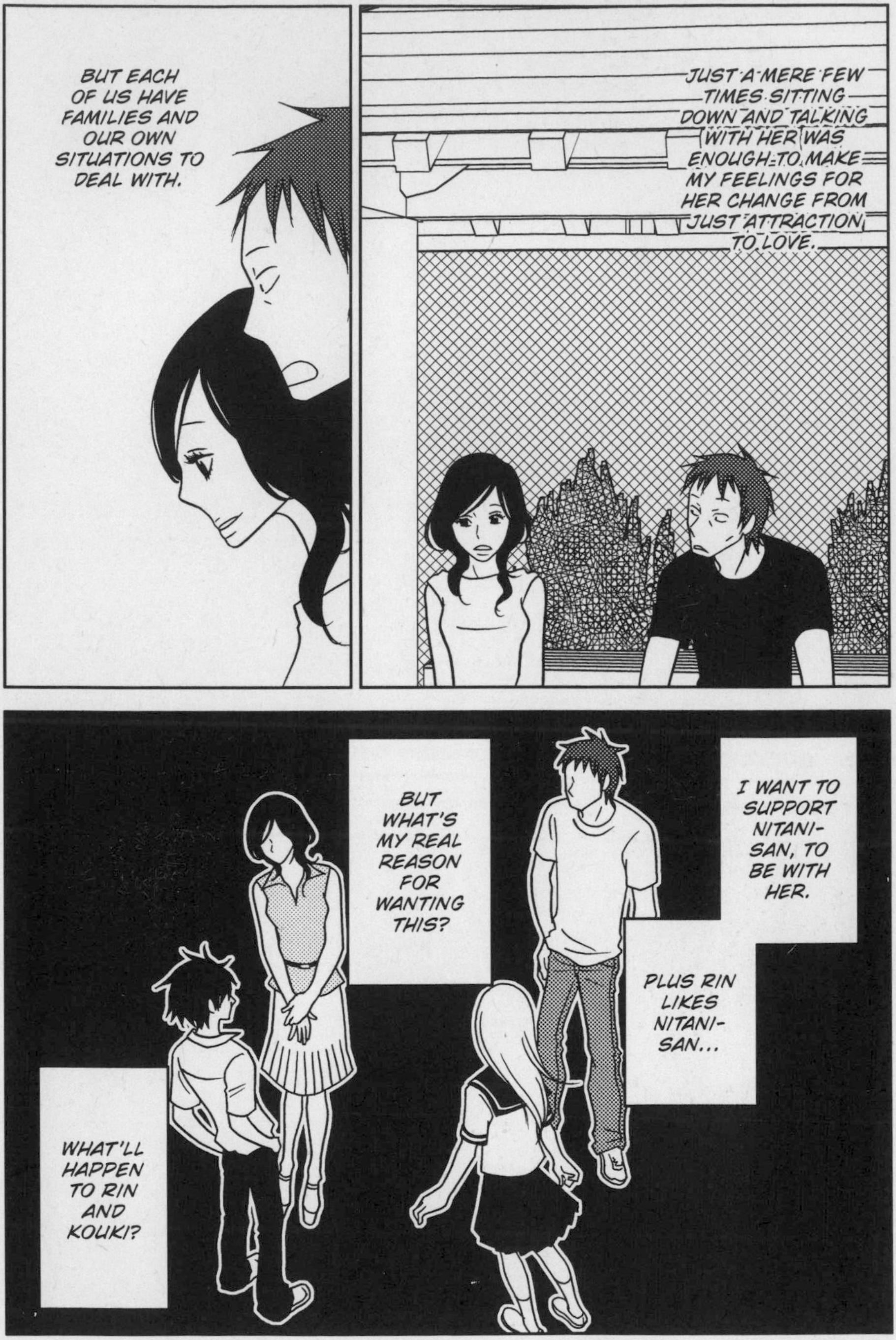
JUST A MERE FEW TIMES SITTING DOWN AND TALKING WITH HER WAS ENOUGH TO MAKE MY FEELINGS FOR HER CHANGE FROM JUST ATTRACTION TO LOVE.
BUT EACH OF US HAVE FAMILIES AND OUR OWN SITUATIONS TO DEAL WITH.
I WANT TO SUPPORT NITANI-SAN, TO BE WITH HER.
BUT WHAT'S MY REAL REASON FOR WANTING THIS?
PLUS RIN LIKES NITANI-SAN...
WHAT'LL HAPPEN TO RIN AND KOUKI?

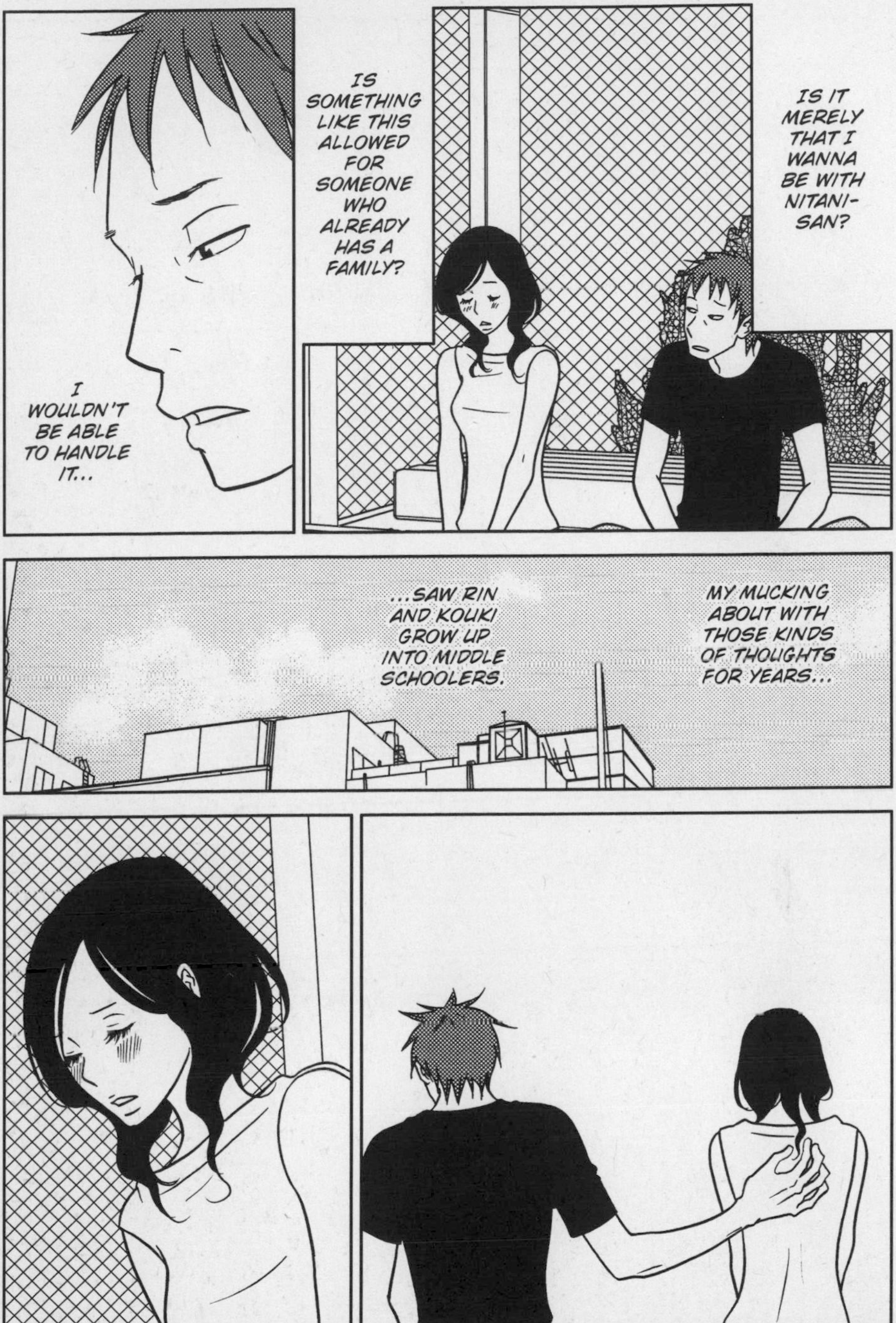
IS IT MERELY THAT I WANNA BE WITH NITANI-SAN?
IS SOMETHING LIKE THIS ALLOWED FOR SOMEONE WHO ALREADY HAS A FAMILY?
I WOULDN'T BE ABLE TO HANDLE IT...
MY MUCKING ABOUT WITH THOSE KINDS OF THOUGHTS FOR YEARS...
...SAW RIN AND KOUKI GROW UP INTO MIDDLE SCHOOLERS.

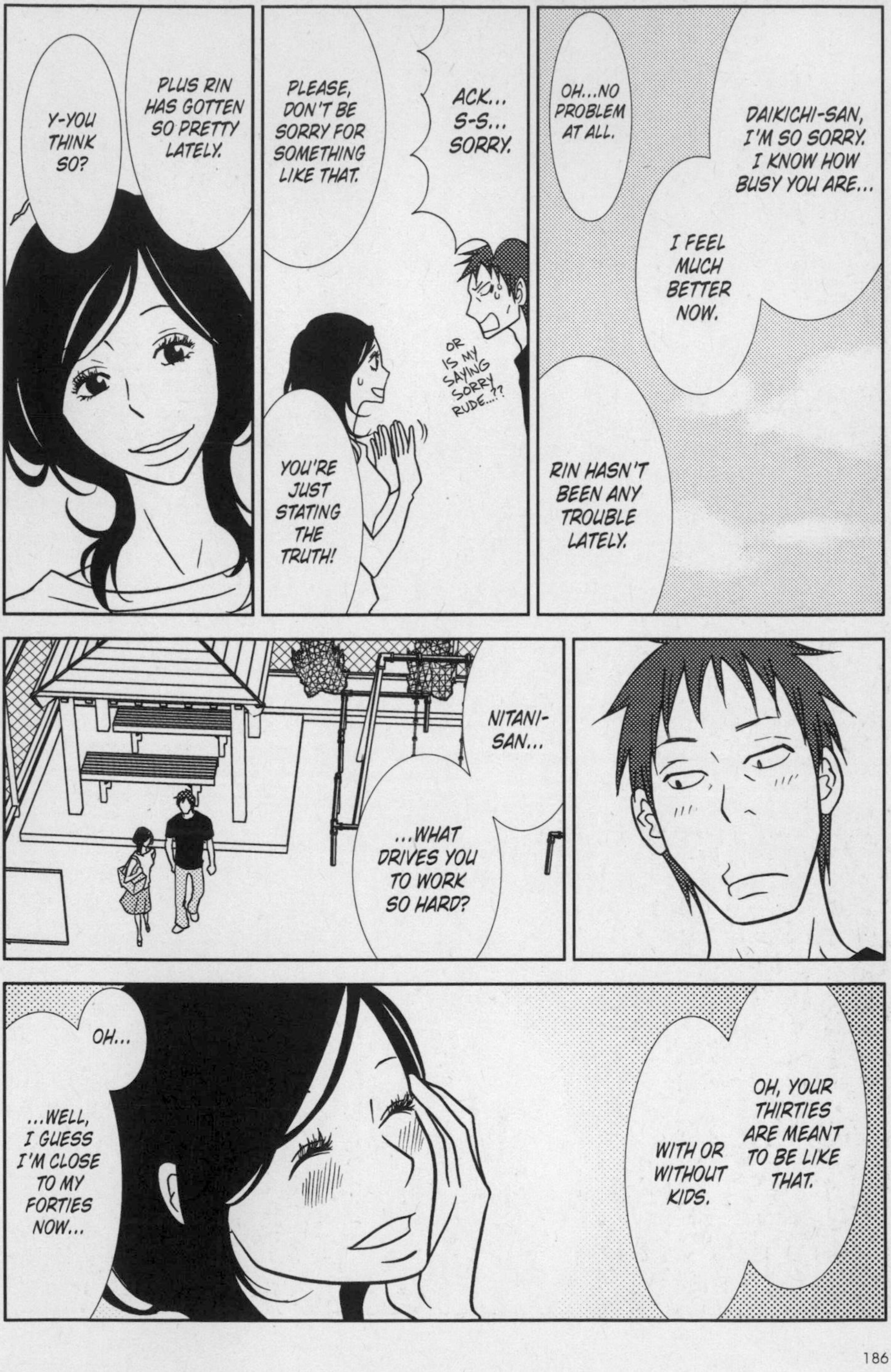
DAIKICHI-SAN, I'M SO SORRY. I KNOW HOW BUSY YOU ARE...
OH...NO PROBLEM AT ALL.
I FEEL MUCH BETTER NOW.
RIN HASN'T BEEN ANY TROUBLE LATELY.
ACK... S-S... SORRY.
PLEASE, DON'T BE SORRY FOR SOMETHING LIKE THAT.
OR IS MY SAYING SORRY RUDE...??
YOU'RE JUST STATING THE TRUTH!
PLUS RIN HAS GOTTEN SO PRETTY LATELY.
Y-YOU THINK SO?
NITANI-SAN...
...WHAT DRIVES YOU TO WORK SO HARD?
OH, YOUR THIRTIES ARE MEANT TO BE LIKE THAT.
WITH OR WITHOUT KIDS.
OH...
...WELL, I GUESS I'M CLOSE TO MY FORTIES NOW...

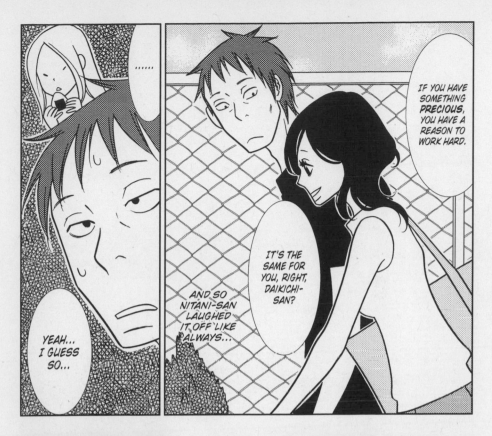

IF YOU HAVE SOMETHING PRECIOUS, YOU HAVE A REASON TO WORK HARD.
IT'S THE SAME FOR YOU, RIGHT, DAIKICHI-SAN?
AND SO NITANI-SAN LAUGHED IT OFF LIKE ALWAYS...
......
YEAH... I GUESS SO...
BUT STILL ...
...SHE SEEMS RUN DOWN...
EVEN AFTER THAT DAY (FROM WHAT I HEARD FROM RIN), KOUKI KEPT CAUSING TROUBLE ON AND OFF...

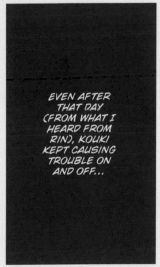

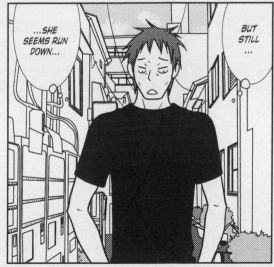

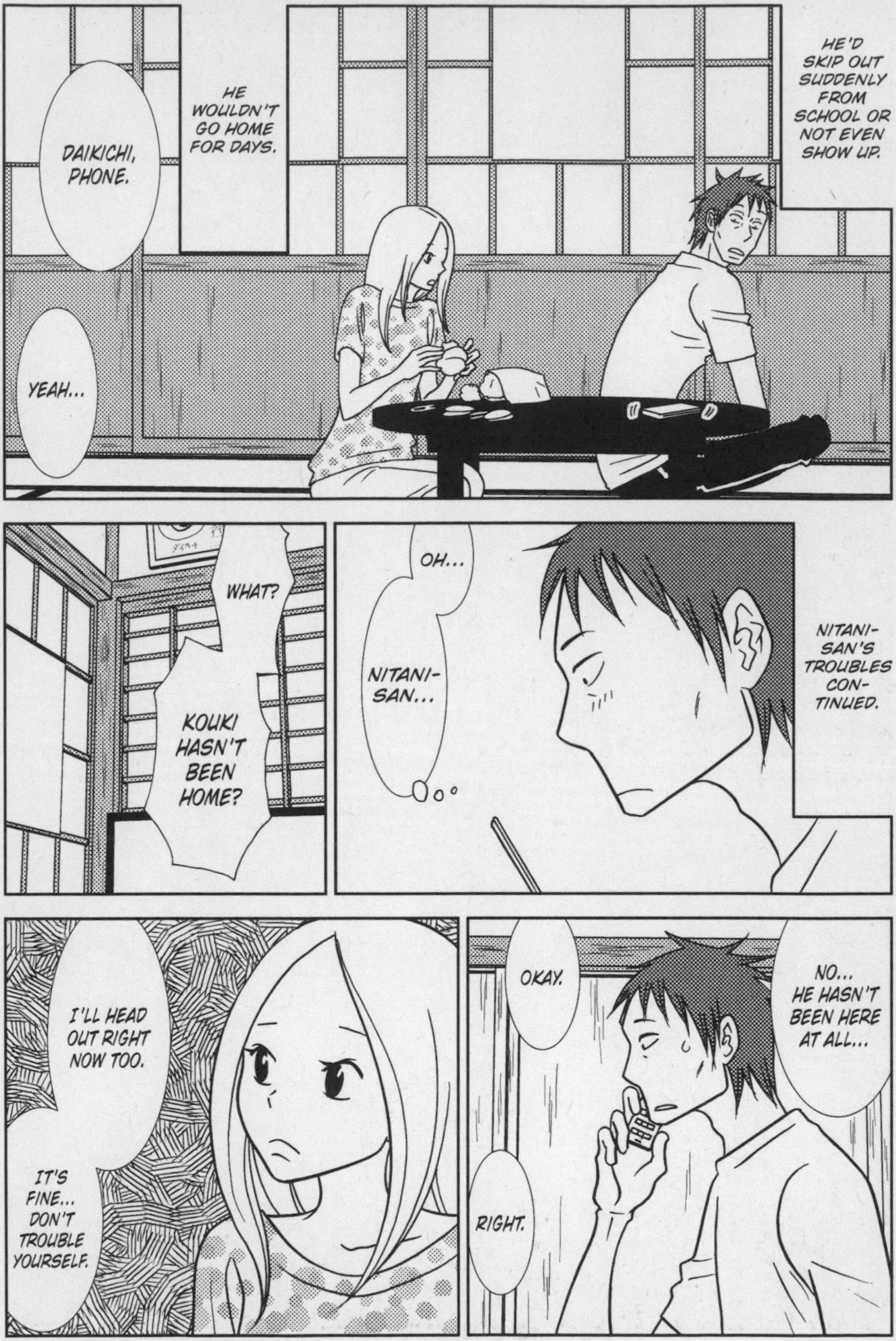
HE'D SKIP OUT SUDDENLY FROM SCHOOL OR NOT EVEN SHOW UP.
HE WOULDN'T GO HOME FOR DAYS.
DAIKICHI, PHONE.
YEAH...
NITANI-SAN'S TROUBLES CONTINUED.
OH...
NITANI-SAN...
WHAT?
KOUKI HASN'T BEEN HOME?
NO... HE HASN'T BEEN HERE AT ALL...
OKAY.
RIGHT.
I'LL HEAD OUT RIGHT NOW TOO.
IT'S FINE... DON'T TROUBLE YOURSELF.

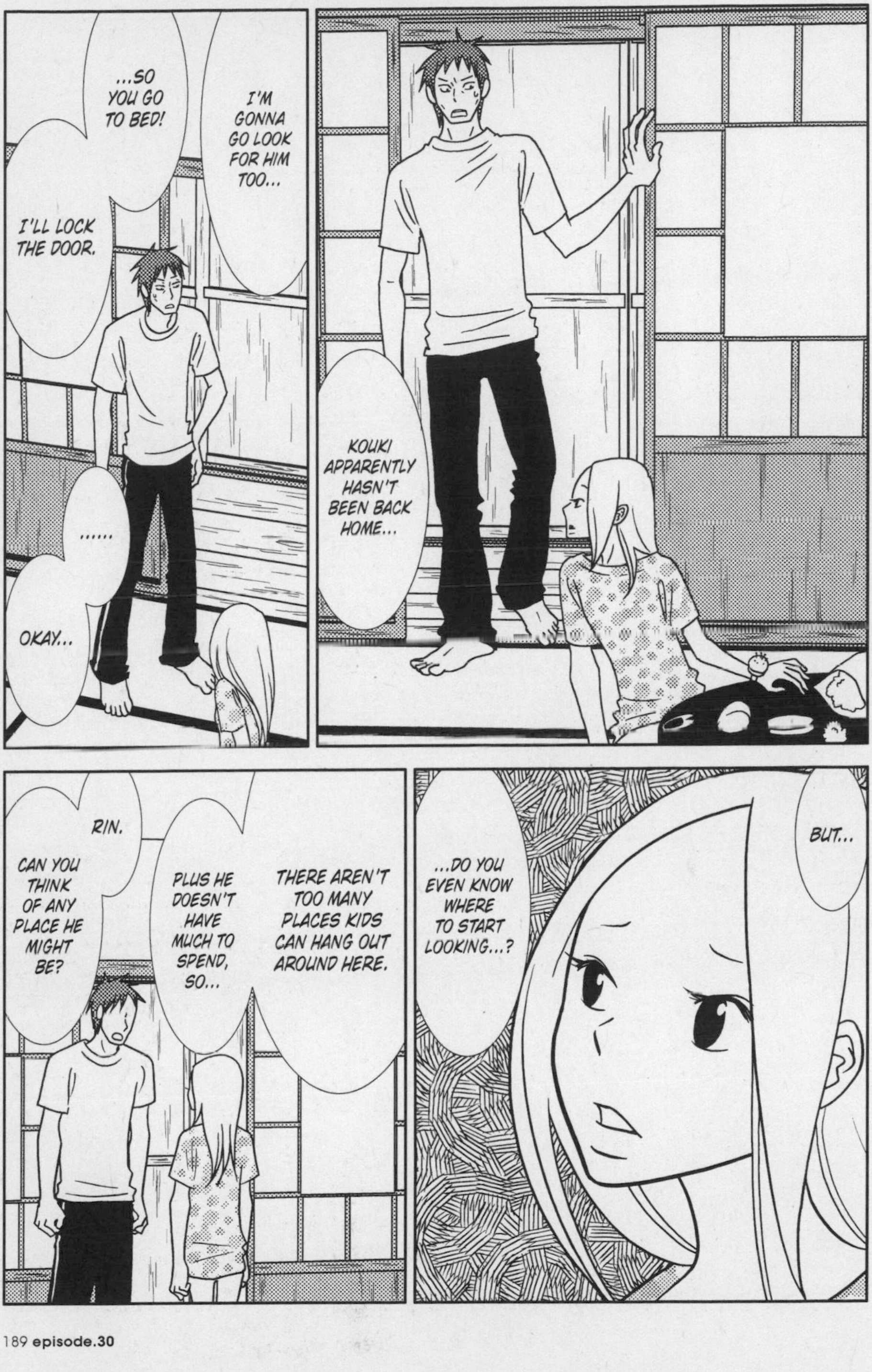
KOUKI APPARENTLY HASN'T BEEN BACK HOME...
I'M GONNA GO LOOK FOR HIM TOO...
...SO YOU GO TO BED!
I'LL LOCK THE DOOR.
......
OKAY...
BUT...
...DO YOU EVEN KNOW WHERE TO START LOOKING...?
THERE AREN'T TOO MANY PLACES KIDS CAN HANG OUT AROUND HERE.
PLUS HE DOESN'T HAVE MUCH TO SPEND, SO...
RIN.
CAN YOU THINK OF ANY PLACE HE MIGHT BE?

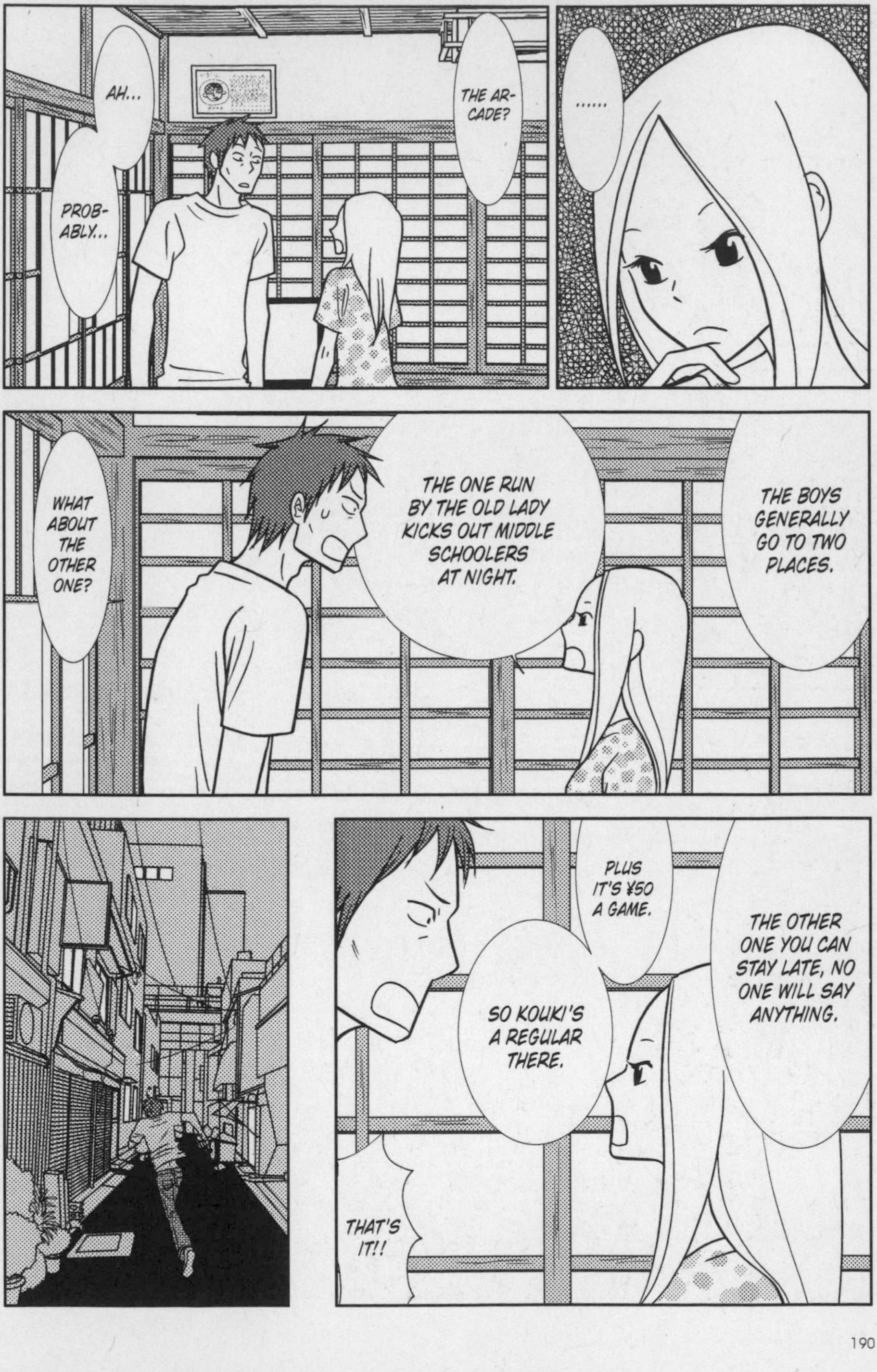
......
THE AR-CADE?
AH...
PROB-ABLY...
THE BOYS GENERALLY GO TO TWO PLACES.
THE ONE RUN BY THE OLD LADY KICKS OUT MIDDLE SCHOOLERS AT NIGHT.
WHAT ABOUT THE OTHER ONE?
THE OTHER ONE YOU CAN STAY LATE, NO ONE WILL SAY ANYTHING.
PLUS IT'S ¥50 A GAME.
SO KOUKI'S A REGULAR THERE.
THAT'S IT!!

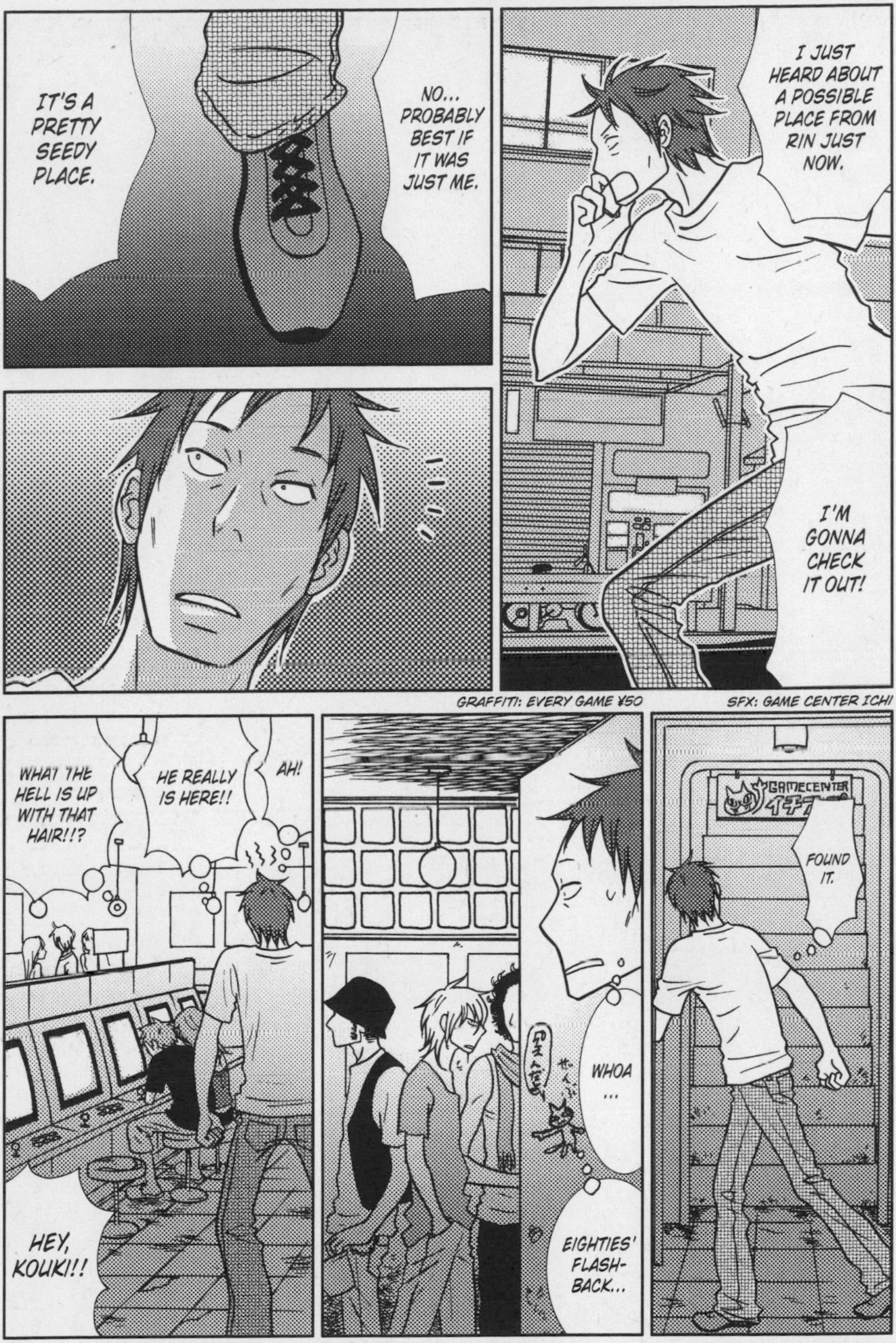
I JUST HEARD ABOUT A POSSIBLE PLACE FROM RIN JUST NOW.
I'M GONNA CHECK IT OUT!
NO... PROBABLY BEST IF IT WAS JUST ME.
IT'S A PRETTY SEEDY PLACE.
SFX: GAME CENTER ICHI
GRAFFITI: EVERY GAME ¥50
GAMECENTER
FOUND IT.
WHOA ...
EIGHTIES' FLASH-BACK...
AH!
HE REALLY IS HERE!!
WHAT THE HELL IS UP WITH THAT HAIR!!?
HEY, KOUKI!!

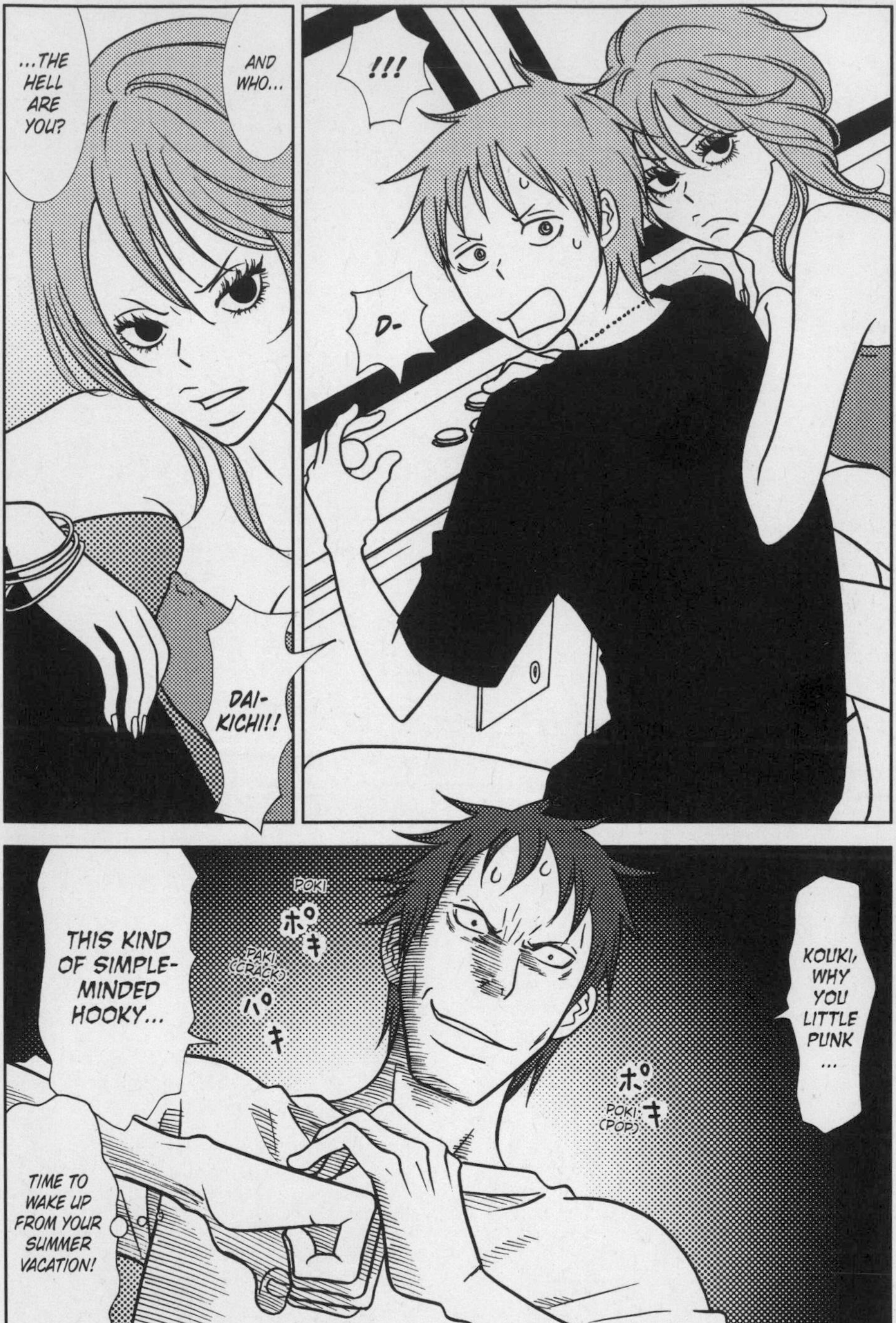
!!!
D-
DAI-KICHI!!
AND WHO...
...THE HELL ARE YOU?
KOUKI, WHY YOU LITTLE PUNK...
ポキ POKI (POP)
ポキ POKI
パキ PAKI (CRACK)
THIS KIND OF SIMPLE-MINDED HOOKY...
TIME TO WAKE UP FROM YOUR SUMMER VACATION!

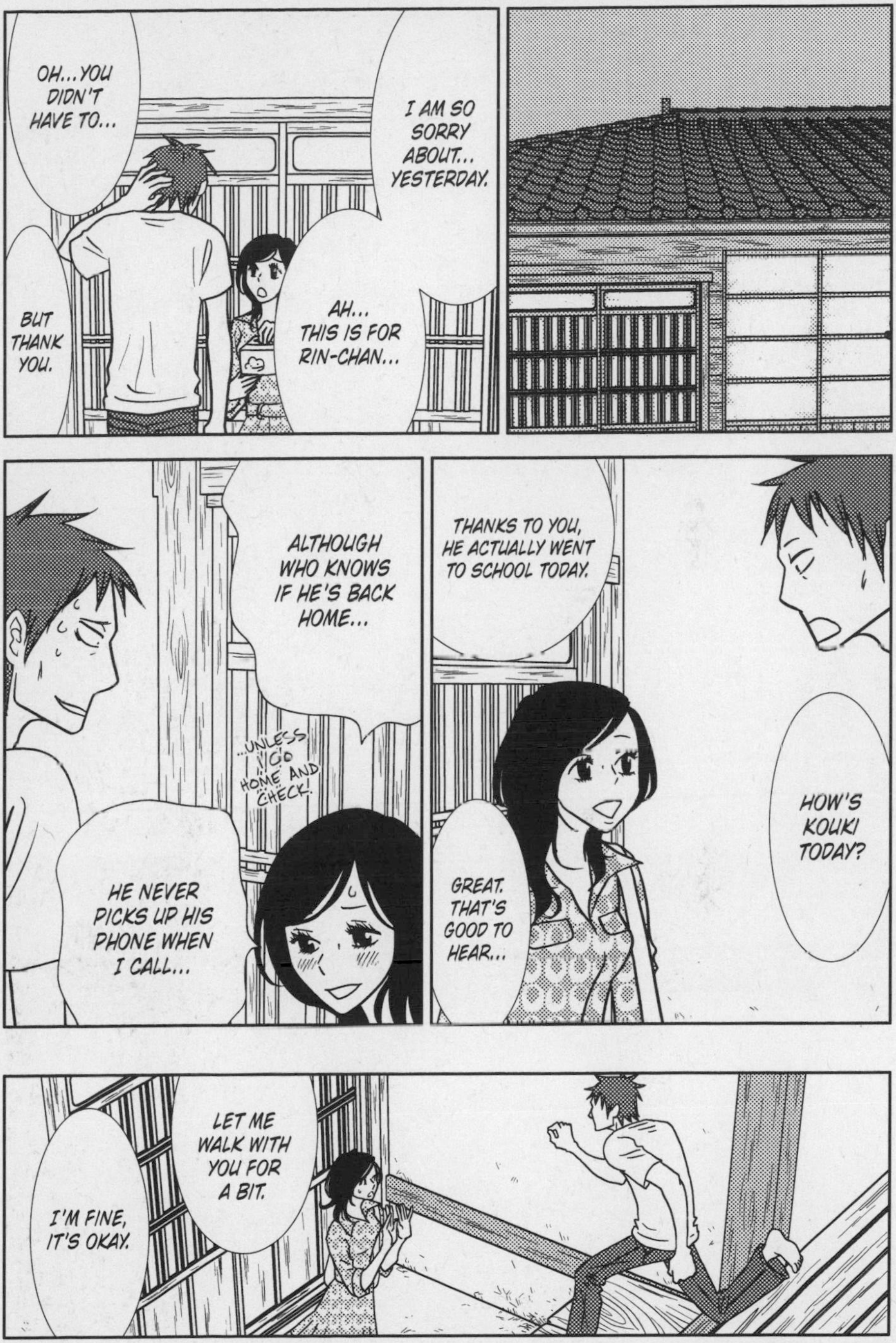
I AM SO SORRY ABOUT... YESTERDAY.
OH...YOU DIDN'T HAVE TO...
AH... THIS IS FOR RIN-CHAN...
BUT THANK YOU.
HOW'S KOUKI TODAY?
THANKS TO YOU, HE ACTUALLY WENT TO SCHOOL TODAY.
GREAT. THAT'S GOOD TO HEAR...
ALTHOUGH WHO KNOWS IF HE'S BACK HOME...
...UNLESS I GO HOME AND CHECK!
HE NEVER PICKS UP HIS PHONE WHEN I CALL...
LET ME WALK WITH YOU FOR A BIT.
I'M FINE, IT'S OKAY.

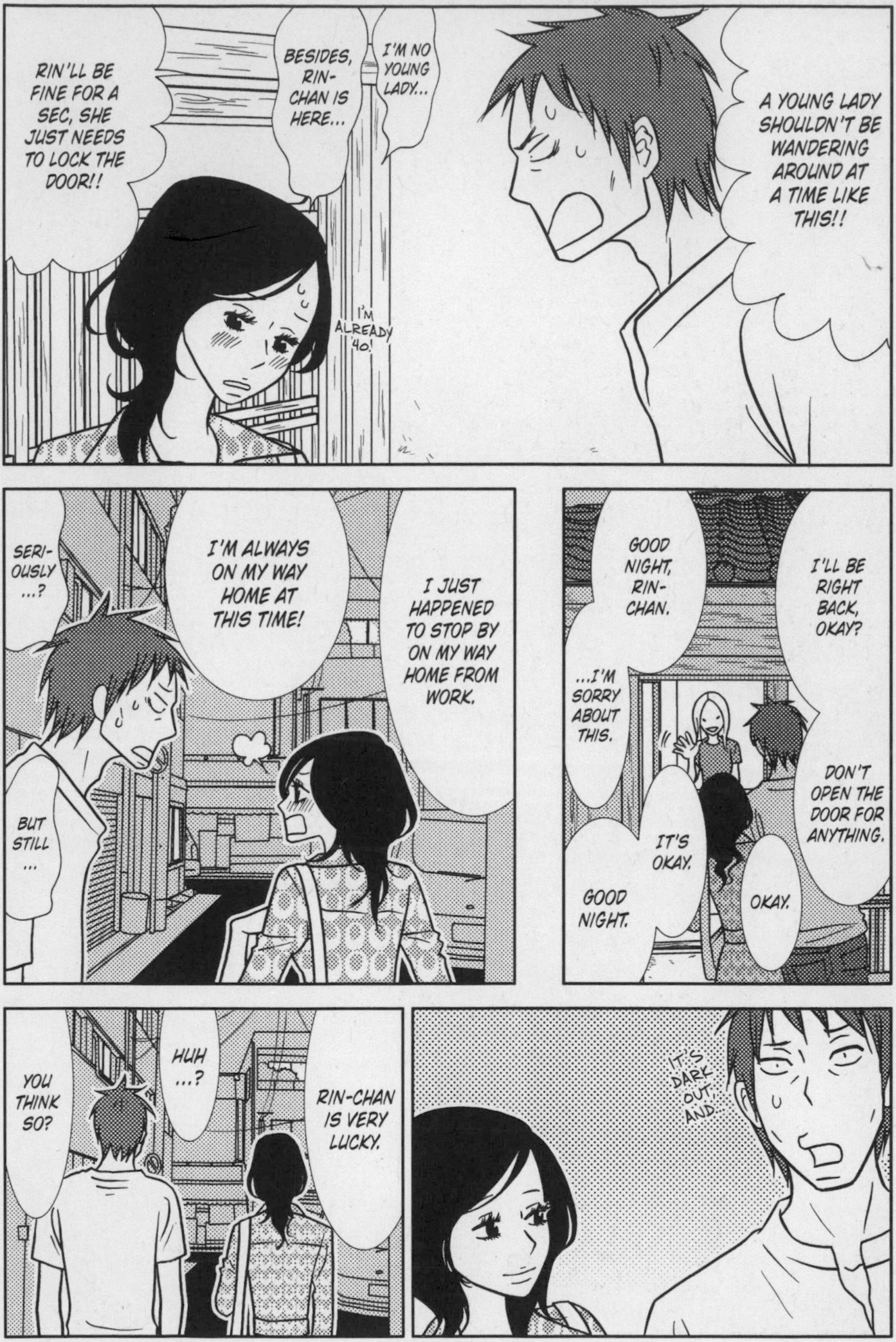
A YOUNG LADY SHOULDN'T BE WANDERING AROUND AT A TIME LIKE THIS!!
I'M NO YOUNG LADY...
BESIDES, RIN-CHAN IS HERE...
RIN'LL BE FINE FOR A SEC, SHE JUST NEEDS TO LOCK THE DOOR!!
I'M ALREADY 40!
I'LL BE RIGHT BACK, OKAY?
GOOD NIGHT, RIN-CHAN.
DON'T OPEN THE DOOR FOR ANYTHING.
...I'M SORRY ABOUT THIS.
OKAY.
IT'S OKAY.
GOOD NIGHT.
I JUST HAPPENED TO STOP BY ON MY WAY HOME FROM WORK.
I'M ALWAYS ON MY WAY HOME AT THIS TIME!
SERIOUSLY ...?
BUT STILL ...
IT'S DARK OUT, AND...
RIN-CHAN IS VERY LUCKY.
HUH ...?
YOU THINK SO?

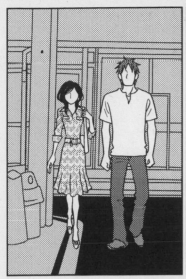

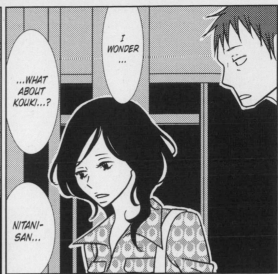

I WONDER ...
...WHAT ABOUT KOUKI...?
NITANI-SAN...
WILL I EVER SEE THE DAY...
...WHEN WE CAN TALK TO EACH OTHER PROPERLY AGAIN...?
UM... NITANI-SAN.
I KNOW THIS IS SUDDEN, BUT...

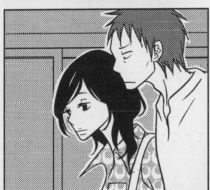

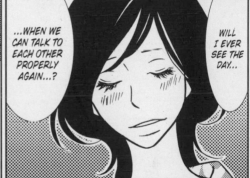

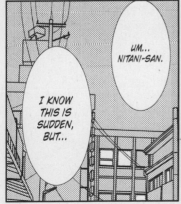

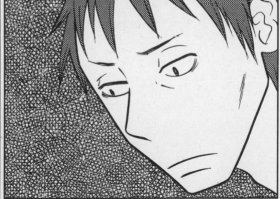

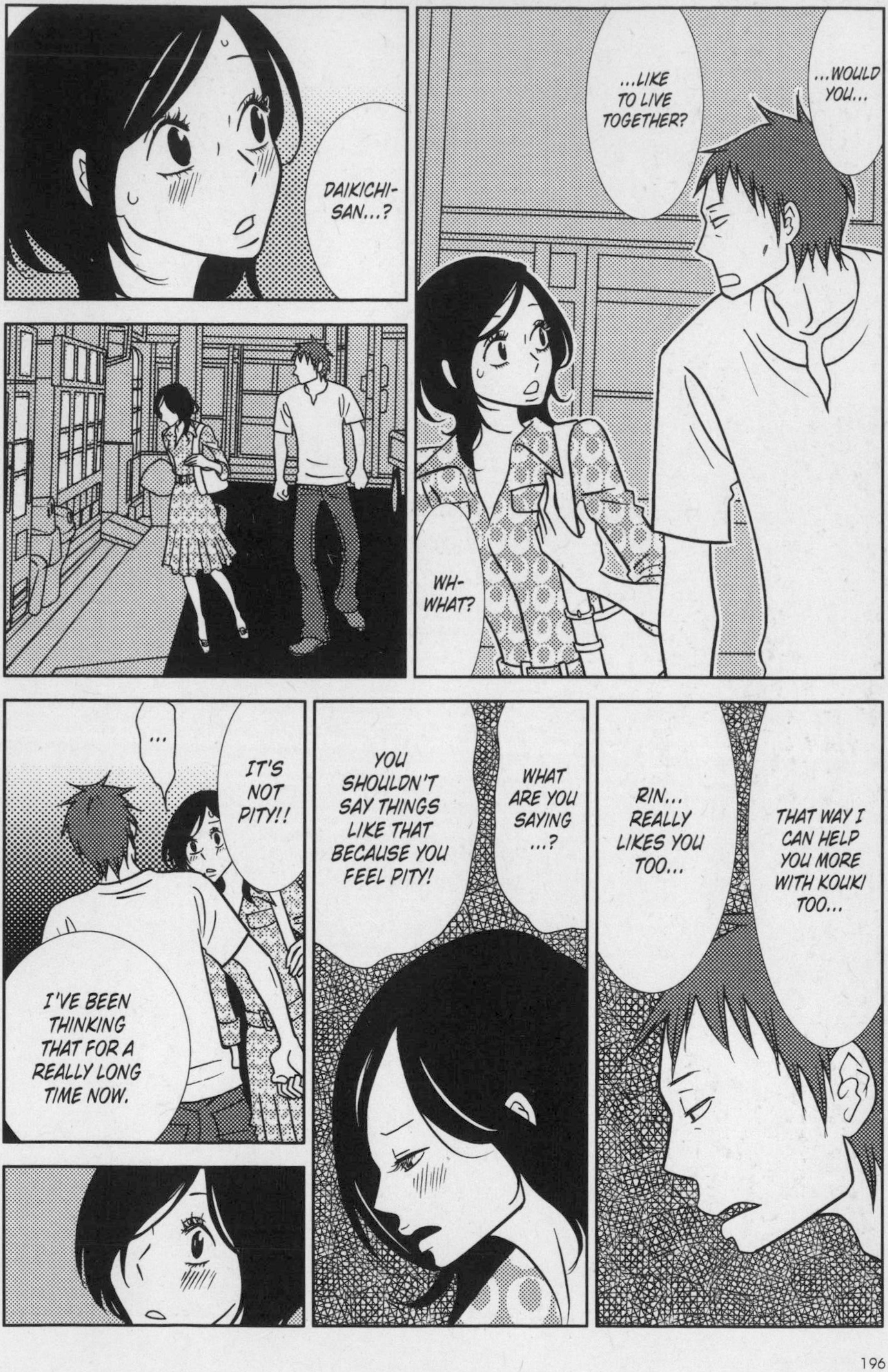
...WOULD YOU...
...LIKE TO LIVE TOGETHER?
WH- WHAT?
DAIKICHI-SAN...?
THAT WAY I CAN HELP YOU MORE WITH KOUKI TOO...
RIN... REALLY LIKES YOU TOO...
WHAT ARE YOU SAYING ...?
YOU SHOULDN'T SAY THINGS LIKE THAT BECAUSE YOU FEEL PITY!
IT'S NOT PITY!!
...
I'VE BEEN THINKING THAT FOR A REALLY LONG TIME NOW.

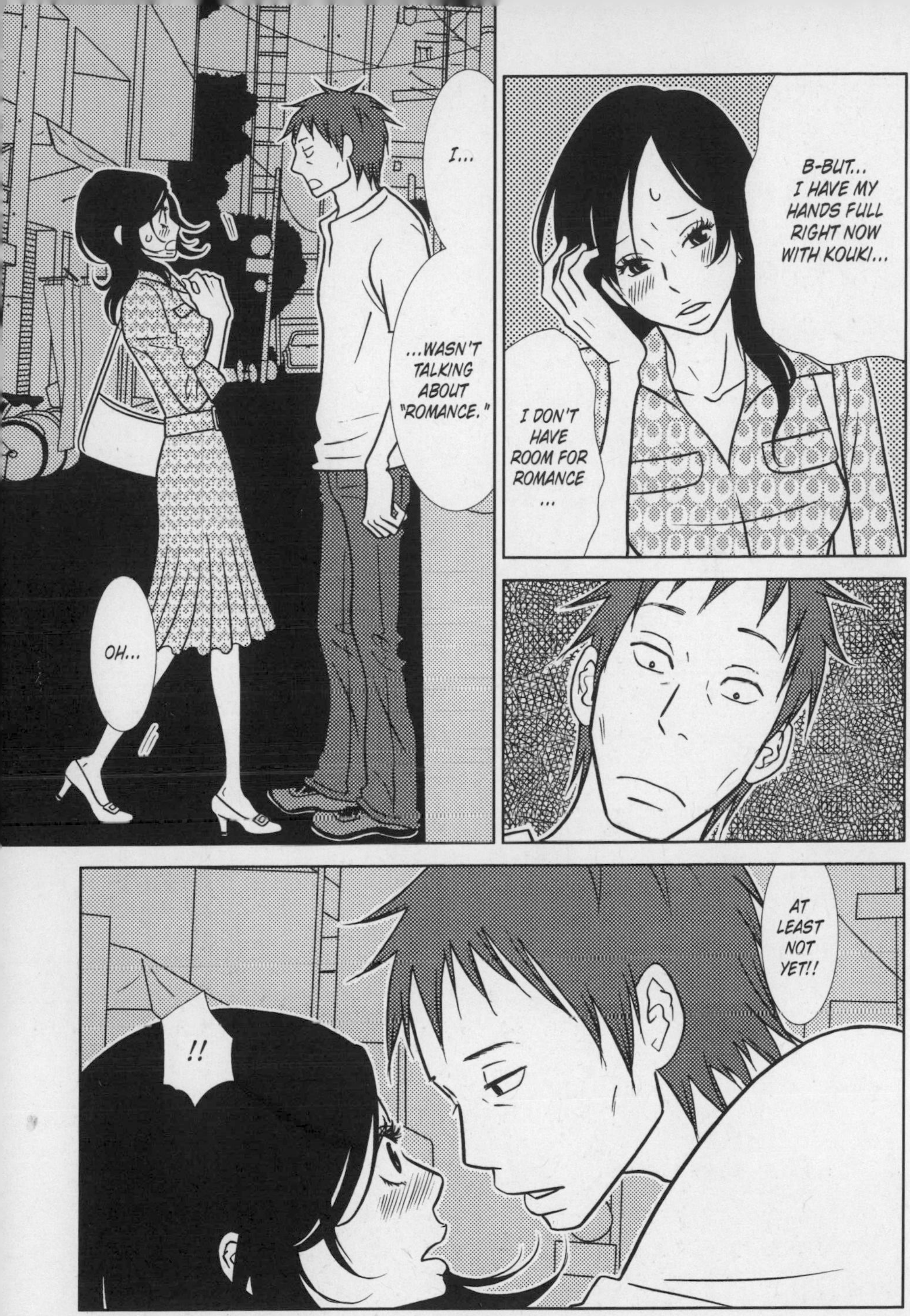
B-BUT... I HAVE MY HANDS FULL RIGHT NOW WITH KOUKI...
I DON'T HAVE ROOM FOR ROMANCE ...
I...
...WASN'T TALKING ABOUT "ROMANCE."
OH...
AT LEAST NOT YET!!
!!

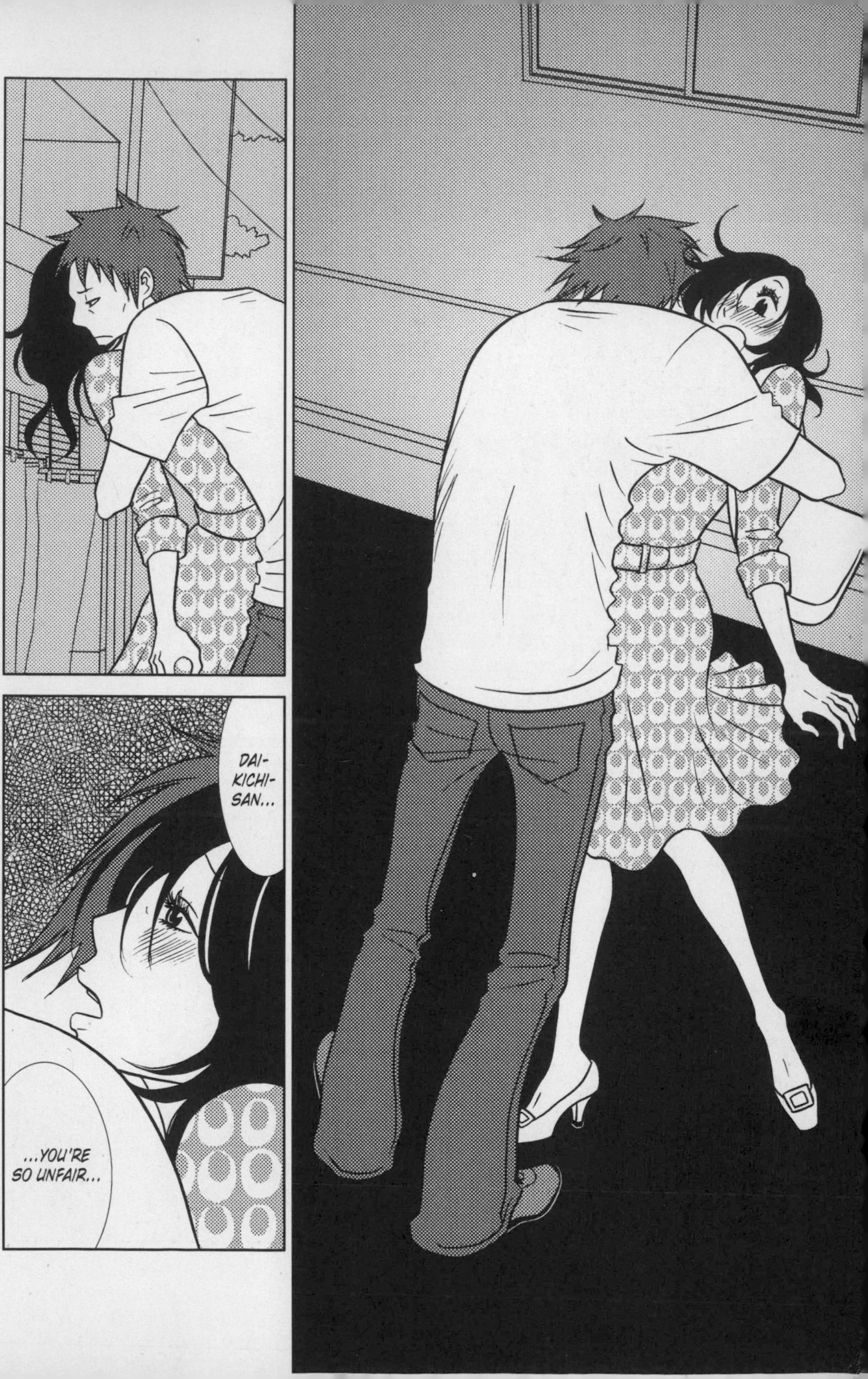
DAI-KICHI-SAN...
...YOU'RE SO UNFAIR...

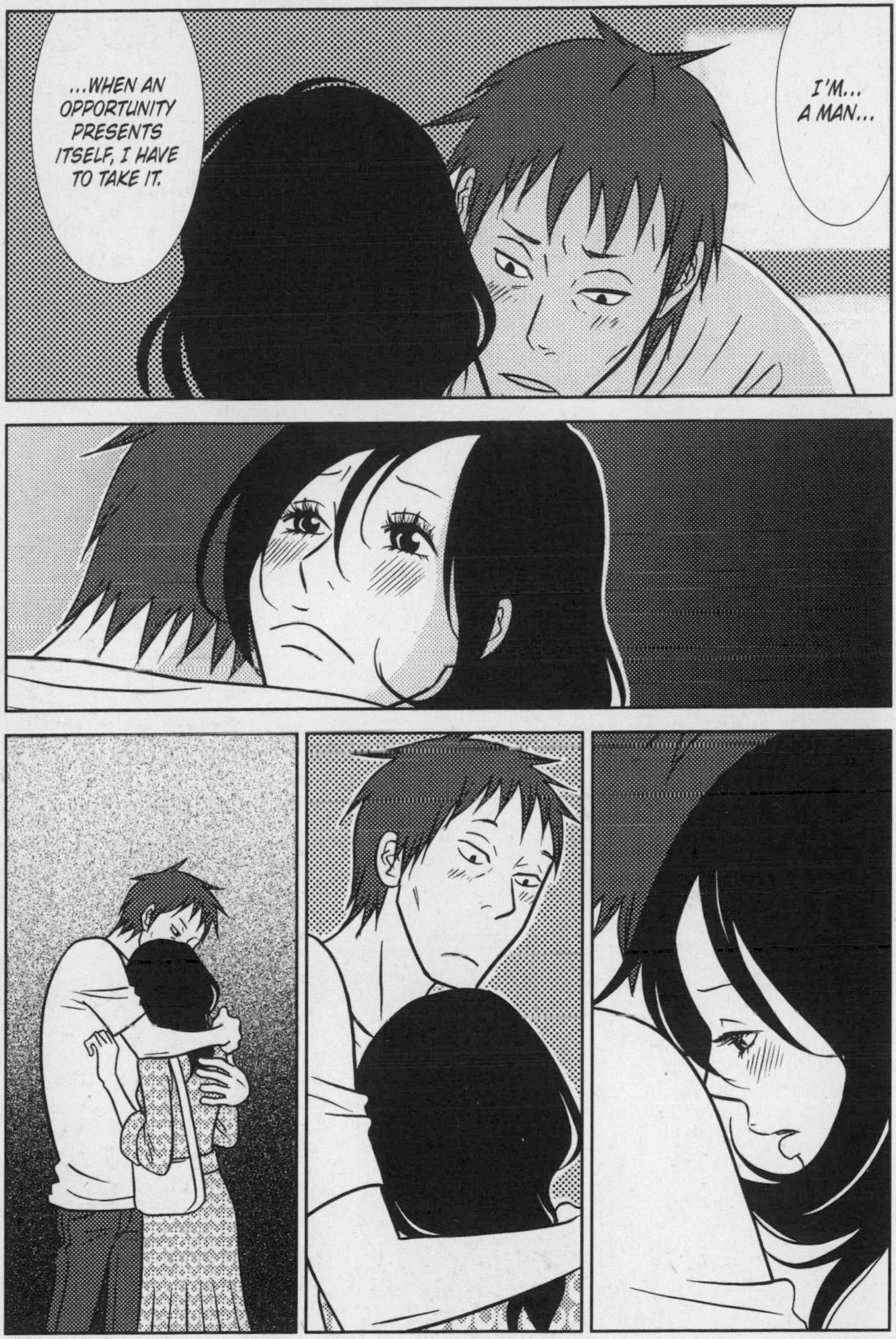
I'M... A MAN...
...WHEN AN OPPORTUNITY PRESENTS ITSELF, I HAVE TO TAKE IT.

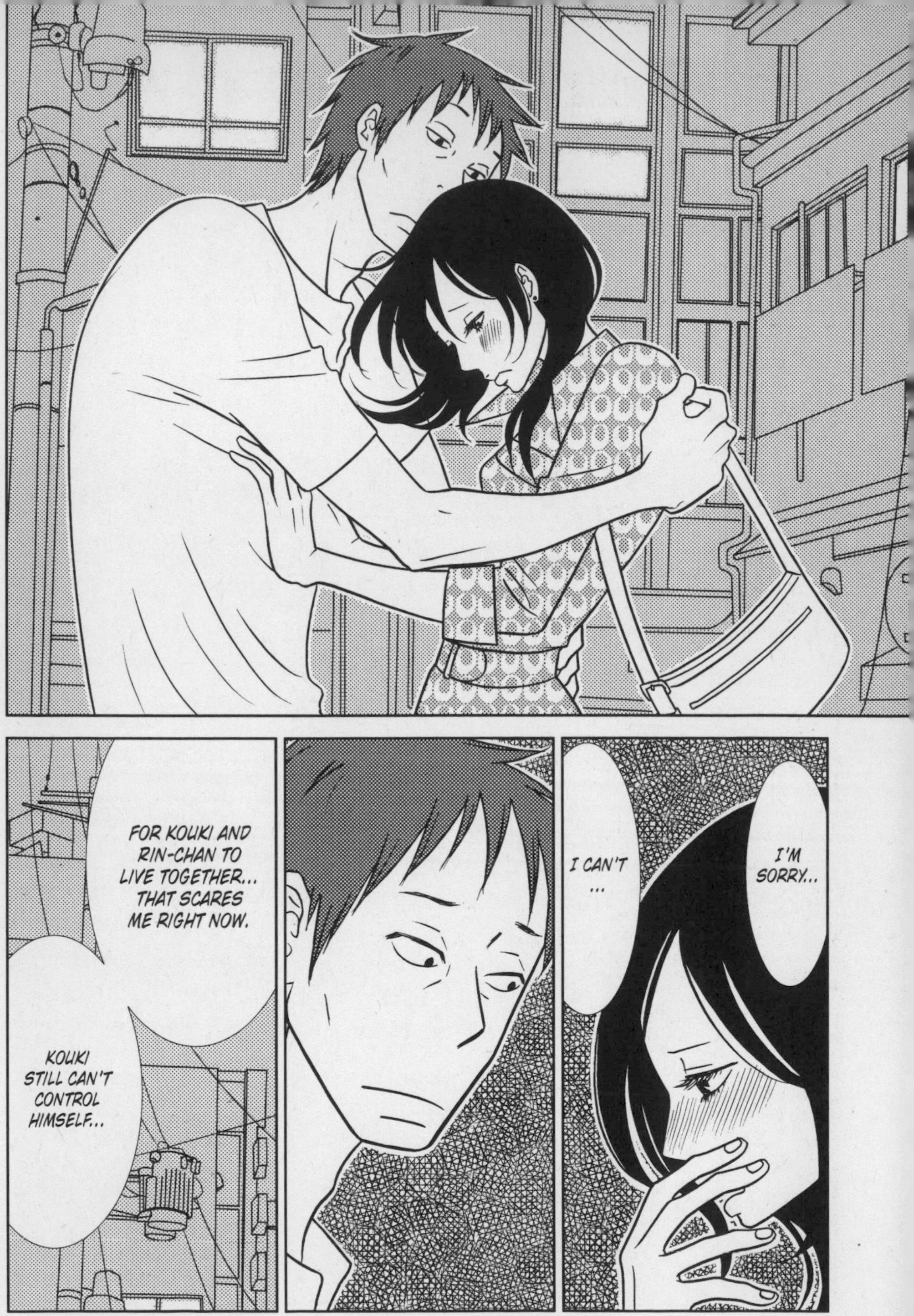
I'M SORRY...
I CAN'T ...
FOR KOUKI AND RIN-CHAN TO LIVE TOGETHER... THAT SCARES ME RIGHT NOW.
KOUKI STILL CAN'T CONTROL HIMSELF...

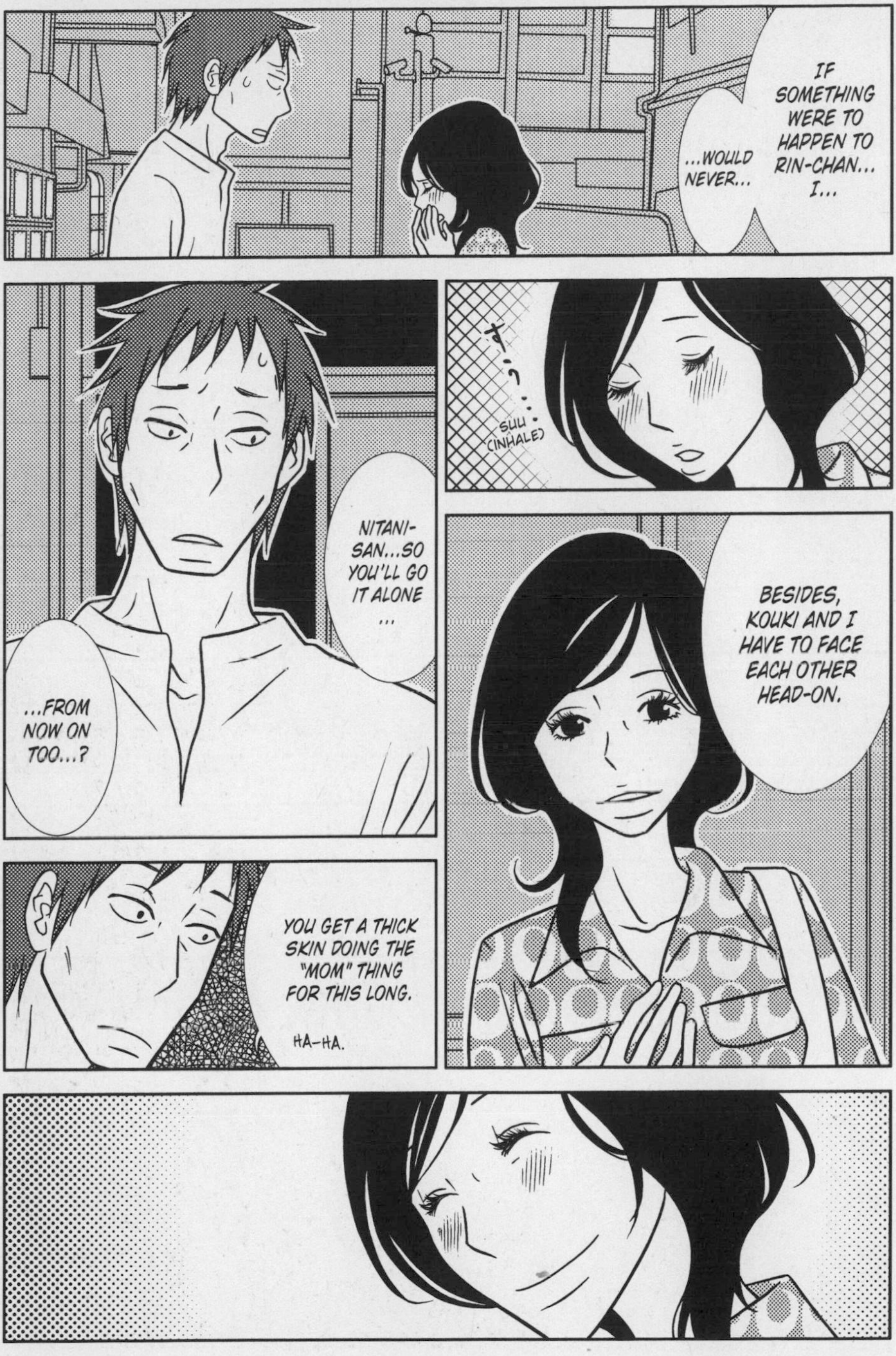
IF SOMETHING WERE TO HAPPEN TO RIN-CHAN... I...
...WOULD NEVER...
SUU (INHALE)
NITANI-SAN...SO YOU'LL GO IT ALONE ...
...FROM NOW ON TOO...?
BESIDES, KOUKI AND I HAVE TO FACE EACH OTHER HEAD-ON.
YOU GET A THICK SKIN DOING THE "MOM" THING FOR THIS LONG.
HA-HA.

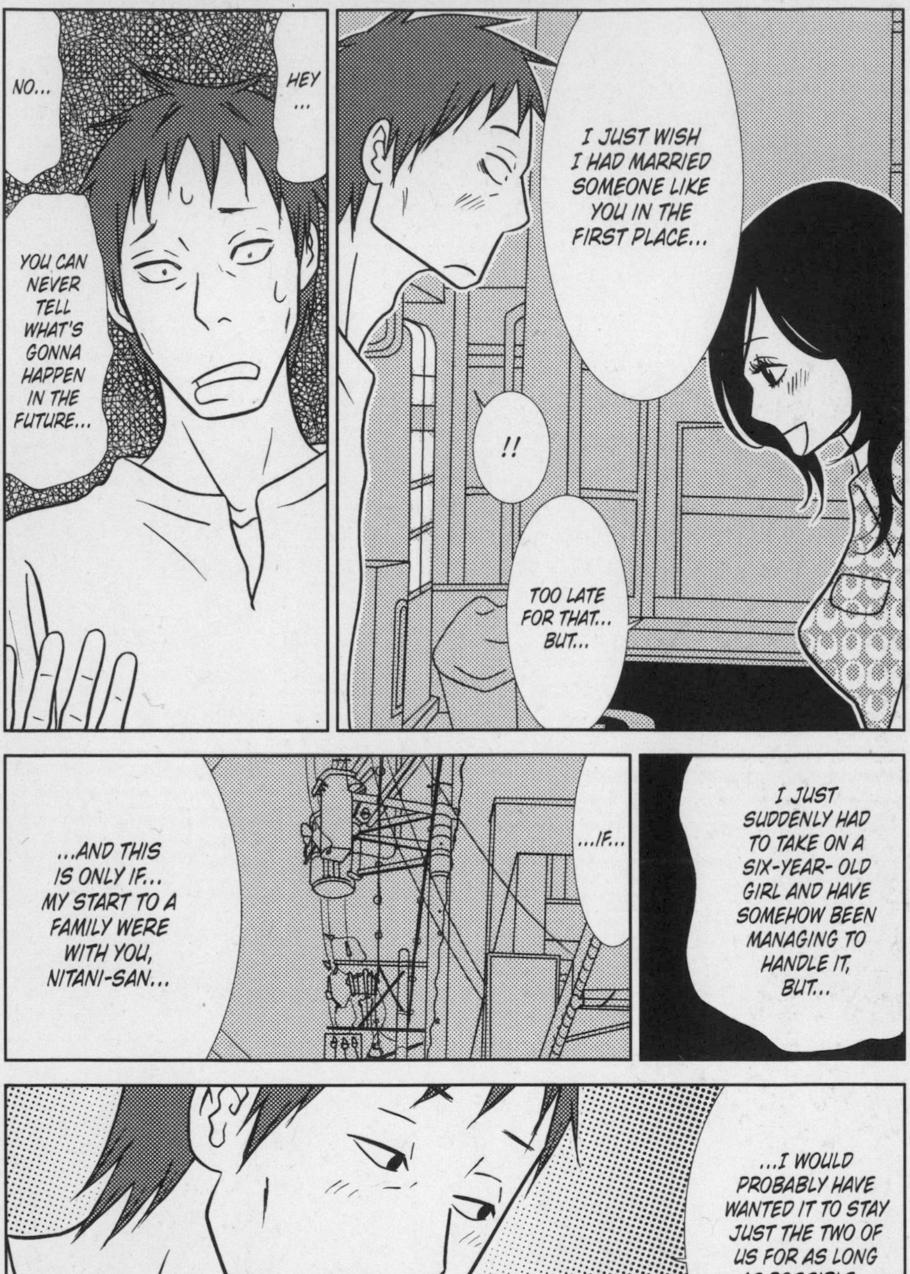
I JUST WISH I HAD MARRIED SOMEONE LIKE YOU IN THE FIRST PLACE...
!!
TOO LATE FOR THAT... BUT...
HEY ...
NO...
YOU CAN NEVER TELL WHAT'S GONNA HAPPEN IN THE FUTURE...
I JUST SUDDENLY HAD TO TAKE ON A SIX-YEAR- OLD GIRL AND HAVE SOMEHOW BEEN MANAGING TO HANDLE IT, BUT...
...IF...
...AND THIS IS ONLY IF... MY START TO A FAMILY WERE WITH YOU, NITANI-SAN...
...I WOULD PROBABLY HAVE WANTED IT TO STAY JUST THE TWO OF US FOR AS LONG AS POSSIBLE...

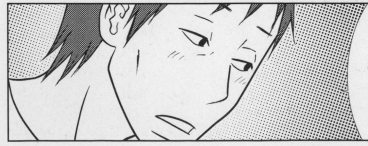

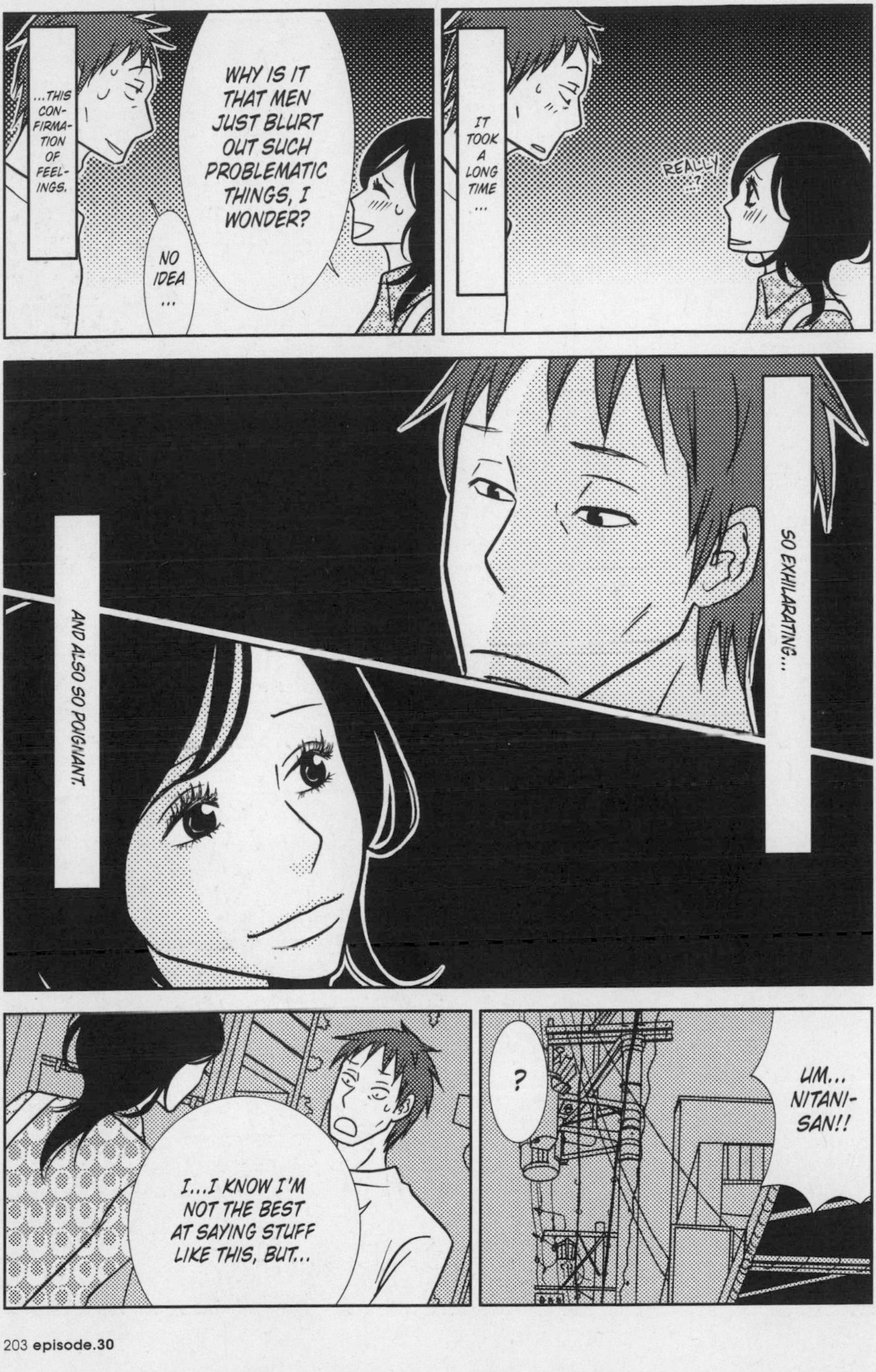
REALLY ...?
IT TOOK A LONG TIME ...
WHY IS IT THAT MEN JUST BLURT OUT SUCH PROBLEMATIC THINGS, I WONDER?
NO IDEA ...
...THIS CONFIRMATION OF FEELINGS.
SO EXHILARATING...
AND ALSO SO POIGNANT.
UM... NITANI-SAN!!
?
I...I KNOW I'M NOT THE BEST AT SAYING STUFF LIKE THIS, BUT...

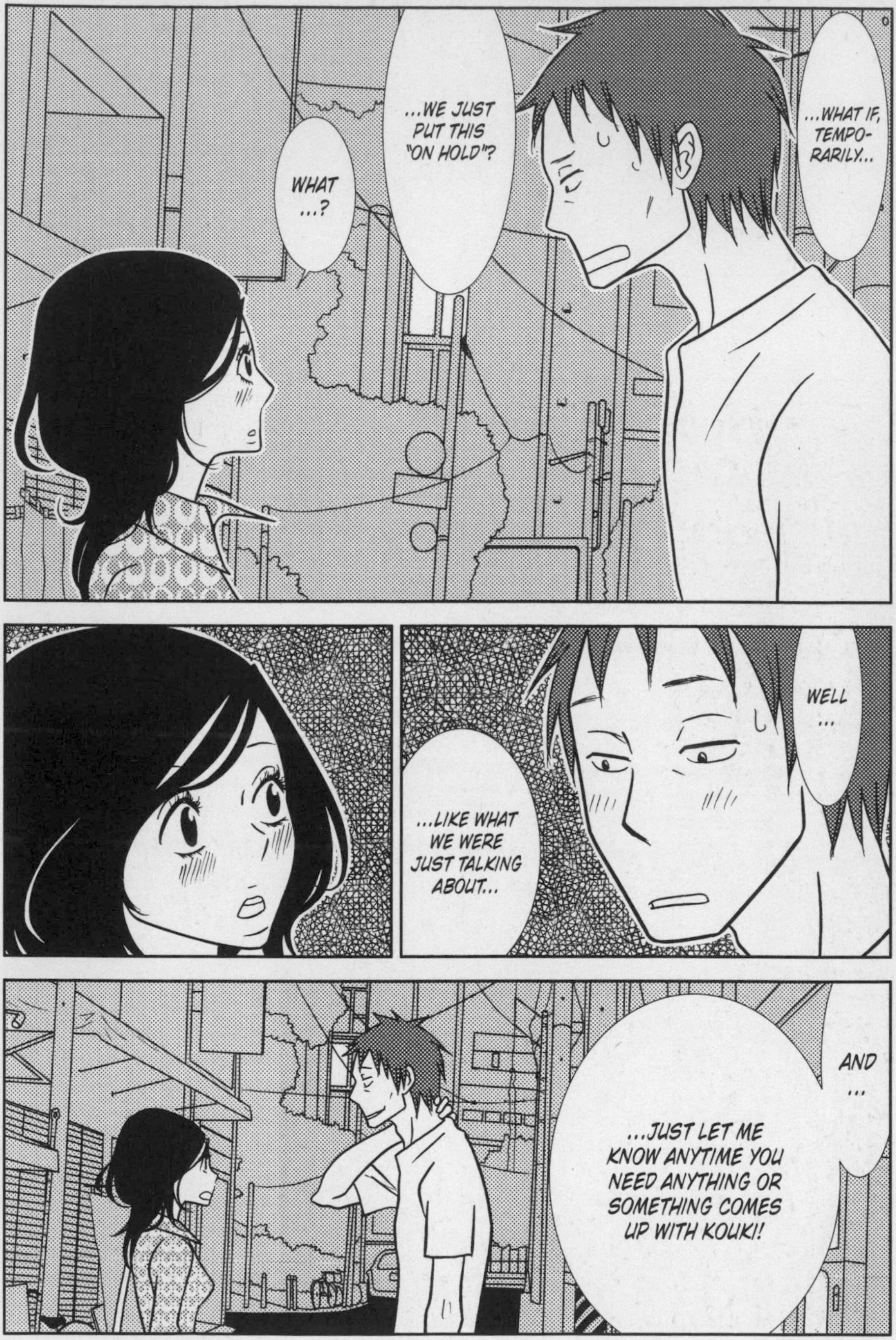
...WHAT IF, TEMPO- RARILY...
...WE JUST PUT THIS "ON HOLD"?
WHAT ...?
WELL ...
...LIKE WHAT WE WERE JUST TALKING ABOUT...
AND ...
...JUST LET ME KNOW ANYTIME YOU NEED ANYTHING OR SOMETHING COMES UP WITH KOUKI!

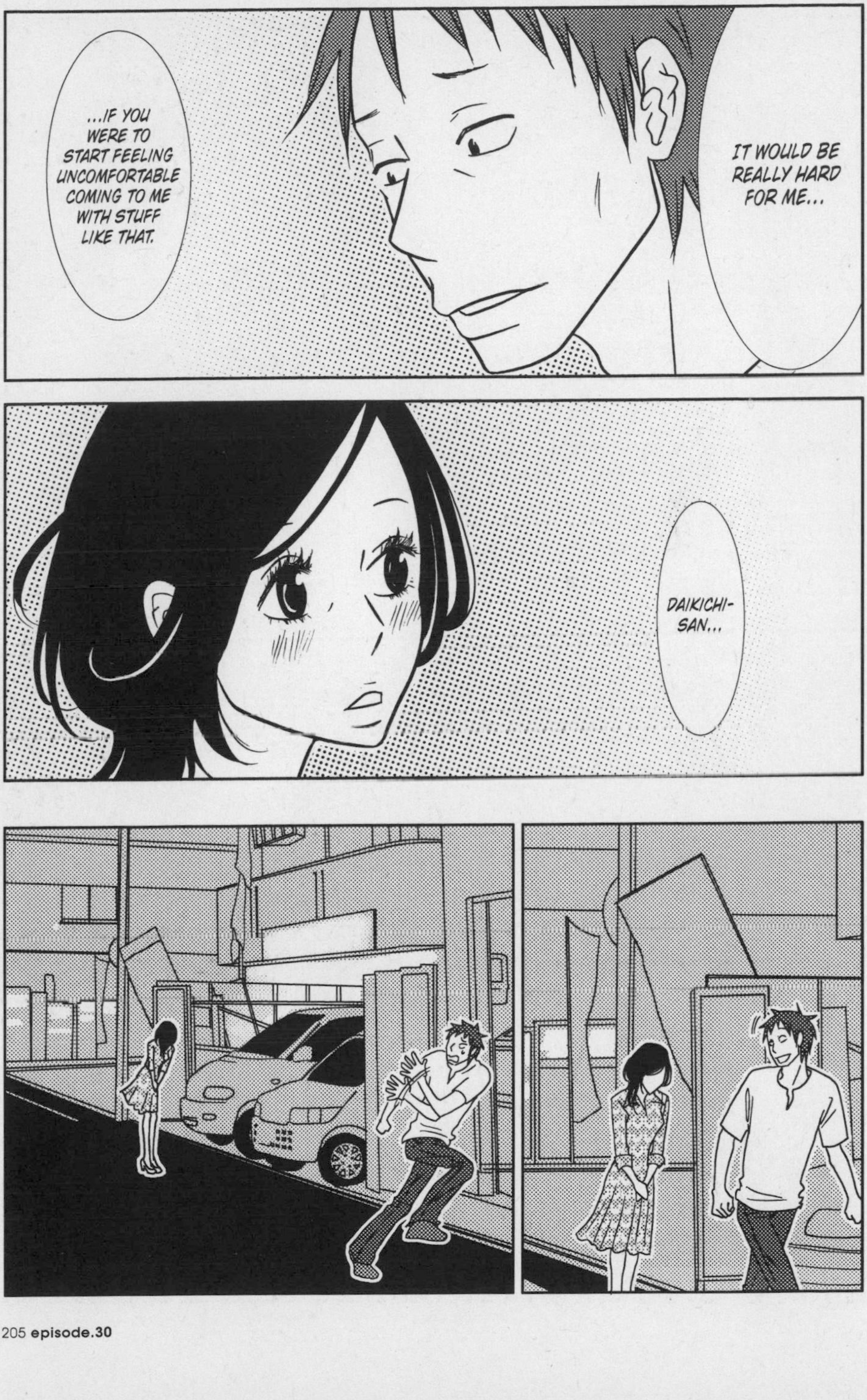
IT WOULD BE REALLY HARD FOR ME...
...IF YOU WERE TO START FEELING UNCOMFORTABLE COMING TO ME WITH STUFF LIKE THAT.
DAIKICHI-SAN...

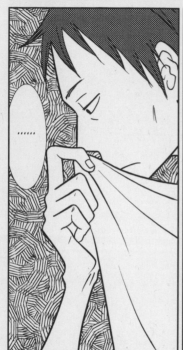

......

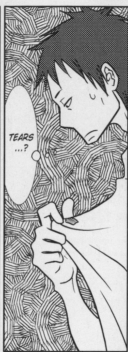

TEARS ...?

HM?

DO I SMELL ...?

FUGA (SNFD) FUGA

SHOOT... I HADN'T TAKEN A BATH YET...

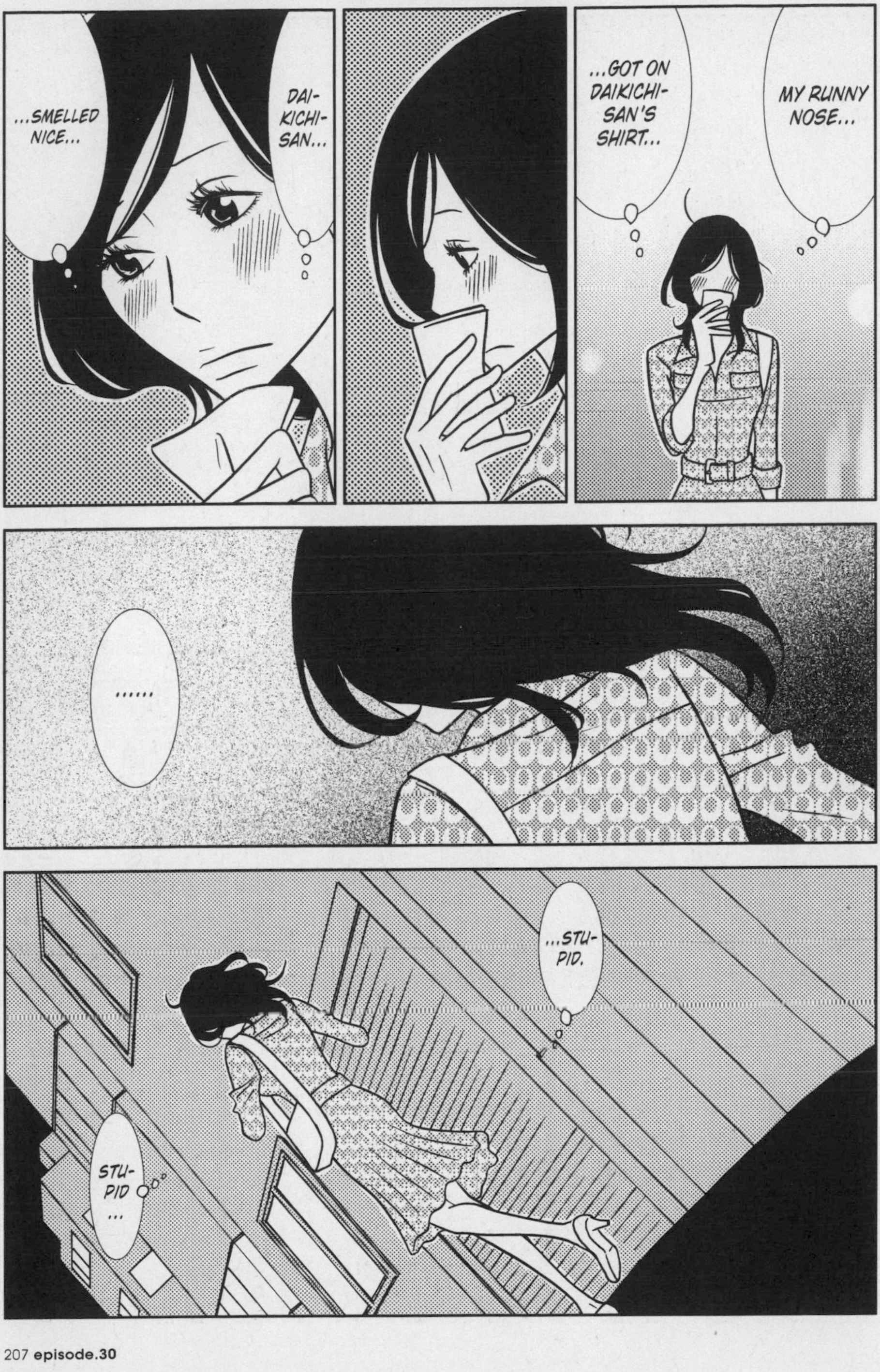
MY RUNNY NOSE...
...GOT ON DAIKICHI-SAN'S SHIRT...
DAI-KICHI-SAN...
...SMELLED NICE...
......
...STU-PID.
STU-PID ...

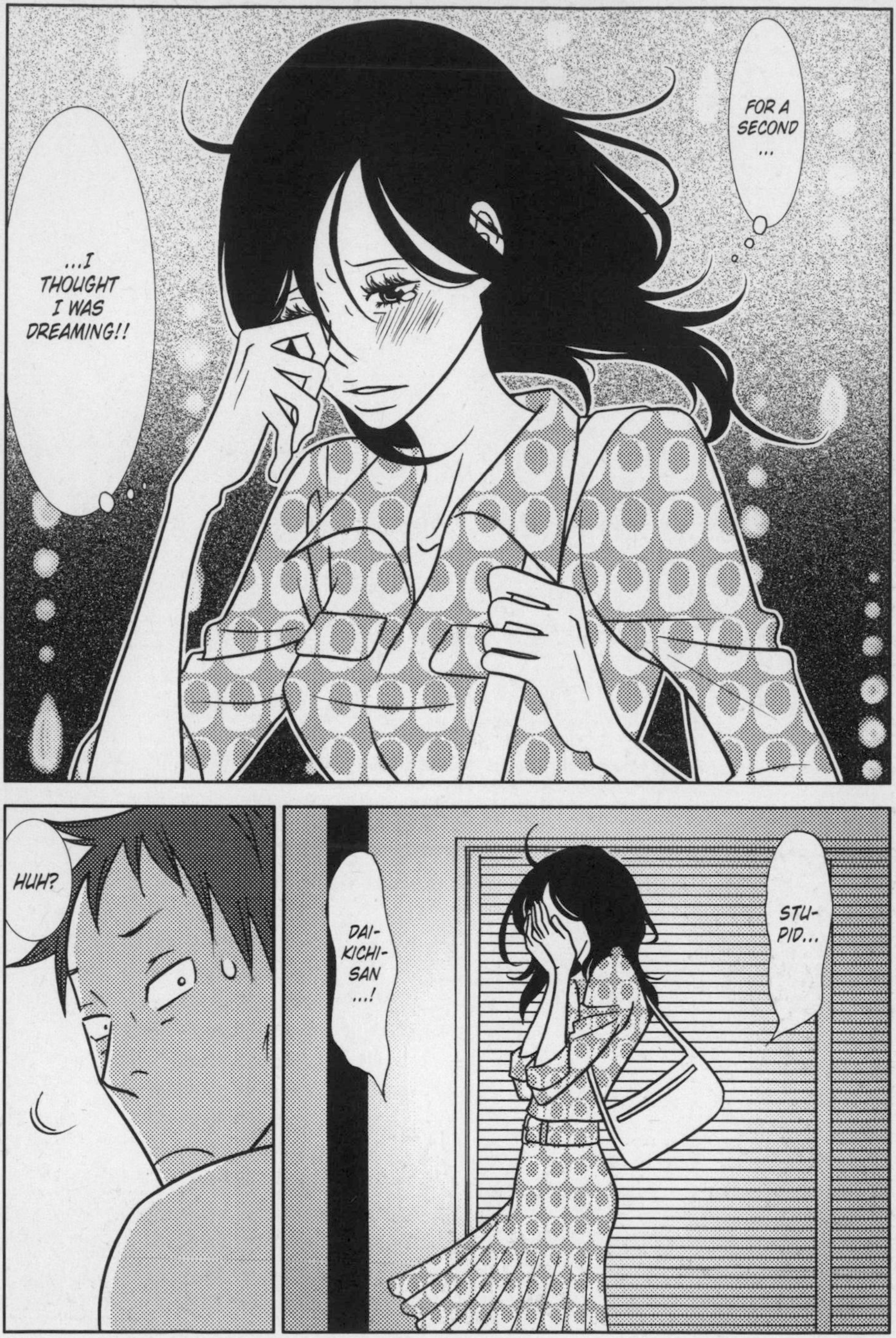
FOR A SECOND ...
...I THOUGHT I WAS DREAMING!!
STU-PID...
DAI-KICHI-SAN ...!
HUH?

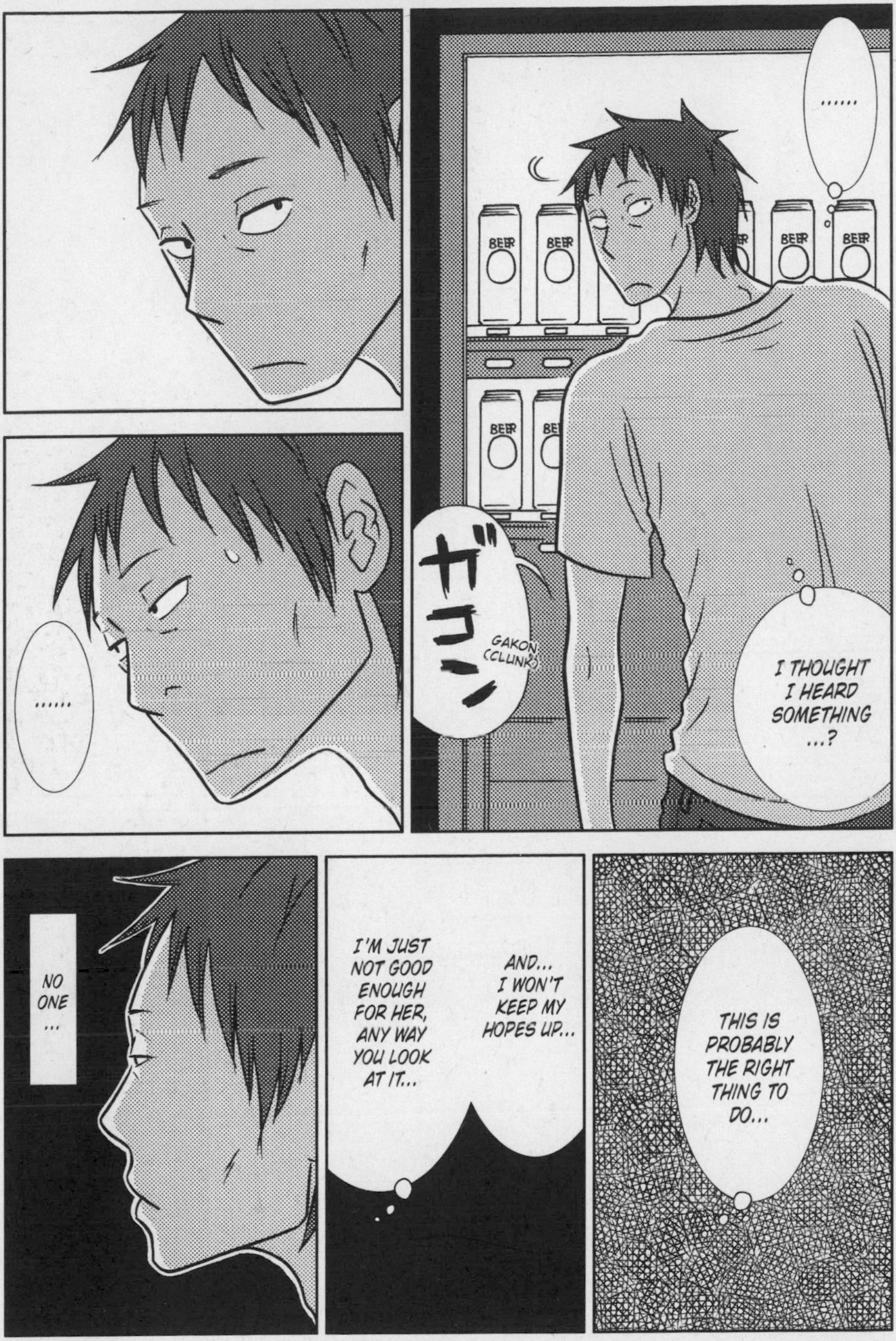
......
I THOUGHT I HEARD SOMETHING ...?
ガゴン
GAKON (CLUNK)
......
THIS IS PROBABLY THE RIGHT THING TO DO...
AND... I WON'T KEEP MY HOPES UP...
I'M JUST NOT GOOD ENOUGH FOR HER, ANY WAY YOU LOOK AT IT...
NO ONE ...

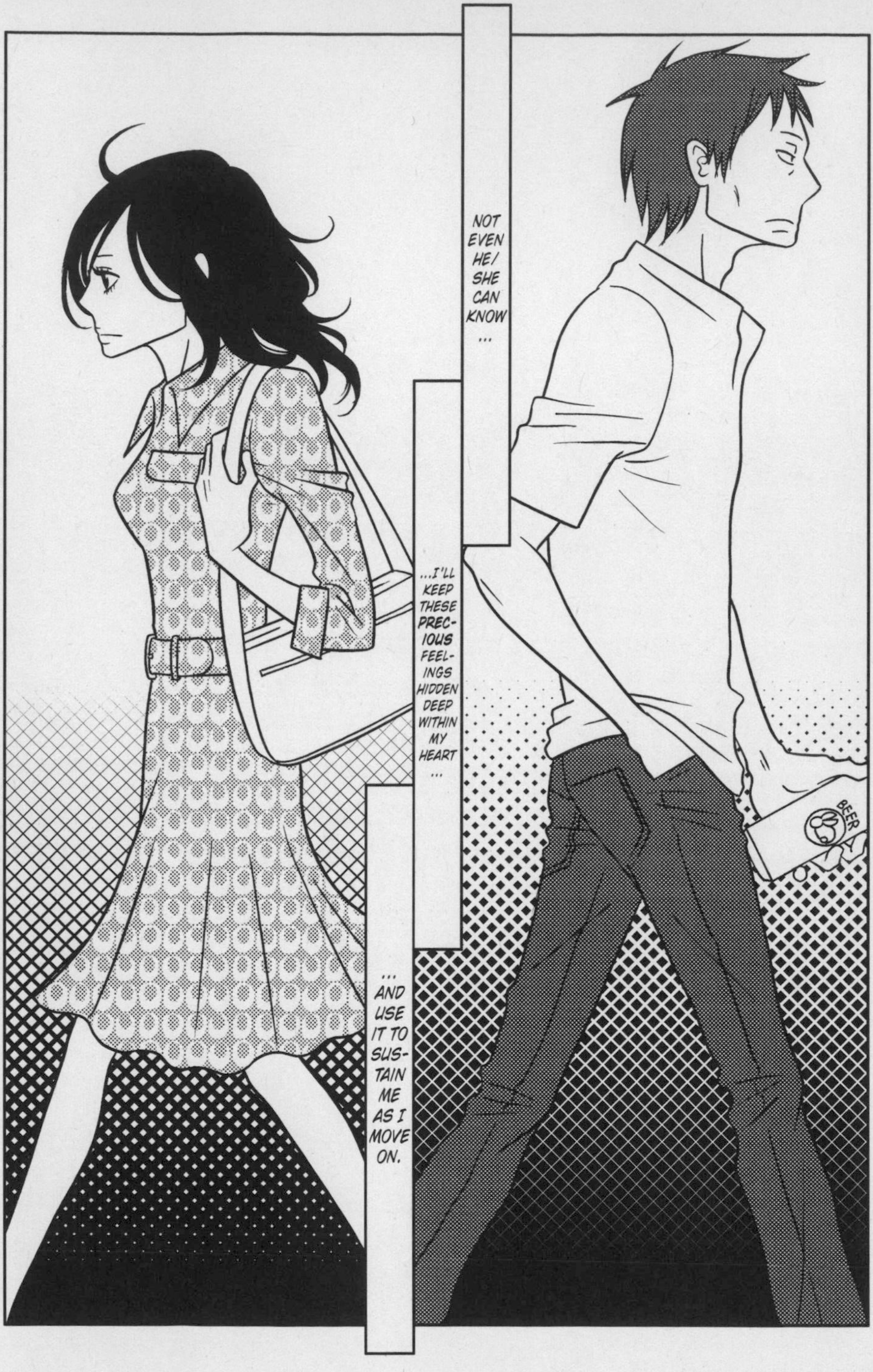
NOT EVEN HE/SHE CAN KNOW...
...I'LL KEEP THESE PRECIOUS FEELINGS HIDDEN DEEP WITHIN MY HEART...
...AND USE IT TO SUSTAIN ME AS I MOVE ON.
BEER

to be continued...

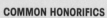

·TRANSLATION·NOTES·

COMMON HONORIFICS

No honorific: Indicates familiarity or closeness; if used without permission or reason, addressing someone in this manner would constitute an insult.

-san: The Japanese equivalent of Mr./Mrs./Miss. If a situation calls for politeness, this is the fail-safe honorific.

-kun: Used most often when referring to boys (though it can be applied to girls as well), this indicates affection or familiarity. Occasionally used by older men among their peers, but it may also be used by anyone referring to a person of lower standing.

-chan: An affectionate honorific indicating familiarity used mostly in reference to girls; also used in reference to cute persons or animals of either gender.

Page 15
Onigiri: A rice ball with different kinds of fillings.

Page 37
Meat-and-potato stew: Called *nikujaga* in Japanese, this dish is a bit different from a Western dish that might have the same name. In Japan, it is a common comfort food dish of thinly sliced meat, potatoes, onions and other vegetables in a sweetened soy sauce-flavored broth.

Page 57
Super Saiyan: A term referencing the manga *DragonBall* by Akira Toriyama. It refers to an advanced level transformation by members of the powerful Saiyan race, beings from another planet.

Page 86
Momma's boy: In the Japanese version, Nitani-san refers to this as boys with a "mother complex." In the context of Japanese popular culture, however, the phrase can go beyond the typical momma's boy and take on a less wholesome meaning, referring to men who find mother figures sexually attractive.

Page 88
Major: In the Japanese version, the play on words references musical scales (do-re-mi).

Page 117
Mock exams: Exams conducted throughout the year in preparation for college entrance placement. Different colleges and universities also have special preparation exams.

Page 134
Designated school: A school that is highly ranked academically.

Page 145
Oyakodon: A rice bowl dish that literally means "parent-and-child bowl" in reference to the chicken and egg main ingredients. These main ingredients, along with green onions and a soup base are simmered together and served atop a bowl of rice.

Page 145
Kijiyakidon: Grilled chicken rice bowl.

Page 145
Katsudon: Deep-fried pork cutlet with egg rice bowl.

Page 158
Obon: A Buddhist custom honoring one's ancestors. This has evolved into a holiday where families visit family gravesites and attend celebrations.

Page 162
Eternal employment: Getting married and being a wife.

Page 167
Imasogari...imasogare: Ancient Japanese grammar conjugation of "to be...to come" stated in honorific mode.

Page 169
Old Japanese grammar conjugations:
       * K-irregular: k- "come"
       * S-irregular: s- "do"
       * N-irregular: sin- "die", in- "go, die"
       * R-irregular: ar- "be, exist", wor- "be, exist"

BUNNY**DROP**

Can't wait for the next volume? You don't have to!

Keep up with the latest chapters of some of your favorite manga every month online in the pages of YEN PLUS!

WITCH & WIZARD

MAXIMUM RIDE

DANIEL X

SOULLESS

K-ON!

Visit us at
www.yenplus.com
for details!

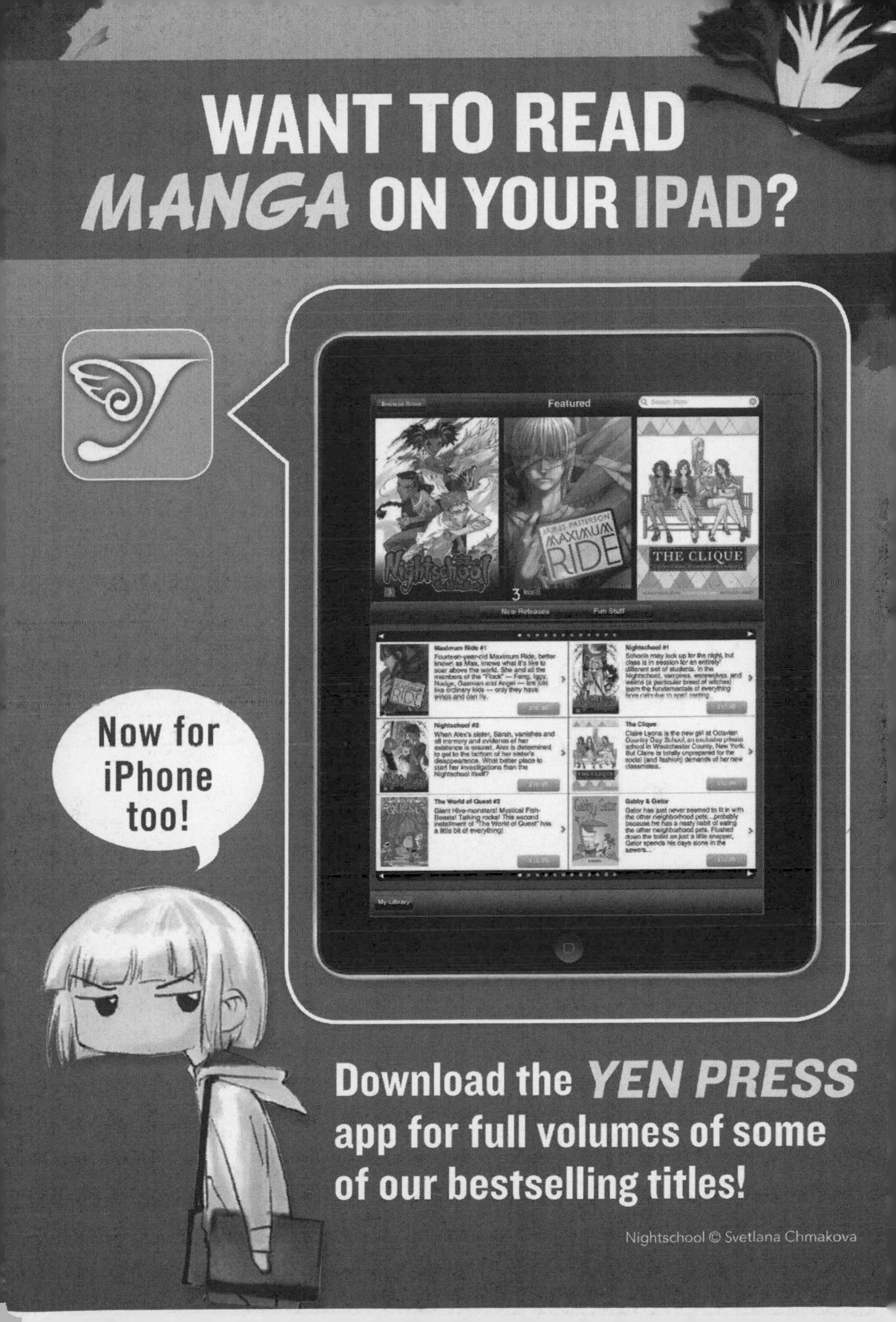
WANT TO READ
MANGA ON YOUR IPAD?
Featured
JAMES PATTERSON
MAXIMUM RIDE
THE CLIQUE
Now for iPhone too!
Download the YEN PRESS app for full volumes of some of our bestselling titles!
Nightschool © Svetlana Chmakova

Hello! This is YOTSUBA!

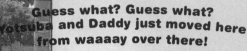

Guess what? Guess what?
Yotsuba and Daddy just moved here
from waaaay over there!

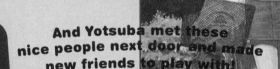

And Yotsuba met these
nice people next door and made
new friends to play with!

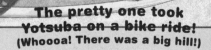

The pretty one took
Yotsuba on a bike ride!
(Whoooa! There was a big hill!)

And Ena's a good drawer!
(Almost as good as Yotsuba!)

And their mom always
gives Yotsuba ice cream!
(Yummy!)

And...
And...
OHHHH!

ENJOY EVERYTHING.

Seeking the love promised by destiny . . .
Can it be found in the thirteenth boy?

13th ★ BOY

After eleven boyfriends, Hee-So thought she was through with love . . . until she met Won-Jun, that is . . .

But when number twelve dumps her, she's not ready to move on to the thirteenth boy just yet! Determined to win back her destined love, Hee-So's on a mission to reclaim Won-Jun, no matter what!

VOLUMES 1-11 IN STORES NOW!

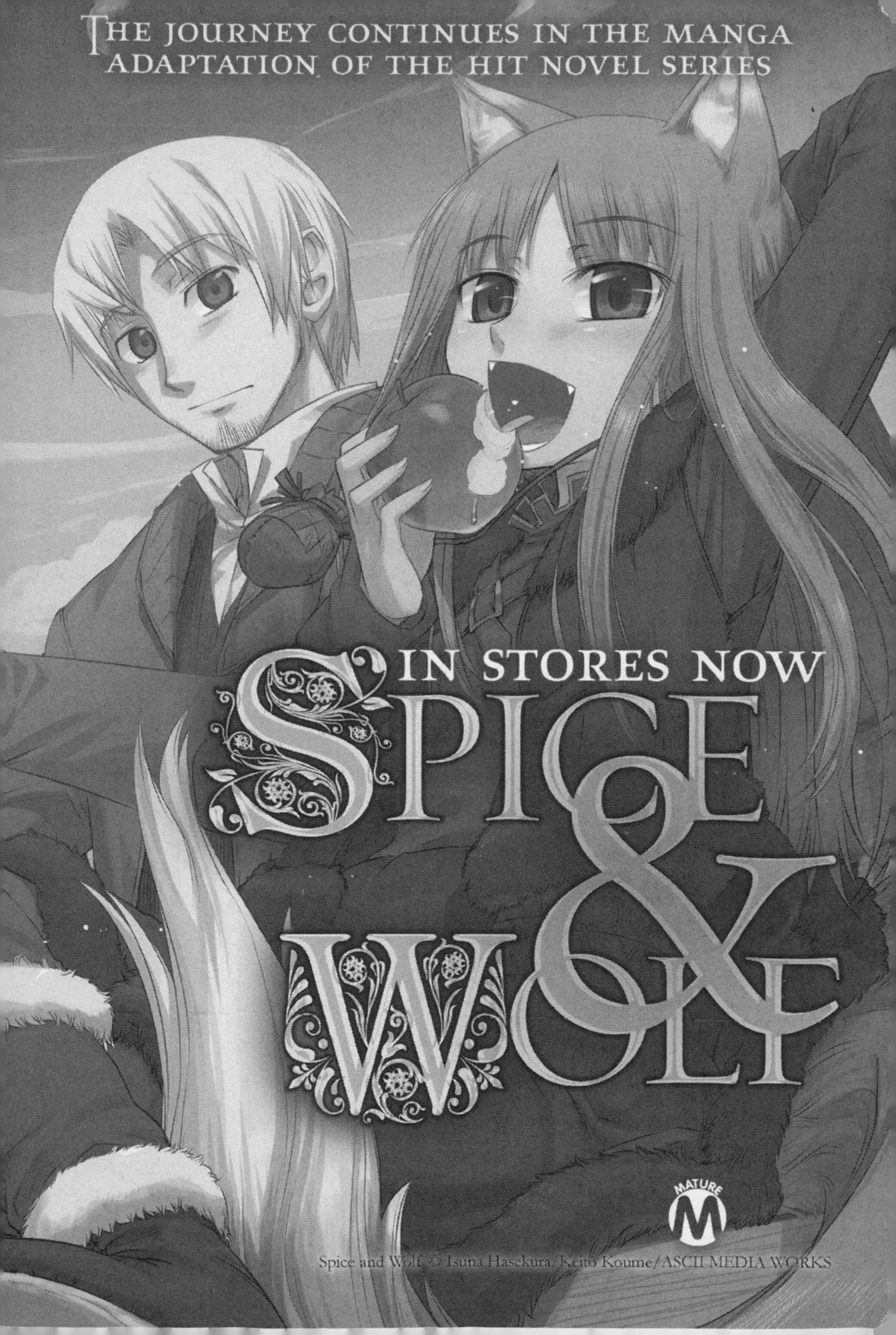
THE JOURNEY CONTINUES IN THE MANGA
ADAPTATION OF THE HIT NOVEL SERIES
IN STORES NOW
SPICE & WOLF
MATURE
M
Spice and Wolf © Isuna Hasekura/Keito Koume/ASCII MEDIA WORKS

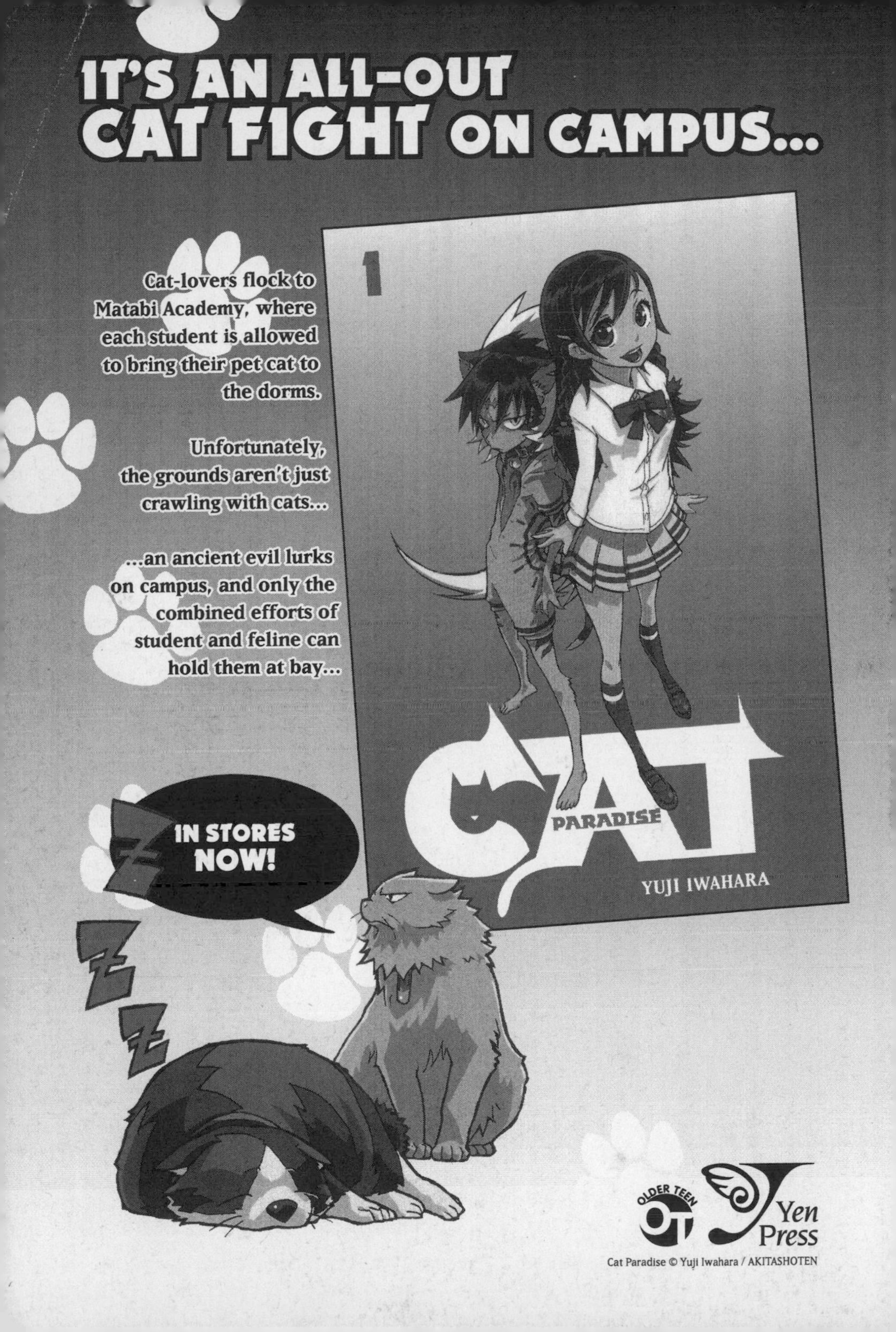

IT'S AN ALL-OUT CAT FIGHT ON CAMPUS...
Cat-lovers flock to Matabi Academy, where each student is allowed to bring their pet cat to the dorms.
Unfortunately, the grounds aren't just crawling with cats...
...an ancient evil lurks on campus, and only the combined efforts of student and feline can hold them at bay...
1
CAT PARADISE
YUJI IWAHARA
IN STORES NOW!
OLDER TEEN OT
Yen Press
Cat Paradise © Yuji Iwahara / AKITASHOTEN

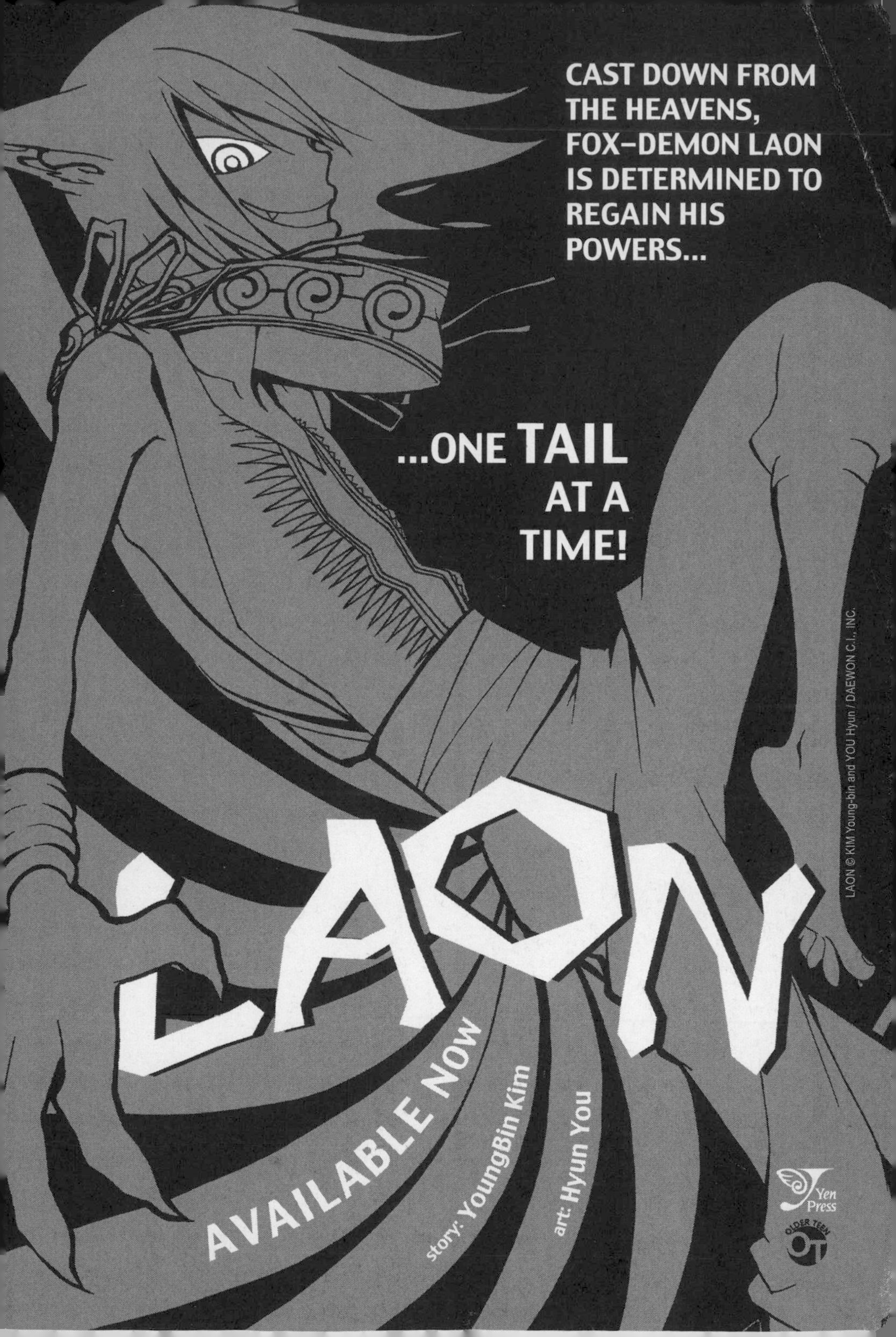
CAST DOWN FROM THE HEAVENS, FOX-DEMON LAON IS DETERMINED TO REGAIN HIS POWERS...
...ONE TAIL AT A TIME!
LAON
AVAILABLE NOW
story: YoungBin Kim
art: Hyun You
LAON © KIM Young-bin and YOU Hyun / DAEWON C.I., INC.
Yen Press
OLDER TEEN OT